WITHDRAWN

THE FASCIST REVOLUTION
IN TUSCANY
1919–1922

THE FASCIST REVOLUTION IN TUSCANY
1919–1922

FRANK M. SNOWDEN

*Lecturer in History, Royal Holloway and Bedford New College
University of London*

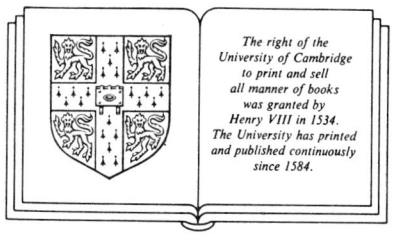

CAMBRIDGE UNIVERSITY PRESS
Cambridge
New York   Port Chester
Melbourne   Sydney

Published by the Press Syndicate of the University of Cambridge
The Pitt Building, Trumpington Street, Cambridge CB2 1RP
40 West 20th Street, New York, NY 10011, USA
10 Stamford Road, Oakleigh, Melbourne 3166, Australia

© Cambridge University Press 1989

First published 1989

Printed in Great Britain at the University Press, Cambridge

British Library cataloguing in publication data
Snowden, Frank
The fascist revolution in Tuscany, 1919–1922
1. Italy. Fascism, 1919–1945
1. Title
320.5'330945

Library of Congress cataloguing in publication data
Snowden, Frank M. (Frank Martin), 1946–
The fascist revolution in Tuscany, 1919–1922.
Bibliography.
Includes index.
1. Tuscany (Italy) – Politics and government.
2. Fascism – Italy – Tuscany – History – 20th century.
1. Title.
DG38.7.S64 1989   945'.5   88-35278

ISBN 0 521 36117 6

FOR ELAINE AND FRANK

CONTENTS

Preface   *page* ix
List of abbreviations and Italian terms   x
Map of Tuscany   xii

Introduction   1

PART I THE COUNTRYSIDE

1   Partnership and love   7
2   The appeal of the right   70

PART II THE CITIES

3   Big business and Mussolini   121
4   The petty bourgeoisie and the Squads   157

PART III THE STATE

5   Compromise and collusion   183

Conclusion   205

Notes   210
Bibliography   267
Index   281

PREFACE

Like all historical research, this book was in many ways a collective enterprise, and I am indebted to many people for their advice and assistance. Most of all I would like to thank Adrian Lyttelton, who was my teacher and whose suggestions at every stage were invaluable. Giovanna Procacci was my first guide to the Italian state archives, and Giorgio Mori was both gracious and wise in his advice on the location of sources in Tuscany. To both of them I am grateful. Research is impossible without the support of the staff of archives and libraries; I am fortunate that the personnel at the institutions listed in the bibliography were generous with their time and assistance.

Academic work also has financial bases. I conducted the research for this book with grants from the Danforth Foundation, the Council on the Humanities at Yale University, and the Central Research Fund at London University. I thank these institutions for their support.

Finally, I have been aided enormously in the completion of the typescript. Donna Koontz typed the text with endless patience and skill, and my parents were helpful critics of my use of the language. The errors that remain are my own.

ABBREVIATIONS AND ITALIAN TERMS

ABBREVIATIONS

AAT	Tuscan Agrarian Association
AIT	Tuscan Industrial Association
ASLU	Archivio di Stato di Lucca
CGL	General Confederation of Labour
FIOM	National Metalworkers' Union
PNF	Fascist Party
PSI	Socialist Party
SMI	Società Metallurgica Italiana

ITALIAN TERMS

affittuario	peasant leaseholder
agrari	landlords
arditi	shock troops in the Italian army
arditi del popolo	non-party anti-fascist armed resistance movement
bracciante	day labourer
camporaiolo	semi-proletarianized sharecropper
capoccia	head of a sharecropping family
caposquadra	head of fascist action squads
carabiniere	military policeman
collocamento di classe	roster of union men for employment in agriculture
colono	sharecropper
Confindustria	Italian Confederation of Industry
consiglio di fabbrica	factory council
consiglio di fattoria	farm council

Glossary of Italian abbreviations and terms

direttorio	executive committee
famiglia colonica	legal peasant family
fascio	branch of the fascist movement
fattore	bailiff
fattoria	estate
imponibile di mano d'opera	compulsory employment of agricultural labour
latifondo	great estate
massaia	wife of the head of a peasant family
mezzadria	sharecropping system
mezzadro	sharecropper
podere	peasant family farm
popolari	members of the Popular Party
questore	local chief of police
ras	local fascist boss
sottofattore	assistant bailiff
sottoprefetto	deputy prefect
stime	estimates of debt between sharecropper and landlord
terrazziere	day labourer
ufficio del lavoro	fascist employment office

Tuscany at the period under study

INTRODUCTION

The central Italian region of Tuscany played a major role in the rise of fascism to power. In the years leading to the March on Rome, only Emilia surpassed it in the number of fascist members and branches. Tuscan fascism, moreover, was second to none in its violence, organizational strength, and intransigence. Far from depending on outside support, Tuscan fascists undertook the export of squadrism to neighbouring Lazio and Umbria, even to distant Apulia.

Despite its prominent role in Mussolini's 'revolution', however, Tuscan fascism has been largely neglected by historians. The historiography of the postwar crisis and the rise of fascism has suffered from a pronounced northern bias. The experience of regions to the north of the Apennines has attracted a disproportionate scholarly interest, with an outpouring of excellent monographs on Emilia and the Po Valley. The same seminal period in the history of central and southern Italy has been underdeveloped. There is no extended study of the 'Red Years' and the rise of fascism in Tuscany. There are local studies of particular cities and provinces, but no attempt to explain the features that make the region as a whole a fruitful and substantial case study. This book is an effort to fill a large gap in the literature.

In addition to its importance as a region where fascism exploded in its most extreme and violent form, Tuscany has other claims upon the attention of the historian. The first of these is the unusual opportunity it provides of examining all of the chief components of fascist support within a single region. Other zones of fascist strength were overwhelmingly either agricultural or industrial. Tuscany is unique among Italian regions in offering the chance of confronting both agrarian and industrial fascism in their most powerful forms.

Tuscany was above all a major agricultural region. Rural Tuscany was dominated by the institution of sharecropping known as *mezzadria*. *Mezzadria* held undisputed sway in the countryside of the provinces of

Arezzo, Florence, Pisa, and Siena, and here especially squadrism flourished. The region was also, however, one of the foremost industrial zones in the nation. Livorno, Grosseto, Florence, and Massa-Carrara provinces were the sites of some of the leading Italian companies in such sectors as mining, textiles, steel, chemicals, shipbuilding, and marble quarrying. Tuscan big business, moreover, was unusual in the depth and enthusiasm of its involvement in reactionary extremism. An important task is to explore the profitability constraints and political calculations that informed the pro-fascism of so many industrialists in the region. Finally, the regional metropolis at Florence and the provincal capitals were major commercial and retailing centres, and this fact poses the question of the role of the petty-bourgeoisie in fascism.

Who then supported fascism in town and countryside, and why? To what extent did Tuscany conform to national patterns? What are the implications of the pattern of support for fascism in this important case for the wider interpretation of the movement? The attempt to answer these questions with regard to each of the major groups in Tuscan society has determined the structure of the book, which is organized thematically. Part I deals with agrarian fascism, turning first to the nobility and then to peasants and farm workers. Part II examines industrial and urban Tuscany, beginning with big business and then moving to the mass popular support for fascism, particularly within the ranks of the petty bourgeoisie. Fascism, however, could never have won power if it had relied solely on the strength of its membership. What enabled Mussolini's movement to win the civil war with the left so rapidly, to deploy a private paramilitary force with near impunity, and then to stage a successful March on Rome was the extensive collusion of the state apparatus throughout the region. Part III, therefore, explores the relations between the blackshirts and state officials.

Such a thematic approach facilitates the job of weighing the significance of the fascist militancy of particular social groups and classes with regard to some of the major issues of interpretation. Does the Tuscan evidence confirm the view that fascism was a weapon of big business in the defence of Italian capitalism? Was it a product of the extremism of the lower middle classes in a time of world war and social dislocation? Did the movement emerge as a product of modernization and the commercialization of agriculture? Is fascism simply a synonym for counter-revolution and repression? Was squadrism an extension of the divisions and methods of the First World War to domestic politics? Was it a 'parenthesis' in Tuscan history caused by 'accidents' imposed from without, or was it a possibility deeply rooted in the social structures of the region?

The period covered by the book requires some explanation. The chief sources of Italian fascism lie in the frontal clash between landlords and peasants over the issue of control over the land, the labour market, and local government. In zones apart from Tuscany where fascism became a powerful force — the Po Valley and Apulia — this conflict gathered momentum from the first organized agricultural strikes at the turn of the century to the all-out confrontation of the postwar years. Fascism marked the violent suppression of the contest and the re-imposition of the prerogatives and power of property. To separate the final stage in this process from its long gestation period is to omit the deep, long-term origins of fascism. The struggle for power in the countryside was a continuous contest for the quarter of a century after 1900.

Tuscany, however, had its own very different tempo. There was no history until 1919 of a challenge by the peasantry to the power of the landlords. In the Giolittian era when there was turmoil in the countryside elsewhere in the peninsula, the Tuscan provinces remained untouched by agricultural strikes, land occupations, and the counter measures of landlords. In a sense that was unique in Italy, the history of the contest for power in the countryside of central Italy was confined to the four years 1919–22. This book is a history of the crisis of these years in Tuscan society, from the first mass strikes in 1919 to the end of labour militancy marked by the beginning of the fascist dictatorship. Every conflict, however, has a prehistory, and in the first chapter I attempt to define the long-term processes which silently prepared the post-war explosion.

The concluding date of 1922 has a similar explanation. The March on Rome marked a watershed in Tuscan history with the crushing of the labour movement throughout the region as a mass force for a generation. It is this process which is the subject of this study. I have not attempted to examine the means by which property owners took advantage of the dictatorship to secure their power and to prevent the re-emergence of labour unrest. The years after the seizure of power merit a full-scale investigation in their own right, and I hope to return to the fascist regime in Tuscany in a future work. The question here is not how fascism used its power, but how it gained it. This question too is complex, and the attempt to provide an answer for these eight provinces is the purpose of the pages that follow.

PART I

THE COUNTRYSIDE

CHAPTER I

PARTNERSHIP AND LOVE

CLASSICAL SHARECROPPING

The system of sharecropping or *mezzadria* was the dominant institution of the Tuscan countryside, and the vast area where it held sway was the zone where fascism was strongest. There were, however, provinces where sharecropping was not the rule, and these must be mentioned in order to explain the geography of fascism. In the industrial provinces of Massa-Carrara and Livorno, agriculture was poorly developed and was conducted in the main by small proprietors who were never successfully unionized on a large scale. Here agrarian fascism was a negligible force. Lucca and Grosseto provinces, by contrast, posessed important agricultural zones, but they were entirely different both from each other and from the rest of Tuscany. Grosseto province was an area of backward great estates worked by migrant day labourers. In its social and economic structures, therefore, Grosseto was the northernmost extension of southern Italian latifundism rather than a characteristic representative of central Italy. Lucca resembled Grosseto in possessing social structures that were very different from the rest of the region. Lucca, however, stood apart in a very contrasting manner. Grosseto was the realm of latifundia; Lucca was a province of dispersed landownership in which the peasant direct cultivator was the dominant figure.

None of these provinces – Lucca, Grosseto, Livorno, and Massa-Carrara – stood in the storm centre of the conflict between landlord and peasant that produced agrarian fascism in its most powerful and violent form. In the industrial provinces the countryside was calm, and fascism emerged chiefly as an urban movement. The latifundia of the Maremma in Grosseto had instead a turbulent history, but fascism there was slow to evolve, and did so as an importation from Florence rather than an indigenously based phenomenon. Lucca, finally, was *sui generis*, and merits attention, but as a small and atypical zone.

The central focus of our concerns is the four major agricultural provinces of Arezzo, Pisa, Florence, and Siena. These provinces dominated Tuscan farming and played the principal role in the rise of agrarian squadrism. Since *mezzadria* was the backbone of the social structure of these provinces in the centre of Tuscany, and since fascism arose in response to the crisis of the sharecropping system, it is important to begin by examining this key institution of Tuscan society.

Landlord and tenant

Under the traditional pattern of *mezzadria* the property of the landlord was divided into one or more estates. Each estate, or *fattoria*, was considered a single administrative unit and was subdivided into a series of peasant farms, called *poderi*.[1] The *fattoria* was the centre of administrative control, which was the exclusive prerogative of the proprietor; the *poderi* were the units of actual cultivation. The working of the land was governed by contract between the landlord and the peasant tenant (*mezzadro*) under the legal form of a partnership in a joint venture. Put most simply, the lord provided the land, and the *mezzadro* the labour, while the entire produce and the expenses of cultivation were divided equally. The proprietor's share of the crop was either consumed in whole or in part, or sold for profit; the peasant's share was his sole source of subsistence.

Here it is important to observe in greater detail the workings of the system because a whole ideology of lordly inspiration concerning *mezzadria* has been propagated which renders Tuscan history incomprehensible. According to this 'official' view, which dominated the discussions of the Accademia dei Georgofili, the landlords' technical and agronomical society, and became the creed of propertied classes in the region, Tuscany in *mezzadria* had found the solution to the social question. In industry and in the northern countryside where wage labour prevailed, there was continual class conflict, and constant danger to social order. Not so in Tuscany, where peasant and landlord were equal partners united by a common interest in the greatest productivity of the soil. The increase of either party was the benefit of both. Thus Pasquale Villari, exemplifying the 'official' doctrine, wrote,

> The contract of *mezzadria*, as has been repeated a thousand times over, has here achieved its best form, and makes the peasant happy, honest, and at ease; it puts him in perfect harmony with the landlord, who has become his partner. This is the true solution to the social question; here socialism has not penetrated, and never will. If something similar could be done in industry, how many reasons for discontent, how many dangers could be avoided.[2]

Much earlier, in 1847, another spokesman of the Tuscan landed aristocracy, Vincenzo Salvagnoli, declared:

> The owner prefers the well-being and dignity of the tenant to the highest income; he cares not for a machine, but for the man; he desires not a servant but a comrade ... In such a relationship there is no desire on the one side to oppress, and no occasion for vengeance on the other. This benign economic relation has joined landlord and tenant together in a moral bond of civil harmony ... These partners in agriculture would never stand as brother against brother in civil war.[3]

Moreover, the 'official' view continued, the tenant, beneficiary of such a salutary moral relationship with his betters, could have no material ground for complaint. The standard of living of the Tuscan *mezzadro*, it was asserted, was the envy of the working classes of the world – honest, secure work; comfort; nourishment in abundance; and a model family life. Thus, in 1920, the official paper of the landlords' association of the Mugello in Florence province reminded its readers that

> No class of workers in the world today has been able to achieve, or perhaps ever will be able to achieve, a standard of living equal to that which *mezzadria* provides the peasants.[4]

Singling out the tenant cottage for special praise, the landlords' correspondent reported that it was 'located on a healthy site, and [was] provided with animals, with ventilation, and with every comfort'.[5]

A moment's reflection reveals the implausibility of such a vision.[6] It was the landlord who held power in the form of the ownership of the means of production – the land, the peasant cottage, the seed, the fodder, the tools and machinery of cultivation, and the work animals – and in the form of the right of eviction; the *mezzadro* possessed only his own labour power and perhaps a few simple implements such as a hoe and rake, and the odd farm animal. It would have been surprising if the formal contractual equality of the 'partners' had negated the effective economic supremacy of the landlord, In fact, a number of secondary pacts supplementing the primary *mezzadria* relationship bear witness to the power vested in ownership. The specifics varied, but nearly everywhere the *mezzadro* was bound, beyond the surrender of half of the crop of his plot, to render a number of tributes and special services to the lord of the estate. Typical additional duties were: to work for a period of the year off the *podere* without compensation, transporting the landlord's share of the harvest to market or digging ditches to improve the property; to provide the owner with established quantities of olive oil or wine, or a given number of fowls; to gather wood for the landlord's hearth; and to wash the landlord's linen. Moreover, the lord exercised the right to regulate the private life of his partner, superintending his dress and religious observance, forbidding him to marry without consent, to attend cafés and gaming rooms, and ordering him to work off the estate. The sanction was eviction.

In addition, the provision that the tenant should assume 50 per cent of the expense of cultivation meant that his entitlement to half the product of his own labour was but a legal fiction. The reason was that the peasant had no capital, so that he was compelled to receive advances of seed, fodder and fertilizer from the landlord's storehouse, to employ work animals from the owner's stables; and to use the equipment and tools of the proprietor's shed. The use of these items then figured at harvest time as so many deductions from the *mezzadro*'s due. The bookkeeping system of estimates (*stime*) by which the lord's capital was assessed allowed ample room for profit by the owner. The value of the advanced capital – seed, equipment, animals – was reckoned at the start of the agricultural year at current market prices and then at the end when accounts were settled, any difference in price making a difference in the way the crop was apportioned. Here, of course, was an opportunity for speculation, and it seldom worked to the disadvantage of the proprietor, as the market value of the landlord's capital was likely to be high when items were provided to the tenants and low at harvest time when accounts were settled. Not unknown was the practice of advancing inferior grains against a return in full-value crops.[7] In any case, the fact that pacts were not written but based on informal agreement and local custom allowed ample scope for abuse by the powerful. In the quiet but unending struggle over the respective shares of the product, the economic power of the landlord decided the issue in his favour.

Beyond this silent conflict over the division of the product, there was another equally important opposition with regard to the actual size of the harvest. The landlord's claim was that there was no possibility of discord as both parties to the contract could only gain by the largest possible output, with the harmonious result that each worked spontaneously for the greatest good of the other. In fact, however, in the long run this formal symmetry of interest was overbalanced by the asymmetry of economic power. For the tenant, the stake was survival as he cultivated for subsistence; for the lord, it was a question of profit. The landlord over a period of time, was able to exploit this difference of emphasis, together with his right to re-order his estate and its division into *poderi*, for his private advantage. The landlord, that is, stood to gain by increasing the intensity of cultivation by reducing the size of the *podere* to the minimum indispensable for the tenant family to subsist. From a smaller plot the requirement of survival was unchanged for the peasant, so that the landlord could obtain a greater exploitation of labour. Moreover, it was easily discovered that the possible minimum size of the *podere* was elusive: the labour the *mezzadro* could extract from himself and his family had a high upward elasticity. Thus there was a long-term tendency for the condition of the *mezzadro* to be reduced to a bare subsistence, obtained by ever-greater toil within a family context in which hours limitations, legal holidays, and child-labour legislation did not apply. Already in 1858, a student of Tuscan agriculture, P. Cuppari, observed:

> If the *podere* is too small, the landlord benefits at the expense of the sharecropper. Truly in such cases the peasant will be bound, by dint of industry and extraordinary labour, to seek to squeeze from his small *podere* a sustenance for his now excessive family ... The gross product increases in this case as a result of the overwork of the peasant, who none the less gets no more than half of the product.
> From this is derived the tendency of the Tuscan landlords to draw ever more narrowly the boundaries of the *poderi* and to make investment in land rather than agricultural improvement. A limit to the trend continually to reduce the area of the *poderi* is provided only by the expense necessary to effect the division...[8]

If the tenant fell into arrears in his annual account with the estate, the landlord had a further instrument with which to extract a surplus or, as the Catholic theorist Giuseppe Toniolo commented, a 'supplementary income'.[9] In such cases the *mezzadro* was able to settle accounts only by working in the off-season for the landlord at disadvantageous wage rates well below those earned by day labourers. This was the phenomenon one author terms 'debt labour', by means of which the proprietor secured cheap labour year-round for the estate.[10] In bad years the landlord could partly offset this loss of revenue by squeezing forced labour from the tenant through the debt mechanism.

It was this ability by various devices endlessly to intensify labour that was the magic economic secret of *mezzadria* which enabled it to survive into the modern world in the face of competition from more rationalized and advanced systems of agriculture.[11] Already in 1836 Marquis Capponi, one of the largest of Tuscan landlords, pointed accurately to unrelenting toil by the tenants as the vital economic underpinning of *mezzadria* – a toil that was as dear in human terms as it was cheap to the lords. 'Regarding man as an instrument of labour,' wrote Capponi,

> our agriculture is costly in the extreme; but, under any other system, man would do less and cost more. The cultivator is always on the spot, always careful. His constant thought is, 'This field is my own' ... The amount of labour bestowed by the cultivator would prove too costly to the proprietor if obliged to pay for it; it would not answer his purpose.[12]

Moreover, contrary to the 'official' view of sharecropping life, recent studies of the *mezzadria* system have concluded that by the early twentieth century the remuneration of sharecroppers was not only low, but actually lower than that of any category of industrial worker.[13]

Finally, if the landlord compensated for low productivity by the overwork of the peasant family and by the low level of remuneration of its members, he further fortified himself against adversity by a minimum of outlay on transfer and welfare payments. The *mezzadro*, that is, received no pension, no sickness and disability compensation, and few attentions from costly charitable or public institutions. Thus, comparing the welfare condition of *mezzadro* and worker, the socialists of Florence addressed the peasants in 1900 to point out the disadvantages of their position. Take one example, the socialists began,

> When a worker falls ill – since the labourers in the town have made themselves heard, and intend to be aided in their needs – he is received *free of charge* by the hospitals, and the commune pays the bill with the money of everyone – that is, also with the money of you peasants who pay taxes. But, if one of you peasants takes ill, he must bear his suffering and cause his family to suffer in toil. Or if the peasant wants to come to the hospital, perhaps for an operation, then he must meet the fee of 2.50 lire a day. It is as if you peasants were not impoverished labourers who need to be cared for by society ... when, because of sickness, you cease to work and therefore to earn.[14]

For the peasant unable to work, the tenants themselves would provide through the institution of the extended family – a solution at once thrifty and conducive to public order.

Of the benefit of their savings in welfare payments the Georgofili were, of course, well aware. Carlo Massimiliano Mazzini discussed at length the welfare legislation of 1883 and 1898 that provided accident, disability, and old-age compensation for workers in industry.[15] For Mazzini such benefits for industrial workers were a necessary means to combat socialism,[16] but he understood that 'it is not light this new burden that weighs on Italian industry',[17] and he rejoiced that there was no need to extend welfare payments to the sharecroppers, who posed no subversive threat.[18]

Such aspects apart, *mezzadria* was a highly vulnerable system, as a variety of factors produced a tendency towards backwardness and inflexibility in its production methods – a fact noted by nearly all students of the Tuscan countryside. Speaking at the Accademia dei Georgofili in 1837, Cosimo Ridolfi seized on the essential point when he remarked:

> Neither is our land fertile, nor are we abundant in our use of fertilizers, and if production continues it is due solely to the great labour and diligence of cultivation which is obtainable only on estates held in *mezzadria*.[19]

The organization of *mezzadria* production for subsistence – a sort of miniature autarky of the *podere* – effectively precluded specialization of cultivation and a developed and rational division of labour.²¹ The contract itself also discouraged investment because half the return, at least in principle, went to the partner. In fact, *mezzadria* was best adapted to an environment such as that of Tuscany where the facts of geology – a predominance of hills and mountains, and a thin rocky topsoil²² – made the prospect of investment relatively unenticing and created very tangible difficulties for agricultural machinery. Moreover, the division of the estate into *poderi*, though it necessitated relatively small increments of on-going capital investment, required a very substantial initial outlay in peasant cottages, terraces, fences, trees, vineyards, and irrigation systems. Much of this original investment was not readily convertible into the structures necessary for the working of the entire estate as a single agricultural unit. To transform the *fattoria* required of the landlord not only a new outlay of capital in a difficult physical environment, but also the abolition at a stroke of a substantial part of his inheritance of previous investment in the land.²³ *Mezzadria* was suited to the cultivation of crops which, like the Tuscan olive trees and vineyards, required close application throughout the year. Thus, *mezzadria* tended towards backward methods and slowness of change, for which the system compensated by its particular ability to secure diligent and unending toil and to require of the propertied classes a low level of continuing investment and welfare expense.²⁴

But, even if the idyllic and mendacious picture of rural social relations described by men of property was belied by the reality of class opposition of interests, there was still good reason for concurring with the Georgofili in their evaluation of the political usefulness of *mezzadria* in preserving the traditional appearance of social harmony. The real explanation, however, is not advanced by the landowners. The idea of genuine class concord in the Tuscan countryside was contradicted by the underlying structure of opposing economic interest. It was mocked by the unbridgeable social distance between the partners and disproved by a whole history of class guerrilla warfare by the *mezzadri* in the form of petty theft, fraud, and poaching. Even murder had a long subterranean history as the final recourse of desperate men.²⁵ Class harmony was further refuted by the landlords themselves, who did not trust so far in the community of interest between themselves and their tenants as to fail to provide their estates with the so-called *fattore* (bailiff) and his assistants (the *sottofattori* and guards) whose duties were those of policeman and judge. Their task was to enforce the landlords' exactions upon a less than enthusiastic tenantry.

The *fattore* was generally of humble rural origin – a *mezzadro* or household servant who, on the strength of years of reliable submission, had been promoted by a long series of stages as guard and *sottofattore* to the trusted position of chief overseer. The fact that the main qualification for the post was political reliability rather than expertise in agriculture is testimony to the nature of the office as the eye of the lord. The traditional *fattori*, in the words of the agronomist Professor Rampazzi, 'come from all the most diverse social classes. It is hoped that they will be honest, but they need to be more alert than capable. They have no technical functions.'[25] A particularly clear statement is that of an anonymous Tuscan *fattore*, who thus described the position for the socialist paper of Siena:

> The *fattore* belongs to the category of men without class. He is the man who knows how to serve for little reward, who gains from the most abject servility a life without a future, if he be an honest man.
> None the less, this man without prospects ... lends himself to all manner of shifty, evil, and sometimes brutal conduct towards the peasants.
> Is there a trick to be played, a deed of violence to be done, a whim to be imposed? Call the *fattore*. Is there a peasant to be found for a dealing that will be happy and profitable for the landlord? Call the *fattore*. Is there a bargain to be struck with not overly scrupulous middlemen? Call the *fattore*.[26]

None the less, despite the evidence of a subterranean current of class antagonism, there is hardly a trace until after the First World War of genuine class warfare. There is no history in Tuscany (excluding Grosseto province, where *mezzadria* was not the rule) of large-scale brigandage or of sporadic Jacqueries as in the South. Nor was there a record of large-scale peasant strikes or subversive organizations as in the North. It was this history of peasant docility that was dear to the Tuscan aristocracy.

Now, to understand the roots of this docility and the developments which undermined it is essential to the task of explaining the rise of agrarian unrest and the advent of fascism. Fascism in Tuscany was directly linked to the crisis of the *mezzadria* system. To explain fascism, one must begin by examining the conditions underlying the stability of *mezzadria* and the influences which produced a major upheaval.

Means of social control

Although there was little reason to accept the ideology of the 'bond of love and gratitude'[27] between landlord and *mezzadro*, still the first factor which accounts for the outburst of unrest was the serious decline in the relationship between the partners. The landlord, despite the assertions of the Georgofili, was hardly inclined to desire a comrade in the person of his tenant, or to value the well-being of the peasant above profit. None the less, there was, historically, a close personal link of a kind between the two classes in the countryside. The landlord, first of all, often resided on his property, played some part in the agricultural cycle, and interested himself in the affairs of the peasants. There was, of course, an antagonistic side in this involvement, as the lord sought to influence peasant affairs, morality, and religion in the interest of the 'public quiet'. The other side of such involvement, however, was a tradition of lordly paternalism, that 'fragile bridge of community' across unresolvable contradictions of interest.[28] In time of sickness, the lord, traditionally, provided medicine and advice. In the event of a bad harvest, he might mitigate hard times by extending credit or making a gift. In the event of the marriage of a tenant's daughter, the proprietor assisted in the provision of a dowry. In addition, he gave advice in the peasant's infrequent contacts with authority and, on occasion, interceded. It was the landlord who financed the few grand festivities of village and parish life. The impulse to rebellion was thus blunted by the moral authority of the owner, by the conviction of his inevitability and usefulness, and perhaps by the memory of an act of largesse.[29]

On the value of paternalism as an antidote to subversion, Gasparin had written in 1833 to remind the Tuscan landed classes that

> The necessity of always having interests in common with the *mezzaiuoli*, of discussing every aspect of cultivation with them, and of listening to their opinion makes relations friendly and authority inoffensive.
>
> Here authority is more that of the father of a family than that of a boss, and this leading characteristic is seen everywhere.[30]

The power of the aristocracy was buttressed by the legitimating force Max Weber terms 'patriarchal authority' – the force of immemorial custom. Peasants acquiesced in the existing order because it was the world in which they were born and because there were strong bonds to the landlord that extended across the class divide that separated owner and tenant.[31]

In addition to this tie to the person of the landlord, the *mezzadro* was strongly bound to the land. In the first half of the nineteenth century Simonde de Sismondi, an attentive observer of the Tuscan countryside, stressed this point. The *mezzaiuolo*, he wrote,

> lives on his *podere* as if it were his own inheritance. To it he gives his love ... trusting in the future and feeling certain that after death his fields will be kept and worked by his sons, and by the sons of his sons. Most *mezzaiuoli* are born of fathers and grandfathers born on the *podere*.[32]

Even in the new century, when security of tenure had been seriously undermined, Toniolo claimed that the hold of Tuscan *mezzadri* on the land was more secure than that of the owners, and Gino Sarrocchi, the Liberal deputy from Siena announced in parliament that, 'we have a large number of families who have been on the same *podere* for two hundred years'.[33]

In such statements Sismondi, Toniolo, and Sarrocchi, accepting the official wisdom of the Georgofili, made grossly insufficient allowance for eviction, the ultimate sanction and ever-present threat of lordly power. Recent studies suggest that, even in the mythical golden age of *mezzadria*, eviction was regularly used to guarantee obedience and maintain productivity. A tenant family that did not perform to expectation had no future on the estate. Nevertheless, in comparison with other regions and with the casual day labourer, the Tuscan sharecropper did enjoy a relative security. Until the end of the agricultural cycle the *mezzadro* was safe, and on the annual day of reckoning a hardworking and deferential tenant could expect to have his contract renewed. Thus the peasant felt an attachment with the past and cherished the hope of future advancement by dint of hard labour. Whatever the reality of his living standards, the *mezzadro* had at least a precarious niche in the social order.

Moreover, at least until the late nineteenth century the *mezzadro* felt a sense of independence on his plot. Objectively, of course, the landlord established the entire context within which the tenant laboured, providing tools and seed, building and maintaining the cottage, physically marking off the boundaries of the *podere*, determining the intensity of labour and the degree of remuneration, and linking the whole structure to the broader influences of the market. But the reality of lordly control was partly veiled and hidden from sight. There was little need for fiats from above. The crops grown – chiefly wheat, corn, olives, and grapes – were those that had been cultivated for centuries according to methods well known and sanctioned by tradition. Thus the task confronting the peasant was directed by an ineluctable and impersonal necessity. The fact that the tenant produced for his own sustenance with frequently no other source of income ensured application without the interference of the owner and his agents in day-to-day affairs. Certainly the *fattore* was a reminder of lordly power, but his supervision was distant and his interventions sporadic. He was traditionally bookkeeper and policeman rather than manager or foreman. Thus the system of *mezzadria*, from the standpoint of the peasant, acquired an appearance of inevitability, as if the only obstacles to enrichment were nature and the niggardliness of the Tuscan soil. The forces which impinged on the tenant's life seemed, in comparison with other systems of cultivation, as impersonal as the laws of nature. If the *mezzadro* was discontented, against whom was he to revolt?

The sense of peasant independence was reinforced, first, by the reality of the looseness of the economic relation of the *podere* to the *fattoria* and then by the internal organization of the peasant family. Historically, the dependence of the tenant was veiled. In a traditional agrarian system such as that which dominated central Italy with backward biennial crop rotations, scarce use of mechanical equipment or fertilizer, and a very stunted development of animal husbandry, little capital was advanced centrally by the *fattoria*, and the peasant's recourse to the lord's capital was intermittent. The tenant family felt itself in large measure self-sufficient.

The feeling of self-reliance was further underscored by the extended *mezzadro* family, which was composed of as many as twenty members.[34] Since its task was self-sufficiency in the context of non-specialized cultivation, the patriarchal peasant family undertook a developed division of labour in the work of providing the necessities of life under the authority of its head or *capoccia*. The *capoccia* was the legal representative of the family in all dealings with the landlord and the state, and he was its effective and often authoritarian head. He determined the tasks to be performed in the fields, while his wife, the *massaia*, apportioned domestic industry among the members of the family. Domestic industry was a major element in the traditional sharecropping family economy. The women of the household made all of the clothing worn by the family from wool, hemp, and cotton-waste. Thus Simonde de Sismondi, observing Tuscany before Unification, wrote of his astonishment at the number of articles the peasants possessed – sheets, shirts, jerkins, trousers, skirts, dresses, and all in sufficient supply. It was the ability of the extended family to carry on such household production that lifted the *mezzadri* above the destitution of the wage labourers.[35] In a variety of ways, then, independence was reinforced while the attachment of the *mezzadro* to the existing order was secured by the whole network of the bonds of filial piety and family affection.[36]

More was involved, however, than affection and the sense of independence created by the autarky of the *podere*. In addition, the patriarchal family was an institution that blunted the force of rising social protest, fostered divisions among its members rather than between the family and the landlord, and decentralized the burden of estate management. This is the more comprehensible if we recognize that both the sharecropping family and the institution of the *capocciato* were contractual and juridical rather than natural entities.[37] The peasant family (*famiglia colonica*), that is, was legally defined as all those who lived upon and cultivated the *podere*. Ties of blood relationship inevitably formed the nucleus of the peasant family, and often the natural family and the legal family were coextensive. Frequently, however, the legal family was not united throughout by blood ties, but consisted of three or four family units living under the same roof. In this case the law sometimes referred not to the *famiglia*, but to the 'tenant partnership' (*società colonica*).[38] It was to this composite entity rather than to its individual members that the *podere* was entrusted. The 'family' was collectively responsible for all contractual obligations. Thus neither the death nor the flight of single members of the clan could deprive the lord of his due. Legal fiction served as an instrument of discipline over a large and scattered work-force.

The interests of the proprietor were further guaranteed by the institution of the *capocciato*. Like the family itself, the internal hierarchy of the family was a legal creation. The head of the family did not owe his position and influence simply to age and personal ascendancy. He was initially selected by the members of the family to represent them in their dealings with authority, but with the important proviso that the landlord could veto the choice of his tenants. Only a person acceptable to the owner and his agents could be invested as *capoccia*. That the landlord could thus intervene to determine the outcome of the selection process altered the nature of the office. The *capoccia* represented the owner as well as the tenants.

The legal powers of the office further distanced the head from the members of his family. The law stipulated that only the *capoccia* could reach juridical maturity: regardless of age, the other members of the family were locked in a permanent minority. Like children they could not quit the estate, marry, buy land, or establish savings accounts without his consent, whether or not there was a blood relationship. Only the *capoccia* could incur obligations in the market or conclude business with the landlord, and his decisions were binding on all. The head alone directed the division of labour within the family. In the civil code and in local contracts the *capoccia* was truly the 'head and representative of the tenant family'.[39]

Thus within the peasant household a position of genuine privilege – a 'little tyranny' in the words of one landlord[40] – was created and sanctioned by law. As a result, the established order acquired a position of leverage and influence inside the family. The *capoccia* was aware not only of the divide which separated him from the owner but also of his own small pedestal of authority and domination. It is hardly surprising that in practice the *capocciato* became a force of moderation in the countryside, a buffer between lordly power and peasant discontent. Patriarchy institutionalized work discipline in the home.

At the same time that latent opposition from below thus failed to emerge as open conflict and the impulse to rebellion shrivelled before it had acquired purpose and target, there was a virtual absence of horizontal links among the peasants themselves. As a result, the material premises for the forging of that sense of community indispensable to collective political action were missing. Marx writes that men cannot master their social relations before they have been created in fact. In mid-nineteenth-century

France he argued that the peasantry formed an inert 'sack of potatoes' because the prevailing dispersed pattern of settlement fostered isolation and an incapacity to take collective action. In his words:

> The small-holding peasants form a vast mass, the members of which have a similar condition but without entering into manifold relations with one another. Their mode of production isolates them from one another. Each individual peasant is almost self-sufficient... and the identity of their interests begets no community, no mutual bond and no political organization among them. They do not form a class.[41]

Contemporary central Italy conformed to Marx's vision. The vast majority of peasants lived scattered across the land on family homesteads with few contacts even with tenants on the same estate. There were few bases for the exchange of information, the establishment of bonds of sociability, and the formation of a collective identity. The isolation of the nineteenth-century *mezzadro* could hardly be overstated: he lived as if he were the only peasant in Italy. Travellers to the region were struck by this feature of Tuscan rural society. Thus Sir John Bowring, reporting in 1836 to the British parliament on conditions in the Grand Duchy, wrote:

> But there is a point of view which, it seens to me, has not excited sufficient attention: this is the universal isolation of the peasantry, which is a necessary consequence of the mezzeria system ... Every peasant's family in Tuscany stands as it were alone: this is indeed a great gain for the public security, but it is a tranquillity purchased at a terrible price – the price of a stationary and backward civilization ... I had occasion more than once to see four generations inhabiting the same cottage; but the last had not added a particle of knowledge to the ignorance of the first ... In innumerable cases families have occupied the same farms for hundreds of years without adding a farthing to their wealth, or a fragment to their knowledge.[42]

The economy of the tenant plot reinforced the isolation produced by the pattern of settlement. Autarky excluded the *mezzadro* from communal relationships. Members of the family were cut off from market relations. They had none of the solidarity that arises from working in the large groups that formed so important a part of the life of the day labourer who formed part of a work gang. The Tuscan sharecropping family instead aimed at total self-sufficiency. Historically, there was little tradition of mutual assistance or of the exchange of labour at harvest time.[43]

This lack of contact among the peasants was not only a result of circumstance. It was actively furthered by the landowners, who were well aware of the political benefits of isolating their tenants. Gatherings of all sorts were carefully discouraged as sources of vice and riotous behaviour. It was often within the contractual rights of the vigilant *fattore* to exercise the power of eviction, as one pact stated, 'in the event that a member of the family was in the habit of frequenting taverns, cafés, billiard rooms or other places of dissipation and vice'.[44] Even religious observance, in which the Church conveyed the very same message of class harmony and partnership that the landlords advocated and to which it added its own exhortations to patience and discipline, was meant to be reserved for festival days. The Tuscan *mezzadro*, in so far as it was in the power of the landlords, was not to have the opportunity to conceive of himself as part of a collective rather than as a toiling, self-reliant individualist.

The general social context of sharecropping provided few countervailing influences. The state, even in the form of tax collector and military conscriptor, was a distant force impinging little on the peasant in the Grand Duchy. Education was rudimentary or nonexistent, and communications poor. Emigration was not a feature of Tuscan society, so that broad and possibly subversive influences were unlikely to arrive from peasants who had gone off to work in Turin, Milan, or Switzerland. Altogether, the ignorance of the traditional *mezzadro* was complete. The information available to the Tuscan sharecropper in the middle of the nineteenth century was confined to such events as the *fattore*, the landlord, and the parish priest chose to relate.[45]

COMMERCIAL CHANGES AND THE NEW 'MEZZADRIA'

Beginning with Unification, however, and with increasing force from about 1880, a whole series of changes took place which radically altered social conditions in the Tuscan provinces, upset the entire mythology of partnership in *mezzadria*, and created the premises for conflict. At the most general level, these changes were associated with the development of capitalism as a world system and the way in which Tuscany belatedly became a part of the national and international market. A first major influence was Unification itself, which eliminated internal barriers to trade and thereby created the possibility of a regional division of labour in Italy. From the standpoint of the Tuscan propertied classes, this implied the opportunity of increased profits from more intensive cultivation and the risks of declining returns from the traditional generalized subsistence agriculture. At the same time, Unification under the auspices of the commercially advanced Piedmont entailed the use of the national state to further the development of Italian capital. In particular, the years after Unification witnessed the use of the state as an engine of primitive accumulation drawing capital from agriculture for investment in the industrial infrastructure of roads, railways, and the merchant marine. The means employed were a regressive fiscal system which relied primarily on a variety of indirect taxes and direct taxes on agriculture, which weighed most heavily on those least able to pay. Examples were the family tax, the land tax, the grist tax, the salt duties, the cattle tax. The burden of these fiscal measures fell most heavily on the agricultural provinces and, within them, on the peasantry.[46]

By 1907 a leading representative of the Tuscan landed aristocracy, Francesco Guicciardini, estimated that in most Tuscan communes the tax burden levied by local authorities alone reached 15–20 per cent of the total income from the land, with nearly the whole being borne by the peasantry. Moreover, Guicciardini continued, taxation, both local and national, was continually revised upwards so that 'the tax system for the sharecropper is a genuine regime of oppression'.[47] As a result of the combination of taxes and protective tariffs, Guicciardini noted, the price of sugar quadrupled and many commodities, once common, became unknown even in the most prosperous peasant households. Salt in particular became the 'torment of the *massaie*' that eliminated other items from the diet. At the same time the duty on oil forced the peasants to do without light, to the point of shortening their evenings and doing without family discussions. Thus the development of Italian capitalism meant further impoverishment for the *mezzadri* and the creation of greater market outlets for the landlords, who now possessed vastly increased incentives for investment. In the long run, these developments proved subversive of the much praised 'public quiet'.

In the 1880s, moreover, the international market made its influence keenly felt in Tuscany with the large-scale arrival in Europe of grain from America. This transoceanic competition spelled a long-term decline in the price of wheat, and therefore a crisis of the *mezzadria* system, which was largely based on extensive wheat cultivation. This crisis was worsened at the end of the century by a tariff war with France, which was a major importer of two other leading products of Tuscan agriculture – wine and olive oil. Thus, with new market outlets to attract investment and declining prices there was a penalty for the continued reliance on the traditional crops and means of cultivation. From about 1880, therefore, there were major changes in the countryside.[48]

To understand these developments, however, one must keep in mind certain limitations which set outer boundaries to the new influences. The contrast between the continuing calm of central Italy and the open class antagonisms of the Po Valley and Apulia greatly strengthened this consciousness. Tuscan landlords viewed the development of rural trade unionism as the danger to be feared from the introduction of wage labour in the countryside. For political reasons, therefore, there was an abiding opposition from the landlords to the idea of dismantling the institution of *mezzadria*. The Tuscan aristocracy was determined to resist the example of the modern commercial farm employing rootless proletarians. The sharecropping system was to be preserved.

What allowed the political preferences of the nobility to prevail was the fact that there were, as we have seen, other more narrowly economic considerations that worked in the same direction. There was the obstacle to change of the investment already embodied in *mezzadria*, an obstacle which proved a serious impediment to the dismantling of the old traditional structures. Then there were the facts of Tuscan soil and topography which were not inducements to the introduction of mechanized equipment or the re-organization of the estates as large-scale farms. Investment in Tuscany was attracted primarily in small increments.

Thus, in the period down to 1922, investment occurred in Tuscany *within* the framework of the *mezzadria* system. Commercialization of agriculture followed a course radically different from the classical pattern of the Po Valley. Nevertheless, it did proceed rapidly from 1890 with profound, if not immediate visible, political consequences. To appreciate these political consequences, we must explore the differences that separated the new *mezzadria* from the traditional pattern.

The most obvious symbol of the new commercial trend was the introduction of such industrial crops as tobacco and sugar beet and of fodder crops for artificial pasture.[49] These were first planted in the fertile river valleys where physical conditions most nearly resembled the Po Valley. Already in the 1880s in the Chiana and Tiber Valleys of Arezzo and Siena provinces and in the lower Arno Valley of Pisa province, there were in use developed four-year rotations (corn–wheat–clover–wheat or corn–wheat–broad beans or vetch–wheat) with refined irrigation techniques, in place of the traditional biennial alternation of wheat and corn, though at this time these were still 'so many exceptions to the general rule of biennial rotation that prevails in Tuscany'.[50] It was in 1881 that a Ministry of Agriculture report on Tuscany revealed the recent introduction of many of the changes associated with commercialized farming in the most fertile valleys where investment was first attracted. In these areas the plough, and especially the iron plough, was just beginning to replace the hoe, and at Siena public demonstrations had been made of a 'most powerful' plough drawn by several pairs of oxen that was capable of tilling the soil to a depth of 50 centimetres. Similarly, the report noted the very first quadrennial rotations then being adopted on an experimental basis and the introduction of the first tobacco plants, as well as a more widespread use of animal fertilizers and the first tentative trials of chemical fertilization.[51]

With such hesitant beginnings in the last quarter of the century, Tuscan agriculture rapidly absorbed the new methods of cultivation, at least in zones where soil, climate, and topography favoured capitalization. By the postwar period, for instance, in the lower Arno Valley of Pisa province less than one third of the land under cultivation was still sown with wheat.[52] A greater area was instead devoted to tobacco and sugar beet, and to artificial pasture for cattle. By 1922, progress having advanced beyond the iron plough, there were over 400 threshing machines in operation in Arezzo province alone.[53]

Thus, in 1914, G. Gastone Bolla, summarizing the changes which had occurred in Tuscan agriculture, wrote:

> No one can any longer deny that agriculture has become industry, and that agricultural production has become industrial production.
>
> This is proved by the fact that ... the art of cultivation, once empirical, has become scientific. It is proved by the use of fertilizers, machines, and electricity; by the breeding of animals and the selection of seeds; by the expansion of industrial crops and of the means of exchange and transport; by the existence of storehouses and places for the first refining of goods; and by the industries that are today tightly linked to and dependent on the primary agricultural enterprise.[54]

Clearly such major developments in the methods of production were associated with important changes as well in the social relations between the classes in the countryside, and in the entire position of the *mezzadro*. The landlord, now involved ever more deeply in production for the market and spurred on by the imperatives of profit, tended to rationalize not only his methods of cultivation but also his relations with his tenants. He gradually became an absentee figure relying on the management of his employee, the *fattore*. The relation between lord and tenant became ever more impersonal, and the tradition of lordly paternalism atrophied from disuse. Leading landlords, from Guicciardini at the turn of the century to Pier Francesco Serragli in 1920, noted this devaluation of the traditional personal bond between landlord and tenant. Recognizing its dangerous effects on rural labour relations, they called for a return of the owners to their estates and for a revival both of paternal aid to the peasants in time of need and of the traditional lordly interest in the details of production.[55] Already by Guicciardini's time, however, the former personal bond between owner and *mezzadro* had frequently become a mere 'cash nexus'. The landlord, indeed, came to be regarded as a rapacious absentee oppressor whose claims were no longer legitimized by personal authority and a visibly useful role.[56] A suggestive illustration of the transformation in rural social relationships was the change in the tradition of paternal assistance in moments of hardship. In the new *mezzadria* the advances extended by the proprietors took on the character of loans bearing interest.

Guicciardini's appeal to the enlightened paternalism of the Tuscan aristocracy ran counter to the economic and social evolution of the region. It was, in effect, the swan song of a traditional relationship fallen into abeyance. The sincerity of Guicciardini's belief in the political value of lordly paternalism was demonstrated in practice by his attempt to elaborate a whole code of aristocratic behaviour towards the peasantry. But the very effort to re-impose such a code was an indication of the irrelevance of the old relations to the new conditions. The next generation of landlords represented by Serragli combined a merely half-hearted appeal to the efficacy of paternalism as an antidote to subversion with a new and altogether more ominous call for an alternative politics of repression and retrenchment. By 1921 Serragli, the former mayor of Florence, was a key figure in the organization of squadrism.

At the same time that the link between tenant and proprietor deteriorated, so the bond tying the *mezzadro* to the land was seriously weakened. In the past the security of the *mezzadro's* tenure had been a major factor in the stability of Tuscan rural society, despite hardship, toil, and a depressed standard of living. By contrast, insecurity and declining living conditions were marked features of the new commercial system. The growing tax burden, of course, played an important role here. The closer relationship between city and countryside now linked through the person of the tax collector, was not, however, the sole source of a slow expropriation of the *mezzadri*. The new agricultural methods involved ever-increasing expenses for the peasant. Inherent in the sharecropping contract was the obligation of the peasant to divide not only the harvest but also the costs of cultivation. Historically, these costs had been comparatively small as agricultural methods in central Italy had been backward. The decision of the landlords to initiate more intensive farming for the market here marked a radical change. There was now a much greater outlay for seeds and plantings, for fertilizers and fodder, for tools and machinery. Taken together with the increased tax burden, the new expenses created a rapidly growing peasant indebtedness as the landowner became ever more a creditor rather than a partner. Guicciardini, for example, reported from his own estate of Cusona that of 31 *mezzadro* families seven had been in debt in 1895 for a total of 1,422 lire, whereas in 1911 the total debt had risen to 20,654.85 lire.[57] Guicciardini also indicated a major source of the worsening economic condition of the sharecroppers: the return to the tenant from the new crops was not sufficient to compensate for the growing costs of cultivation. Such was the logical result of a system in which expenses were equally divided between the partners, but the harvest, through a series of arrangements beneficial to property, went in larger proportion to the owners. As costs increased, the tenant was caught in a form of scissors crisis between a fixed share (50

Table 1.

Podere	Tenant's total share of the expenses of cultivation (in lire)	Tenant's share of the cost of the ensulphuration of vines (in lire)
Apparita	217.50	125.30
Bellosguardo	83.39	50.89
Belvedere	284.23	186.11
Bruceto	52.48	28.08
Buzzotto	162.18	89.31
Campo al Castagneto	74.58	53.73
Casa nuova	184.42	108.67
Case	115.22	76.83
Casedoniche	67.76	31.16
Casi (1)	138.16	72.53
Casi (2)	86.87	46.89
Collina	130.55	67.82
Colombaia	98.04	63.39
Fonte a Solano	189.37	127.23
Gabbiana	77.56	39.66
Granchiaia	277.64	170.09
Grisciavola	183.63	144.11
Masso all'Anguilla	99.06	50.64
Mulino all'Americana	168.51	68.54
Mulino del Vado	52.98	22.05
Palagio	65.54	53.17
Palagio-Sacchi	71.08	58.68
Pianaccio	91.77	71.33
Piani	56.10	51.08
Poggiale	200.84	112.46
Poggio (1)	108.49	69.14
Poggio (2)	83.67	50.70
Poggiolino	297.52	153.71
Riposo	178.89	128.91
Serilli	39.74	24.86
Solano	221.17	152.83
Strada	136.80	80.13
Tafanaia	104.80	56.50
Terravistio	186.46	131.64
Villa	85.82	70.40

ACP, FVR, (Fondo Vai Rurale), Filza 421, 'Mulinaccio conti colonici', 1 June 1912 – 31 May 1913.

per cent) of increasing expenses and a substantially smaller proportion of the eventual return.[59]

The role of increased expenses resulting from commercial change emerges clearly from the surviving acounts of the Mulinaccio estate of 35 *poderi* belonging to the Vai family in the Prato zone of Florence province. The records for the agricultural year 1912–13 indicate the peasants' share of the expenses of cultivation, together with an itemization of the various costs involved. What is most interesting, as table 1 shows, is that on every *podere* of the estate the most heavy financial outlays, generally accounting for more than half of the total expense for the year, were those for chemical fertilizers (sulphur and copper sulphate) for the ensulphuration of the vineyards.

On the Mulinaccio estate, in other words, the expense of the new intensive methods of cultivation constituted the bulk of the cost of sharecropping production. The point becomes clearer still if we remember that Prato was not one of the zones of most advanced commercial progress and that the tenants at Mulinaccio were not burdened with the major outlays for machinery and mechanical equipment that one would have encountered in the Chiana Valley or the Pisa plain.[60] The accounts of the Mulinaccio *fattoria*, then, help to explain the fact that the question of the division of the new burdens of commercial farming between landlord and peasant became one of the vital points of conflict in the Tuscan countryside.

Together with the increased expenses, conditions of living declined. Here reliable indices are difficult to obtain, but there are several indications that all point in the same direction. One is the direct testimony of such major landlords as Guicciardini, who admitted the decline and analysed some of its causes. Another is the appearance for the first time from the late nineteenth century of a sizeable incidence of the diseases of malnutrition, especially pellagra, and of the diseases of poor sanitation, such as hepatitis and cholera. Descriptions of peasant living conditions in the new century portray a reality of overwork, misery, and squalor for the Tuscan *mezzadro*.[60] In the new *mezzadria* Sismondi's comments on the abundance of clothes possessed by the peasants no longer applied. Thus even the *Intrepido*, the fascist paper of Lucca, which had little political sympathy for the tenants, conducted an investigation in the summer of 1922 into the 'physical, hygienic, and sanitary conditions of the workers of the land'. The conclusions conflicted with the usual optimism of the Georgofili. For the 'generality' of Tuscan sharecroppers, conditions were rather less than the envy of the working classes of the world.[61]

The *Intrepido* noted that about 300 days of the year were devoted to work, 248 in the fields and 52 in the family cottage – repairing tools, selecting seeds, tending to hedges, mending clothes. The work day itself tended towards 14 hours as a year-round average, with a high point in the autumn when the *mezzadri* even slept in the fields and a low of 10–11 hours in the winter.[62] The diet was restricted and deficient in vitamins and protein. Its basis was ground meal prepared from wheat, corn, or chestnuts supplemented with potatoes, beans, and vegetable soup garnished with pigs' fat. Meat and eggs were saved for feasts, and wine was a luxury reserved for the harvest season.[63] Clothing was inadequate, with a weekly change of underwear the rule, and shoes were a refinement saved for winter, for church, and for trips to town. In winter the tenants shivered in the cold.[64] Most striking of all, perhaps, was the description of peasant housing:

> The walls are not plastered outside, and they are blackened with smoke inside. The rooms are narrow, very low, and insufficient in number, so that it is impossible in the bedrooms to separate the sexes, and often even to separate the married couples from the others. There is no toilet. The floors are often formed of planks through whose cracks there spreads throughout the house the pestilential stink of the squalid pig sty underneath. The roof is covered with broken tiles ... which admit the rain and sometimes the snow as well. The narrow windows often lack both frame and glass, and are closed only by wooden boards, so that in the winter even by day one must sit in the dark or brave the elements. The furniture is sparse and in disrepair. On the bed sometimes there is a mattress of wool or more frequently of chicken feathers, but very often this is missing and what passes for a bed is a miserable mat of straw. In a word everything bears the mark of poverty and hardship.[65]

Even the Mugello landlords' paper was capable of a far from sanguine account. It admitted that

> many landlords have made the maintenance of the peasant dwelling their last concern, whether from the point of view of the structure of the building or the appurtenances, not to mention the question of propriety and hygiene.[66]

More broadly, a leading Catholic paper noted that

> *mezzadria* ... in the last decade of the last century and the early years of this, has undergone a transformation wholly to the detriment of the peasant and to the advantage of the proprietor.[67]

Still another indication of growing hardship was the suddden beginning, from the turn of the century, of peasant emigration from the region – a phenomenon which until that time had been virtually nonexistent.[68] The idea of peasant security had become a mockery.

So, too, the earlier independence of the peasant cultivator had become only a memory. We have already seen that there was a long-term tendency for the landlord to restrict the size of the *poderi* in order to gain a greater intensity of labour. Now the increase in productivity associated with the new methods afforded the possibility of subsistence from a much smaller area. Hence the commercial revolution in the Tuscan countryside was accompanied by a drastic reduction in the average size of the peasant plot. Furthermore, together with the smaller *podere* went a break-up of the extended patriarchal sharecropping family. Estimates of the size of the traditional family vary – as large as 20–30 members according to some authorities,[69] as small as 10–15 members according to others.[70] What is clear, however, is that the large families of 20 or more members which had once existed and that some authorities consider typical of traditional Tuscan *mezzadria* were wholly disappearing. The new average of 7 members by 1930[71] marked a sharp decline. Indeed, still smaller families were common in the zones of most advanced commercial change. With good reason the bulletin of the Tuscan Agrarian Association warned of the 'systematic dissolution of the share-cropping families' as a 'new danger for *mezzadria*'.

There was a rough inverse correlation in postwar Tuscany between the size of the *podere* and the intensity of cultivation – from the *poderi* of 2 to 4 hectares in the irrigated valleys to those of 60 hectares or more in the Maremma.[72] Moreover, the small plots of the fertile river valleys were of recent formation, resulting from the tendency, there most advanced, towards the ever-greater fractioning of the *fattoria*. In these areas, reports of the situation by the 1920s give the impression of a feverish activity in the dismemberment of *poderi* and the break-up of peasant families. Thus Camparini and Bandini reported from the Chiana Valley that,

It [*mezzadria*] presents ... the general feature of a scarcity of manpower owing to the dismemberment of the large peasant families and to the strong attraction of industry, particularly on the young.

The size of the *podere* tends to become continually smaller, and there is an ever-greater need for new peasant housing and the formation of new *poderi*.[73]

The decline of the extended family was not simply a reduction in size but also a degeneration of the moral bonds among the family members. As increasing economic pressures were exerted upon the tenants, disputes over the internal division of labour and of the crop became pronounced and often bitter. Divisions began to separate the generations as youths grew impatient of the traditional authoritarian rule of the *capoccia* at a time when hardship was increasing, and the prospects of an improved future seemed ever more remote. Indeed, announcing the 'funeral of *mezzadria*', the Mugello landlord, A. Giovannini, mourned:

Between landlord and peasant, and among the members of the same household, harmony has been broken. Conflict dominates thought and attitude, gives rise to quarrels, and builds a wall of separation ... The elders are unable to adapt to this state of war after having lived in relations of peace, so dear to the heart and conscience and also so useful to the furtherance of legitimate interests. The *massaie* as well, devoted and attached to disciplined tranquillity in the family, refuse to accept the arguments that inflame the young. The old patriarchal household traditions suffer and fall into disuse. Words are sometimes spoken that bite; and quarrels and disputes arise and are embittered by differing political beliefs and conflicting ideas, even in religion.[74]

In addition, the break-up of the extended peasant family worsened peasant economic security by decreasing the possibility for a developed division of labour within the family. As a result, the number of ancillary tasks performed by the family declined, particularly domestic industry. This in turn forced the *mezzadro* into greater reliance on market relations and thus into greater indebtedness.[75] A downward spiral was begun in which economic hardship and the declining family were each at once cause and effect of the other. The process was accentuated where specialization of cultivations was most advanced and industrial crops were grown. Then, by definition, the traditional subsistence farming gave way to extensive relations of exchange. The near-autarky of the *podere* was at an end.[76]

In any case, the independence of the *podere* had also been abolished from another point of view – that of the relation of the peasant farm to the estate management. Traditionally, this relation was one of day-to-day independence for the *podere* and limited responsibilities for the *fattore*. As the landlord invested more capital in agriculture, however, the dealings of the *mezzadro* with the central estate underwent a marked change. The concentration of the ownership of the means of production in the hands of the proprietor made the sharecropper ever more similar, in fact if not in legal form, to the rural proletarian of the North. The independence of the tenant vanished as he grew increasingly reliant on the machines, the fertilizers, and the technical knowledge of the landlord and became increasingly subject to the supervision of the owner's agents. Indeed, the changing functions of the *fattore* were among the most conspicuous features of the commercialization of Tuscan agriculture. On modernized estates he became the agent of rationalizing directives from above and was made responsible for the technical direction of production. He overcame tenant reluctance, introduced industrial crops, supervised the establishment of new systems of rotation, selected seeds, and attended to the use of fertilizers and machinery. The *fattore*, in a word, had become a manager.[77]

Certainly the *fattori* saw themselves, in the changed circumstances, as a rising class of rural agricultural specialists with new claims to security, prestige, and improved treatment from their employers. In the new century they founded an association of *fattori* to press their claims and a paper, the *Fattore toscano*, to spread the glad tidings of the new dignity of the landlords' agents.[78] The chief point here, however, is that a corollary of the increasingly managerial position of the *fattore* was the declining independence of the tenants.[79]

The new position of the *mezzadro* was given clear expression in the worsening contractual terms to which he was subjected as commercialization advanced. Here an important example is the contract in force at the turn of the century on the estates of Count Giovanni Angelo Bastogi in the Chiana Valley of Siena province.[80] What is striking is that modern methods of cultivation and industrial crops had given rise to important new clauses in the contract, all embodying new and onerous burdens for the tenant.

The influence of commercialization upon the substance of the contract is evident from the very title of many of the clauses. Thus, article 16 was entitled 'Threshing and the cost of machines', article 20 'The turning over of the ground for vines', article 21 'Sulphuration of vines', article 24 'The turning over of the ground for corn', article 25 'Tobacco', article 26 'Sugar beet', and article 34 'Crop rotations and pasture'. In each case there were additional obligations for the peasant, further occasions for supervision by the *fattore*, and fines to sanction non-compliance.[81] The landlord, making heavy new outlays of capital in crops requiring greater attention and application, was not content to rely on the diligence and judgment of the tenant. Instead, he was intent on having his agent present to supervise every phase of the agricultural cycle. Thus the clause on tobacco was endlessly porous in its single statement that, 'For the cultivation of tobacco the Peasant will prepare a part of the land ... in the way indicated by the Landlords or their agents, and carry out such deep tillings as are ordered by the above mentioned, in accord with the applicable rules or special dispositions of the directing authority.'[82] Similar in spirit was the article on sugar beet,[83] while the article on crop rotation intimated that the lord and his agent would determine what area of the *podere* would be devoted to what crops, and how they would be grown.[84] The article on threshing outlined new expenses to accompany the new methods and machinery.[85]

In these provisions the former independence of the *podere* vanished. Bastogi confesses that the new crops had to be introduced against the stubborn resistance of the tenants.[86] At times he attributes this resistance to a simple peasant-like superstition and fear of change. More substantial reasons, however, are easily inferred from the contract itself, which provides for more work, increased expense, and strict discipline under the watchful eye of the *fattore*. Furthermore, Bastogi admits that the peasant growing industrial crops was subject to a much increased insecurity in accord with the vicissitudes of the market, and suggests that the *mezzadro*'s need to market rather than consume the produce of the land provided the less than scrupulous landlord with the opportunity to defraud the tenant of a portion of his share of the harvest.[87] Clearly all of this put a strain on the bond of partnership and love.

The declining position of the sharecroppers was further illustrated by the emergence in sizeable numbers from the end of the century of a variety of new sub-categories of semi-proletarianized tenants known variously as *camporaioli, logaioli, vignaioli,* and *mezzaioli.*[88] Most important were the *camporaioli.* Like *mezzadri*, these new peasants worked on stable *poderi* whose produce they divided in half with the landlord. There, however, the similarity with classical *mezzadria* ended. The new sharecroppers did not live on their plots, which were now too small to provide accommodation. Instead, they commuted to the fields from neighbouring villages or from labourers' barracks, where they paid rent. Furthermore, they did not work the land in family units, but as single workers. Nor did they grow enough for subsistence as their plots were not sufficiently large. Most, therefore, supplemented their income by working part-time as day labourers or as operatives in industry. Significantly, too, the longevity of tenure which had been a major factor in the stability of *mezzadria* no longer existed for the *camporaioli.*[89]

The origin of the new contracts was simple: existing *poderi* were subdivided and given to tenants under radically different and less advantageous conditions. The *camporaioli* formed a category of transition, a temporary halting place for peasants in the process of being reduced to the status of day labourers. The new quasi-proletarians first appeared in the commercially advanced valleys of central Tuscany, where they cultivated specialized crops with machinery and tools they did not own but rented from the lord. They were a growing and, in some areas, already large work-force. By 1930 they accounted for about 10 per cent of all the sharecroppers of the Chiana Valley in Arezzo province.[90]

Beyond the *camporaioli*, more obvious products of the commercial pressures at work in the countryside were the stable nuclei of full-time wage labourers (*braccianti*) of the Chiana and Arno Valleys. These farm workers marked the final step in the dissolution of *mezzadria*. In key zones of the region there was formed that class of rootless rural proletarians against whom the Tuscan aristocracy had long warned as the chief carriers of the socialist contagion.

Day labourers, of course, had been far from unknown even in the mythological golden era of *mezzadria* in the form of casual hands working on the fringes of the estates, tending to the woods, doing the heavy tasks of digging ditches or terraces, and helping during the harvest.[91] Working on the edges of the *fattorie* and returning at intervals to alternative arrangements on the land or in industry, these landless peasants were ancillary to the *mezzadria* system. What is significant is that the increase in the number of wage labourers and their concentration as a major proportion of the work-force in certain zones suggests a fundamental change in social relations. Most frequently the *braccianti* found work on land drainage and reclamation projects, but increasingly in the great river valleys they were employed directly in the cultivation of capitalist farms run along the lines of the Po Valley.[92]

Together the *camporaioli* and *braccianti* were the clearest examples of a very general process of the proletarianization of the sharecropping class as their living standards and security of tenure declined; as they were gradually dispossessed of any meaningful control of the means of production; as they were pushed into broader relations with the market and their families were broken up; and as increasing numbers of them were finally driven from the land and forced to sell their labour power. What must be stressed is that what had occurred was not a series of separate and unrelated developments: the major changes taking place in the substance of *mezzadria* were the interlocking aspects of the single process of the commercialization of Tuscan agriculture.

Not surprisingly, these developments had political consequences which reduced the once pronounced difference between labour relations in central Italy and in the great zones of capitalistic agriculture in the North. The bonds which had linked the *mezzadro* to the social order – ties to master, land, and family – had been severed or seriously weakened, while the causes for discontent had multiplied through the growing burden of debt and taxation, through an increasing insecurity of tenure, and through worsening conditions of health and housing.

At the same time that the vertical bonds of the *mezzadri* to the existing order were overthrown, a new network of horizontal class bonds was forged that provided the collective consciousness that was a major premise of revolt. The traditional isolation of the *mezzadri* was overcome. In part this new communal spirit was the result of the greatly improved means of communication that linked the Tuscan countryside with impulses and influences from outside. In part it was the result of simple demographic increase.[93] Then, too, there was the development of increasing market relations by the sharecroppers as their economic self-reliance was overthrown and they went to market as purchasers of goods and as sellers of labour. Perhaps most important, the development of a collective consciousness was not simply a result of external influences but was created by the peasants themselves. That is, as the family declined in size, there arose during peak periods such as the threshing season a shortage of labour which began in part to be remedied by the mutual exchange of labour. Thus in the zone of the Casentino (the upper Arno Valley in Arezzo province) it was reported by the postwar period that threshing was done almost entirely through the reciprocal exchange of labour among the *mezzadri*.[94] As a result, common action became possible as the peasants came to view their condition as a collective one.

Finally, it should be added that, with the advance of modernization, the conservative influence of the Church in conditioning the political and social beliefs of the peasantry greatly waned. Ernesto Ragionieri, in a study of the comune of Sesto Fiorentino in the new bourgeois Italy, writes of the 'disintegration of parish life'.[95] Whereas the parish church had once been a focus for the few great occasions of peasant life, in Liberal Italy the multiplication of contacts and occasions of a commercial, political, and lay character diminished the awe and importance of the Church and created other rival repositories of attention, loyalty, and hope – the town hall, the party, even the market place. By the propagation of a secular culture and ideology, United Italy weakened the esteem in which the clergy were held. At the same time, changes in the productive process associated with the capitalistic penetration of rural Tuscany evoked a non-religious response. In traditional *mezzadria*, the relation of the *podere* to broad economic forces and to the powers of the landlord had been partly veiled as the peasant felt that his struggle was largely one with himself and with the forces of nature – the soil, the rain and wind, the health of domestic animals and of seed plants. In this setting, one surmises, the power of intercession with divinity was of greater value than at a later time when the exactions of landlord and state, and the vicissitudes of the market had both increased absolutely and become ever more apparent. The landlord was ever more visibly the source of orders and directives, and was clearly responsible for the introduction of new crops and methods that changed the face of the countryside. In all this the peasant came to know his position as the product of human agency, and his response was not religious but political. An important prop of the social order had been quietly removed.

WAR

Collective consciousness was given tremendous impetus by the War, the greatest catalyst of all in the emergence of a mass movement in the countryside. Nowhere in Italy was the contrast between the Giolittian years of untroubled labour relations and the great clashes of the 'Red Years' (1919–20) more striking. Unfortunately, a word of caution is necessary. The social and economic history of the war years is still an underdeveloped subject in Italian history, and one made particularly tentative by the fact that some of the most important sources – the archives of the army and of the economic ministries – have not been made public. Of special relevance for our purpose here is that there is as yet no extended study of the war years and their consequences for the population of central Italy. Such a study would constitute a major research project in the available communal and parish archives that lies beyond the scope of a work on fascism. In the absence of such a work, conclusions on the impact of the conflict on Tuscany are necessarily provisional.

Nevertheless, there is ample evidence to suggest several important considerations.[96] The first is that any overly simple economic determinism is inadequate for an explanation of the political behaviour of the sharecroppers. The *mezzadri* were not propelled into political activism by any clear process of increasing economic hardship during the war. The relationship between economic discontent and peasant political and union militancy in the Tuscan provinces is more complex. In purely financial terms, the *mezzadri* were better able to defend their interests in the maelstrom of the war than the mass of landless farmworkers, for whom the conflict was ruinous throughout Italy.

Farm labourers suffered in part as a result of the effects of war-time economic policies on the agricultural sector. Since the priorities of the government were to maintain industrial production and to supply the army, there was a systematic draining of resources from agriculture to the cities and the front. Grain and livestock were requisitioned; food prices were regulated; and manpower was conscripted, while chemical fertilizers, sprays, machinery, spare parts, and metal tools became impossible to purchase.[97] The contraction of animal husbandry in the Tuscan provinces is illustrative of the processes involved. By 1918 the number of horses and mules on the region declined by 30 per cent, sheep by 17 per cent, pigs by 16 per cent, and cattle by 11 per cent.[98]

At the same time, agricultural prices during the war lagged far behind a galloping rate of inflation. There were, of course, differences from crop to crop. The prices of such industrial crops as grapes and olives were buoyant, while the price of the traditional extensively cultivated staple – wheat – languished. The general price index of wholesale goods (1913 = 100) rose to 502 in 1919–20, but the price of wheat reached an index of only 368 and other food stuffs 405.[99] In general, therefore, there was a significant redistribution of income and resources away from the countryside. The inevitable result was that the productive methods of an already vulnerable sector of the economy were further undermined everywhere in Italy. As investment withered, machines broke down, and fertilization was neglected. Soil erosion advanced, productivity declined, and yields were inferior to prewar norms in both size and quality.

If farming was thus the stepchild of the war effort, the hardship within the agricultural population was very unequally distributed. The landless labourers, the most numerous class in the nation, were most badly affected. Whether they lived through the war as soldiers or as producers, their income in real terms declined sharply. The private soldier's basic pay, set in 1915 at 0.65 lire a day plus an allowance of 0.30 lire for a wife and 0.15 lire for each child, was not raised in line with the cost of living.

For *braccianti* who remained on the land, economic prospects were no more favourable. Wages, like soldiers' pay, failed to keep pace with inflation. It was true that conscription produced a shortage of hands, but the effect was not to raise pay scales in real terms because the workers found that they lacked the means to defend their position. Union structures were decimated in the wake of mass mobilization, and the strike weapon in any case was perilous in the state of emergency. Strikes were also discouraged by the socialist movement, which expressed moral disapproval of the war, but refused to condone actions which could be construed as unpatriotic. 'Neither support nor sabotage!' was the party slogan. Employers, in the meantime, found new methods of wage control in such devices as the massive hiring of women, who cost little; in the use of Austrian prisoners of war to cultivate the fields; and in the decision of some to leave their fields unplanted.

Farm workers who found themselves newly exploited in the fields and in the trenches discovered that they fared no better as consumers and citizens. The war effort entailed not only a decline in purchasing power but also severe shortages in the shops, bread of inferior quality, ever-lengthening queues, and periods of hunger. The government intervened with rations and price controls, but these measures were only partially effective. The state had neither the will nor the means to police the economy in a systematic fashion. The war, therefore, produced a thriving black market where hoarders and speculators added a sharp note of bitterness to the experience of hardship.

The living standards of the mass of the population were further undermined by the effects of the emergency upon local government. From the time of Unification in 1861, the provision of welfare and public services had been largely allocated to the commune. It was the commune which provided health facilities, education, hygiene, and public works. In the Giolittian period, moreover, there was a widespread program of municipal reform in large areas of Italy. Under the influence of socialists, republicans, radicals, and democrats, many communes sought to redistribute wealth through the reform of local taxation, to improve rates of literacy, to combat unemployment, and to improve health. From the date of intervention in 1915, not only did reform cease but town councils also found that they were no longer able even to maintain existing levels of provision. The central governmment dramatically cut their budgets and imposed new and onerous tasks related to the war effort and the administration of the war-time economy. The result was a further sharp decline in living standards, as the representatives of socialist-administered townships throughout Italy explained at a congress in 1916. From Bologna in Emilia to Gravina in Apulia, the assembled mayors and councillors agreed that there was a stark choice between war and welfare, and that Italy had chosen war.[100]

For a variety of reasons, then, the most vulnerable and impoverished sectors of the rural population emerged from the conflict in weakened economic circumstances. In this catalogue of widespread and growing hardship, however, the *mezzadri* were a partial exception. The evidence is still fragmentary, but it suggests that the sharecroppers were able, on average, to maintain their economic position, even to accumulate modest savings.[101] The explanation is uncomplicated. Most important was the fact that, unlike many categories of labour, the croppers received their remuneration in kind rather than in cash. They were insulated, therefore, from the price revolution that followed intervention. For those on capitalized estates who tended vineyards and olive groves, there was still less difficulty in sustaining prewar patterns of consumption as industrial crops kept pace with inflation. Furthermore, living scattered across the countryside rather than in agglomerated settlements and towns, the *mezzadri* were far less affected by the crisis in municipal finances.

A more technical feature of the *mezzadria* contract worked in the peasants' favour in these years of galloping inflation. This feature was the traditional system of 'estimates' (*stime*) for livestock and seed. During the 'normal' years of relative price stability since Unity, the estimates had been a source of indebtedness to the proprietors, as we have seen. Advanced at the outset of the peak-season, animals and seed possessed a higher value than in the off-season when accounts were settled. In the abnormal conditions of the war, however, the months between the opening and the closing of accounts marked a rise in the value of the capital advanced as well as a general devaluation of outstanding debts, so that *mezzadri* found themselves in the unusual position of being able to write off debts instead of accumulating them.

The great threat to the position of the sharecropping family during the war, then, was not the pressure of inflation but the danger of declining yields owing to the shortage of hands resulting from conscription and to the decline in capital investment by the landlord. Capital investment, however, had long been a burden for which the *mezzadro*, as we have observed, was charged half at the discretion of the owner. The inability of landlords to supply copper sulphate was a temporary relief and a saving. With regard instead to manpower, as all authorities on *mezzadria* agreed, one of the strengths of family production was the elasticity of labour.

Sharecropping families maintained output by the prodigious overwork of those who remained on the plot. A human cost was involved, but it could not be measured in financial terms. Furthermore, family production implied that, unlike the *braccianti*, the sharecroppers of central Italy could receive the devalued salaries and family allowances from the front not as their primary means of subsistence but as small additional savings.

Finally, in considering the position of *mezzadri*, one must remember that state intervention had the effect of temporarily increasing their security of tenure and therefore of buttressing their bargaining power in dealings with the proprietor. The state, that is, decreed the freezing of contracts and the postponement of eviction until after the armistice. One of the weapons of lordly power was momentarily suspended.

If the available evidence suggests that the Tuscan *mezzadri* emerged from the holocaust of the First World War with small savings or reduced debts, then the explosion of postwar agitation seems difficult to comprehend. The difficulty, however, is only apparent. The amelioration in the sharecroppers' financial accounts was only a minor and transitory improvement in a position that was in crisis. Furthermore, the existence of savings could further weaken the crumbling structures of traditional *mezzadria*. A relaxation in the constant pressure of the debt mechanism and the possession of some reserves provided the peasants greater margins of resistance and greater means to fund their own organizations. Savings, moreover, accelerated the crisis of the patriarchal tenant family. Men who had spent years in the army and women who had gained independence through working in industry or managing production were unwilling to hand their pay to the *capoccia* or to submit to the old authority. The family headship was further eroded as an institution for preserving the social order.

Most important, however, is the conclusion that the essential contribution of the war to labour militancy in central Italy was not economic but moral. The war transformed the mentality of the soldiers who took part. Peasants emerged at the end of hostilities with a burning sense of injustice. An important reason is that the Italian army was composed disproportionately of peasants in uniform. Of the 2,200,000 men in the army in 1916, over half were peasants, and the proportion increased dramatically among the combat troops. The men in the trenches were overwhelmingly of peasant origin.

Thus the experience at the front taught a bitter lesson in the implications of inequality. The First World War placed a profoundly unequal burden of suffering on the peasantry. It was the peasants who filled the lists of the dead, the wounded, and the disabled. The countryside suffered far more than its share of the pain of mourning the loss of husbands, fathers, brothers, sons, and lovers, while landlords enjoyed exemption from service and joined the hated ranks of the 'shirkers' (*imboscati*).

It was the peasants, too, who endured the nightmare of the Isonzo front. Of all the armies on the western front, the Italian paid the least attention to the well-being of its men. Italian soldiers were the worst equipped to face the ordeal of trench warfare with inadequate rations, medical provision, clothing, and firepower. Furthermore, they endured the longest tours of duty at the front. Uniquely Italian, furthermore, was the absence until 1917 of any attempt to provide the humble infantryman with a sense of purpose or mission. Rigidly autocratic in its structures under the command of the old-fashioned martinet Luigi Cadorna, the Italian army regarded the private soldier as an infinitely expendable commodity. Schooled in the outmoded doctrine of the offensive and imbued with the aristocratic ideology of war as a test of valour, the High Command wantonly hurled its men against superior Austrian positions.

Cadorna, moreover, gave no thought to the problem of morale. There were few recreational facilities, inadequate leaves, and no military newspapers to explain the reasons for the conflict. On the contrary, the High Command relied on military discipline to provide the will to go on. Where discipline alone seemed inadequate to persuade the men to attack, the army provided liquor, especially *grappa* – soldier's 'petrol'. When discipline cracked, there was terror. The army established draconian measures to deal with insubordination. These measures culminated in the placing of élite military police detachments behind the lines armed with machine guns 'to encourage the others', in the summary justice of the regime of 'special tribunals', and in the barbarism of the practice of *decimazione*, by which every tenth man in a rebellious unit was taken at random and shot.[102]

It was in these conditions that conscripted peasants experienced the surrealism of the Isonzo front, where two years of combat and hundreds of thousands of casualties produced no movement along the whole extent of the border with Austria-Hungary. Even the names of the battles were eerily repetitive as no fewer than twelve battles of the Isonzo were fought. Here peasants endured cold, disease, hunger, and lice in alternating bouts of numbing inaction and murderous but futile assaults. Here too they increasingly lost confidence in the High Command, the state, and the *signori*.

If isolation and the lack of a collective sense of identity were traditional means by which social order in Tuscany had been preserved, the years of soldiering went a long way towards creating a new consciousness. Conscripted peasants were transported by train and by truck. They travelled to cities in the North, where they saw at first hand alternative ways of living. Brought together in large numbers from different provinces, they shared ideas and experiences, listened while literate comrades read newspapers aloud and explained their meaning, and learned of the aspirations of men who had taken part in strikes and organizations. In the trenches too the peasants learned to cooperate and to depend on one another. Certainly it was this awakening of consciousness in the slaughter at the front that the organizers of the left underlined in explaining the sudden explosion of agrarian unrest after the war. With special reference to the situation in Tuscany, the *Difesa*, the socialist paper of Florence, averred,

> It is the war that brought the peasant into contact with modern life. It pushed him into the factory side by side with the workers... It placed him in the trenches along with the clerk and the professional men who explained the war. It transported him to the hospital ward, to the cities and towns, by train and by automobile. The peasant came to know at first hand the humbug of the press, the honeyed promise, and the hatred for socialism. And he experienced the corruption of the sisters of charity.[103]

More subtly, the war taught the lesson that the power of the state could be used to transform daily life. The regime of 'war-time agriculture' produced a massive intervention of the state in every detail of agricultural life. The state requisitioned, set prices, conscripted, rationed, froze contracts. It was no great leap of imagination to suppose that such immense power could be put to other purposes. The world made by the landlords could no longer be regarded as immutable. It is not too much to suppose, for instance, that the idea of security of tenure, which played a central role in the sharecroppers' demands in the 'Red Years', was first suggested on a wide scale by the state, which set the precedent of freezing contracts and blocking evictions.

Most importantly of all, however, the war years put the question of the land as the first item on the Italian political agenda, challenged the legitimacy of the existing distribution of property in the minds of all, and taught the peasant that he had rights and expectations to be honoured. The great postwar explosion can be seen as the attempt by peasants to claim what they had been promised.[104] The promises came from a variety of sources. One vital element in the new political awareness came from abroad – the experience of the great revolution in Russia. The point is that the events of 1917 in the Russian Empire were seen and interpreted in Italy as a peasant revolution by which the humble Russian *muzhik* had seized the land. It was in this fashion that the socialist press, the party, the cooperatives, and the farm workers' union Federterra, presented the Russian revolution to their members.[105] So too did four representatives from the Petrograd soviet who toured Italy in August 1917 and used their platform at Florence to extol the grand vision of the socialist minister of agriculture, Victor Chernov.[106] The myth of Russia was a potent force in the Italian peasant army.

At the same time that the idea of land reform pressed from outside, the state itself took the initiative in promising the peasants a social revolution. The reason was that the Italian front collapsed in 1917. From the start of the year there were clear signs that the troops had lost the will to fight and die in an unpopular war. There was a wave of self-mutilations, of desertions, of officers shot from behind, and of rebellions by units that refused to obey orders to return to the line. Morale collapsed finally and dramatically in the autumn in the great rout of Caporetto that some even called the 'soldiers' strike', when the Italian army was put to flight all along the front. At the same time disaffection and subversion spread on the home front. Demonstrations and mass protests took place across Italy, escalated into riots, and reached a crescendo in August in the full-scale uprising at Turin. To the governing classes it seemed that Italy was indeed following the Russian example, and that the same combination of discontent at home and defeat at the front that had toppled the Romanovs was about to overturn the House of Savoy.

The regime survived in the end, but it did so at enormous cost. In order to persuade mutinous troops to return to the fight and rioters to be patient, the state offered a great vision of an agrarian law and of major social reform. It was accepted that the peasants had earned a 'promissory note of suffering' which would be redeemed in land when peace returned. To take the message to the men in the trenches, the military established soldiers' newspapers on a large scale for the first time and set up a propaganda service, whose mission was to spread the glad tidings of the coming social order. 'Land to the peasants!' and 'Save Italy, and she's yours!' were the slogans that junior officers were commissioned to circulate among the troops.

Behind the lines the same message was heard in every public forum. Parliament announced the intention of requisitioning uncultivated land, which would be placed at the disposal of the veterans' associations for distribution among the ex-combatants. The landlords' press, taking its cue from the major national organ of the proprietors, the *Resto del Carlino*, affirmed the commitment to provide the peasants with land, while agrarian associations and chambers of commerce held meetings with trade-union representatives to explain the vision. Parish priests took the message to their faithful, and the socialist movement used its full resources to inform the people that a new deal had been promised. The General Confederation of Labour (CGL), socialist-controlled communes, the cooperatives, and the party held conferences, rallies, and congresses, and the socialist press reported the initiatives. From Venice to Palermo the air was alive with the pledge of land. The peasant was encouraged to view the land as his due.[107]

The idea acquired further substance because of events in Lazio that were given national prominence. With premature zeal to cash the blank cheque they had been issued, the peasants and labourers of the latifundia in the province of Rome began to occupy land from 1915 onward in a local preview of what was to become a vast postwar movement of national proportions. Undoubtedly the circumstances of Lazio were particular – the recent date of the enclosure of common land and the extinction of common rights that made the land question a burning local issue, the presence of vast tracts of uncultivated fields that were a provocation to the landless, the brutally exploitative nature of latifundism, the history of sporadic land invasions during the Giolittian era, the intense agitation for land by the local socialist organizations, and the acute problem of chronic unemployment. The important feature of the movement in Lazio for our purposes, however, is that it was taken up nationally and acclaimed by the left as an example of just action in defence of rights that the peasantry had earned in the trenches. Lazio, moreover, was a precedent that was far closer to home than Petrograd.[108]

In this climate of supercharged expectations, the nation limped to the armistice. Demobilization throughout the peninsula was followed by one of the great periods of agrarian unrest in modern Europe. Led by the returning veterans, peasants everywhere laid claim to rights they regarded as theirs. When the state reneged on pledges, there was a vast explosion. Even in Tuscany, with its long history of stability and deference, the silence of the peasantry was over.

POLITICAL EFFECTS AND REACTION

With these considerations in mind it should cause little surprise that after several decades of intense commercial development, the 'public quiet' in central Tuscany was finally and dramatically broken by the *mezzadri*, the very class on whom so many hopes had been placed by the aristocracy of central Italy.[109] This postwar explosion had been heralded by two earlier events of 1902 and 1906 which had been insufficiently appreciated at the time, but had marked the end of an era in Tuscan history. In 1902 the first strike of *mezzadri* ever to occur in the region took place, and it occurred precisely in the area where commercial changes had first been introduced and had gone furthest – the Chiana Valley communes of Chiusi, Chianciano, and Montepulciano. In the same year the socialists noted that 'even in our Tuscany the peasants are beginning to understand the necessity of organization', and reported the establishment of the first peasant League.[110] The first agitation in 1902 was then followed in 1906 by further strikes of sharecroppers in some of the most advanced zones of Florence and Arezzo provinces.[111]

With these dress rehearsals of 1902 and 1906, the burst of political militancy after the war among the *mezzadri* should perhaps have caused little surprise. In fact, however, the 'official' view of *mezzadria* as guarantor of social stability had so dominated discussion of the social question in central Italy that neither right nor left of the political spectrum was prepared to confront the new situation. Even the socialist party shared with the landowners the view of the impermeability of *mezzadria* to socialist influence. The revolutionary paper the *Difesa*, for instance, greeted the sudden emergence of vast rural agitation with unconcealed astonishment. Commenting on the postwar development of political militancy among the *mezzadri*, the Florentine paper exclaimed,

Anyone who has followed the phases of the agrarian struggle in Tuscany ... can only be amazed by the mental transformation of our peasants.
Who could have foreseen it?[112]

In a similar vein the socialist paper of Siena wrote of the sharecroppers, 'no one would ever have believed them capable of a demonstration of strength, determination, and solidarity'.[113] And the Empoli socialists remarked that 'It seems like a dream'.[114]

In fact, however, the movement, which began in the spring of 1919 as a series of largely spontaneous local strikes throughout the commercially advanced areas of central Tuscany, demonstrated considerable 'strength, determination, and solidarity'. The impulse to a radical re-ordering of rural social relations came from below. Indeed, the essential demands first advanced in a hundred different localities were a response to broad pressures which were similar all over the region and remained largely unaltered throughout the postwar struggles. It was true that the movement was rapidly channelled and led by the two rival parties of the rural Tuscan left – the Socialist Party (PSI) and the Catholic Popular Party (PPI) – but what was notable was that the parties adopted a range of demands for contractual reform that they found in large measure already formulated. Their tasks from 1919 to 1921 were to unify and generalize the struggle that had already begun, to provide it with continuity and organizational framework, to broaden it to include much wider political purposes and class allies, and to direct it towards more fully articulated ends.

With political direction and especially socialist leadership, the movement which began on the land became more consciously subversive and politicized. Moreover, as the first strikes proved successful and major concessions were won from a landholding class that was still unorganized and ill prepared to resist, the sharecroppers became more aware of their power and felt increasingly confident in advancing wider claims. The old order was visibly vulnerable, and this fact in itself was a powerful fillip to popular militancy.

Ironically, the direct source of the ideas used by the peasants to put forward and defend their aspirations for change was the landlords' ideology of *mezzadria*. The ideology that inspired the sharecroppers' movement did not come primarily from outside. Tuscan *mezzadri* read neither Marx nor Leo XIII. The vision that informed the union struggle was based on material much nearer to hand. For centuries the landlords had elaborated a doctrine of sharecropping as a form of partnership, and the peasants were deeply familiar with its tenets. The ideology of the Georgofili was embedded in the law, in contracts, in social relations themselves. For the landlords, the doctrine was a powerful instrument of hegemony that veiled the realities of power from the tenants, provided a psychological reassurance for aristocrats that their social position was not only just but was even loving, and rallied proprietors in defence of a common creed.

For the purpose of social stability, however, the ideology of *mezzadria* contained a fatal flaw. The doctrine of partnership was one that could be interpreted very differently by the two opposing classes in the countryside. For the landowners, partnership was a declaration that the status quo was perfect. For the tenant, on the other hand, partnership could be seen as a pledge, a description of sharecropping not as it was, but as it could become. In this sense, the whole militancy of the *mezzadri* after the war can be seen as an attempt to transform partnership from an ideal into a reality. If landlord and peasant were partners, the sharecroppers argued, then they should both enjoy economic security and have equal rights in the direction of the estate. Partners, furthermore, should not be able to evict one another. The mystery of the sudden emergence of powerful mass union movements among the sharecroppers of the region can be understood if one notes that they were not based on the slow spread of new ideas. Tuscan socialism and Tuscan political Catholicism were the application in a novel and subversive way of ideas long familiar to everyone. The commercialization of *mezzadria* provided the croppers with grievances; the First World War firmly established the conviction that they had a right to a fundamental transformation; and the well-known ideology of partnership provided the vision of an ideal to be won.

The demands first articulated in 1919 formed the basis for the entire postwar struggle. The political problem of the *mezzadri* in 1920 and 1921 became one of unifying the struggle into a single regional movement based upon a uniform set of demands, and of extending the movement from the direct question of the land to the whole range of key centres of the landlords' power. For all of this, however, the reforms of the *mezzadria* contract first advanced in 1919 were the focus, and one should note that even between the competing socialist and Catholic parties, whose ultimate social aims were starkly opposed, there was a great similarity in the contractual demands they proposed – a similarity based on a general community of aspirations in the doctrine of partnership which united the *mezzadri* as a class. Taking this community of aspirations as a starting-point for evaluating the threat posed to the Tuscan aristocracy by the tenants, we can sum up the reforms urged by the peasantry in a set of demands advanced throughout the area of Tuscany where *mezzadria* prevailed, demands which served throughout to demarcate the lines of class division. There were, of course, local variations initially, but the chief reforms called for by the *mezzadri* in 1919 in the four central provinces where the new agitation was strongest (Siena, Pisa, Arezzo, and Florence) were:

(1) union recognition.
(2) a written rather than oral contract.
(3) the expenses of threshing to be met by the landlord.
(4) direction of the estate to be exercised by mutual agreement and with equal rights of the landlord and the tenant.
(5) reduction of the obligation of the tenant to supply the landlord with chickens, and recognition of the right of the tenant to raise one or more pigs for his own exclusive use without the obligation to give the landlord the leg.
(6) the expenses of sulphuration and spraying with copper sulphate to be met by the landlord.
(7) eviction of the tenant to be carried out only in case of violation of the Civil Code, with disputes to be referred without appeal to an arbitration board with representation of both parties.
(8) establishment of arbitration boards for the resolution of all disputes concerning the interpretation of the contract.
(9) work done by the tenant apart from his own *podere* on behalf of the landlord to be paid by the latter at the current market rate.
(10) right of first option to be given to the sitting tenant in the event of the sale of the property or the decision to let it.
(11) insurance to be provided by the landlord.
(12) wine and olive-oil duties owed by the tenant to be abolished.
(13) work tools to be included in the *stima*. The expense of evaluation to be paid by the landlord.
(14) expenses for the sale of livestock to be divided equally between landlord and peasant. Veterinary expenses and cattle taxes to be met by the landlord.

(15) for special crops, payment in proportion to the net income of the hectares planted.
(16) the expense of new crops to be met by the landlord for the period of time necessary for them to enter production.
(17) abolition of all *corvées* and other obligations whether of labour or in kind. The duty of the tenant to transport the share of the produce belonging to the landlord to extend only as far as the storehouse of the estate. All other transportation of goods to be paid for at the current market rate.
(18) expenses of chemical fertilizers to be met by the landlord, or at least to be borne mainly by the landlord, and reimbursement to be provided for the expense of fertilizers in the last year of planting in the event that the tenant leaves the *podere*.[115]

These demands of the striking sharecroppers fall roughly into three categories.[116] The first includes those which attempted to resolve the traditional question of the precise amount of the produce of the *podere* accruing to each party to the contract by fixing the division more nearly in accordance with the theoretical proportion of 50/50. Thus a number of demands called for the abolition of particular obligations of the *mezzadro* to the landlord which either served as additional burdens on the peasant or figured as deductions from the peasant's share of the harvest. Such demands included the call for the abolition of chicken duties and wine and olive-oil duties, for the abolition of *corvées* and of the obligation to provide transportation for the landlord's goods. Similar in spirit were the demand that the contract be written and the demand for the establishment of arbitration boards to settle disputes. Falling partly also in this category was the demand that the landlord provide insurance and veterinary care for livestock. The common feature of all these provisions was that they did not affect the substance of the traditional contract, but were designed to protect the tenant from the arbitrary exercise of unequal power.

Taken together, the claims pressed by the *mezzadri* in this first category, though unwelcome to the landlords as they threatened a certain redistribution of wealth between the two partners, were nevertheless considered negotiable by most. Although they corrected a number of abuses and ended a variety of useful prerogatives of property, they did not disturb the substance of lordly power. Indeed, the reforming advocates of enlightened paternalism, represented by Serragli, actually pressed for prompt concessions on these issues as they hoped that such action would remove a number of needless causes of tenant discontent without affecting the vital questions of power and principle. An astute proprietor, so it was reasoned, could maintain his position despite a few new constraints.

A second category of peasant demands attempted to deal with the additional burden of expense which had fallen upon the tenants as a result of modernization and the continuing rationalization of production in agriculture. These included the demand that the landlord alone assume the expense of providing chemical fertilizers, threshing machines, and sulphuration, together with the tools needed for such tasks and for the maintenance of mechanical equipment. Related in spirit was the demand that the owner meet the cost of planting new crops up to the moment when they became productive. A special case, but one that had a similar effect and was intended to deal with the increasing exploitation of the *mezzadri*, was the call for union recognition.

This set of demands was considered unacceptable by the landlords and was met by a firm resolution of intransigent opposition. One clear reason was that such concessions would seriously affect profits, and were the more bitterly resented by the landowners as they were put forward at a time when farmers in Italy were in straitened financial circumstances. On the whole, Italian farmers in this period were in no mood to be generous. Agricultural production as a whole had declined as a result of the war. The national wheat harvest – 52 million quintals before the war – had declined to 46 million in 1919 and 38 million in 1920, while corn production fell from 25 million quintals before the First World War to 22 million in 1919. Sugar beet followed the same pattern, showing a fall from 21 million quintals to 11 million in 1919 and 12 million in 1920.[117] Worse, in the inflationary 'monetary revolution' that began during the war and continued into the postwar years, agricultural prices lagged behind the rise of the general price level. During the war the general price index (1913 = 100) rose from 100 to 287, but agricultural monetary income only from 100 to 221. Summarizing the effect of the war in this regard, Arrigo Serpieri writes,

Comparing the two indices, we must conclude that in the four years of the war the effective buying power of the total agricultural income declined by about one fourth.[118]

The postwar period worsened the position for farmers. The Bachi price index (1913 = 100) shows this clearly (see table 2).[119] When agricultural production did increase in 1921, so too did competition from abroad, so that prices for agricultural products did not improve their position.[120]

In Tuscany, more particularly, production fell less steeply, but two of the great staple crops of the region – wheat and corn – were among those whose prices showed the least buoyancy relative to the general price inflation. Another of the four main agricultural products of the region – olive oil – showed a marked price increase, but for long months in the postwar period was subject to price controls as the government sought,

Table 2.

	1919–20	Second half of 1920
General price index of whosesale goods	502	610
Grains and meats	368	456
Other food stuffs	405	518

after the food riots in 1919, to assuage popular discontent by limiting the prices of certain goods of major mass consumption. In these conditions, the landlords of Italy were not willing to make concessions lightly.

It may be objected here that the same consideration applies to the demands of the first category. And, indeed, there were many landlords, particularly small landlords, who failed to make a distinction and rejected the demands of the peasant unions in their entirety. A major problem of the Tuscan Agrarian Association was to win acceptance for its policy of selected concessions from its more uncompromising members. A distinction, then, is useful in order to explain the decision of leading landlords to reject one set of demands and accept the other, and in order to illuminate the extent of the conflict in postwar Tuscany. The difference is that the first set of demands affected profits primarily in the short term, whereas the second set of demands threatened to undermine *profitability* as such, and in the long run. Certain of the prevailing provisions of the *mezzadria* contract, that is, allowed lordly speculation at the expense of the tenant and were useful to the owners, but were not essential to the system as such. The provision, however, that the peasant meet a fixed share of the expense of cultivation was, especially in the context of a competitive world market, an essential underpinning of the whole system. To have removed this feature would have compromised the ability of the landlords to modernize agriculture without undoing *mezzadria* – without, that is, following the path of Emilia. What was at question was the whole direction chosen by Tuscan capitalistic development.

Similar was the question of who was responsible for the cattle tax. Undoubtedly there was no enormous issue at stake in the cattle tax itself, but the question of burden of the whole series of such taxes threatened to raise the whole question of capital accumulation in Tuscany. In the raising of the problem of the cattle tax, the landlords correctly saw the thin edge of the wedge. This danger was made most explicit in the peasant strikes in the Mugello, where it was not only the question of cattle tax that was raised. In the Mugello, the demand was advanced that all land taxes be paid by the landlord.[121]

Partly similar, too, was the question of the obligatory provision of insurance and veterinary care by the landlord. Again, as in the case of the cattle tax, it was not just the immediate issue under dispute which separated the two sides. Rather the problem here was that such demands touched upon the thornier and wider issue of welfare payments under *mezzadria*. An important source of the profitability of the system seemed to be called into question. Thus the *mezzadro* Nincheri of the Empoli zone of Florence province, when interviewed by the agricultural investigating committee of the Ministry for the Constituent Assembly, referred to a situation of conflict over the question of peasant security and welfare that had apparently existed for some time. As he put it,

We *mezzadri* are considered sharecroppers, but, practically speaking, we are just labourers. In fact, we find ourselves in this situation: we begin work in the morning, and by evening we still have no guarantee of earnings for the family. And since the yield [of the land] is certainly not enough to support the family we ask that the owners run the estate by the wage system ... At least that way we shall have a guaranteed income and a pension that will allow us, after 60, not to live completely dependent on our children. This problem was hotly discussed after the other war [i.e. the First World War], but then fascism hushed it up.[122]

More broadly, the demands in the second category led the landlords to intransigence because the margins for reformist concessions in the *mezzadria* system were particularly narrow. *Mezzadria* had survived in an era of world competition by its capacity to exact a high level of exploitation of labour, as we have seen. To press for major reforms in the substance of the contract was to reverse this process and to threaten the competitivity of the system. Serragli himself declared that *mezzadria* would cease to function if the peasant appeared no longer 'as a partner who is concerned for the common interest, but as a day labourer who thinks of the amount of his own remuneration and who therefore argues, debates, and protests'.[123]

Most important of all in the postwar conflict, however, was a third category of peasant demands that were incompatible with the existing system of property relations. The economic demands of the second type threatened indirectly to undo *mezzadria* by removing the sources of its profitability. In addition, the Tuscan sharecroppers, in common with other sectors of the labour movement, advanced claims to direct control over the workplace – claims that were *per se* revolutionary. Two demands in particular became the central focus of contention between the opposing sides in the struggle. These were, first, that eviction be made illegal except for the provisions of the Civil Code. Since eviction was the ultimate sanction which ensured compliance with the other exactions of the system, this demand was fundamentally subversive of the power of private property. Eviction, in Serragli's words, was 'the sole means of restoring discipline among the sharecropping masses'.[124] Secondly, the Leagues called for equal rights for the *mezzadri* in the direction of the estates. In some areas – most notably Siena province – farm councils of the peasantry (*consigli di fattoria*) were established as the instruments for the exercise of this right.[125]

These two demands were the Tuscan equivalents of the *imponibile di mano d'opera* and *collocamento di classe* set up by the Po Valley *braccianti* in their confrontation with the *agrari*. The *imponibile* was a practice by which the unions determined the number of men to be assigned to each hectare of land for each crop and season of the year, while the *collocamento di classe* set up a roster of labourers to work the fields in turn. Together these two devices created a monopoly of the labour market, depriving farmers of their ability to pick and choose their men and to use the competition for work provided by chronic rural overpopulation as a lever to drive wages down. Thus, to the extent that they became effective, the two measures rendered much of the title to property nugatory by abolishing one of its central prerogatives. Furthermore, the ability of the unions to regulate the labour market implied the power to influence critically, although indirectly, the whole range of managerial decisions from the level of investment and the type of crop grown to the intensity of cultivation and the direction of production. In a very real sense the *imponibile* and *collocamento* were a revolutionary challenge to the control of the farmers over the land, and were at the centre of the postwar conflict in Emilia.

If anything, however, the two proposals regarding eviction rights and peasant participation in management put forward by the Tuscan Leagues raised more overtly still the questions of control and power. It is no accident that they became the chief issues in the struggle for power in the countryside. As the socialist paper the *Difesa* of Florence commented at the height of the great peasant strike of 1920,

> These [i.e. eviction and equality of right between landlord and peasant in the direction of the estates] are the two questions that are the centre of the peasant battle, and it is here that the landlords have committed themselves to the staunchest resistance. In fact, this attitude is to be understood if we remember that through victories on these questions of a moral and legal order the peasants hope to achieve the abolition of *mezzadria*, which is the most typical form of the ancient domination of the bosses.[126]

With unforeseen speed and clarity the issue was drawn between the two partners to the *mezzadria* pact.

If this struggle between the partners was the central issue in the Tuscan provinces, an important secondary struggle was waged in a more restricted zone between the landlords and the *braccianti* in areas where full-time wage labour played a major role in the economy. In these areas the *braccianti*, as the Georgofili had long predicted, were heavily under the sway of the much feared 'new ideas'. In these zones they were massively organized by the socialist party and waged a struggle analogous to that of the Po Valley, pressing, first of all, for such economic provisions as the eight-hour day, the abolition of piece work, wage increases, time-and-a-half for overtime, and official recognition of the Leagues.[127] More significantly, the *braccianti*-led Leagues, as in the North, demanded the same *imponibile* and *collocamento* that had proved so politically explosive north of the Apennines. Thus, for example in the Pisan-plain commune of Pontedera, Alessandro Martelli, who drew up the official position of the Tuscan Agrarian Association towards the demands of the *braccianti*, wrote in distress in 1921 that

The number of *braccianti* has more than quadrupled since 1915, and the farms, even when run entirely by *mezzadria* and therefore not in need of wage labour, employ an average of one worker for every seven hectares of land at a daily wage of sixteen lire.

The various local Leagues and Chambers of Labour have so completely come to dominate the landowners that they now send, with or without prior notice, as many wage labourers for employment as they deem fit...[128]

Thus, summarized Martelli, the future fascist minister,

The serious *braccianti* question places many landlords in the Region in the impossible position of being no longer able to bear an expense that often far exceeds the total income of their estates.[129]

Clearly the landlords regarded the *braccianti* Leagues as intolerable, and there was no meeting of landlords in postwar Tuscany or communication of their Association to the Ministry of the Interior that was complete without reference to the seriousness of the question and without a demand for government action through public works programs to relieve the economic burden of employment falling on the lords[130] and through police repression to deal with the political dangers.[131] It was as the socialist movement continued to expand and the government failed to provide a remedy of either an economic or a police character that the determination of the landowners to resort to self-help began to take shape.

The Congress of the Agrarian Association meeting at Florence in late November 1920 gave a measure of the importance attached to the problem of the *braccianti* and of the political conclusions then being drawn by the Tuscan farmers. In the morning of the congress, Serragli had warned that in general 'it would be a foolish illusion to expect from the state a solution to the grave problems affecting agriculture'.[132] That same morning, Salvadore, representing the branch of the Association at Pontedera, where as we have seen the *braccianti* were particularly numerous and powerfully organized, proposed that the assembly 'make up its mind to take energetic measures. The farmers can stand no more, and long to take up their freedom of action in order to tell the *braccianti*, "Enough".'[133] Significantly, too, in the afternoon session, the *braccianti* question was the first item on the agenda.

Here there is a difficulty to be explained. If one examines the area affected by the *braccianti*-led movement and the numbers of workers involved in proportion to the total agricultural population,[134] the concern of the landlords seems inexplicably disproportionate. The numbers of *braccianti* were restricted, while the area affected was discontinuous and constituted only a small fraction of the total agricultural zone of the region. The *braccianti* problem would seem to involve principally a number of local disputes hardly worthy of the deep and continuous concern of the highest officials of the AAT. What such a view misses is that, in the areas where they were concentrated, the Tuscan *braccianti* were among the most compact and militant sectors of the socialist movement, exerting an influence out of proportion to their numbers. More important, the *braccianti* Leagues threatened to win control of the most fertile and profitable farming land in the region – the Pisan plain of the lower Arno valley, the Chiana Valley, the Tiber Valley, and western Florence province towards San Miniato.[135]

In general, whatever the actual contractual demands brought forward by the *mezzadri* and *braccianti*, the landlords saw their whole social position menaced by the new organizational force of the peasant union and political movements. The demands advanced and the strikes which secured their acceptance were rapidly directed and channelled by a whole network of peasant Leagues and Chambers of Labour under the aegis of the PSI and the CGL, or of the PPI. These organizations, which rapidly gained a vast following, aimed, in the areas where they were strong, at the creation of an effective monopoly of the labour market. Since such a monopoly threatened to revolutionize the effective bargaining-power relations between the classes, and since the Tuscan landlords were accustomed to an uncontested domination over their estates, the unions themselves, even apart from the specific radical demands they advanced, were grimly opposed by the landlords. The question of union recognition was one of the bitterest issues in rural postwar Tuscany, and the creation of an alternative labour organizational structure was to be one of the first priorities of the reaction.

Once begun in 1919, the strike movement led by the Leagues, initially involving a series of local disputes, became increasingly powerful and widespread. By the autumn of 1919 and early spring of 1920, a series of massive province-wide strikes had wrung major concessions from the landlords' organizations. And in the summer of 1920 the decisive victory of the unions was won. Conscious of the aroused militancy of the tenants, frightened by the advances made by the unions during the provincial strikes of the preceding months, and desirous above all of yielding as little ground as possible on the vital issue of the right of the tenants to a share in the management of the estates, the Association sought to outrun events and to play upon the rivalry between the competing socialist and Catholic League organizations. As a tactical manoeuvre, it summoned both sides to Florence in June to discuss a possible unified regional pact.[136] When the Catholics and socialists were unable to cooperate, and when its own intransigence over the issue of control caused a collapse of the negotiations, the Association at least found itself in the advantageous position during the ensuing strike led by the socialists of having the Catholic peasants acting as strike breakers by continuing to thresh the wheat under the watchful eye of the police, who turned out in force for the occasion in order to protect the 'right to work' of those who refused to support the strike.[137]

None the less, the solidarity created by the strike throughout the region was wholly without precedent. This was the largest agricultural strike in Italian history: over 500,000 peasants (72,000 families) in eight provinces took part, out of the total of 710,793 Tuscan *mezzadri*.[138] Under the circumstances, virtually the entire wheat crop was in jeopardy, and during the third week of July the Association capitulated, signing the famous 'Red Pact' that granted the tenants in all of Tuscany the right to security of tenure and a voice in the direction of the estates, together with virtually all the other improvements in their contractual standing first put forward the year before. The property rights of the Tuscan landowners had been seriously breached. On the question of actual control, a compromise was worked out with an acceptance of the right of the tenants to participate in management, but with a number of important qualifications. The relevant clause of the new pact read:

Direction of the *podere* will be exercised in agreement with the tenant in the spirit of cooperation. The landlord, however, has the right, without appeal:
(1) to establish crop rotations
(2) to determine the kind and extent of the various crops, orchards, and vineyards
(3) to set the type, quality, and quantity of cattle in relation to the resources of the *podere* and to the conditions of the environment, with reference also to the requirements of commerce.[139]

Despite these qualifications over one of the major issues in dispute, the new contract decreed a revolution in rural social relations. To have accepted the new pact, the landlords would have needed to have resigned themselves to the demise of the old social order. Instead, they accepted their defeat as only provisional and used the time they had gained by concessions to organize to destroy the threat of rural socialism.

The need felt by the Tuscan aristocracy to organize its own self-defence was underscored by what it regarded as the patent failure of the government to defend the rights of property. Beyond police measures to protect the 'right to work', the government had done little to reassure the landlords. Indeed, the fall of the Liberal majority in parliament and the crumbling of the Liberal parties in the provinces indicated that the state was no longer able to defend property, while the failure of the government to intervene during the Occupation of the Factories in the autumn raised doubts about government resolve. Of particular effect on the growing disillusionment of landowners with the state was the attempt by the Liberal ministry to outrun peasant discontent by introducing a series of reforms into rural labour relations. By a series of decree laws the state began to operate a welfare program for the benefit of agricultural workers, including *mezzadri*. The chief features of the program were compulsory accident, old age, and disability insurance, all involving major contributions from the proprietors. Accident insurance for the tenants was to be financed entirely by the landlords through a tax surcharge of 3 per cent of taxable wealth.[140] The premiums for the old-age and disability schemes were to be equally divided between the employer and the insured. The cost to the landlord was 24 lire per year for each adult male sharecropper, 18 lire for women, and 12 lire for minors.[141]

These provisions, taking effect at a time of agricultural crisis, raised a storm of outrage from the proprietors. Every meeting of the Agrarian Association until the March on Rome raised the issue and condemned the initiative of the government.[142] The view of the Tuscan landlords was that they were being crushed between the unions and the state. According to the AAT, the government was attempting to gain popularity by bartering away the profitability of Tuscan agriculture. The position of the association was uncompromising. Welfare payments for *mezzadri* were an intolerable burden. As G. Chiostri, secretary of the AAT, explained,

The *mezzadro* has no need for insurance against disability and old age. For him, the solidarity binding the various members of our peasant families is the best form of provision.[143]

The new burden demanded of landed property was 'an absurdity'.[144] From the start, the landlords' conversion to reaction was an attempt to destroy not only the threat of bolshevism but also the belated rural reformism of the Liberal state.

In any event, whatever its intentions, the Liberal state seemed on the verge of being overwhelmed. Already after the elections of 1919 the leading national newspaper representing agrarian interests, the *Resto del Carlino*, had written with evident gloom that the results

> appeared to be the political liquidation of the Liberal bourgeoisie that ... has governed Italy.
> The defeat, which is the defeat not just of the government, but of the Liberal and secular state, the crisis of a regime, and the end of a historical era, are all apparent.[145]

With such a feeling of crisis already in 1919, one can easily imagine the mood of the landlords after the major defeats in the strikes of the summer of 1920. A gauge of their attitude was provided in August when a national agrarian congress took place at Rimini among representatives of the Agrarian Associations of Veneto, Emilia-Romagna, Tuscany, the Marches, and Umbria. The mood of the congress, as described by the correspondent of the *Resto del Carlino*, was one of defiance towards the government and of determination to resort to self-help.[146] Among the most militant, Marchi, the representative of the Tuscan Agrarian Association, said:

> If the farmers of Italy cannot find in themselves the strength to face the dangers that threaten them, we are wasting our time in discussion. We must realize that by now the state has no authority to help us and that only the farmers themselves can rectify the present situation.[147]

The gloomiest reflections of the landlords in 1919 and the middle of 1920 were more than confirmed in the autumn local and provincial government elections of 1920 when the PSI won 2,162 of Italy's 8,059 communes (it had held only 300 in 1914) and 25 of the 69 provinces.[148] More particularly in Tuscany, six of the eight Tuscan provincial councils (Lucca and Massa-Carrara being the exceptions) had socialist majorities, as did 149 of the 290 communes, while of the remaining communes the PPI had secured 52. The most alarming results of all, from the standpoint of the ruling classes, came from Siena province, where of 36 communes the PSI won 30 as well as 32 of 40 seats on the provincial council.[149]

The results of the local elections not only confirmed fears of the continuing socialist advance but also – and this was crucial – they overturned the traditional local control of the ruling classes. The landlords now saw a vital element in their domination overthrown and themselves ousted from local bodies they had come to regard nearly as much their own as the land. Whole networks of influence, patronage, and clientele relations were suddenly jeopardized. Further, with control of local political power, the bargaining power of the union movement was greatly enhanced. Above all, the landlords now found themselves the objects of an unwonted use of the powers of local taxation. A whole series of levies was placed upon men of wealth. In a large number of communes the new mayors ordered major sanitary improvements to be made to peasant cottages, at the landlords' expense.[150] From the landowners' viewpoint, the most menacing development was the decision of the now socialist-controlled communes to impose a new expropriatory surcharge upon the land. In November 1921 Arrigo Serpieri, the agricultural expert and friend of property, calculated the cost to landlords of a year of socialist local government. He reported that in 1920 proprietors paid a total of 323 million lire in local surcharges on land. In 1921, by contrast, the burden of land surtaxes levied by local government had climbed to over 802 million lire.[151] In April 1921, for example, the Florence provincial council voted to increase the land surcharge from 9,949,930 lire to 25,400,000 lire.[152] Not surprisingly, the Agrarian Association announced that the 'ferocious social-communist fiscal initiative' was the object of its 'special interest'.[153]

In this climate of revolutionary crisis, it is understandable that the fascist movement made its first appearance in rural Tuscany at the end of 1920 and the beginning of 1921 as the instrument of lordly retrenchment. Moreover, as the socialist threat had challenged lordly power at three interrelated but different levels – the contractual, the economic, and the political – so the reaction intended to overturn the socialist local councils, to replace the socialist and Catholic Leagues with a network of fascist unions deeply responsive to the concerns of property, and to introduce a new regional pact that sought to regularize the contractual relations between landlords and tenants through an authoritarian re-assertion of lordly rule. A strategic difference between the conduct of the peasant advance and that of the fascist-agrarian counter-revolution was the reliance on organized military violence through the squads.

Here a word of caution is needed. The landlords were always to claim that fascist violence, though regrettable, was merely the resort to self-defence after the socialist reign of terror in 1919 and 1920. It should be stated categorically that the claims of socialist violence were either simple invention or referred to the 'violence' of socialist rhetoric. Police reports, certainly guilty of no sympathy for the socialist cause, leave no room for equivocation. During the vast agrarian agitations of the 'Red Years', there was no planned or systematic use of force by the socialist movement. The few physical clashes that did occur during the agitation were isolated scuffles with strike-breakers and *fattori*. Of bloodshed there is no mention.[154] Even the prefect of Siena, the 'reddest province in Tuscany',[155] Emilio D'Eufemia, whose sympathy for the landlords' cause was unconcealed, and who directed police action during the strike to protect the 'right to work', reported that the great agitation of 1920 'took place without too violent a shock, nor, in general, was public order seriously disturbed'.[156] By contrast, fascist violence in 1921 and 1922 was systematic, creating a tidal wave of murder, assault, and intimidation. An open civil war was fought to destroy every vestige of peasant influence and of socialist or Popular party power. It was during the fascist offensive that the very unpreparedness of the socialists for a trial of force, even for self-defence against the squadrist onslaught, became apparent, revealed the emptiness of the landlords' claim, and played a major role in the fascist success.

The leading part played by the Tuscan landlords in the fascist movement is beyond dispute. The *fasci* that mushroomed in the countryside from the spring of 1921 were the creation of the *agrari*. The landlords financed the movement both individually and collectively through the Association. The Tuscan Agrarian Association, like its counterparts in Emilia, set up an internal system of taxation among its members on behalf of the movement – the famous 'resistance fund' – and liberally supplied it with funds.[157] The official papers of at least two of the provincial branches of the AAT (Florence and Siena) openly declared that the *fasci* were their creation.[158] So close was the relation of the Association to fascism that in July 1921 Count Alfredo di Frassineto reported in alarm to the Central Committee of the AAT that membership was beginning to falter because proprietors, 'seeing in other organizations the security that until yesterday they had lacked, feel that perhaps they can do without their natural organization of self-defence'.

Founding members of the Association and presidents of its branches – perhaps most notably the Liberal deputies of Siena and Grosseto, Gino Sarrocchi and Gino Aldi Mai – toured the region to argue the fascist cause before the unconvinced, presided at ceremonial occasions organized by the movement, and participated in public demonstrations of pro-fascist sympathy.[159] Sarrocchi in particular used his position as deputy to defend fascism – 'the purest form of social defence'[160] – in parliament. As he declared in the Chamber in March 1921,

The nation today has the right to defend its institutions and its liberties, and the marvellous organization of the *fascisti* is contributing to this end.

Continuing with a modesty unjustified in view of his importance to the movement, he added,

If I were not, by feeling, reluctant to use violence ... I too should be enrolled among the fascists.[161]

Indeed, the Siena deputy predicted that the *fasci* would soon enlist 'all the healthy forces of the nation'.[162]

In addition, leading property owners took the initiative in organizing the fascist unions, and the president of the AAT, Pier Francesco Serragli, campaigned on behalf of the fascist corporations.[163] Most openly of all, in Grosseto province the wealthy proprietor Ferdinando Pierazzi was the prime mover of Grossetan squadrism, and became president of the fascist branch at Civitella Marittima and secretary of the fascist provincial federation.[164] The secretary of the Grosseto branch of the AAT, Dino Andriani, was at the same time secretary of the local *fascio* and *caposquadra*, and for a time the *fascio* and the AAT operated from the same office.[165] In Arezzo province the important *fascio* of Montevarchi, which played a leading role in the organization of squadrism throughout the upper Arno Valley, was founded 'on the initiative of the local *agrari*'.[166] One of the Montevarchi proprietors was the Duke of Aosta, and at his *fattoria* of Borro the squads were cordially entertained on their expeditions.[167]

At Siena, Count Girolamo Piccolomini, in 1920 president of the Siena communal subsection of the AAT and in 1921 vice-president of the provincial branch of the Association, was a squadrist,[168] while his relatives, Counts Enea and Alberto Piccolomini, were secretaries of the *fasci* of Chiusure and Castelnuovo dell'Abate.[169] Similarly, the *fattore* of the Piccolomini estate at Sovicille, Angelo Tiezzi, was *caposquadra* and secretary of the local fascist branch.[170] Rolando Bocchi Bianchi, member of the Siena branch of the Association and candidate for the provincial committee, was secretary of the *fascio* at Colle sul Rigo.[171] At Fauglia (Pisa province) the secretary of the fascist branch was Marquis Enrico Giustiniani.[172] Or again at Empoli (Florence province), the executive committee of the *fascio* included representation of one of the leading landholding families of the area, Tito Capoquadri,[173] while at the public ceremony for the dedication of the standard of the local branch the principal speakers were yet another Capoquadri and Luigi Del Vivo,[174] member of the famous Del Vivo family, which was a dominant force in the economic and political life of the commune.[175] At same time, Count Carlo Guicciardini was a member of the electoral committee of the Florence *fascio*.[176] Marquis Luigi Ridolfi, meanwhile, was *caposquadra* at Florence, where the *fascio* 'had him present in the moments of action and saw him take posts of the highest responsibility at times of difficulty'.[177] In the Mugello the squadrist offensive began at the summons of Countess Cambrai Digny.[178] Similarly, the founding father of fascism in the Nievole Valley of Lucca province was the wealthy landlord Evaristo Armani.

Certainly the (incomplete) lists of Tuscan squadrists provided by G. A. Chiurco include the names of many of the most powerful families of the

Tuscan landed nobility. Among known squadrists, in addition to Luigi Ridolfi, were, for example, Count Ildebrando Scroffa, Marquis Alfredo Bargagli, Count Fulvio Bargagli Petrucci, Counts Leone, Niccolò and Piero Guicciardini, Marquises Roberto and Carlo Lodovico Incontri, Count Ugurgieri della Berardenga, and Counts Valfredo and Uguccione Della Gherardesca.[179] Furthermore, among the women enrolled in the Florence *fascio* were such names as Countess Luisa Capponi, Maria Cristina Guicciardini, Marquess Cristina Malenchini, Countess Laura Scotti, Countess Maria Grazia Vannicelli, and Chiara Corsini.[180] And, if we enlarge the definition of fascism to include the Citizens' Defence Alliance, of which we shall say more later as an important force in the reaction, we may mention as well Prince Andrea Corsini, Count Guiseppe Della Gherardesca, Count Lorenzo Bini Smaghi, Baron Luigi Ricasoli, Marquis Luigi Torrigiani, Count Pio Guicciardini, and Count Guglielmo Bonbicci Pontelli.[181]

Another clear indication of the active involvement of the Tuscan landed interest in the fascist reaction is the close collaboration with the movement of the Liberal parties, the exponents of the Tuscan governing classes. We have already observed the leading role of the Liberal deputies Sarrocchi and Aldi Mai in the organization of squadrism. Their action, however, was far from being the result of mere personal preference. In Grosseto province, a recent study of the reaction concludes that the Liberal Association became so closely identified with the *fasci* as 'to become virtually a single movement'.[182] At Siena the Young Liberals' Association, the Fascio d'Azione Giovanile Liberale, was particularly active on behalf of the fascists, even forming squads of its own to accompany the blackshirts on their expeditions. Such activity, moreover, had the full approval of the parent organization, which in the spring of 1921, in the presence of Gino Sarrocchi, took the decision to admit the compatibility of simultaneous membership in the Liberal party and *fasci di combattimento*.[183] Similarly, writing in the spring of 1922, the prefect of Florence, Pericoli, noted:

> It is certain that the democratic and Liberal elements, especially in Florence but in general throughout the province, are at the moment oriented towards the fascist party that maintains a notable power in this city, partly because more or less openly belonging are the foremost personalities in political and administrative life.[184]

The provincial Liberal press leaves little doubt that Pericoli's observation was valid not only for Florence, but also for Tuscany as a whole. Thus the official Liberal paper of Siena, the *Fiamma*, wrote of Mussolini in early 1922 that, 'There is no difference between his thought and ours',[185] and called for the formation of a 'National Right' of Liberals, nationalists, and fascists as the embryo of a future national government.[186] Still more openly stating its entire solidarity with the movement, the Siena Liberal paper announced:

> It is useless to prevaricate: fascism has saved Italy, and whoever is against fascism is against his fatherland ... Let us bless fascism and let us join with all our strength to help this proud awakening of the energies of the Italian race.[187]

In much the same spirit the *Rinnovamento* of Pisa observed of fascism — that 'beautiful Garibaldian militia' — that

> It is the healthy, good, and patriotic part of Italian youth, who desire to save the nation from arrogance, criminality, and factionalism ...
> Let us therefore give full and complete credit to fascism.[188]

Despite such enthusiastic and powerful endorsement, the agrarian organization of fascism did not simply spring into being overnight. In April 1919 when the rapid spread of subversion in the Tuscan provinces was already apparent, 1,000 of the larger landowners of the region together with their *fattori* had gathered in Florence to found the Tuscan Agrarian Association with the express purpose of 'halting the spread of unions in agriculture and defending production'.[189] The task of organizing the landlords in Tuscany was, in comparison with other areas of the peninsula, greatly facilitated by the concentration of Tuscan landholding. Often the point passes unnoticed, but landownership in Tuscany was very highly concentrated, perhaps more so than in any other region.[190]

This concentration of ownership favoured personal contact among the proprietors and eased their problems of orgnization. In addition to being relatively few, the Tuscan landlords were easily organized because of their keen awareness of their common interests. In the Accademia dei Georgofili they already possessed a virtual landlords' parliament, and in *mezzadria* they had a unifying ideology. These in turn reflected the traditional personal involvement of the Tuscan landlord with his estates. This direct contact undoubtedly waned as the lords withdrew to Florence and were transformed into absentee entrepreneurs. None the less, this tendency had not yet completed its course. By contrast with the rest of the peninsula, the Tuscan lords were still deeply involved with their properties. It was notable, for example, that no generation of middlemen had yet interposed itself between land and owner. Even in the Chiana Valley, the most commercially advanced zone of Tuscany,

> The large and medium estates are run directly by the landlord as entrepreneur; letting is all but unknown.[191]

It was still the landlord who usually

> hires technical specialists, organizes market operations, takes care of the selection of cattle, makes experiments, and tries to make improvements...[192]

The land in Tuscany, then, was held by a select handful of noble families who were far from having lost all contact with rural affairs. In such a context, a whole network of personal contacts still existed among men of property, contacts that proved convertible into the structures of political militancy. As political antagonists, the Tuscan landowners were still a formidable class.

Certainly the establishment of a powerful landlords' organization proved relatively easy. From its founding in April 1919 with about 1,000 members, the AAT grew rapidly. In November 1920, after just seventeen months, the Agraria had a membership of 5,330 landlords representing a taxable income of 11,000,000 lire or approximately one third of the landed property in the region. Like Tuscan landownership itself, the Agrarian Association was a highly centralized regional oligarchy. The proprietors had long regarded Tuscany as a region apart, distinct from the rest of Italy. It was logical that they should respond to the crisis of *mezzadria* as a common regional problem. For large landowners with substantial holdings in more than one province, only a regional organization provided an adequate safeguard for their interests. Thereafter, the strategic necessities of civil war reinforced the bias towards centralization and confirmed Florence as the hub of lordly politics. So marked was the preponderance of the capital within the AAT that the agrarian congress of October 1921 expressed concern at the local branches of the Association, which had adopted the attitude that 'what needs to be done will be done at the Florence headquarters'.[193]

The founding of the Agraria was not as such the call for violent reaction. This potential, however, was present from the start. The AAT explained to its members from the beginning that it intended to function as a militant instrument for the defence of private property and that it would confront rural subversion 'strong in numbers and means, and based above all on iron discipline'.[194] The violent possibilities of such a stance were rapidly made clear in Florence province by the support the Mugello branch of the AAT gave to the Citizens' Defence Alliance from 1919. The Alliance, a direct precursor to the Florence *fascio*, was an anti-socialist militia with nuclei in the capital and in such neighbouring agrarian centres as Borgo San Lorenzo. The purpose of the Alliance was described by A. Giovannini, a spokesman for the Mugello Agrarian Association. 'A war to the death', he wrote in February, 1920,

> has been declared against the bourgeoisie, to whom the world owes all its scientific, technical, and political progress, and in the program against this bourgeoisie there figures organized violence, collective and individual, of thought and of action...
> The government, unable to defend the state, allows the nation to suffer the

blows of the trade union movement, and subjugates it before the ills of a policy at once anti-national and harmful to the state.

It is this system of yielding and surrendering rights, duties, and power ... which has promoted the organized violence of classes and parties.

From this observation of fact, and from this sense that the government is abandoning the most vital interests and rights of society, has arisen the idea of citizens' defence.[195]

The new organization was a 'union of all the healthy forces' of the region.[196]

Under the aegis of the Alliance, a group of landlords, including Count Paolo Guicciardini and Marquis Peruzzi de' Medici, began to meet in Florence with some of the future leaders of Tuscan squadrism, such as Dino Perrone Compagni, Umberto Banchelli, and Michele Terzaghi. The purpose of the meetings was to plan armed resistance to the union advance in the countryside. The intentions of the group were admirably unequivocal. 'Machine guns', wrote Banchelli, 'were often the preferred topic.'[197]

Here in the Citizens' Defence Alliance and in the more informal group assembled in Florence there were direct links between the Agrarian Association from its founding and the future leading cadres of the *fasci*.[198] For a time, however, there was an effort made in two other directions. In the first place, the Association made a rather clumsy effort to overtake the politicization of the *mezzadri* by a re-assertion in a new form of the old paternalism. The continuing emphasis on the traditional ideology of *mezzadria* as a genuine partnership and as a solution to class divisions was not just a long-term attempt to justify a system which had served the landlords well. There was also a more immediate purpose. The Agrarian Association, that is, offered itself as a paternalistic alternative to the Leagues. In keeping with the putative communitarian spirit of *mezzadria*, membership was announced to be open not only to men of property, but to the peasants as well, who were warmly invited to join. (At the same time, perhaps in deference to the real class antagonisms at stake, elaborate internal arrangements were devised through the division of membership into categories that were intended to ensure that the reality of control from above within the Association should not be threatened.)[199] Appeals were then made to the peasants to enrol in the Association, and backed up by incentives to demonstrate the benefits of class cooperation.

The trouble with this paternalistic strategy in the postwar years was the stubborn refusal of the *mezzadri* to take it seriously. The Association was far too blatantly the organization of the lords. Two years after its founding, the AAT was forced to acknowledge that the membership category open to tenants existed only on paper. It was the recognition of the failure to revitalize paternalism *in extremis* that underlined the need for an alternative that could combine energetic repression with at least an appearance of independence from the lords. It was this alternative which took shape as fascism.

There is a dividing line between the early period of the Association when it contemplated armed reaction but still preferred to rely on a combination of its own efforts at paternal persuasion and government intervention to safeguard property interests, and a later time when the AAT embarked on a subversive resort to violent self-help. The watershed is the congress of the Association mentioned above that met in Florence in late November 1920. At that congress, the vice-president of the Association, P. F. Serragli, warned that 'it would be a foolish illusion to expect from the state a solution to the grave problems affecting agriculture ...'.[200] Even at the time, the *Nazione*, the Florence paper that proved well informed of the concerns of men of property, recognized that the congress marked a turning-point, and that the *agrari* had resolved upon a policy of intransigent retrenchment and self-help.[201] Agrarian squadrism was the new course adopted by the landlords. The purpose, Serragli announced, was 'the economic and moral reconstruction of the nation'.[202]

COMPANY UNIONS

The close relations that existed between the landlords and the *fasci* are the more readily comprehensible if we recall that fascism, in addition to crushing subversion in the short term, offered to replace the socialist and Catholic union organizations entirely and permanently with its own network of unions which were more solicitous of the interests of landed property. The landlords were well aware that squadrism alone was too clumsy an instrument for rule in the long term. A more adaptable instrument of vigilance, control and re-education was needed. The *Difesa agricola*, the agrarian paper of Siena, explained its conception of the limits of squadrism and outlined the role to be fulfilled by the new union structures. Even after the destruction of the socialist revolutionary threat, the countryside in late 1921 had not yet been pacified to the satisfaction of the lords:

The usual orators, once the exploiters of bolshevism, no longer dare to hold forth in the public squares. But they are tireless in attending even religious festivals, meeting places, and dances where peasants gather. And with blandishments, slander, and threats they plant the evil seed of rebellion.

Now repressive means alone are not enough to bring beclouded minds to reason. We must oppose propaganda with propaganda, and spread, with the benevolent forms of class solidarity, the feelings of law and order and of morality which are the foundation and the safeguard of the general well-being.[203]

The instrument required, one that would be in continuous contact with the peasants, spreading propaganda and demonstrating the tenets of class collaboration, was provided by the fascist unions, variously known as 'economic unions', 'national unions', 'autonomous unions', and 'Peasant Brotherhoods'. These unions first appeared in the Chiana Valley of Siena province in February 1921. Their appearance was an early and clear indication that fascism intended not only to prevent revolution but also to establish a whole new regime in the countryside, a new moral and economic order in which the unsteady foundations of a decaying *mezzadria* system were to be buttressed by the institutions of an ongoing repression. Fascism was anti-Liberal as well as anti-socialist.

That the landlords should have been interested in establishing such institutions is easy to understand, as the AAT itself had attempted to become a pseudo union when in 1919 and 1920 it had thrown open its membership to the tenants. The difficulty with the union experiment of the Association was that the *mezzadri* stubbornly refused to take part.[204] The Association terminated the effort at its regional conference in October 1921. The Liberal deputy Sarrocchi, a founding member of the AAT and one of the early proponents of the 'interclass' experiment, declared that the time had come to liquidate the attempt as well as to reject the proposal of Donini, president of the national Confagricoltura, that a National Agrarian Party be created. Carrying with him the overwhelming majority of the assembled congress (5,177 against 1,676), Sarrocchi explained:

To orient the political contest in a direction unlikely to succeed is, I believe, an error. We shall only be accused of organizing as landlords among ourselves and the peasants will move even further from us just now that we can detect a certain re-awakening among them, a re-awakening that is our only hope of winning them to us by reason. Otherwise we shall provide weapons for our enemies. For the moment ... only the Economic Unions are carrying out the work of breaking up the Red Leagues.[205]

The failure of the AAT to become at once the instrument of lordly reaction as well as a viable rural trade union reveals something of the nature of fascism and its usefulness to the landowners. The AAT, to be successful as a mass labour organization, had three fatal disabilities. First, on its own, it lacked the necessary means of coercion. Secondly, it was far too clearly the direct creation of the bosses to compete even nominally with the rival Catholic and socialist unions for credibility and support among the masses. Thirdly, it was, as an organization of the landlords themselves, an unwieldy and improbable instrument for flexible and demagogic measures. It was unlikely, for instance, that the AAT could organize the standard weapon of trade unionism, the strike: the bosses could hardly lead a strike against themselves.

All these deficiencies were made good by the *fasci*. Squadrism, in the first place, was an indispensable support for the advance of the fascist unions. In the course of 1921 socialist Leagues passed wholesale into the labour organizations of the *fasci*, often under threat of physical violence. Terror was generally the forerunner of the 'economic unions' and 'Peasant Brotherhoods', which followed in the wake of the squads. Moreover, the link between the activities of the two complementary instruments of fascist policy was clearly shown by the many instances in which leaders of the action squads were also the principal labour organizers. Perhaps nowhere was this close relation clearer than in Siena and Grosseto provinces. At Siena the leading person in the propaganda and establishment of the fascist unions in 1921 was none other than Giorgio Alberto Chiurco, secretary of the Siena *fascio* and squadrist *par excellence*.[206] Similarly, at Grosseto the head of the directing centre of the fascist unions, the Camera Italiana del Lavoro, was Dino Andriani. Andriani was secretary of the Grosseto *fascio*, 'the most active of squadrists', and secretary of the provincial branch of the AAT.[207]

At the same time, however, mere physical duress was an unstable basis for the new unions, and a major effort was made to portray the new institutions as the genuine defenders of peasant interests. The class surrender involved in taking out membership in the 'Peasant Brotherhoods' was camouflaged to a degree at least by the fact that formally they, unlike the AAT, were independent of the employers. Much propagandistic use was made of one of the titles of the fascist labour organizations – the 'autonomous unions' – and it was a major advantage that many of the foremost fascist labour organizers, such as Idalberto Targioni, Nazzareno Mezzetti, and Patrizio Oddi, were former socialist union officials. Indeed, an attempt was made to keep the unions 'autonomous' not only from the landlords, but also from the *fasci* in order to soften the sense of capitulation involved in enrolling in the new unions. The separation, of course, was fictitious as the leading cadres of the 'economic unions' were frequently also members of the directing bodies of the *fasci*.[208] The fiction of independence, however, was actively furthered, even by the occasional organization of local strikes and, more frequently, the threat of such strikes.[209]

Furthermore, genuine material benefits were used as incentives to join the unions. The fascist unions recommended themselves by the immunity they offered from fascist raids and harassment; by the possibility to those enrolled of finding continuous employment; and by the important wage differentials often granted by employers to fascist union members. Typical was the meeting of landlords at Rapalano (Grosseto province) at which, according to the fascist press, it was agreed that the landlords will guarantee work to those enrolled in our unions and a wage sufficient to meet the cost of living. For this purpose, moreover, it was decided to link the salary to the provision by the employers of the articles of first necessity at prices and conditions below the market level.[210]

At the same time there were other benefits which the fascist unions offered. Membership – and this was a demagogic stroke of which the most was made – was often free, in contrast to the standard dues system of the socialist and Catholic unions.[211] There were competitions open to members by which substantial monetary awards could be won. Peasant members were entitled to hospital insurance and to insurance for their cattle. There were fascist distributive cooperatives for clothes and agricultural equipment. Wage labourers who gave proof of political reliability were sometimes promoted to the tenancy of a *podere*.

Such benefits were meagre by the standards of the regional pact of 1920. The point, however, is that they had an entirely different appeal in late 1921 and 1922 as the aspirations of the 'Red Years' gave way to despair, as the economic crisis deepened, and as the socialist and Catholic Leagues made ever more evident their growing inability even to defend the gains won at such sacrifice. In these circumstances, the patronage available to the *fasci* through their connections with the landlords offered the opportunity, if not certainly of solving the crisis, then at least of personally escaping its harshest consequences. In exchange for this possibility, however, the new members – and this was the aspect dear to the Agrarian Association – were obliged to abandon the moral and political demands on which the original agrarian agitations had been founded and to accept instead the regimentation of an articulated system of political coercion.

The new unions from their inception took great pains to reassure property owners that their role was not to challenge but to reinforce hierarchy and the domination of property over labour. In February 1921, at the establishment of the very first 'national unions', the fascist Giacomo Lumbroso explained the new development in the *Riscossa* for the benefit of uneasy landlords:

There are many peace-loving members of the bourgeoisie who, when they hear the mention of trade unions, make the sign of the cross and shudder as if the devil had been named. These distinguished gentlemen may take heart: 'union' in the true sense of the word means only a corporation or association of workers belonging to the same category...
Furthermore, the union idea, even if understood in a wholly revolutionary sense, is always a hierarchical and aristocratic concept in contrast to idiotic bolshevik levelling: a hierarchy of class and not of individuals, but always a hierarchy; an aristocracy of intelligence and not of birth, but always an aristocracy.[212]

Furthermore, the unions guaranteed their own 'economic', 'apolitical', and 'autonomous' character. In part, as we have seen, such qualifications were a demagogic manoeuvre to proclaim the independence of the new unions from the *agrari* and even from the *fasci*. There was, however, a deeper significance as well. The fascist unions were apolitical and economic in the sense that the claims they put forward on behalf of their members could concern only immediate monetary issues rather than the array of broad political and moral questions that had been at the heart of the demands of the 'Red Years' – security against eviction, participation in the direction of the estates, effective control of the land. Indeed, the Tuscan fascist unions in 1921 and 1922 made such broad political demands virtually impossible by radically splitting the labour movement into isolated geographical and category compartments.[213] Thus the peasants and wage earners could no longer face the landlords as a class united by a common platform, organization, and experience.

Indeed, in so far as the new unions served to advance the claims of their members, their task was to further individual advancement 'according to talent and merit'[214] rather than to support collective and class interests. The fascist union movement, in Idalberto Targioni's words,

> wants to arrange human values in a hierarchical sense. That is, it intends to place everyone in the station he deserves and to reward the individual according to his merit.[215]

And in practice even within a single union, the effort was made to establish differentials of every description among the labourers and to create competition through a series of prizes. When the very first 'economic union' was established among the peasants in Siena province,

> The first deliberation of the Union was the opening of a competition for prizes to be awarded for the best cultivated *podere*.[216]

In that particular instance, seventy-five prizes were at once established for a total of 7,000 lire and a 'diploma of honour'.[217]

In any case, the 'economic unions' were unlikely to present any claims subversive of the established relations of power in the countryside because, backed by the squads, they were hierarchical and unresponsive to pressure from below. The officials were appointed from above and saw their mission as one of inculcating in the peasants the values of work, discipline, and patriotism rather than one of furthering the interests and claims of the membership. In fact, even within the 'economic' sphere which the fascist unions had, as a matter of principle, claimed as their province, there was considerable reason to doubt that the Peasant Brotherhoods were committed to the protection of anything beyond the actual physical survival of the peasant – and that only because it was also in the interest of production. Here the provincial secretary of the *fasci* of Florence province, Carlo Romagnoli, and the inevitable Targioni explained quite clearly that the 'key idea' of fascist trade unionism was to find the proper balance between capital and labour in which neither overwhelmed the other. Now, however, they reasoned that capital oppresses labour in only one circumstance:

> when the employer places the worker in such a situation that he does not possess sufficient means to satisfy the elementary needs of existence.[218]

As the subversive threat receded and as the need to compete with the socialist unions for membership faded with it, the fascist organizations began to accept in good grace very severe reductions in the standard of living of their members. In early 1922 the Italian Chamber of Labour, the organizing centre of the fascist labour movement in Siena province, directed by Chiurco and Oddi, was content to take note that 'the landlords, the industrialists, and the employers in general tend to reduce wages and salaries, and by no small amount'. Far from taking action, the fascist organization reminded the employers that it too opposed 'artificial and harmful rises in wages'.[219] Chiurco, meanwhile, actually appealed to the Agrarian Association as a fellow 'economic' organization 'acting outside and above all political tendencies and parties' to help the Italian Chamber of Labour in the pursuit of its goals and,

> to serve as a connecting link in the settling of economic differences between capital and labour – all in accordance with the principle of class collaboration on which our whole union program is based.[220]

The landlords demonstrated a very clear appreciation of the purposes and functions of such organizations as the 'Peasant Brotherhoods' and the Italian Chamber of Labour. Francesco Nicolai of the Mugello branch of the Association unequivocally outlined his understanding of the functions of the Brotherhoods:

> They intend to develop and maintain close bonds of solidarity and fraternity between the partners with the sole purpose of achieving a gradual and continuous economic improvement by means of a technical perfection of work, an increased yield from the land, and a growing love for thrift.
> With the proprietors the Brotherhood maintains relations of harmony and collaboration while it proposes to combat with every means all the subversive elements that act against the good of the nation and against the real interests of the partners.[221]

That the Brotherhoods should have acted in such close harmony with the landlords was a foregone conclusion as it was the landlords themselves who had taken the initiative in introducing the new unions to the Tuscan countryside. The earliest rural fascist unions in the region were established in the Chiana Valley of Siena province, as we have seen, in February 1921 at Montepulciano, Bossona, and Fila with 800 members.[222] What should be added is that these early organizations of the *fasci* were set up by important local employers and leaders of the AAT, such as Marquis Ridolfo Bichi Ruspoli-Forteguerra, Count Ildebrando Scroffa, and the ubiquitous Sarrocchi, all of whom cooperated extensively with the Sienese fascist leaders Chiurco, Oddi, and Mezzetti in the setting up of the 'national unions'.[223] And the AAT officially, on both the provincial and the regional levels, gave its support to the new organizations.[224] Serragli confirmed that 'the Association is establishing friendly relations with the independent peasant organizations and with the Economic Unions'.[225]

The importance of the fascist unions should not be understated. Through them the landlords gained a virtual monopoly over the labour market, an efficient means of dividing the peasants and wage labourers into isolated categories and competing individuals, a vast instrument of surveillance and propaganda, and a whole network of patronage. The official view of the Agraria was that the new order of which the unions, as extensions of the squads, were a part, was essentially a return to the harmonious golden age of *mezzadria* with love and cooperation between the partners. Then, however, the economic power of the landlord in the form of ownership of the means of production had been sufficient to guarantee the exploitation of the sharecropping class and the creation of a surplus for the landlord, while a variety of traditional bonds had tied the tenants to the social order and prevented the emergence of open rebellion. These bonds had been destroyed by the commercialization of agriculture, and the old class disparities, no longer sufficient alone to guarantee the social position of the landlords and their ability to extract a surplus from the *mezzadri*, were now supplemented by the instruments of political coercion in the forms of the squads and the unions.

The new order was given legal expression by the adoption from late 1922 of a new regional pact to be applied and enforced by the unions. In August 1922 T. Pestellini, Serragli's successor as president of the AAT, announced that the Association had decided unilaterally to denounce the pact of 1920 then in force and that a new pact had been drawn up which was to be applied from March 1923. This new pact, drawn up by the fascist union organizations and drafted in large part by the ex-socialist Mezzetti, gave expression to the new regime in the countryside.

This fascist pact abolished at a stroke the gains of the tenant class in 1920. Eviction was re-affirmed as the indisputable prerogative of the landlord. The entire tenant family was legally tied to the *podere*, and only the landlord could give permission for the size of the family to be modified. The entire expenses of cultivation were to be divided equally between the partners. Insurance was no longer an obligation of the landlord. Direction of the estate was to be the exclusive right of the proprietor. The tenant was obliged to work for the owner off the *podere* upon request when the latter 'lacked a way of proceeding otherwise'. The arbitration boards were abolished, and all disagreements over the interpretation of the pact were to be 'referred for solution to the local, provincial, and national agrarian and tenant organizations' (i.e. the AAT or the fascist unions).

Perhaps the most revealing clause, however, was Title VI, Article 38, entitled 'Rights and duties of the tenants', which read:

The tenant has the duty to cultivate the land according to the criteria of a good head of the family, and with a strict obedience to the orders given by the landlord or his representative. Within the framework of these orders and directives, and in accordance with past usage, the tenant, as partner and collaborator of the proprietor, has the right of an appropriate initiative in the manual execution of his work.[226]

CHAPTER 2

THE APPEAL OF THE RIGHT

EMILIA AND TUSCANY: THE LIMITS OF TUSCAN POPULISM

The fascist movement in the Tuscan countryside began as an instrument of class repression organized by the large landowners. From the early weeks of 1921 the *agrari* unleashed a violent civil war against the union and political organizations of their tenants. Throughout the spring and summer the eight provinces witnessed an unending succession of raids by fascist squads against town halls with recently seated socialist councils; against the branches of the socialist and popular parties; against the offices of the subversive press; and against the homes of union officials. Activists were harassed, assaulted, and murdered. When resistance was offered, whole villages were plundered and set aflame.

That the sheer violence of the fascist onslaught was a major factor in its success is obvious. The use of terror was pervasive, systematic, and well organized. Socialist mayors and town councillors resigned their posts. Union leaders went into exile or fell silent. Opposition newspapers closed down. Individual members of the socialist and Popular organizations abandoned the cause, even accepting instead membership in the new fascist unions as the only guarantee of physical security. In Tuscany in particular we must not understate the efficacy of the fascist 'redemption' administered at night with the pistol, the cudgel, and the flaming torch, for the region achieved a sad national primacy in counter-revolutionary terror. Florentine squadrism, in the words of Paolo Spriano, was 'the most savage and arrogant ... that ever took root in Italy'.[1]

We need not rehearse the dreary history of squadrist exploits, which are well known in outline and differ little from similar events elsewhere in Italy. A more important task is to understand the political context in which the fascist offensive proved effective. Violence in itself was no novelty in Italian history. What set fascism apart from simple repression and enabled the proprietors to re-establish their political domination on more stable foundations was the capacity of the movement to counter subversion with a mass following of its own. The *fasci* emerged victorious in the civil war because they were able to create a plebeian base for reaction. To understand fascism, then, we must explore the recruitment of a mass membership in the provinces.

In the composition of its following, Tuscan fascism was radically different from the movement on the national level. The sources of support for reaction in the region and the agrarian program with which the fascists sought to gain adherents were unlike those of Emilia, the 'classic' region of agrarian fascism. The social structure of the Tuscan countryside made the national agrarian program, based on the experience of the Po Valley, unworkable. Florence thus became the centre for the elaboration of an alternative rural strategy, which was applied in most of the region. On the other hand, there were two restricted zones in which the *fasci* chose Emilia as their model. The fascists of the Chiana and Arno Valleys adopted the agrarian program not of Florence, but of Ferrara. In this chapter, then, we must consider first the rural heresy of Florence and then the return to orthodoxy proclaimed in Siena. Our argument will be that the advance of capitalistic farming methods had so altered the pattern of class relations in the great Tuscan valleys as to make them more readily comparable to the Po Valley than to the areas of traditional *mezzadria*.

In the North, there were latent divisions within the rural labour movement among different and partly competing categories of peasants. Developing and exasperating these tensions, the fascists were able to undermine socialist unity and to mobilize a peasant following of their own. The main line of cleavage that proved so perilous for Emilian socialism was the divergence of interest between, on the one hand, the landless *braccianti* who aspired to revolution, and, on the other, the various strata of 'middle peasants' – sharecroppers, peasant leaseholders, and small proprietors – who preserved a stake in the existing order. The opposition between the two groups reflected objective differences of interest. The possibility of conflict was woven into the social fabric of the northern provinces. It was embedded in the incomplete modernization of the northern countryside which had given rise to the lingering juxtaposition of traditional tenure patterns and some of the most modern capitalist estates in Europe. The extent of the conflict that actually developed, however, was in no sense inevitable, but was the result of a series of more immediate factors – the defect of a divisive socialist agrarian program, the vast expansion of small peasant proprietorship after the war, the soaring rate of rural unemployment, and skilful fascist propaganda. Capitalizing on potential divergences of interest, the *fasci* of Emilia rapidly built their own agrarian support.[2]

In Tuscany, by contrast, the factors which enabled the fascists to win peasant support in the North applied either not at all or to a much smaller degree. In the first place, in central Tuscany as a whole, the relative social homogeneity of the region militated against an easy fascist fomenting of the same sorts of internecine divisions which undermined peasant unity in Emilia. In Tuscany capitalist development had transformed rural social relations. A major difference from Emilia, however, was that this development, for a variety of economic, geological, and political reasons, had taken place *through* the traditional sharecropping contract, drastically altering its social content but preserving intact its form. As a result, there was in Tuscany an overall uniformity of tenure based on *mezzadria*. Within the provinces of Florence, Siena, Arezzo, and Pisa that chiefly concern us here, there was an overwhelming numerical predominance of *mezzadri* over all other categories of labour. Tuscany provided, therefore, a structural basis for greater unity within the labour movement than existed in the North, where tenure patterns and social stratification were heterogeneous. The Tuscan landlords confronted a peasant front within which the ancient formula for ruling by dividing was of difficult application. By comparison with the Po Valley, the Tuscan countryside was relatively impermeable to fascist penetration.

There is a seeming problem here, however, which must be explained — the difference in political behaviour between the sharecroppers of central Italy, who formed the backbone of the rural socialist movement, and their counterparts in Emilia, so many of whom joined ranks with the reaction. The long-term factors which transformed the Tuscan *mezzadri* from the guardians of social stability dear to the Georgofili into the revolutionary social force of the postwar years have been examined. Unfortunately, there are not sufficient studies of the contrasting evolution of Emilian sharecropping to make firm judgments on the evolution of the contract and the condition of the peasants. Presumably, however, the same sorts of commercial pressures at work on the Tuscan *mezzadri* affected Emilian tenants as well. Certainly in Emilia, too, the *mezzadri* gave proof of their discontent by their early participation in the socialist Leagues. What later conditioned their vacillation with regard to the socialist cause and then led to their growing enthusiasm for reaction was their position of *relative* privilege with respect to the surrounding sea of destitute wage labourers. But the division between the two categories was not inevitable; it was in part created by the socialist movement itself which, by adopting the program of socialization of the land and denying thereby the land hunger and aspirations of the *mezzadri*, gratuitously alienated a social category whose sympathies for a new order in the countryside might have been more fully developed had that order taken a different form. Furthermore, beyond the long-term aim of socialization, which to the *mezzadri* was anathema, spelling misery, enforced idleness, and the loss of their remaining sense of independence and security, the more immediate policies and methods of the northern Leagues were often such as to produce further grounds for reciprocal bitterness and recrimination and, from the standpoint of the sharecroppers, proof that the Leagues were controlled by the *braccianti* in pursuit of narrow category interests rather than common unifying concerns. Examples here were the application of the *imponibile* to employing sharecroppers as well as to landlords and the ban on the exchange of labour among the sharecroppers themselves, so that they were forced to turn to the labour market, where they confronted the Leagues not as the guardians of their interests against those of the landlords but as an alien power. Similarly, the Leagues, concerned mainly with the wage labourers, applied sanctions – boycotts and fines – against recalcitrant sharecroppers unwilling, in contrast to the *braccianti*, to jeopardize their crop by joining the agitation. Such sanctions, useful in the short term in breaking the resistance of the employers, in the long run revealed a dangerous division of interest between the ostensibly allied labourers – a division which was felt by the whole class of *mezzadri*, who came to resent the discipline of the Leagues as an imposition.

In Tuscany, the militancy of the *mezzadri* was far more developed and sustained than in Emilia. This was true, first of all, because the Tuscan *mezzadri*, far from being a privileged category of rural labour, stood at the base of the social pyramid. Tuscan sharecroppers constituted a social category different from their Emilian counterparts because they had virtually no ownership of the means of production. Nowhere was the difference more apparent than in the question of livestock. The Emilian *mezzadri* tended to own cattle, whereas in Tuscany such ownership was an indication of considerable relative prosperity. Here was the practical result of that contrast in social evolution by which primitive accumulation in central Italy occurred within the framework of *mezzadria*, while in the North the proletarianized *mezzadro* became a wage labourer.

In relative terms, moreover, the Tuscan *mezzadri* had no interests to defend against encroachment from below. Apart from a few restricted zones, the Tuscan sharecroppers looked down upon no surrounding mass of organized wage earners as in the North. Where there were nuclei of *braccianti* and *camporaioli*, they lived either on the fringes of the great estates as scattered and destitute labourers, economically marginal and politically unorganized, or in the restricted zones of the Chiana and lower Arno Valley. Where the *braccianti* did find political expression, it was as an appendage of the movement of the *mezzadri*. The Tuscan *mezzadri*, then, had little sense of privilege to defend against assault from below.

Such considerations were perhaps not sufficient to guarantee the political militancy of the Tuscan *mezzadri* in contrast to their Emilian counterparts, but they produced a number of important corollaries that worked towards the same result. Of great importance here was a vital modification of the socialist program and of socialist union practice in the region in favour of the interests of the sharecroppers.

To begin with the agrarian program, we must not expect to find in the Tuscan socialist leadership any great theoretical or organizational preparation for the tremendous postwar militancy of the *mezzadri* of the region. Indeed, the official analysis, which considered the aspirations of the sharecroppers petty bourgeois and unrelated to the exigencies of socialism, made the party systematically unprepared for the rapid postwar politicization of the countryside. Surely no one expressed greater surprise than the Florence weekly the *Difesa*, the most combative socialist paper in Tuscany, at the overwhelming response of the *mezzadri* to the great agitations of 1920. 'Who could have foreseen it?' was the comment of the paper.[3] The Tuscan socialists faced the coming postwar crisis blinkered by the official party view of agrarian social relations. One should not expect, therefore, any sort of fully elaborated alternative analysis or an overt rejection of the party program. What did occur, however, was that, inevitably, in postwar Tuscany the inadequacies of the socialist program to confront the crisis of *mezzadria* were revealed dramatically and inexorably. The call for socialization of the land, based as it was on the experiences and struggles of the Po Valley *braccianti*, could have been pressed in this region of newly revolutionary sharecroppers only by men who resolutely closed both eyes to reality. It was not coincidental that one of the leading voices raised to query the party program in the matter was that of Argentina Altobelli, the Federterra secretary, who had a close knowledge of central Italy and played a major role in the great postwar Tuscan strikes and in the drawing up and negotiating of the new regional pact.[4]

The objective constraints of working in the Tuscan countryside caused the local party and union officials quietly in practice to drop the call for socialization in favour of the demand 'The land to the peasants!'[5] Again, this step was not taken uniformly, nor was there an absence of those within the party who saw the new development with alarm. But even such protectors of party orthodoxy on the issue as the paper the *Falce* of Arezzo, which denounced the new watchword as dangerous anti-socialist heresy, appealed, interestingly, less to the formula of socialization than to local intermediate experiments at collective rent contracts and productive cooperatives as the guide to correct socialist practice in the Tuscan countryside.[6] There is reason to suppose, then, that the adoption of a long-term objective which responded to the traditional aspirations of the sharecropping strata was an important factor in the commitment to the League movement on the part of the tenants of the region and in the preservation of a united peasant front in the long spring of 1921. Certainly, D'Eufemia, the prefect of Siena, emphasized the importance of the land program in winning the allegiance of the Tuscan *mezzadri* to socialism. Thus, during the high tide of socialist success in the middle of 1920, he informed the Ministry of the Interior that

the peasants gladly follow the socialist party as long as it promises them the ownership of the land.[7]

He also reported:

Taking advantage of the ignorance of the agricultural class and of its attachment to the land, and holding before its eyes the prospect of an imminent revolution that will give it possession of the landed estates by expropriating the present owners, the leaders of the revolutionary movement in this province have succeeded in attracting into their ranks the overwhelming majority of the peasants...[8]

Or again, D'Eufemia informed his superiors of his conviction that the *mezzadri* enrolled in the socialist Leagues were

attracted less by political conviction than by the mirage of the ownership of the land shortly promised them ... by the socialist propagandists in their continual meetings.[9]

The agrarian program, perhaps, was but one important example of a broader process by which the socialist Leagues in Tuscany adopted a socialist practice which enabled them to be regarded by the *mezzadri*, not, as in Emilia, as an alien power, but as the instrument of their faith and the weapon of their emancipation. Because the Leagues, first of all, were in fact the creation of the sharecroppers and not of another social category and because they pursued an objective consonant with the *mezzadro*'s own vision of social reform, there was little need for the sort of disciplinary sanctions applied in the North to buttress faltering sharecropping solidarity. It was true that during the great strikes of 1920 there were 'Red Brigades' that patrolled the countryside to see that the strike was not broken, but the conflicts that arose seem to have arisen chiefly with *fattori* or with the members of the rival Catholic organizations.[10] Strikingly, there was, in comparison with Emilia, only a relatively weak pre-existing League bureaucratic structure to direct the postwar struggle. Perhaps partly as a result, given the prevailing bureaucratization of the General Confederation of Labour and its associated unions, there was a greater degree of improvisation and responsiveness, a greater relationship between organizer and organized.

Certainly, in terms of the relation between union officials and union members, the Turin communist paper the *Ordine nuovo* stressed the difference between Emilia, where the socialist rural organizations collapsed before the fascist advance with hardly a blow being struck in their defence, and Tuscany, where the fascist penetration was stubbornly and desperately contested. One of the major reasons that the paper underlined in its analysis of the débâcle of 1921 in the Red provinces of the North was the distance that had developed between the unions and their supporters. In Emilia, the paper emphasized, the unions had become undemocratic centralized bureaucracies standing over and above the masses like a new state power that levied taxes, sanctioned noncompliance by the uncommitted, and administered fines for violations. Between the old state power that was the expression of the hegemony of property and the new reforming order represented by the socialist Leagues the choice of the masses in the northern countryside, expressed clearly in the massive socialist electoral victories, was never in doubt. The reasoning of the *Ordine nuovo*, however, was that the new social order was being introduced in the North from above, without the active personal participation of the agricultural workers. Adopting a polemical tone, the paper sometimes exaggerated the 'despotic' nature of union power. The point, though, is clear. Thus, for instance, the Turin paper declared:

The organization [of the Leagues] was heavily concentrated in the persons or the very small circle of the leaders. To bring chaos into the unions it was enough to strike down a few individuals and, worse still, this provoked no serious reaction from the masses ... The reason was that the organization, in its recent colossal and bureaucratic growth, became increasingly nothing more than an enormous central administrative office which had lost all direct contact with the masses, to such an extent that they no longer considered it the arm and standard of their faith ...

'Power' was centralized in the person of the leaders without the masses' being able in any way actively to participate in the power of 'their' organization.[11]

Here it is useful to bear in mind that constant themes of fascist propaganda were the 'tyranny', 'bureaucratization' and 'regimentation' of the Leagues, and the autocratic rule of the union 'bosses' (*capilega*).[12] Such propaganda by the fascists obviously must not be taken as a valid description of union reality, but, instead of simply dismissing it, we should ask the more relevant question of why the fascists found such themes so useful as debating points.

In Emilia an important factor in fascist success was surely the fact that the unions had so wrested the initiative from their following that, when the necessity came to reverse the process in order to resist the onslaught of the squads, the task proved impossible. Even the most revolutionary demand of the northern Leagues – the closed union shop –

required no direct action on the part of the workers, but was essentially an administrative measure to be run by the union officialdom. The socialist order was to arrive only through union mediation.[13]

Very much by contrast, in Tuscany it was the *mezzadri* themselves who were invited by the Leagues to take control of the land in person. A new and radical democracy was to be introduced in which the rural labourers themselves assumed a major share in the direction of production. The 1920 regional pact on Tuscany made this point without ambiguity. The peasants were to participate directly in the management of the estates. In this sense, even the 'petty-bourgeois' program of land to the peasants had its own revolutionary significance – the direct control of the labourers over the means of production. Most strikingly, the Siena Chamber of Labour adopted as its official goal throughout the province the effective establishment of a council movement in which 'farm councils' (*consigli di fabbrica*) would function as agrarian soviets for the radically democratic control of the land.[14]

For a combination of circumstances, then, the task undertaken by the *agrari* and the fascists of turning the flank of the peasant movement proved a peculiarly arduous task in Tuscany, despite the fact that the landlords in the region were among the best organized in the kingdom as well as among the earliest to stress the need for self-defence as an alternative to reliance on the police powers of the state. There were few divisions within the ranks of the socialists that could be exploited to create opposition between rival categories of labour. Furthermore, the commitment of the socialist membership to the institutions of their faith had little parallel in the Red provinces of the North. The fascist attacks on the socialist organizations were not accepted with resignation as so often in Emilia, but provoked a fierce and determined resistance. For the *Ordine nuovo*, Tuscany served as the very example of the sort of popular resistance to the advance of the *fasci* which, if properly led, had a chance of success. Comparing Tuscany with Emilia, the paper observed that

> The fascist experiment was first tried in the city considered the Red stronghold of Italy, Bologna, and the proletariat there knew no way to react except weakly and half-heartedly. There was an ooccasional scuffle, the odd fight by a group, and nothing more. Bologna, like the other centres of Emilia, did not lend itself to the effort.
> At Florence, instead, every time that the fascists attempted an exploit, the workers responded immediately and energetically, with a united movement, with the most rigid and active general strike.[15]

Certainly the determination of the Tuscan working classes, urban and agrarian, to resist the fascist advance was clear and impressive. At Florence, fascist terror provoked an armed insurrection. From 27 February

1921, when the communist leader Spartaco Lavagnini was killed at his desk, to 3 March the city was the scene of a revolt with barricades and pitched battles in the suburbs. The working-class quarters of the city and the industrial suburbs – in particular Santa Croce, San Frediano, and Scandici – improvised a desperate self-defence. The uprising was put down only with the tanks, heavy artillery, and armoured vehicles of the regular army, which crushed the centres of rebellion and left the squads in its wake to carry out the work of punishing and 'mopping up'.[16]

Florence, moreover, was no isolated example. The news of the bloody repression in the capital and the continuing waves of fascist violence touched off a series of similar spontaneous insurrections in the spring of 1921 across the provinces. Each reproduced the same outburst of blind popular fury, and each was put down by the same collaboration and division of labour between the army and the fascist squads. Pisa, Siena, Livorno, Empoli, Pontedera, S. Giovanni Valdarno, all had the same story. Everywhere, too, the revolts were similar: the workers' quarters were breached by tanks and cannons, and the fascists followed to carry out reprisals.[17] Even these, however, were only the large-scale and well-known highlights of this period of Tuscan resistance. 'The same', Togliatti reminds us,

> occurred in the countryside. What is more, the revolt of the countryside, which was equally spontaneous and without organization, teaches the lesson of the force of the rural areas.[18]

With such a united peasant front, the fascist movement found the task of splitting the socialist base a long and difficult process. This difficulty was compounded by the relative numerical paucity of those categories of 'middle peasants' that, unlike the *mezzadri*, had never been part of the rural union movement and in the Po Valley were among those in the forefront of the reaction – the peasant leaseholders (*affittuari*), new peasant proprietors, and the unemployed. With regard to the leaseholders, it was a simple fact that in most parts of Tuscany peasant leaseholds were all but nonexistent.[19]

The case of the peasant proprietors requires some explanation.[20] Peasant proprietorship would seem to offer an abundant source of potential fascist support in the region as this form of tenure was predominant in several provinces of the northwest, and in the mountains. In fact, however, neither in Tuscany nor in the North were such peasant landowners of much significance to the fascist cause. They were, first of all, geographically removed from the areas of socialist strength which therefore hardly affected them directly. Further, among established peasant proprietors the attachment they felt to the land was highly unstable. Many must have been aware less of the future security and prospects ownership offered than of the inexorable economic forces that were slowly forcing them from the land. Such, for example, would have been the case of the tiny mountain proprietors whose economic plight was as desperate as that of any category of rural labour and who were forced seasonally to leave their plots in search of other employment. The proprietors who contributed to fascist strength were the many thousands of *new* peasant owners who had been lessees, *fattori*, sharecroppers, or even wage labourers before the war, but who had found in the war-time economy an opportunity to accumulate savings which they then used to purchase land. These new owners were concentrated, significantly, in the most commercialized zones of both the Po Valley and of Tuscany where the Leagues and the rural socialist movement were most powerful. Moreover, these new proprietors, unlike many of the declining prewar peasant owners, found their political identity through the land, which they saw as the realization of a lifetime of sacrifice and the key to future security, now jeopardized by the threat of socialism. These peasants believed that in the *fasci* they had found an instrument of self-defence. Now the point here is that the expansion of peasant proprietorship was not comparable to that in Emilia in either relative or absolute terms. As a result, the vast movement of landownership into peasant hands which had played such an important part in fascist success in the North provided a far more restricted base of support in the Centre. And, finally, yet another major factor in the success of the *fasci* in the rural North – mass unemployment – could not, in a region of sharecroppers, create the same army of idle and discontented wage labourers who found in fascism the guarantee of a job.[21]

For a combination of reasons, then, the fascists in Tuscany were unable either to undermine the solidarity of the rural socialist movement led by the *mezzadri* or to find mass allies in social reaction among conservative peasant categories – new peasant proprietors, *affittuari*, and the desperate unemployed. These groups were relatively much less numerous in Tuscany than in the 'classical' fascist provinces of Emilia. It was largely for this reason that Tuscan fascism was so slow in establishing its influence. In no other region in which the movement eventually became a powerful autonomous political force before the March on Rome were the *fasci* so tardy in overcoming socialist resistance and in building a stable following of their own. As Palmiro Togliatti noted in the spring of 1921, Tuscany was notable for the 'narrow natural bases that fascism established in the region and for the slight correspondence of its program and methods of struggle to the character of this [i.e. Tuscan] people'.[22]

This narrowness of its 'natural bases' accounted for some of the leading features of the action and strategy of Tuscan fascism. Thus, for example, the marked centralization of the movement under Florentine leadership was not only a result of the concentration of Tuscan landholding, of the prior centralization of the AAT, and of the organizational advantage that the Florence *fascio* derived from the Citizens' Defence Alliance, but also reflected strategic necessity. Since local support was often weak and local recruiting arduous, the struggle in the provinces could often be decided in favour of property only by the strength of the organization at the centre, and, in particular, by its ability to support the provincial *fasci* by mobilizing and deploying men and arms throughout the region. Thus the provincial *fasci* often found their success dependent on Florentine assistance, a factor which naturally reinforced and extended the influence of the *fascio* at the capital. An especially clear statement of the role of Florence as the guiding force in the reaction throughout Tuscany is that of the *caposquadra* Bruno Frullini, who knew his subject well. Frullini wrote:

> The calls for help, so many times full of anguish, on the part of the first groups of fascists in the province and throughout Tuscany were never unanswered. Florentine fascism, conscious of being the Father of Tuscan fascism ... hurried where there was need. With its best men it shielded its comrades in every quarter. It defended, it raised up, it encouraged, it struck, and it punished.[23]

The extreme violence of the Tuscan squadrists was caused by the difficult environment in which they operated. Everywhere, of course, force and intimidation were key elements in fascist success. What was remarkable in Tuscany was not the resort to violence as such, but the particular ferocity of the Tuscan squadrists, whose brutality was proportional to the narrowness of their success by conventional political means and their ineffectiveness at moral suasion. Furthermore, in a region where resistance sprang up spontaneously it was often not enough as in Emilia to harass the union leaders into exile, to coerce the local socialist town councils into resignation, and to pillage party, union, and press headquarters. The Tuscan squads often found it necessary to conduct their missions not as lightning raids but as ponderous military operations in which they occupied whole towns and villages. If the most striking example was the occupation of Grosseto by thousands of squadrists in the summer of 1921, the nature of the operation, if not its scale, was all too common.

The Tuscan social structure also dictated a general political strategy different from that followed in the 'classical' areas of fascist success. Far more than in Emilia the Tuscan fascists dispensed with their populist mask and abandoned the hope of enlisting the support of the mass of *mezzadri*. Considering the sharecropping *poderi* hostile terrritory, the fascists concentrated on the task of winning support instead at the very margins of the *fattoria* and at the great house at the centre. In many respects Tuscan fascism evolved as an anti-*mezzadro* crusade. And nowhere, perhaps, is this anti-*mezzadro* practice of the Tuscan movement better illustrated than in the agrarian program developed at its centre, in Florence.

CENTRAL TUSCANY: POPULISM REJECTED

The national agrarian program of the fascist movement was first outlined at the Milan Congress by Alceste De Ambris,[24] then developed by Gaetano Polverelli and Mussolini in the spring of 1921, and first and most systematically applied in Ferrara province. The great success of the program was its ability to outrun agrarian socialism by seizing on its weak point of socialization and proposing instead a broad agrarian reform that would create a new class of peasant proprietors and peasant lessees as a bulwark of social conservatism. Thus already at Milan De Ambris called for 'greater social justice' and the 'maximum intensification of production' by the distribution of land, through the granting of freeholds or long-term leaseholds, to those most interested in production – the agricultural workers. Proposing confiscation, De Ambris launched the slogan, 'The land to the peasants!'[25]

A year later, as fascist expansion began in the provinces and the need for an agrarian program grew more pressing, Polverelli and Mussolini obliged with a fuller elaboration of fascist policy.[26] The fascists, they explained, were opposed to the socialist call for the socialization or nationalization of the land, on the grounds both of productive efficiency and of social justice. Socialization, in their view, would hinder production by giving the direction of the estates not to a skilled technical class but to distant politicians and bureaucrats. Similarly, they argued, the interests of justice would be compromised by the vesting of control in a central political oligarchy. 'In opposition to the social-communists', Mussolini declared in February,

> we want the land to belong not to the state but to the cultivator. Whereas social-communism tends to disinherit all, and to transform every cultivator into an employee of the state, we wish to give the ownership of the land and economic freedom to the greatest number of peasants. In place of the sovereignty of a central political caste, we support the sovereignty of the peasant.[27]

The fascists, in their own expression, aimed at the creation of a new 'rural democracy' based on peasant landownership.

Opposed to the vision of the 'social-communist' oligarchy, the fascists claimed to be equally opposed to the existing class of big idle and parasitic landlords. Fascism, said Mussolini, was to become 'rural' but not 'agrarian'.

> The *agrari* are one thing: the *rurali* are another. The *agrari* are the big landlords and, with a few praiseworthy exceptions, they are strongly conservative; the *rurali* are sharecroppers, lessees, small proprietors, day labourers. Between *fascismo* and the *agrari* there is no love lost ... They can hardly, in the long run, sympathize with a party that has no respect for their narrow interests, but subordinates them to the interests of production and of the Nation.[28]

Agrari who left their land uncultivated or were absentee owners, Polverelli explained, 'lose the right of property, which presupposes a social function'. Above all, therefore, fascists were the enemies of '*latifondismo*'. The land of the *latifondisti* and absentee farmers, therefore, should be confiscated, with compensation, and distributed to 'those directly concerned, that is, the actual cultivators'.

> We are, moreover, firmly convinced that all those peasants who have no direct interest in the fruits of their labour ... are in no condition to be deeply attached to the land, committed to intense work, and devoted to the best results of agricultural practice. Wage labourers inevitably make up a fluctuating rural social mass susceptible to the most extreme consequences of dogmatism.
> We, instead, desire that every cultivator should be deeply and continuously bound by the ties of affection to the land, to work, to the best production methods. And therefore, in this period which ... is necessarily only one of transition, we will support ... all the best and most equitable forms of profit-sharing ... But, as a general guiding principle, fascism openly and decidedly proposes the gradual elevation of every peasant – through the necessary technical, administrative, financial and political preparation – to the dignity and national responsibility of landownership.[29]

What made the fascist program, with its slogans 'Land to those who work it!' and 'To every peasant the entire fruit of his sacred labour!'[30] the more convincing was that it was backed by a real, if strictly limited, experiment at partitioning among the peasants some marginal areas of land that the agrarian associations were willing to concede to demonstrate the effectiveness of 'class collaboration' rather than antagonism. This experiment went furthest at Ferrara, where the provincial Agrarian Federation under the leadership of Vico Mantovani placed thousands of hectares of land at the disposal of the local *fascio* for the transformation of disgruntled wage labourers into lessees and tiny proprietors. Thus in March 1921 the Land Office of the Ferrara *fascio* announced two initial distributions respectively of 4,000 and 3,000 hectares, followed by successive lists of smaller areas.[31]

In the northern countryside, the fascist agrarian program, in addition to delighting men of property with its prospect of a class of new conservative rural allies – in Mussolini's words, 'a new rural petty bourgeoisie'[32] –

possessed a substantial popular appeal for the rising 'intermediate' strata of peasants anxious to defend a position of relative security and fearful of proletarianization when the revolution ended the regime of private property.

By contrast, the Tuscan agrarian program accepted as immutable the inability of the fascists to find the same deep fissures within the peasant ranks as among the heterogeneous following of Emilian socialism. The Tuscan agrarian program was developed above all by the ex-socialist leader Idalberto Targioni, the official fascist propagandist for Florence province and editor of the two major fascist papers of the province, the *Riscossa* of Florence and the *Giovinezza* of Empoli. Targioni transformed the populist position of the national movement into a consistently authoritarian and explicitly anti-*mezzadro* doctrine. Far from stressing the opposition of *fascisti* and *agrari*, Targioni deliberately took up the main points of the 'official' lordly ideology of *mezzadria*. Giving up entirely the idea of outflanking the socialists in appealing to the potential grievances and fears of the mass of Tuscan sharecroppers, the fascist rural propagandist proclaimed that the conditions of the *mezzadri* were already 'good and satisfactory in every respect'.[33] Indeed, being already the partners of the landlords, they could have no right to ask for more. Adopting a still harsher tone, Targioni argued that, by destroying the 'friendly relations' and 'mutual respect' that had always bound owner and tenant, the *mezzadri* stood in all justice to lose the position and benefits they had. The ex-socialist-turned-agrarian-moralist had no doubt that, when the tenant behaved 'against the laws that govern the rights of property' and 'associates himself with those parties that leave no means untried to create hatred and discord among the social classes', then it was 'only humanly understandable that the landlord should use all his force to free himself as soon as possible of a tenant now become an adversary and an enemy'.[34]

Whereas the national leaders emphasized the populist tendencies of the *fasci*, underlined the distinction between the narrow 'selfishness' of the *agrari* and the collective good of the *rurali*, and stressed the 'bad blood' between *fasci* and *agrari*, the Tuscan fascists openly associated themselves with the defence of the Tuscan Agrarian Association. In Tuscany the national slogans with their reforming ring were replaced by watchwords of far less popular appeal. Thus, for instance, 'The land to the peasants!' was replaced by 'The land to those who know best how to cultivate it!'[35] It was indicative that, when in the spring of 1921 Gaetano Polverelli, architect of the national agrarian program, addressed the regional congress of the Tuscan *fasci* at Livorno on the agrarian question, he was received with general dissatisfaction and informed of his ignorance of the Tuscan countryside.[36]

Even when Targioni used the very guiding concepts of the national program which seemed most to offer advancement to the peasant and the opportunity to rise in the social scale, he so twisted their meaning in reference to Tuscany that they came to signify instead only sacrifice for the peasants and further gains for the lords. Two examples are Targioni's use of Polverelli's program of 'elevation' of the rural workers through *compartecipazione* to the 'dignity' of landownership, and his use of the fascist call for 'rural democracy'. Targioni uses the same words, but with a radically altered meaning. Calling for a 'return to the land', Targioni explained that

> The landlord must cause the peasant to embrace the land, by designing ever new forms of *compartecipazione* and by morally elevating him, in such a way that the peasant may understand that his work is not complete when he collects his income, but exists in strict correlation with the total output of the enterprise.[37]

Similarly, 'rural democracy' in Tuscany had a meaning quite different from its apparent interpretation. Apostrophizing the peasants, the *Giovinezza* declared,

> You peasants who work the land, who are never satisfied with the land you have and often cultivate an area beyond your productive capacity and therefore cultivate badly, be less greedy, give up some of your land to those who have none.[38]

Equally uncompromising in its stand against the *mezzadri* was the *Intrepido* of Lucca. Raising the question 'To whom should the land belong?', the fascist paper suggested that very often land,

> in order to produce and be cultivated, requires landowners with a broad agricultural training, with substantial funds, and with a wide use of machines and mechanical equipment.

What the Lucca fascists advocated in practice was the concentration of the land in the hands of the great proprietors. In theory, the *Intrepido* acknowledged that there were many areas where peasant cultivation was viable, but stressed that such land should be given 'not to the peasant of today, but to the peasant of the future':

> The direct cultivator, we find today, is in the great majority of cases not ready to run even small plots of land.[39]

Furthermore, the 'future peasant' was to appear slowly and only as a result of his own individual efforts and savings. Any external assistance negated the necessary 'moralizing value' of property, and the *Intrepido* specifically rejected 'concessions and favours' as well as 'violent confiscation' on behalf of the peasant.[40] The only immediate aid the Lucca fascists were prepared to offer the tenants was the advice to emigrate.[41]

That the *Riscossa* , the *Giovinezza*, and the *Intrepido* in their rural policy gratified men of property is clear. This, however, is not a sufficient explanation of the pains to which the papers went to modify the national program. What seems to account for the differences in the Tuscan agrarian program is that, paradoxically, in the land of *mezzadria* the *fasci* had found, in an assault on the *mezzadri* as a class, a means of recruiting a measure of scattered popular support in the interstices of the Tuscan social fabric. Our task is to examine the support which, first of all, was found at the centre of the *fattoria*. A key figure in Tuscan fascism keenly responsive to the anti-*mezzadro* animus of fascist propaganda, was the *fattore* with his entourage of *sottofattori* and guards. The opposition of the *fattori* to the Leagues and to the threat of rural socialism was deep and irreconcilable. In part, this opposition by the *fattori* was simply a reflection of the political stance of the landowners. To this extent, the *fattori* merely extended to fascism their traditional role as the direct representatives of property.

What is more interesting is that there were also substantial interests which drew the *fattore* to fascism independently of the interests of property and occasionally even somewhat at odds with the will of the landlords. There were frequently, in the first place, old accounts to settle between the *fattore* and the tenants. It was the *fattore* who had felt most acutely the effects of peasant organization and resistance for it was he who was the visible symbol of the repression of the old regime in the countryside. The landlord was a more distant, often absentee, figure, and the traditional armed defender of existing social relations in Italy, the *carabiniere*, was seldom present on the remote estates. It was the *fattore*, then, who had been the target of such violence as had occurred during the vast strikes of 1920, and the lingering humiliation still rankled in his mind. There could hardly have been any outcome save conflict in the relations between the *fattore* and the Leagues. His authority, his social preferment, and his livelihood were bound up with the traditional rural hierarchy. The levelling and democratic goals of the Leagues, and the institution of the 'farm councils' imperilled his existence. The security of the tenants against eviction established by the regional pact, and the establishment in some areas of *collocamento di classe* for the wage labourers undermined some of the power of sanction and patronage that buttressed his ascendancy and control over the labour force, and reduced the possibilities for sharp dealings. In addition, both in fact and in conscious outlook, the *fattore* was the very personification of a struggling rural petty bourgeoisie that had risen in the social scale through a lifetime of personal sacrifice and endless servility to the *signori*. His success was an individual triumph. To the *fattore*, therefore, collective solidarity was alien and threatening, while the socialist idea of abolishing the tiny ladder by which he measured his long climb above hardship and insecurity meant the destruction of a lifetime's achievement. In many cases, too, the *fattore* had concrete material interests to defend – a bit of land purchased through savings, a regular income, and a tiny web of patronage. He did not propose to stand quietly by at the time of his undoing.

What fascism offered the *fattore*, however, was not simply the defence of existing privileges through a reassertion of discipline and 'natural hierarchies'. In addition the *fasci* catered to the insecurity and discontents that were inseparable from the post. In many respects the *fattore* was in a most contradictory position: from the standpoint of the *mezzadri* he was the symbol of authority, but, having few skills and little training, he was, in the view of the landlord, a highly expendable servant with no security of office.[42] Furthermore, the landlord had no intention of allowing his overseers to form attachments that would compromise their allegiance to their employer. For this reason, when seeking a *fattore*, a proprietor might well select a candidate from a distant commune.[43] For this purpose, too, the *fattore* was subject to a whole range of lordly restrictions, generally including either an absolute prohibition of marriage or at least of marriage to a tenant of the estate, with the right of the owner to veto any prospective fiancée from a family whose 'morality' or 'conduct' gave cause for concern.[44] Now such restrictions were hurtful to pride, especially as they were combined with modest remuneration and with a vast social distance from the *signori* whom one *fattore* termed 'my Lords and Masters'.[45] Moreover, once appointed as *fattore*, a peasant with ambition had reached the summit of plebeian social advancement, and it would hardly be surprising if the inability to rise further in the social scale was for some a cause of disgruntlement. Indeed, the whole range of overseers' discontents led in the early years of the new century to the creation of an Association of Fattori as a kind of union to defend the interests of the agents against their masters.[46]

The differences that separated the *fattori* from the landlords should not, however, be overstated. It was from below that they saw the chief danger to their position; from the employers what they sought was less to change their lot than to secure it. The creation of the Association of *fattori* did not prevent a sizeable number of overseers from remaining at the same time active members of the AAT. But this miltancy in the Agrarian Association in one way heightened the contradictions inherent in the post because it underlined the unlikeliness that the *fattori* alone could apply effective pressure on the proprietor. In any case, as a political force the *fattori* were both widely scattered and few in number.[47]

What the *fasci* seemed to offer was an escape from the dilemma. In the first place, the essential mission of fascism was to crush the rural labour movement which was such a menace. On this there is little need for further comment. At the same time, the *fasci* astutely seized on the insecurities of the *fattore* in their elaboration of a vision of fascist order in the countryside. For fascist propaganda, the *fattore* was a vital figure in a new mythology – the rustic hero who had achieved success through individual self-advancement rather than by the anti-national and unpatriotic methods of the Leagues, or through unending and fruitless agitation.[48] Indeed, in fascist rhetoric the *fattore* was more: he was the rural representative of the new technocratic élite that was to be the fascist ruling class. In industry and administration, the famous *gruppi di competenza* composed of the most highly skilled technocrats were loudly proclaimed as the training grounds for the efficient cadres who were to govern the fascist order, sweeping aside privilege, corruption, and even politics to run the state in accordance with the dictates of productive rationality, and who were, in contrast to the socialist council movement, to take power from above.[49] Perhaps in industry and the state apparatus such a program was at least intelligible, and certainly it had an appeal for the expanding generation of aspiring meritocratic bureaucrats. Applied in terms of efficiency and productive rationale to the Tuscan countryside, the concept was highly ironic, for the *fattori*, untrained and frequently illiterate, were themselves a powerful obstacle to the rationalization of economic production, were inescapably linked with a system of agriculture that was itself backward and wasteful. In political terms, however, the *gruppi di competenza* held out the promise of resolving the insecurities and grievances that the *fattori* were unable to overcome through membership of the AAT, an organization which was unalterably the guardian of the interests of the proprietors. Fascism, by contrast, offered the vision of a future in which the *fattori* would have not only dignity and security but also a powerful role as the new ruling class. In the Siena meeting which took the decision to join the *fasci* and to secede from the AAT, the *fattori* and *sottofattori* noted that

the Partito Nazionale Fascista, with the establishment of *gruppi di competenza* within their 'corporations', recognizes the great importance that *tecnici* and experts will have in national reconstruction.

And the Siena fascist paper the *Scure* replied in large headlines that

The *tecnici* will be the brains of the Fascist Agricultural Corporation.[50]

It is not surprising, therefore, that throughout central Tuscany the *fattore* played a major role as the local backbone of the fascist movement, often as political secretary or *caposquadra* of the smaller rural *fasci*. And in the spring of 1922 the fascists scored a major triumph when the Sienese *fattori* seceded *en masse* from the AAT to join the *fasci di combattimento*. The *Difesa agricola*, the landlords' paper of Siena, gloomily recounted and explained the occurence:

> The bailiffs... acted in perfect unity [with the landlords] in all the agitations; and, since they were in direct contact with the excited and tumultuous peasant masses, they were the object of violent hostility and painful vendettas...
>
> Have we ever considered the irreparable consequences that might ensue ... if this class had felt a moment of disheartenment and had sided with the rebels?
>
> Apparently not, since, in explaining the collective resignation of the bailiffs from the Agrarian Association and their membership in the National Corporation of Agricultural Labour, a creation of the fascist party, it is claimed ... that the demands for economic and moral improvement of their situation advanced by the bailiffs, were never even listened to by the leaders of the Agrarian Organization.[51]

For the *fattori*, fascism, unlike the Agraria, seemed peculiarly *their* organization. And through the active membership in force of the Tuscan *fattori* the fascists gained an asset valuable beyond the bare numbers involved, for the *fattore* was a powerful figure, with the everyday management of the land in his hands and, therefore, power to dispense reward and punishment, as well as to aid in the spinning of a web of patronage in which to ensnare less enthusiastic potential followers of the movement. What was more, the official *fattore* was surrounded and followed by his inevitable and more numerous satellites – the *sottofattori* and guards, some of whom, in addition to simple membership, could provide the *fasci* with a long apprenticeship in the use of physical force.

In addition to the allegiance of the men gathered at the *casa fattorale*, the *fasci* won a measure of sympathy from the landless labourers on the margins of the estates. These were not the highly concentrated and politically organized *braccianti* of the fertile river valleys who worked on the land improvement, drainage, and irrigation schemes, and on public works programs. Instead, these were the so-called *terrazzieri* or semi-*braccianti* who were employed as secondary labour on the large estates. As we have seen, this category of rural labour was numerous throughout Tuscany, though there is no acurate estimate of their numbers. Unlike the valley *braccianti*, however, these labourers were not able to find an adequate union or political organization. They were a scattered and shifting population that, through its separation from the means of production, constituted a rural proletariat 'in itself' but which was not a class 'for itself'. Economically, they worked as adjuncts of the *mezzadri*, whose labour they only complemented, while politically, in so far as they were organized at all, they were part of the movement led by the *mezzadri*. Certainly among this category of labourers the *fasci* were able to make inroads. The causes for discontent among these workers were evident, but the point is that the fascists were able to divert some of this discontent away from opposition to the long-term forces (most broadly put, the process of capital expansion which used the state and the existing property relations in the countryside as vehicles of primitive accumulation) that, objectively, created their conditions of existence. Instead, fascist practice assiduously courted their discontent to channel it instead into the narrow, short-term, and divisive politics of category rivalry. For at least some of these *braccianti*, that is, a veil was thrown over their opposition of interest with landed property while their more immediate divisions with the *mezzadri* were enlarged and played upon. And the ploy succeeded – to a degree – because landed property itself cooperated in the ruse, because economic crisis placed immediate interests in relief, and because no history of political struggle and organization provided them with a clear understanding of the real forces at work in the countryside.

The fascist appeal to these *braccianti* was a variation of the anti-*mezzadro* ideology that was standard in central Tuscany. With regard to the *braccianti*, the *mezzadro* was depicted as a rapacious exploiter. Here it was possible for the *fasci* to capitalize upon two differences of interest between the sharecropping and wage-earning strata in the countryside. One difference was that between the wage labourer, who lived principally by purchasing his necessities in the market place, and the *mezzadro* who, to a greater or lesser degree, was still a subsistence producer and therefore was less apparently affected by inflation. The trick then was to convince the *braccianti* that it was the exorbitant economic gains made in the postwar years by the *mezzadro*-led Leagues which were responsible for the astronomically rising cost of food. Here was one crack in the socialist unity of the Tuscan countryside. The sharecropping class, Targioni explained,

runs the risk of seeing itself exposed to the hatred of the *braccianti* and the city proletariat, who have good reason to note that the rising cost of living that so largely consumes their modest earnings is caused by the food products ... that every day are put up for sale by the peasant class.[52]

At the same time the fascists were able to play upon the division of interest that often existed between the *mezzadro* as employer (since the sharecroppers were obliged to meet 50 per cent of the cost of hiring salaried labour) and the *bracciante* as wage earner. Discreetly leaving aside the question of remuneration, the *fasci* simply demanded of the *mezzadri* that they hire more labour. 'Hire a few *braccianti*!' was one of the 'duties of the peasant' that the fascist press announced to the sharecroppers.[53] Such a bald attempt to play off the two categories of labour against each other might well have failed except that it was backed by concrete evidence that demonstrated the alleged effectiveness of the *fasci* in solving the employment problem of the *braccianti*. The fascist injunctions to the *mezzadri* were not exhortations, but threats. 'Remember', Idalberto Targioni counselled the *mezzadri* in their dealings with the wage labourers,

> that these people could also move against you. They are a reserve army for the working of the land, and one day they could even be called upon to to replace you.[54]

And, in fact, there is good evidence that the fascist unions executed the threat. The landlords, in the first place, launched a massive program of politically motivated evictions, ousting thousands of militant *mezzadri* between 1921 and 1922, and replacing them with men provided by the local *fasci*. At the provincial congress of Federterra in Pisa province held in the middle of August 1921, the delegates noted that in that one province alone since the signing of the regional pact some 500 *mezzadri* had already been evicted from their plots – in defiance of a law then in force prohibiting evictions. The same lot had fallen as well to over 300 tenants in Florence province.[55] Indeed, already in February the prefect of Florence, Olivieri, had reported,

> For some time, a lively discontent has been simmering among the peasants enrolled in the provincial Federterra organizations on account of the way that evictions have been carried out ... The ferment is most serious in the Prato area where the tenants claim to be the victims of the proprietors...[56]

Invariably the evictions were carried out first against the leading activists of the peasant Leagues.[57] So serious was the effect on morale that the 1921 Federterra congress at Pisa decided that eviction 'represents for us the most serious question that, if not resolved, could undermine our organization'.[58] Such evictions, backed by the squads, had the double advantage for the Agrarian Association of both inflicting a major blow on the League organization and of creating a grateful class of recipient *braccianti*.

As an alternative tactic, which both avoided possible legal complications arising from the existing temporary legislation providing security for tenants against eviction and also reduced the potential political conflict of overt victimization, the Association and the *fasci* operated another policy. This was the reduction of the size of the *podere* on which the *mezzadro* worked, with the additional land thereby made available being used to create new, if much smaller plots for new tenants – *braccianti* now 'elevated' according to the principles of fascist 'dignity' and *compartecipazione*. Indeed, this stategy was proposed as official policy of the AAT at its Florence congress in November 1920 by Barneschi, the president of the sub-section of the Association at Cetona, who 'in order to lift the weight of wage labour from the shoulders of the proprietors, proposed the reduction of the peasants' land and the creation of new *podere* units'.[59] The political objective was obvious – the creation of a class of aspiring allies of property who now had clear proof of the efficacy of 'class collaboration'. This policy of fractioning existing *poderi* was no new departure, but was part of the long-term process by which *mezzadria* adapted itself to the modern world by drastically increasing the intensity of peasant labour. On the process in action in the Tuscan countryside, Gino Sarrocchi in 1921 was as candid as ever. 'I have always held', reasoned the founding member of the Agrarian Association,

that there is an absolute necessity to encourage the initiative of the landowners in the fractioning of the units of cultivation.[60]

Explaining his position further, Sarrocchi continued:

The shareholders' plots in our Tuscany are entirely too large, both absolutely and relatively. They are too large in an absolute sense because the intensity of cultivation is hampered by the extent of the holding ... they are too large in a relative sense, especially since the war, because the labouring capacities of the sharecropping families who work the plots have diminished.[61]

The only point Sarrocchi concealed was the urgency of the political imperative behind the procedure he advocated. Here was a practical application of the fascist agrarian program in Tuscany by which not the landlord but the peasant gave up land.

Nevertheless, the strategy of rallying the *terrazzieri* as part of the anti-*mezzadro* crusade was in no sense a total or automatic success. On the contrary, the *terrazzieri* were initially inclined to support the Leagues and the socialist movement. It was only from the winter of 1920–1 as unemployment bit deeper and armed reaction was organized that defections began. The first fascist unions of *terrazzieri* were established in January 1921. The initial desertions became more massive as it became evident that, after the spectacular successes of 1920, the Leagues and the PSI in 1921 had no strategy to confront either the economic recession or the political crisis of counter-revolution. As the prospect of a collective solution to the deepening crisis grew even more remote, so the idea of opting for what appeared at least an individual solution became progressively more attractive.

Based, then, on the handful of overseers and on the lukewarm support of a fluctuating and marginal population of wage earners, fascist appeal within the boundaries of the *fattoria* was extremely restricted. By excluding the mass of sharecroppers, fascist propaganda attracted only a small minority of the agricultural population of the sharecropping estates. A vital element in fascist strength, therefore, was the ability of the movement to win adherents from social groups in the countryside not involved in the relationships of the *fattoria*. Of these groups by far the most important was the class of new peasant proprietors. These new owners were not of the same numerical importance in Tuscany as in Emilia. In Emilia, in the years following the First World War, 79,039 hectares of land (5.4 per cent of the arable area of the region) passed into the ownership of new peasant proprietors. Corresponding figures in Tuscany were only 31,250 hectares and 2.8 per cent.[62] A precise estimate of the numbers of peasants involved in these purchases is more difficult, but if, as a rough approximation, we assume that throughout the region the usual size of the new plots in the Pisan plain (2–3 hectares) prevailed,[63] then a guess would be that there were some 10,000 to 15,000 new proprietors in postwar Tuscany.

The bare numbers of new proprietors, however, are not an adequate indication of the importance of these peasants to the reaction because they were not distributed evenly throughout the eight provinces, but were heavily concentrated in the interior and, above all, in the lower Arno and Chiana Valleys. Their local importance as a new social force was unsurpassed anywhere in the peninsula. In the lower Arno Valley of Pisa province alone, for instance, some 5,000 hectares (13.7 per cent of the arable area) were bought by peasant owners – a proportion not exceeded even in Emilia.[64] From the beginning, these peasant proprietors were, in the zones where they were strong, a leading force in social reaction.

The origins of the phenomenon of postwar small peasant proprietorship are of some interest.[65] The accumulation of substantial savings among sections of the Tuscan peasantry in this period is unexpected in view of the general economic recession and the deep crisis of agriculture, in particular caught as it was between rampant inflation and sluggish prices for food stuffs. Despite the general economic gloom, there were still opportunities in the new circumstances for a minority in the countryside to make substantial gains. The classic case is that of the peasant *affittuari* who benefited from the war-time decrees that froze rents during a period in which a steep inflation devalued the outstanding rent. There were few *affittuari* in Tuscany, however, and other opportunites for the fortunate and the enterprising were more important there. In the first place, it is essential to distinguish carefully among crops. Although the staple grain crops of the Italian economy enjoyed far from buoyant prices, some of the specialized industrial crops were less affected or even enjoyed prices that rose faster than the general price index.[66] Another source of possible savings was provided by the war-time labour shortage which gave considerable opportunity to supplement income from the land by secondary employment in industry. At the same time, money sent from abroad by emigrants was an important source of revenue. Since the peak period of emigration immediately preceded the First World War, the amount of money returning to Italy – and Tuscany – reached record levels in this period. Nationally, some 817,317,514 lire flowed into Italy from this source in the four years 1915–18, and 2,712,373,602 lire in the next four, 1919–22.[67]

Nor were other possible sources of savings lacking. Thus, for example, the price of livestock, in contrast to grain products, rose sharply. Hence, *mezzadri* who kept animals for domestic use that were exempt from the usual 50/50 provision of the contract (pigs, poultry, and so on) were often in a relatively favourable position. Similarly, a war-time enactment prohibited the closing of sharecropping accounts until after the war, with the result that outstanding debts, like frozen rents, lost a large proportion of their real value.

At the same time that the fractioning of landed property was thus fostered by increased peasant demand, a great fillip was given to the process by increased supply. The augmented peasant savings were met by a new willingness on the part of the landlords to offer their property for sale. This was, again, a trend that was most marked in the central Tuscan valleys, and the reason was, in large part, political. It was precisely in these areas that the crisis of *mezzadria* relations was most acute and that the threat of socialist expropriation was most feared by the *signori*. There was therefore a major flight from the land by the upper classes, many of whom were frantic to sell their holdings before the advent of bolshevism. Logically, this fear was most pronounced in Siena, the famous 'Red province' of Tuscany where the police reported a massive emigration by men of property seeking to escape 'a systematic persecution and permanent menace'.[68] This flight from the land by many *agrari* was the obverse of the decision of more resolute property owners to organize armed resistance, and was eloquent testimony to the feeling of the landlords that they stood on the edge of the abyss.

In short, although the formation of new peasant ownership in Tuscany was less than in the North, it was far from negligible. Despite the long-term tendency of the crisis of *mezzadria* to proletarianize the Tuscan sharecroppers, there was always a small counter-tendency of *mezzadri* who, through fortune, toil, or cunning were able to improve their lot, save, and possibly invest in land. The war and its aftermath provided the occasion for a vast, if transitory, swelling of this counter-trend as a whole series of new opportunities opened up for luck and shrewd household economy. The new properties were, in the long term, economically unviable and they were to succumb to the pressure from the larger, more economically run, and more specialized estates. The short-term political consequences, however, were considerable.

These consequences were geographically limited but they were often decisive in this time of crisis. The rising revolutionary tide was met headlong by a backlash of militant social conservatism, strongest precisely in those areas of Tuscany where the socialist organizations were most powerful and the crisis of Tuscan rural society most profound. The upwardly mobile categories of *mezzadri*, *affittuari*, and occasionally *braccianti*, who bought land and thereby acquired a material bond to the social order and a conviction of the possibility of self-advancement, were in the vanguard of the reaction. They were joined, moreover, by numbers of other *mezzadri* with savings, who hoped eventually to purchase land but had not yet done so, fearing, perhaps, to buy during the uncertainties of the 'Red Years'. For the new and the aspiring peasant owners there seems to have been very little hope of a *rapprochement* with the Leagues. Already during the mass strikes of 1920 the peasant proprietors had begun to parley, not with the Leagues, but with the *agrari*. Organizations of peasant proprietors and lords were even formed to resist the spread of rural socialism and to press the government for police repression.[69] On this point the prefect of Siena, Emilio D'Eufemia, was explicit. With reference to the Leagues he cabled his superiors:

Facing this multitude of people animated by the most violent passion is a small fringe of men weak and fearful – the small proprietors. The big landlords, nearly all members of the Tuscan Agrarian Association, followed the phases of the struggle under the protection of their organization.

The small proprietors, instead, were disorganized, anxious, and backward in their ideas. They had no idea of what to do, save to call for the aid, the intervention, and the action of the authorities, even when this was neither necessary nor urgent.[70]

The gulf, both material and ideal, that separated the small (peasant) proprietors from the movement of the Leagues was profound. There was a vast economic distance. The new generation of postwar proprietors and aspiring proprietors was an economic élite of 'successful' peasants who had attained what they considered the status and security of individual title to the land. They shared with the *fattori* the outlook of self-made men who had 'made good'. The levelling and collective notions of socialism were antithetical to their long apprenticeship in individual self-advancement. The boundaries of their *poderi* were so many lines of demarcation between them and the landless masses. And they were prepared to defend their plots by force. It is no surprise that when the government failed to provide the repression they demanded, these proprietors were heavily and early recruited into the squads. The Prato zone of Florence province was characteristic of the areas where the movement of land into peasant hands was strong. There the police reported that it was on the strength of the support of small proprietors, who had not belonged to the AAT, that fascism penetrated the countryside. In early 1922 Inspector General Di Tarsia emphasized the political alliance

> that is forming everywhere in the countryside among the small proprietors. As is known, the sharecropping system dominates in the region, and the defence of their own interests and their own land created the necessity of alliance, and the *fascio*, directed and financed by the agrarian and industrial associations, by taking advantage of economic discontent and by carrying out an active propaganda campaign, is gaining control over the countryside.[71]

EMILIA IN TUSCANY: THE GREAT RIVER VALLEYS

The difficulties of recruitment which generally slowed the progress of fascism in the Tuscan countryside did not arise in the lower Arno and Chiana Valleys. These two zones formed the storm centre of Tuscan fascism where the movement was strongest and most broadly based. In terms of popular appeal, the *fasci* of the Chiana and Arno Valleys achieved a degree of success more characteristic of Emilia than of Tuscany. The fascists themselves emphasized the comparison with the North. In marked contrast to the regional movement as a whole, which was heretical in agrarian doctrine and practice, the *fasci* of these two zones returned to fascist orthodoxy, choosing Polverelli's program and Ferrara practice as their models.

A reading of the fascist weekly, the *Scure* of Siena, reveals major differences from the doctrine expounded at Florence by Idalberto Targioni. The agrarian program developed by the *Scure* was a morass of internal contradictions. The Sienese fascists oscillated between the defence of *mezzadria* and the defence of small peasant proprietorship as the ideal solution to the agrarian question. They shifted ground continually between an emphasis on maximum production and an emphasis on social justice. There was a deep confusion between the stress on the necessity to maintain 'natural hierarchies' and the commitment to defend peasant interests. What *was* consistent, however, and marked the decisive shift from the *Riscossa* and the *Giovinezza* was a definitive turn away from a platform that invariably castigated the *mezzadri* as the villains of the countryside. The *Scure* repeated the populist attempt of northern fascism to placate peasant opinion. Difficulties arose in the effort to apply to central Italy a program developed in a different social context. None the less, the effort to return the original demagogic significance to the concept of 'rural democracy', to restore pride of place to the slogan 'Land to the peasants!', and to replace the veil of modesty that covered the relations between *fasci* and *agrari* was unmistakable. The prospect was clearly held out to *all* categories of agricultural labour, of a gradual progress towards ownership of the land, with the assurance that in the realization of the new social justice it would be the *agrari* who would be called upon to make the necessary sacrifice. The prospect drawn up by the *Scure* was quite unlike Targioni's image of the future:

> In contrast to the utopian [idea of] socialization, the *fasci di combattimento* want *all* cultivators of the soil to be elevated, gradually but rapidly [sic] to the dignity of direct and effective ownership of the land.
>
> We will therefore act with the lightning activity shown in every political battle to achieve a new justice, to establish for every labourer the possession of as much land as he can cultivate.
>
> The *fasci* pledge that from this moment they will take steps to obtain land from the landlords, which will be made available to you at fair terms.[72]

The reworking of the fascist program in the Chiana Valley corresponds to a major difference in social structure which set the lower Arno and Chiana Valleys apart. The selection of Ferrara as the model for agrarian Sienese fascism was not accidental, but reflected the attempt to play the two chief categories of labour – the 'intermediate' peasants (*mezzadri, affittuari* and proprietors) and the *braccianti* – off against one another in the fashion which had succeeded so well in Emilia. In the Chiana and Arno Valleys there was, in a manner reminiscent of the Valley of the Po, an uneasy juxtaposition of different forms of tenure with correspondingly different categories of labour. In such a context there was therefore the hope not simply, as elsewhere in the region, of rallying together relatively marginal social groups (*terrazzieri, fattori*, and guards) against a unified labour front, but also of splitting the labour ranks from within and of pitting group against group. In particular, the attempt was made to divide 'intermediate' sectors of the peasantry against wage labour.

The first and easiest fascist victory was, as elsewhere, the recruitment of new peasant proprietors, who were especially numerous in the valleys of central Tuscany.[73] In addition to the increase in peasant landownership through war-time savings, the number of new proprietors was artfully swollen by the landlords themselves, who in this respect as well demonstrated that they had mastered the lessons of Ferrarese experience. In Ferrara the Agraria under the guidance of Vico Mantovani had provided the *fascio* with over 8,000 hectares of land to distribute among the peasantry to demonstrate 'class collaboration'.

The appeal of the right

Vittorio Pedriali, director of the fascist Land Office of Ferrara and himself a large landowner, expressed the conservative hopes of the lords:

If the will to defend peace and justice in the countryside is to take root among the class of landlords, then may the idea take shape of multiplying small ownership.[74]

It was far from surprising, then, when on 13 and 27 March 1921 the fascist paper of Ferrara, the *Ballila*, duly published two initial lists of 4,000 and 3,000 hectares of land given to peasants under a variety of forms – usually long-term leases. Nor was it remarkable that the new small proprietors had the desired jaundiced view of socialism and stood ready to defend their new station in rural society.

Information on similar policies applied systematically in the Pisan plain is scanty, though at Laiatico we know that the local landowners, led by Prince Corsini and Major Gotti-Lega, arranged for 22 landless labouring families to be given plots of an average size of three hectares apiece at the nominal rent of 40 lire a year with an option after 24 or 29 years of purchasing the property at the current market value. To make the proposition all the more appealing, the landlords offered to assume the full burden of taxation on the property.[75] Meanwhile, in the Chiana Valley the *fasci* and the Agrarian Association sought officially to imitate the Ferrarese precedent on a larger scale. Thus in May 1921 the Siena *fascio* announced:

At a meeting of lessees held at Mantodine it was decided to give 800 *pertiche* to the *fascio*, always for the use of those enrolled in our unions.
Thus up to the present our five peasant unions have over 2,000 *pertiche* [perch] of land at their disposal.[76]

Obviously the largesse of Sienese landlords for such purposes had its limits, and both the total area distributed and the size of the individual plots were severely restricted. The provision that most of the land be distributed in leaseholds rather than freeholds even testified to a residual niggardliness of the nobility. None the less, the value of the exercise was by no means a simple function of the number of peasants directly affected and the size of their plots. In the middle of 1921, when the socialist and labour movements had made manifest their inability to protect their followers from economic crisis and political reaction, the example of practical fascist initiatives of the kind had a disproportionate effect. The significance of such measures is suggested by the use made of them by G. A. Chiurco, the leading organizer of the reaction in southern Tuscany. In his propaganda tours Chiurco made the grants of land to fascist peasants his central theme. The strategy succeeded because the long-term economic viability of the new properties was not a question at issue.

In addition to new proprietors, the reaction in the Chiana Valley eventually won over large numbers of *mezzadri* in a manner reminiscent of Emilia. In the Chiana Valley, however, the task was far more difficult than in the North. One reason was that, even in zones where the *braccianti* dominated the local union branches, it was difficult for the *mezzadri* to regard the whole union movement as an alien imposition in a region where it was the sharecroppers who dominated rural socialism. Perhaps still more important was the point stressed by the prefect of Siena – namely, that in the Chiana Valley, in contrast to the situation in the North, the labour movement had not left its flank exposed, but had adopted a direction which, through the demands for 'Land to the peasants!', workers' control, and radical democracy through the council movement, unified the labour front and minimized the divergences of interest between wage labourers and sharecroppers.

There were, nevertheless, weak points at which socialist unity in the countryside was vulnerable. The first of these was the objective opposition of interest between the upper stratum of 'rich' *mezzadri* who were employers as well as labourers and the unions dominated by *braccianti*. In Tuscany, as in the North, these unions, as we have seen, established a monopoly of the labour market and implemented the *imponibile* and *collocamento di classe*. The resulting obligation of the employing sharecroppers to hire a number of men designated by the unions at increased wages was deeply resented. It was these employing peasants who early joined the reaction in large numbers. On the conflict between the wealthy *mezzadri* in Siena province and the *braccianti* in late 1921, Police Inspector L. Gaudino informed his superiors at the Ministry of the Interior:

> The peasants, so heavily favoured under the old contract of *mezzadria*, have made such major gains that the greatest number of them now possess massive savings. But, whereas the peasants have perserved their advantages, the *braccianti* have lost them. The reason is that with the new pact the expense of paying the *braccianti* is divided precisely in half between landlord and peasant, and is not, as the socialist leagues had first demanded, borne solely by the landlord. The result is that the sharecroppers have withdrawn their solidarity from the *braccianti*, and consider themselves greatly imperilled by the forced imposition of an arbitrary and burdensome number of wage labourers. Therefore when, in imitation of other regions and through the work of strangers to Siena, the fascist organization took root in the province, it was was welcomed not only by the bourgeoisie but also by the peasants, who saw it as a protection from the imposition of the *braccianti*.[77]

Any such conflict between simple self-interest and the collective interest was deepened by the *fasci*, which portrayed themselves as the guardians of individual liberties from the assault of a collectivist tyranny. In particular, the *fasci* made most of the resentment of many *mezzadri* against the sanctions of the Leagues when it was felt that the interests pursued were the narrow category interests of the wage labourers. On behalf of those *mezzadri* who had found themselves subjected to a fine or boycott by the Leagues for flagging solidarity, the Siena *fascio* publicly offered, if any peasant came forward, to denounce the socialist union officials for having applied such sanctions, and to rectify the situation by forcibly collecting the amount of the penalty direct from the pockets of the offending officials.[78]

The generation gap also assumed political importance by creating divisions in the peasant ranks that the fascists sought to exploit. Whereas earlier conflicts within the labour movement had opposed category to category, tension now developed within the multiple *mezzadro* family. In the new commercial *mezzadria* the authority of the *capoccia* came to seem ever more irksome to younger and more politicized members of the family, who had a vision of rural social relations far different from those which had given rise to rural patriarchy. The deepening of the crisis of traditional family relationships was both cause and effect of the impulse to socialism in the countryside. Ironically, the *capoccia*, as the AAT observed, was in part the cause of his own unmaking. As the share-cropping families pressed for more democratic management of the *fattoria*, the younger members of the household failed to see why the same democratic principles should not operate within the narrower confines of the *podere*. By raising the issue of democracy, the *capoccia* set in motion a process of radicalization that they were unable to halt when it began to impinge upon their own privileges.

Thus the great gulf of interest that separated landlord and tenant also ran in a thin line within the peasant family itself, dividing the generations and separating the *capoccia* and the *massaia* from the interests of younger members of the household. In the great summer strike of 1920, for example, the prefect of Pisa pointed out to the interested authorities at Rome that

Already in the peasant families quarrels are developing between the youths and the elders, as the latter have no desire to allow themselves to be dragged along behind the union movement.[79]

It is hardly surprising, then, that the fascists sought to broaden this generation conflict. They aimed their appeal at the 'elders' through an assertion of the value of the traditional relations of *mezzadria*, a defence of 'natural hierarchies', and a determination to re-establish the authority of the 'poor *capoccia*'.[80] Exactly how far this appeal across class lines to conflicts within the tenant family itself succeeded is impossible to determine. Even with little evidence, however, one suspects that the appeal to the *capoccia* was not very successful as an independent force. The class divide between the lords and the tenant family as a whole was more important than the secondary 'quarrels' within the tenant family. Probably, therefore, the fascist appeal along generation lines was most effective as an additional attracting influence multiplying the doubts of *mezzadri* who already had reservations with regard to the Leagues. In picturing the role of the *capoccia* in fascism, one should not imagine the head of the clan calling upon the squads to settle disputes within his own family. Instead, the *capoccia* of the wealthy *mezzadro* families saw in the threat to traditional family values and structure an additional reason to fear socialism and to rejoice that the squads should offer to restore order to the homes of others.

Causes for reservations about the socialist cause in any case grew among many *mezzadri* in the valleys of central Tuscany from the autumn of 1920. In part it was a result of the successful and disciplined application of the provisions of *imponibile* and *collocamento di classe* which became an increasing burden on sharecroppers who hired labour. Paradoxically, however, even the very successes of the Leagues in 1920 helped to prepare the way for the great defeat of 1921. Having come so far, many *mezzadri* began to wonder, perhaps the time had come to be less venturesome, to consolidate what had been gained rather than risk further rural class warfare. New gains, less urgent in any case after the substantial reforms of the new regional pact, could be won gradually, with less sacrifice, and perhaps without the inconveniences of the discipline of the Leagues. At the height of the success of the Leagues, the socialist paper of Arezzo, the *Falce*, had already foreseen the possibility of this evolution:

We must be forewarned, we must not trust in the tide of optimism that follows upon victory, upon the first major success.
The landlords still have several fearful weapons yet to employ...
In addition, the improved *mezzadria* contracts will increase the economic reserves of the peasants. And the result could be that these workers, instead of being won over to socialism, will take their distance from it.[81]

To the *mezzadri* thus grown cautious with success, the fascist program of 'rural democracy' seemed to offer the reassuring prospect of continuing reforms, gradually won, that would not cause unpleasant surprises and would not risk either further conflict with the lords or socialization under the control of Leagues dominated by the *braccianti*. In Tuscany as a whole, the probability that large numbers of *mezzadri* would similarly grow cautious with success was lessened by the fascist agrarian program which blocked off the alleys of retreat into conservatism or passivity by demanding, in effect, the unconditional surrender of the tenants as a class. In the more heterogeneous social conditions of the great river valleys, by contrast, no effort was spared to extend reassurances to the sharecroppers.

The growing impulse to conservatism in 1921, however, was by no means a simple effect of fascist blandishments. From the time that lordly resistance was organized and the initial defections to the reaction by the wealthy strata of *mezzadri* had begun, the process of the collapse of rural socialism gathered momentum throughout the year. Fascist intimidation began the process, and thereafter calculations of expediency in the now shifting balance of power in the rural struggle furthered the tendency. Simple weariness with a long and dangerous struggle played a role as well. After the initial wave of fascist violence in Arezzo province in the spring of 1921, for instance, Police Inspector General Paolella reported that

> Peace now shows signs of returning to Arezzo and its province. The workers' associations are disorganized, and, particularly in the rural masses, a desire is being shown for calm and for work.
>
> In fact, in some communes there are large numbers of sharecroppers who have enrolled in the new organizations promoted by the *fasci di combattimento*.[82]

In addition to those social groups – *fattori*, small peasant proprietors, and wealthy employing *mezzadri* – for whom fascism provided a means of preserving a position of privilege, unemployment helped to attract *braccianti* into the fascist organizations, even in zones where they were normally among the most revolutionary forces in the countryside. In Tuscany, where *mezzadria* prevailed and most rural labourers were assured of work, unemployment was neither as readily apparent nor as severe as in many other areas of Italy.[83] None the less, the number of those officially jobless more than doubled between 1919 and 1921, and the statistics do not measure the growth of underemployment – the loss of supplementary incomes as the economic recession and the closing of emigration routes meant the loss of secondary and seasonal jobs. Certainly, as we have already seen, the landlords and the police authorities considered the high and rising rate of unemployment and underemployment among the *braccianti* a major source of the political unrest among the category and the immediate cause for the demand for the much-feared *imponibile di mano d'opera*. From one point of view, that is, unemployment among *braccianti* was an important contributing factor to revolutionary discontent, and it was for this reason that the Ministry of the Interior was besieged with calls from the Agrarian Association for programs of public works to relieve the pressure of unemployment.[84]

At the same time, however, unemployment among the wage labourers in the long term worked in favour of political subversion in another direction: the jobless *braccianti* of central Tuscany proved an important source of recruitment for the fascist cause. This factor became increasingly important as 1921 wore on. The deepening economic crisis and the accelerating collapse of the socialist movement tempted many to substitute employment for the receding mirage of proletarian solidarity. The one thing that the fascist movement could provide, thanks to its connections with the employers, was a job. Indeed, in the field of employment the fascist unions were organized and energetic, setting up free employment offices *(uffici del lavoro)* for the placing of those willing to give guarantees of their political reliability.[85] The reason that the unions were able to exercise such a function was, of course, that the landlords supported the venture, reserving employment for those enrolled in the fascist unions. Typical was the meeting of the landowners at Fercoli in Pisa province in April 1922, which took two decisions, both of interest here:

(1) In order to aid those enrolled in the fascist Union, it has been decided to employ only them in piecework jobs and in the work of threshing, as well as to hire those who justify the trust placed in them by the employers.
(2) The employers hereby undertake to maintain in continuous employment the members of the Union.[86]

Similarly, in Siena province the landlords simply announced that they would hire only workers who produced proof of membership in the fascist organizations.[87] In this way the *fasci* were able to broaden their base of support through an extensive ability to dispense patronage. Thus, for example, the secretary of the *fascio* of San Piero a Ponti (Florence province), Gaetano Danesi, explained to the central committee in September 1921 that

This branch has formed a Labour Office for the unemployed of the village and is already finding work for a number of them, thus gaining the sympathy of the jobless and of their families, who until now were our bitter opponents.[88]

The Agrarian Association also put land at the disposal of the fascist unions by evicting militant tenants whose places could then be filled by others. Thus the 'economic unions' were able to offer a few the chance to rise in the social scale by becoming *mezzadri* or tiny proprietors. The fascist movement in Pisa province in the winter of 1921, for example, claimed to have performed two tasks, both of which must have appealed to the desperate and the unemployed at the base of the social scale. These tasks were 'guaranteeing work for those enrolled in the difficult past winter' and 'clearing new ground progressively to transform member braccianti into mezzadri'.[89] Thus economic crisis and the interested generosity of the landlords provided the modern fascist *condottieri* with an army of mercenaries. Clearly, the terms of employment and tenancy provided by courtesy of the *fasci* were severe, but in the lean years

1921–2 for many the alternative to acceptance of the new terms was hunger.

Finally, in accounting for fascist inroads among all classes in the countryside, one must allow ample scope for the corrosive effect on morale of the failure of the socialist party to organize armed resistance to the fascist onslaught. Moving backward into revolution, pushed forward by the mass movement rather than effectively at its head, the PSI had no strategy with which to confront the violent opposition it aroused. Not only did the socialist leaders decline to confront the problem of self-defence, they even denounced the spontaneous attempts at resistance made by the workers and peasants themselves. Turati, for instance, the party founder and leader of its reformist wing and parliamentary delegation, had this advice to offer the peasants of Italy at the height of fascist violence in 1921:

> Peasants, a sad and macabre time has come for you. ... Do not despair, brothers; do not allow yourselves to be crushed or intimidated. I promise ... that violence will yield no results to those who practise it. When the storm passes, once again you will be the stronger.
>
> Do not accept provocation; do not provide them with pretexts; do not reply to insult. Be good, be patient, be holy ... Even forgive.[90]

In a similar spirit, the Florentine Gino Baldesi, secretary of the CGL. 'serenely' surveyed the fascist offensive and counselled the masses to disarm as violence was 'an uncivilized weapon'. True socialists, instead, should reply to their enemies only in the ennobling realms of the battle of ideas and the electoral contest.[91] Indeed, judged by the standards of these higher realms, both the fascists and those on the left who sought to reply to violence with force stood equally condemned as 'opposing extremisms'. For Baldesi, 'The two extremes meet': 'the polemical method of the fascist and the communist extremists is perfectly identical'.[92] And meanwhile in the provinces, the local leadership of the party sometimes felt the need even to disavow its own revolutionary past and extreme rhetoric.

The explanation for this extraordinary course of socialist inaction in the middle of 1921 was clearly not simple pusillanimity. It also reflected a mechanistic analysis of fascism as a 'reaction', and a precise political calculation. If fascism was simply an anti-socialist reaction, the 'white guard' of the Italian bourgeoisie, then by definition it would automatically disappear with the ebbing of the revolutionary threat. The socialists failed to realize that fascism was not just a new form of the repression that had punctuated the history of United Italy but signified a definitive settling of accounts, a change of regime. Since the socialist leadership felt that the Italian masses were not yet sufficiently 'mature' to dominate society and since the party leaders also thought that the reaction was a passing wave, then it was logical for them to take the view that all that was necessary was to bide their time until the storm had subsided. Then the cautious socialists could re-emerge as always to exert their influence. The result was that the work of the squadrist expeditions was greatly facilitated.

Nowhere, perhaps, was the socialist strategy of non-defence more puzzling than in Tuscany, where armed resistance was not a movement that had to be created, but one that had sprung up spontaneously. The masses themselves had taken the initiative, as we have seen, in a series of local uprisings. What was needed was that this initiative should be directed and coordinated. An effort was made in this direction even outside the formal party structures through the establishment of the so-called *arditi del popolo*. The *arditi del popolo*, set up by local socialist and communist militants but open to anti-fascists of all persuasions, were meant as a citizen's militia to combat the squads. For the socialists, however, the idea conflicted with the strategy of passively waiting. The new communist party, meanwhile, though committed in principle to armed resistance, was suspicious of an organization that was not 'marxist' and had been set up outside the recognized party framework. In practice the newly founded communist party pursued a policy not greatly different from the socialist strategy of waiting. The PCI rejected the resistance that existed in fact in favour of an ideal resistance yet to be established. As a result, both the socialist and the communist parties folded their hands while the spontaneous resistance movement, deprived of political leadership, collapsed.[93]

PROVINCIAL INDUSTRY

In addition to the actual agricultural population, a vital element in the development of Tuscan fascism was light provincial industry. This point requires some stress because often there is a tendency to over-emphasize the relations between the *fasci* and the board rooms of heavy concentrated industry – the engineering, mechanical, chemical, shipbuilding, and mining sectors. Indeed, some have gone so far as to regard fascism as a simple product of monopoly capital. The importance of modern oligopolistic capital in fascist development must not, of course, be overlooked, and in Tuscany it is a problem we must later take up. In general, however, the emphasis on the role of heavy industry is part of a broad tendency to lay a disproportionate stress on the urban bases of fascist support to the detriment of the countryside. Part of the reason for this distortion of emphasis is ideological, at least for those historians influenced by the theory of the relation between fascism and monopoly capital. It is also a reflection of the urban bias of city-dwelling historians and a product of the methodology of much traditional, narrowly political history. This tendency is further strengthened by the fact that the actors in the countryside have remained relatively anonymous, and relatively few rose to positions of national power within the fascist regime. Most deeply, the dual stress on heavy industry and the urban base serves what can only be called an objectively apologetic interest because it conceals and mystifies the true and deep origins of fascism in the process of the expansion of Italian capital, as a moment in the history of a particular type of capitalistic development. Fascism must be studied as an agrarian phenomenon, though not with the idea that only agrarian problems matter in its origins. On the contrary, fascism, in a sense, emerged as the connecting link in the Italian city–country relation. Fascism arose as a violent means of containing the stresses of primary accumulation and modernization in the context of a week political regime.

Several recent students of Italian fascism have sought to underline the importance of agrarian social relations for an understanding of fascist success. More immediately of concern for us in this chapter, such students of the fascist movement in Emilia have strongly emphasized the central role of agriculturally based sugar refineries in the fascist success in the North.[94] What an examination of Tuscany indicates is that the sugar refineries were but one example of a much broader pattern of deep involvement in the reaction of small-scale provincial industry. In Tuscany the active role played in the organization of the squads by manufacturers in the textile, ceramics, brick-making, food, and quarrying sectors was an essential element in fascist expansion.

The active role of light industry in the reaction seems a contradiction of our thesis of the nature and importance of agrarian fascism. To a degree, certainly, the role of provincial industry is a caveat against too mechanical and absolute a distinction between industrial/urban and agrarian fascism. More importantly, however, the contradiction is more apparent than real. Work on the sugar refineries of Emilia demonstrates the deep connection between that sector of industry and agriculture. Provincial industry in Tuscany was much the same.

In the first place, provincial industry, in terms of simple geography, was deeply affected by the outcome of the class struggle in the countryside. The small industrialists of the provinces saw their economic and political position as inseparable from the survival of established hierarchies on the landed estates. The new socialist local governments elected on the strength of the peasant labour movement deeply affected the profits not only of the landowning aristocracy but also of manufacturing industry. The tax weapon, applied with expropriatory intent to landed property, was used to the same purpose against urban wealth. Capital was to be heavily taxed in town as well as in the country, and the burden was all the more onerous in that the same people often found themselves subject to major levies in more than one capacity.

More than merely geographical, however, the link between light industry and agriculture in the Tuscan provinces was organic. Sometimes the directorships of industry and landownership were interlocking as landholding interests invested in industry or, vice-versa, manufacturers bought the land. More broadly, local industry was often agriculturally based, being concerned largely with the working up of raw materials supplied from the land. In such cases, any changes in rural social relations which affected the cost of agricultural products were of direct material interest to the manufacturers. Furthermore, light industry was materially affected by events in the countryside not only in the commodity market but also in the labour market. The work-force of the small and medium provincial industrial plants was very heavily composed of labourers, largely women,[95] who were part-time peasants or *braccianti* who sought secondary employment in industry to supplement their income from agriculture. They commuted, often at considerable distance, to the towns and villages. In addition, the textile industry, in particular, was still dependent on outwork done by *mezzadro* families in the countryside.[96] Not surprisingly, therefore, the political and union atmosphere in the plants themselves was deeply influenced by the development of agrarian protest. The setting up of an effective monopoly of the labour movement in the countryside and the establishment of the labour exchanges would have increased the bargaining power of factory workers as well.

For a variety of reasons, then, provincial industry shared the landlords' opposition to rural socialism and rural trade unionism. The open involvement of light industry with fascism in its most violent agrarian form contrasted with the political outlook of big industry and the Tuscan Industrial Association. Heavy industry – represented in the region by the mining, chemical, shipbuilding, and iron and steel sectors – was far more concerned with long-term political and industrial stability than were small entrepreneurs, who had narrower margins of security and a shorter time perspective. Large-scale manufacturers were reluctant to identify themselves too closely with the subversive work of the squads. The small producer, whose business horizon extended no further than the boundaries of the province, was more preoccupied with local domination than with national and international repercussions. Furthermore, like the landlord, the provincial entrepreneur felt the necessity to resort to self-help more imperative because he despaired of his power to influence the state to protect his interests, whereas big industry was confident of its influence. In addition, heavy industry refrained from openly advocating terror because it needed the cooperation of a trained work-force whose skills were in short supply. Provincial manufacturers, like landowners, dealt instead with largely unskilled and often illiterate labourers who were readily replaced. Impelled by such considerations, small local industrialists joined the *agrari* in the organization of squadrism. Textile producers and pasta-makers played an active role in crushing subversion in the countryside.

Here the evidence from the Tuscan provinces is fragmentary, and a definitive description of the pattern of fascist support from provincial industry must await a full investigation of the position of each sector of light industry in the region. In the absence of such a study, however, there is still sufficient evidence of the pro-fascist activities of several leading sectors of Tuscan manufacturing to justify our broad conclusion.

Perhaps the most important as well as the clearest instance of the close relations between Tuscan light industry and fascism is provided by the textile industry at Prato in Florence province. Prato was the textile capital of Tuscany and very much a single industry town with over 10,000 workers (80 per cent of the local labour force) employed by the wool manufacturers.[97] Before the war, the local plants, in the words of the Florence daily the *Nuovo giornale*,

> had always been able to exist, but they had never been for their owners the hen that laid the golden eggs. Their life, if not difficult, still had been one without great triumphs, which is to say without great profits.[98]

The war, however, completely transformed the situation. It was a time of booming demand for textile products, of feverish activity in the plants, and of windfall profits for the industrialists, For the wool industry it was generally recognized as the 'golden age'.[99] Some measure of the profit margins obtainable until well into 1920 is furnished by the price of wool. In 1913 a metre of good-quality Prato wool cost 7 lire, while in 1920 the same metre cost 135 lire. Similarly, coarse natural wool rose from 3 lire per metre in 1913 to 8 lire at government requisition prices in 1918 and to 40–50 lire at free market prices in 1920. A man's suit rose in price from a range of 70–140 lire before the war to a new range of 600–1,100 lire in the middle of 1920. Thus it was that some 17 wool companies in Italy with a total capital of 51 million lire, representing about 35 per cent of the total capital of the Italian wool industry, are reported, in the three years 1914 to 1917 alone, to have made profits of nearly 163 million lire.[100]

Even amidst the frenetic activity of the boom years, however, there appeared the harbingers of impending crisis. The wool makers of Prato, mesmerized by the prospect of fantastic quick rake-offs, took no thought for the long-term competitive position of the industry. Production was simply increased to the maximum consonant with the existing plant and exsting production methods. No attempt was made to invest in new equipment or cost-reducing methods of production; no effort was spent on the diversification of the traditional range of local products; and little concern was shown for the introduction of economies of scale. As a result, when the war-time boom ceased and the effects of world-wide recession began to be felt, the Prato wool industrialists found themselves faced with a many-faceted crisis – a reconversion and overproduction crisis, a crisis of general economic stagnation, and a very particular crisis caused by the inability of the local manufacturers to compete with their more efficient, more diversified, and larger-scale competitors in the North[101]

As the crisis approached, it is clear that because of the particular profitability constraints that affected them, the Prato wool producers were very sensitive to the need to reduce costs by holding down wages, to the desirability of reducing their tax burden, and to the necessity of minimizing the cost of raw materials. The development of the new militancy in town and country found them fiercely determined to resist all concessions. Indeed, one feature of the industrialists of the Bisenzio Valley was their very early intransigence and conversion to a politics of subversive counter-revolution. Already in late 1919, after the first wave of wage and union demands by the wool workers, the initial socialist electoral victories, and the initial outbursts of agrarian unrest under Popular Party leadership, the Prato paper the *Patria*, spokesman for the interests of the wool manufacturers, was adamant in its stance and raised the spectre of civil war. The eight-hour day was unacceptable because, the industrialists argued, it would only lead to the dissolution and degeneration of the workers. Health benefits would inevitably be followed by absenteeism as labourers would exploit the system, and wage rises would invariably produce alcoholism and the inability of the local plants to compete with the textile makers of Biella. More broadly, the paper explained:

For so many years our industrialists have been tormented in their plants by ceaseless demands, threats, agitation, labour stoppages, and small partial strikes. For so many years they have had to submit to the tyranny of the internal committees and the Chambers of Labour.

They could tolerate no more, and they have risen up.[102]

In still more explicit fashion the industrialists' spokesman asked, 'Are we our own masters?' and warned, 'Beware of civil war!'[103]

If these were the views of the wool-makers in 1919, 1920 did little to improve their humour. In 1920 within the plants the socialist unions grew rapidly in strength, gaining a vast new membership, leading massive agitations, winning concesssions over wages and hours, and advancing more militant and broadly political demands. Indeed, while the industrialists in 1919 had worried over their competitive position and profit margins, and advanced spurious worries over workers' alcoholism, dissipation, and absenteeism, in 1920 there was a radical clarification of issues through the militancy of the internal committees, and the industrialists became openly preoccupied with the question of actual control in the factories. The question of workers' control had clearly become the centre of the debate even in the small-scale Prato textile industry, and was treated at length and in alarm by the *Patria*.[104] At the same time a socialist local government was elected to office in the town, while the 'white bolshevist' wing of the PPI was in control of the surrounding countryside, pressing for 'direct management of the estates by the peasants.'[105]

In this situation of crisis the fascist movement had much to recommend it. The local *fascio* supported the manufacturers when, in the deepening crisis of 1921, they unilaterally denounced the existing wage contracts, reduced wages, and sacked militants. In these circumstances the *fascio* defended the now sacrosanct 'right to work' and actively recruited blackleg labour at the same time that it used coercion, violence, and intimidation to break the desperate resistance the wool workers attempted when they went on strike against the wage cuts and victimizations, staying out for over 75 days in the darkening autumn of 1921.[106] Led by the firm of Romuald Beretti, the wool industrialists during the strike hired labour provided by the *fascio* and continued production. Praising Beretti's initiative, the *Patria* noted that he 'has demonstrated the will no longer to bend under the yoke of the Red organizations'.[107] And the policy of breaking the strike proved effective as discouragement mounted among the workers, mutual recriminations began, and a slow trickle back to work grew into a broad steady stream until by the end of November the movement was over.

At the same time, under the presidency of the fascist leader Persindo Giacomelli, a committee of taxpayers in revolt against the local socialist-dominated town council was set up to organize tax resistance. On the committee, significantly, sat representatives of the Prato *fascio*, the Prato branch of the AAT, the Union of Wool Manufacturers, and the Prato Union of Industrialists.[108] Meeting in February 1922, the taxpayers thus represented voted to rebel 'in the interest of the nation and in the defence of our own existence', demanded the dissolution of the elected town council, and deliberated to refuse payment of local taxation.[109] In the meantime the squads were active in restoring the social equilibrium of the old regime by destroying the fabric of the socialist and Popular parties in both town and country, and by regimenting the workers within the new hierarchical fascist unions.

What was particularly interesting here was the great awareness shown by the textile manufacturers of the interrelation between the political situations of town and country. The *Patria*, perhaps, gave pride of place to its opposition to the local socialist leadership under the deputy Targetti in the town, but hostility to the PPI in the country was hardly less vehement. The *Patria* wrote:

> the PPI is the most anti-patriotic, anti-national and anti-social party in Italy. And this came about because although it claims to base itself upon the principles of order, of brotherhood, and of patriotism, in its practical activity it shows itself the enemy of order, brotherhood, and fatherland.[110]

Declaring its solidarity with the landlords, the paper continued,

> The landlords of our region, apart from a few rare exceptions, are worthy people and good Catholics, and we fail to understand that another group of Catholics could, or should, hold this class up to public scorn and set forth with so much fury to see the class destroyed.[111]

What is important is not simply the declaration of solidarity with the landlords. In practice the wool manufacturers formed an alliance with the local branch of the AAT under Fortunato Magni. The wool-makers joined hands with the landlords to organize fascist repression throughout the city and the surrounding agricultural zone, forming a common umbrella association with them to finance the Prato *fascio*. Police Inspector General Di Tarsia reported that at Prato the AAT

> has joined the *fascio* in its entirety. Reliable information leads me to the certain conclusion that this association, which has today about 600 members – the leading producers of the area, with great political and financial power – subsidizes the *fascio*, which has become its support and its defender.
>
> To the Agraria are completely joined all the local industrial associations; and here it is well to note that the industrial associations are formed by the whole wealthy section of the area. This wealthy element was formed during the war years through the massive [government] contracts...[112]

Public demonstrations of pro-fascist solidarity also saw the Prato manufacturers present in force. For instance, the ceremonies of mourning at the death in action in January 1922 of the notorious Federico Florio, the guiding spirit of Prato squadrism, provided an opportunity for important interests in the town to demonstrate their support for the reaction. Official delegations representing the AAT and the Prato Union of Industrialists attended the public honours, and the Union of Wool Manufacturers published condolences and notices of support for the dead Florio.[113]

The wool manufacturers gave no evidence of any reluctance to adopt the violent methods usually associated with agrarian fascism. Indeed, Di Tarsia reported that at Prato there was a 'reaction which has exploded in exaggerated violence ... The whole outlook of the fascists is the expression of the will of the agrarian and industrial associations'.[114] In fact, the commander of the Prato squads, Antonio Lucchesi, was himself a rich local industrialist,[115] and the executive committee of the *fascio* included one of the leading names in local wool manufacture in Bruno Calamai.[116] Other important wool makers, such as Edo Rosaliti, Orlando Franchi, and Alessandro Mariotti, were also active fascists.[117] Furthermore, in February 1922 the wool manufacturers gave a collective demonstration of their backing for squadrist violence. They began a lock-out, bringing the entire industrial life of the city to a halt to secure the removal of a single police officer, Commissioner De Bernardinis, because of 'his attitude, which was openly and inconveniently hostile to the fascists'.[118] De Bernardinis was in command of one of the infrequent centres of political impartiality within the Tuscan police hierarchy, and he had the temerity to order the arrest of local blackshirts. The Ministry of the Interior, however, was not prepared to support its subordinate against the textile industry, and the offending commissioner was replaced by a man more congenial to Prato businessmen. The point requires some stress because the Prato *fascio* was one of the most powerful and influential in all of Tuscany, and several of its political leaders, such as Luigi Zamboni and Carlo Romagnoli, at one time or another held positions of regional responsibility.

In explaining the attitude of the Prato manufacturers to fascism and fascist violence, the last word rightfully belongs to the *Patria*. For the wool makers' paper fascism was self-defence, or, more poetically, it was a 'resurrection'. 'Fascism', the paper explained,

has gained strength and expanded because the Government is unable to defend law and order. The day when the Government demonstrates, in action, that it is able to safeguard the regime, to defend liberty ... and keep the competition of political parties within the law, on that day fascism will become superfluous and will disappear automatically. But not before.[119]

More brutally, the paper wrote:

The penal code exempts from punishment a man who kills in self-defence ... Fascism has set fire, has beaten, and has killed ... in the spirit of self-defence.

The fascists well know that violence leads to violence. The fascists, though they use violence, deplore it and, as soon as it is possible, will put away their notorious clubs. But just as they have little, or rather no, respect for insane and aberrant ideas, just so they respect those professing such ideas. When those people refuse to change their minds and insist on propagating in Italy Leninism, thuggery, and murder, when they teach men to deny their country, to outrage the dead, and to destroy civilization, then it is not such an evil that milder counsels give way to a holy, most holy, wielding of the club.[120]

Wool manufacturers at Prato were not alone in the Tuscan textile industry in the extent and nature of their fascist sympathies. Lucca province presents a comparable spectacle. The class struggle that emerged in the postwar province of Lucca never assumed the magnitude it possessed in central Tuscany. The police reported, for example, that

The province of Lucca was one of the most peaceful in Tuscany and continued so in the early postwar period, despite the increase of the forces of subversion...[121]

In industry, there were no great centres of heavy industry, and such great moments of postwar labour history as the Occupation of the Factories were hardly felt in the province, with the exception of the Ansaldo plant at Viareggio and the Società Metallurgica Italiana (SMI) at Fornaci di Barga. None the less, the 'Red Years' did have their reflection in Luccan industry – notably in the textile plants of the capital, in the Serchio and Nievole Valleys, and in the marble quarries of the Versilia.[122] Similarly, in agriculture there were very significant moments of rural unrest in the relatively commercially advanced Luccan plain and the Nievole Valley.[123] Singularly, both in the provincial capital and in the countryside, the movement for the renewal of existing social relations was led by the PPI.

For our purposes here, the point to be stressed is the leading role played in opposition to Catholic subversion by the small industrialists. It was no accident that the first areas of the province where the fascists met with success were the zones where there was most industry – the Versilia, the Serchio Valley, and the Nievole Valley.[124] In the Nievole Valley in particular the Prefect Di Donato underlined that the wave of fascist violence in the villages of the zone was due in large measure to 'the existence of numerous and powerful industrial firms that, seeing in fascist action a means to protect their interests, encourage the movement and support it, even financially.'[125]

Similarly, in the Versilia the police informed the Ministry of the Interior that

In the Versilia the fascists were helped especially by the industrialists of the marble industry, who until now were the victims of the blackmailing strikes of the workers.[126]

Thus it was no mere flattery that led the 'duce' of Lucca, Carlo Scorza, to include 'small industrialists' in his enumeration of the groups which brought fascism to power in the province.[127]

A well-documented case and one of the most important in the province was that of the foremost textile company in Lucca, the thread-making firm S.A. Cucirini Cantoni Coates, under the direction of James Henderson. For Henderson and the managers of the various plants of the CCC the issue at stake in the struggles of 1920–1 was primarily power – the defence of managerial authority in the factory. What Henderson was unwilling to tolerate was the growth in influence of the Catholic unions within the plant and the increasing authority of the internal committees. For these political reasons Henderson became one of the earliest in Lucca to finance the local *fascio*.[128]

Beyond textiles, however, other sectors of Tuscan light industry demonstrated an active involvement in the fascist movement. The food industry, here exemplified by the pasta-making firm of Buitoni of San Sepolcro (Arezzo province), is a case in point. There is no doubt that the San Sepolcro *fascio* was the creation of the Buitoni company owned by Silvio Buitoni, one of the directors of the Arezzo Chamber of Commerce,[129] and managed by his nephew Fosco. The barest statement of fact reveals the role of the company in the life of the local movement. Silvio and Fosco Buitoni not only financed the San Sepolcro fascist branch, but were also active members of its executive committee, while the political secretary, Cesare Cappelletti, and the commander of the squads, Valentino Dindelli, were employees of the firm.[130] Fosco Buitoni in particular made no effort to conceal his fascist connections, but personally played an important role in the squads and made an attempt on the life of the local socialist deputy, Luigi Bosi.[131] As Bosi himself testified, "'Fascismo' at San Sepolcro is 'Buitonismo'."[132] The uses of the squads to the Buitoni family in the town of San Sepolcro were several. The squads provided the means of dismantling the socialist administration[133] and of crushing all opposition to the authoritarian role of Fosco Buitoni over the 250 workers in his plant. Indeed, in 1921 a purge was carried out within the factory in which all workers were sacked who were 'subversive and disloyal to the family in question'.[134] Beyond these benefits, the squads seem to have served darker private ends[135] and to have furthered a series of unscrupulous practices, both political and business, invloving uncle and nephew. Fascist sources themselves indicate, for instance, that the squads practised extortion and managed a protection racket, in addition to covering the 'many political irregularities committed by Fosco Buitoni'.[136]

What is perhaps of still greater interest is that the Buitonis took it upon themselves to preside over the 'redemption' not only of the town of San Sepolcro, but also of the whole area of the Tiber Valley in Arezzo province. The countryside was no less an object of the attentions of the San Sepolcro squads than the town.[137]

Like the textile manufacturers and food producers, the ceramics industry also played a major role in local fascist success. The *fascio* of Sesto Fiorentino, in Florence province, was largely the creation of the famous porcelain company Richard-Ginori.[138] In the Elsa Valley brickmakers seem to have been among the leading figures in the establishment of the fascist union movement.[139] At Empoli a leading promotor of the *fascio* was Luigi Del Vivo, the glass manufacturer. In this case the fusion of interests beween light industry and agrarian reaction was most clearly revealed because the Del Vivo family not only dominated local manufacturing, but also owned vast tracts of the surrounding countryside.[140] And at Siena in the middle of 1922 when the socialist deputies Cavina and Bisogni produced striking revelations of squadrist violence in the province, the Società fra Industriali Commercianti ed Esercenti di Siena e Provincia gave clear support to continuing fascist terror by informing the Minister of the Interior that the charges were false and absurd, because at Siena there reigned 'absolute calm'![141]

Other evidence of support for fascism by small industry is provided by the scattered surviving returns of the fascist movement's internal census of its own social composition in late 1921. This evidence is very fragmentary and there is no way to know how the fascists defined the category of 'industrialists'. None the less, it is significant to note that industrialists were reported to be an important element in the *fasci* of many towns and villages. Of 50 members of the *fascio* of Pozzo della Chiana (Arezzo province), for instance, 10 were classified as industrialists.[142] At Sestino (Arezzo), of 50 members 5 were industrialists.[143] Of 36 members, the Modigliana *fascio* (Florence) claimed 4 industrialists.[144] Again at Pontassieve (Florence) there were 10 industrialists in a membership of 33;[145] 9 of 28 at Premilcuore (Florence province);[146] 27 of 73 at Sancasciano Val di Pesa (Florence province);[147] 23 of 85 at Seggiano (Grosseto province).[148]

Here a case somewhat apart is that of the relations between the fascist movement and the marble-quarrying industry in the province of Massa-Carrara. Both subversion and reaction in Massa-Carrara were above all industrial problems, so that it is somewhat anomalous to refer to the marble quarries in a discussion of agrarian fascism. None the less, the involvement of the marble-owners with the *fasci* does complete our picture of the relations between light industry and fascism – relations that were personal, intense, and violent. The fascists of the northwest exhibited some of the leading characteristics of pro-fascist provincial industry that we have noted elsewhere in the region – an extremist politics associated chiefly with the *agrari*. Still more directly, there were clear links which tied the marble-owners to an extent to the agrarian wing of fascism. The squads of Massa-Carrara took part in expeditions in other provinces in the region. Moreover, in the great debate over pacification which split the movement roughly along the same lines that separated, however imprecisely, the urban and agrarian wings of the movement, the *fasci* of Massa-Carrara joined the *agrari* in militant opposition to the pact.[149]

Fascism in Massa-Carrara emerged as an instrument in the hands of the marble-owners for the restoration of unquestioned rule over their workforce. This rule had been shaken by the militancy of the 12,000 quarry men,[150] organized primarily by the anarchists, who controlled the Carrara Chamber of Labour under the leadership of Alberto Meschi.[151] In a series of protracted and bitter strikes in 1919 and 1920, the quarriers won major wage increases with the award of 5.50 lire a day. More important than the immediate increase, however, was the clause in the new pact which linked the future level of salaries automatically to increases in the cost of living, with adjustments to be made at the end of every month, so that for the workers inflation would be permanently offset by rises in pay. Such a victory threatened to create a permanent redistribution of income between the classes. At the same time, moreover, the workers had established, as part of the new contract, that the employers were entitled to hire only workers belonging to the Chamber of Labour.[152]

For the industrialists, such changes in themselves were dangerously subversive of their traditional unchallenged domination of the quarries. In addition to the actual concessions to which they had been forced, however, the industrialists were deeply concerned over the movement to expropriate the owners and turn the quarries over to the workers to be run as cooperatives. The slogan circulating among the workers was, 'The quarries to the quarry men!'[153] Moreover, the local pressure of the workers was backed in parliament where the republican deputy from Carrara, Eugenio Chiesa, and the socialist Umberto Bianchi had presented bills calling, respectively, for the expropriation of the marble-owners by the commune and for the nationalization of the quarries under the workers' control.[154]

Fascism, as it evolved in the province from the spring of 1921 under the leadership of Renato Ricci, was the means to restore industrial absolutism. The squads were the agents for the purging of the quarries, physically eliminating those who resisted, and harassing and intimidating the rest, while the 'national' unions provided more docile and apolitical members from the ranks of the unemployed and the underworld to take the places of the militants. In early 1922 the leading marble firm of Francesco Dell'Amico, for instance, simply replaced its entire work-force with men supplied by the *fascio*.[155] Further, having obtained from the employers the exclusive right to represent the workers, the *fasci* negotiated new terms and conditions of work that institutionalized the subjection of the labourers by introducing a regime of radical job insecurity. The contract negotiated by the Marmifera Nord Carrara, which with its 600 workers was the small northwest fief of the great industrialist Guido Donegani,[156] was a case in point. Under the agreement reached with the fascist unions, the wage system was replaced by piece-work, at rates not fixed by contract but to be established *ad hoc* by management. Moreover, the new contract stipulated that

> The worker who demonstrates a lack of will or of ability in his work, especially piece-work, will be liable to disciplinary measures, including dismissal without notice.[157]

That the marble industrialists should have received terms from the *fasci* so favourable to themselves is readily understandable if we remember that at every stage Ricci's squads were the direct expression of the policy of the industrialists. The inspiration and purposes behind the Carrara *fascio* were clearly set out by the police. In the words of Inspector General Paolella, the Carrara *fascio*, from the time of its founding in May 1921,

> immediately found ... broad favour with the majority of the population, which was tired of being held to ransom by the subversives and was disgusted by their unpatriotic propaganda. And it enjoyed powerful financial backing from the industrialists, who relied on the new organization to face and put a halt to the growing and excessive claims of the working class, which is nearly all enrolled in the Chamber of Labour, whose leaders are militants in the anarchist party.[158]

The members of the Industrial Association of Carrara and of the Federation of Marble Industrialists were, however, far from limiting their fascist sympathies to financial aid. The major marble-industrialist Guido Fabbricotti, for example, was himself an active squadrist and an 'ardent advocate' on behalf of the 'economic unions'.[159] In his quarries he favoured employees who could produce the membership card of the local *fascio*, and he dismissed anyone who took part in May Day festivities or was known to be enrolled in the Chamber of Labour.[160] Fabbricotti was also known to have clubbed one of his workers, Ottaviano Secchiari, whom he disovered to be a communist.[161] Furthermore, beyond the gates of his quarry Fabbricotti commanded a mounted squad of blackshirts.[162] His pro-fascism, moreover, was not a personal, but a family preference, and the lists of Carrara squadrists include, beyond Guido Fabbricotti, Andrea, Annibale, Bernardo, Francesco, Guidino, and Vincenzo Fabbricotti.[163]

The Fabbricotti firm was by no means exceptional among the members of the Industrial Association in its political sympathies. Bernardo Pocherra, a leading member of the Federation of Marble Industrialists and of the Carrara Liberal party, took an enthusiastic part in fascist public meetings.[164] The Dell'Amico company, as we recall, employed only fascists, while the family provided an extended list of active squadrists – Alessandro, Amedeo, Aristide, Battista, Bernardo, Ezio, Francesco, Gino, Giuseppe, Guglielmo, Raimondo, and Ugo Dell'Amico.[165] Ugo Dell' Amico in addition was a member of the *direttorio* of the Carrara *fascio*.[166] Similarly, the directors of the Valton firm were reported to be chiefly fascists or fascist sympathizers.[167]

When in January 1922 the Prefect Roberto Berti attempted to curb the extreme violence of Renato Ricci, the *ras* or 'boss' of Carrara, by decreeing the confiscation of all firearms, the industrialists rallied collectively to the defence of the squads by announcing a lock-out at all the marble quarries in the province. The lock-out was to continue until the offending decree was revoked.[168] Again, as at Prato, the government yielded to pressure and declined to support its provincial subordinates in the attempt to enforce the law against the *fasci* and their patrons. The prime minister, Ivanoe Bonomi, personally cabled Berti, instructing him to revoke the order owing to 'special personal circumstances and to the special conditions of the area'.[169]

PART II

THE CITIES

CHAPTER 3

BIG BUSINESS AND MUSSOLINI

ECONOMIC VULNERABILITY

If the struggle between socialism and landed property was the principal contest on which fascist success in postwar Tuscany was based, an important secondary source of strength was derived from the urban centres. In this section, then, we must take up the question of the urban support for Tuscan fascism. In the towns, as in the countryside, there was a division between the clearly articulated and powerful interests of capital on the one hand and the popular rank and file that swelled the squads on the other. It is important to examine each of these groups in turn, in order to answer both the empirical question of who supported the *fasci*, and the interpretative question of the significance of each source of fascist strength for an analysis of the movement. Does the evidence from Tuscany support the idea of fascism as the armed militia of monopoly capital or the notion that the movement was the political extremism of the petty bourgeoisie? To answer these questions, we must turn first to the Tuscan board room.

Fascism for heavy industry,[1] as for landed property and provincial manufacturing, was a response to the combined pressure of economic crisis and political challenge. It is useful, however, to treat the pro-fascism of the giant companies as a case apart because it had its own characteristics and special limitations. Fascism was a movement that industrial capital viewed as a possible political ally in the defence of the social order against the threat of Italian bolshevism; and from their founding the *fasci* enjoyed substantial monetary contributions from the highest circles of Italian business and finance. What distinguished the fascist sympathies of heavy industry from the commitment to armed reaction of the *agrari* was the way in which the industrialists hedged their bets and refused to become inextricably linked with Mussolini's movement. Big industry, unlike the *agrari*, the pasta-makers, and textile manufacturers was concerned with winning the cooperation of a skilled work-force, and found squadrism a clumsy instrument for labour relations. At the same time, heavy industry was more long range in its planning and felt reluctant to rely on a movement whose violence and unpredictability were corrosive of the atmosphere of ordered regularity best suited for the transaction of business. Large companies with widely dispersed assets and international dealings looked well beyond the local domination that was the chief concern of the landlords. For this reason as well, the industrial leadership was unwilling to identify itself too closely with any political movement, preferring to maintain working relations with the dominant party in order to survive with a profit whatever the colour of the government. The *fasci* were a force with which business could, and did, come to terms, but not one that it embraced without reserve. This was particularly true since the industrialists were powerfully organized nationally through their peak organization, Confindustria, and were confident of their ability to take a common stance as well as to influence the ministries and the government. As a result, the impulse to resort to armed self-help was diminished, particularly as squadrism, so effective against the local League and socialist branch, was incoherent in its national political and economic strategy.

For these reasons, the leaders of Italian industry were cautious in their approach to the fascist movement. In the first place, they preferred financial support to direct membership. Fiat, Ansaldo, and Ilva, to mention just the three greatest industrial complexes in Italy, all opened their purses to Mussolini as did a host of other major companies in the peninsula, but their directors seldom enrolled in movement or publicly campaigned on its behalf. There were exceptions, of course: Guiseppe Broglia, one of Agnelli's foremost collaborators at Fiat, was active in the Turin *fascio*;[2] Edoardo Rotigliano, a leading spokesman for Ilva, was widely known to be a 'fervent fascist'; and the Perrone brothers of Ansaldo appeared on public platforms with Mussolini. On the whole, however, industry preferred not to compromise itself by an open espousal of the fascist cause. The aid industrialists were prepared to give did not generally include active political militancy. Instead, they gave money; applied pressure on the government to close an eye to fascist illegality; and provided encouragement and favourable negotiating terms to the fascist unions.

Even the financial support provided to the *fasci* by the industrialists differed in its source, regularity, and direction from that of the landlords. The *agrari* often gave funds individually, but they were also prepared to subsidize the movement on a regular collective basis through their associations. Moreover, they more often directed funds to the provincial fascist organizations rather than to the Central Committee in Milan. By contrast, the industrial paymasters of the *fasci* donated money sporadically and on a purely individual or company basis, without the official involvement of Confindustria and its provincial counterparts. Moreover, there was a tendency for leading industrialists to subsidize Milan rather than the local movement, to prefer Mussolini and the *Popolo d'Italia* to the local *ras* or *caposquadra*.[3]

These differences in strategy between the agrarian and the industrial bourgeoisie reinforced a major division within the fascist movement itself. This division was complex and shifting, so that the lines of fissure appeared at different points on different issues. There was, none the less, a general distinction to be made between the two great currents – the 'two fascisms' in the words of the fascist theorist Lanzillo – which nearly split the movement in the middle of 1921.[4] Both were repressive, authoritarian, and violent. The 'moderate' urban current favoured by industry, however, contrasted sharply with the 'revolutionary' and 'heroic' fascism of the *agrari*. The 'moderates' preferred conventional political methods to a squadrism they found difficult to control; they supported the national leadership of Mussolini against the anarchic provincialism of the *ras*; and they sought a political solution to the postwar crisis that would disturb as little as possible the ordered regularity of business as usual. Urban fascists viewed squadrism as a surgical necessity rather than as a permanent means of rule, and they distrusted trade unionism even in fascist guise.

Now, what was notable was that in Tuscany the relationship between the *fasci* and industry was less cautious than was the norm in Italy, while the broad and general distinction between agrarian and urban fascism was correspondingly more blurred. Here it is useful, in beginning to understand the particular pro-fascism of the Tuscan board rooms, to recall Poulantzas' general claim that fascism is not characteristic of advanced capitalism, but constitutes a 'state of exception'.[5] Fascism was not the normal state form of the advanced capitalist powers which had consolidated their internal rule, achieved a class domestic 'hegemony' through the evolution of social and economic structures supportive of a bourgeois polity, and attained a colonial status with respect to an international market. Instead fascism arose, Poulantzas continues, in the 'weak links' in the world-market chain, the industrial 'latecomers' (e.g. Italy, Germany, Japan). These states were 'weak links' in the chain first because, with a new and precarious industrial structure, they were forced to compete with far more advanced imperialist powers. Secondly, these regimes had in common an internal fragility because in each the bourgeoisie had not succeeded in carrying out its industrial revolution with the speed or thoroughness of the established powers, had not completed the process of transforming the domestic social fabric in accordance with the requirements and logic of advanced capitalism. And thirdly, the nations that turned to fascism shared the position of parvenus in an already established colonial network. As a result, the path of foreign expansion was effectively blocked, and the possibility of successfully transposing internal conflict on to the international arena was foreclosed.

Here, in a study of a single region, there is no possibility of evaluating a theory of such scope and wide-ranging implications as that proposed by Poulantzas. It is impossible even to assess the applicability of the theory to Italy as a whole. We need merely note that Poulantzas' argument helps to explain the pro-fascism of the great Tuscan industrial complexes because Tuscan industry itself was a 'weak link' in the narrow and stunted chain of Italian capital.

We have already seen considerable evidence for this conclusion in our study of the Tuscan countryside. Tuscan agriculture had become, in essence, a form of capitalist enterprise in which the relations between the 'partners' were explicable in terms of the concepts of political economy. The lord had achieved by our period full control of the means of production and faced an expropriated labourer who received a wage for his labour power (advanced, however, in kind rather than cash). From him the lord extracted a surplus through a series of devices that ensured a high exploitation of labour as measured by both the length and intensity of the work day. The landowner, moreover, farmed for the market, treated his produce as a commodity, and sought to run his estates in accordance with the dictates of profit maximization. A deep contradiction was that the structures of *mezzadria* formed an intolerable obstacle to the productive rationale of a commercialized agriculture and made traditional Tuscan farming unable to compete in the national and international markets. From an economic standpoint, then, the Tuscan agricultural sector was unable to withstand the impact of a world market. At the same time, the system was politically in crisis because, under the weight of the changes introduced by the new commercial methods, the traditional devices of social control by the Tuscan ruling classes (e.g. the isolation of the tenant families, the influence of the clergy, the institution of the *famiglia colonica*, the bond of lordly paternalism), had broken down, but the institutional and ideological mechanisms of control characteristic of a capitalist bourgeoisie had not yet been evolved. To these contradictions fascism was a repressive and authoritarian solution.

The crisis of Tuscan agriculture was not, however, restricted to the countryside, but affected the entire regional economy and social system, including industrial capital. For industry, the implications of a dominant agricultural system based on *mezzadria* were serious. Agriculture hindered industrial expansion. The depressed standard of living characteristic of the mass of the population in the countryside was a severe impediment to the formation of an expanding consumer market. At the same time, the inherent aim of *mezzadria* was the self-sufficiency of the *podere*. To the extent that the system achieved this goal, the rural population was removed from the market place. In addition, the backwardness of the productive methods of Tuscan sharecropping, its reliance on the intensive exploitation of labour rather than on enhanced productivity, meant that the Tuscan estates were not active creators of industrial demand. The *fattorie* were not large-scale purchasers of agricultural machinery and equipment, of chemical fertilizers and electric power. As a result, there was a far-reaching conflict between the demand requirements of industrial growth and a stunted regional market. This problem of market outlets for industry was not, of course, exclusively Tuscan. It was one of the fundamental weaknesses of Italian capitalism as a whole. Nationally, this contradiction was expressed most clearly in the North–South relation, in the barrier to the northern development of the backward Mezzogiorno. What made the contradiction especially clear in Tuscany was the juxtaposition in a single region of modern monopoly capital and a traditional social structure.

No more direct or important example of the organic relation between the prospects for expansion of Tuscan industry and the purchasing power of the agricultural estates can be found than that of the giant Montecatini complex. Originally founded in 1898 as a small copper-mining concern, the company dated its own transformation into an important economic force from its purchase in 1910 of the pyrite mines in the Maremma of the Unione Italiana Miniere Pirite. Pyrites, used in the production of sulphuric acid and phosphate fertilizers, were a vital base for the production of chemicals, which were henceforth the foundation on which the fortunes of Montecatini rested. During the war the company developed into an industrial colossus as a supplier of munitions. Montecatini's prospects of conversion to peace-time production and its long-term hopes of continued expansion, however, were indissolubly linked to the sale of chemical fertilizers. In 1920 Guido Donegani, the authoritarian chairman of the board, staked the whole future of Montecatini on the modernization of agriculture by investing 100,000,000 lire in the purchase of the two most important companies producing artificial fertilizers in Italy, the Unione Italiana Concimi and the Colla e Concimi. At the same time Montecatini bought interests in a whole range of mining ventures (copper, marble, lignite, sulphur, lead, zinc, and iron), but the productive core of the complex was firmly oriented to supplying the farms of central Italy with fertilizers.[6]

It was no aberration that Donegani proclaimed agriculture the foundation of national wealth, and that the company adopted the attitude of the *agrari* towards the threat of social revolution in the countryside. The Montecatini board did not share the cautious reserve of Confindustria towards the *fasci*, but fully endorsed the counter-revolution. We have seen Donegani's decisive intervention in defence of the squads in Massa-Carrara. This occasion, however, was only an incident in a close and mutually profitable relationship between Montecatini and fascism. As Donegani informed the company shareholders after the March on Rome,

When in October 1922 the blackshirts arrived in Rome, we industrialists rejoiced and welcomed Benito Mussolini's government that gave back to the state and its laws the necessary authority.[7]

Speaking more directly of the interest of Montecatini in the fascist success, the chairman linked the future of sales of fertilizers to the 'cessation of social agitation' and praised the squads for undertaking the task of restoring order.[8] To demonstrate his faith in the reaction more publicly, Donegani undertook a mission abroad as Mussolini's personal envoy to reassure the international business community about the intentions of the new regime.

Montecatini is a conspicuous example of the political convergence of Tuscan industry with the politics of the *agrari*. Few other companies shared so direct and overwhelming a dependence on farmers as purchasers, but there were respects in which Montecatini was illustrative of the close bonds between industry and the Tuscan aristocracy. One indication is the concentration of Tuscan heavy industry as a whole in the mining sector. With its rich deposits of iron, mercury, pyrites, lignite, and marble, Tuscany became a region of extractive industry more than of manufacture, although other sectors developed as extensions of the original mining nucleus. Steel mills were natural offshoots of the iron mines, just as chemicals were of pyrite and mercury extraction. Docking and shipbuilding revolved around the port of Livorno and the need to ship Tuscan raw materials.

Now, two obvious peculiarities of mining should not be forgotten as they were of considerable importance in orienting Tuscan industry towards political stances more typical of the *agrari* than of Italian big business. The first is that the mines, being located beneath the soil, often required the consent or active involvement of the landed interest. The second is that mining required enormous initial outlays of capital that in Tuscany only the landed aristocracy could provide. A marked feature, therefore, of Tuscan heavy industry was the extensive involvement of major landlords, both as sleeping partners and active entrepreneurs. This close interlocking of the industrial bourgeoisie and the modernizing aristocracy was one of the mechanisms that compensated for the chronic shortage of capital and the limited market outlets of the region.

The tendency to form an organic bloc between industry and agriculture was perhaps most obviously visible in the great holding company launched by the *agrari* – the Società per le Strade Ferrate Meridionali, commonly known as the Bastogi after the great Sienese landowning family. The Bastogi held vast interests throughout Tuscan industry, and was the prime mover of the electrical sector.[9] The expansion of agrarian capital into industry was also apparent in the key positions held by leading aristocrats in the board rooms of the major Tuscan companies. P. F. Serragli himself, vice president of the AAT, was a director of the Società Boracifera di Lardarello, as were Prince Piero Ginori Conti, Marquis Lorenzo Ginori Lisci, and Count Francesco De Larderel.[10] Ginori Lisci was also a director of the Monte Amiata, and had close links with the Orlando shipyards.[11] Marquises Emanuele and Vincenzo Trigona were leading figures in the steel company Magona d'Italia and in the Tuscan Industrial Association.[12] Prince Ginori Conti, beyond the Boracifera, was a director of Ilva and of the Monte Amiata. Through his leading position at the Marmifera Nord Carrara, a subsidiary of Montecatini, he was also closely associated with Guido Donegani. Industry and agriculture in Tuscany were bound tightly together.[13]

In addition to the tie to the countryside, a direct consequence of the need to mobilize and concentrate capital to overcome the deficiencies of the Tuscan home market was a marked and precocious tendency of Tuscan industry towards monopoly. A very few pairs of hands controlled the industrial economy of the region. In virtually every sector one or two giant enterprises dominated production. Iron and steel were practically synonymous with Ilva. Mercury was the domain of the Monte Amiata and the Società Mineraria del Siele. Boric acid was the province of the Boracifera, as lignite was of the Società Elettrica e Mineraria del Valdarno. The electrical industry was shared between the Mineraria and the Società Ligure-Toscana; shipbuilding was dominated by the Orlando yards, Ilva, and Ansaldo; and precision instruments were known primarily through the Officine Galileo. Only marble quarrying, fossil fuels, and provincial industry were competitive.[14]

The predominance in each sector of a single company, or pair of companies, however, gives only a hint of the real degree of concentration achieved. Such giant concerns as Ilva and Montecatini were both vertically and horizontally integrated with interests in several sectors at once.[15] Furthermore, the directorships of the leading companies were endlessly overlapping. The great Livorno shipbuilder Luigi Orlando, for example, was a member of the board of the SMI, of the Credito Italiano, and of the

Mineraria, in addition to being president of the Ligure-Toscana and of four of the nine small Tuscan electrical companies that were nominally the 'competitors' of the Mineraria and the Ligure-Toscana.[16] Marquis Ginori Lisci, whom we have encountered as a director of the board of the Monte Amiata, was also a director of the Boracifera and of the Società Marmifera Nord Carrara, and had links with both Guido Donegani and the Orlando brothers.[17] Prince Piero Ginori Conti, president of the Boracifera, was also a director of Ilva and of the Mineraria.[18] Arturo Bocciardo, the rising star of Ilva who was president of its subsidiary Elba and then succeeded Count Orlando as president of the entire complex in May 1922, was tied to the Credito Italiano and the Banca Commerciale, and was a leading figure at the Magona d'Italia and the Ligure-Toscana.[19]

Such a concentration at the top echelons of the industrial hierarchy contrasted with the slenderness of the economic base. Furthermore, it testified to an overstretching of financial resources that became apparent when the period of boom ended. It had the effect, when the crisis came, of multiplying the interests affected and of facilitating a common political direction of the Tuscan bourgeoisie.

If Tuscan industry was a 'weak link' because of the structural deficiencies of its regional market, its sectoral concentration in extraction, and its tendency towards an overreaching of its financial resources, it was all the more vulnerable because of the tempestuous and disordered character of its boom period during the war. The war was a period of quick profits, unprecedented output, and extreme velocity of turnover. A combination of lucrative government contracts, militarized discipline in the factories, almost unlimited demand, and a rampant rate of inflation that devalued wages, created unparalleled opportunities for prosperity in business, and in particular for the arms manufacturers.[20] What was striking, however, was the contrast between the relatively ordered growth of the national industrial 'establishment' on the one hand and the breakneck expansion of the aggressive new generation of speculative Tuscan manufacturers. We have already seen the contrast in the textile industry between Prato and Biella.[21] The Prato wool makers, preoccupied with the short term, had taken no care to prepare for the return to peace as their great northern competitors had done, increasing their range of products, introducing new plants and equipment, and rationalizing their methods in order to raise productivity. The Prato manufacturers had been concerned only to produce *more*, with great resulting waste and inefficiency. Part of the explanation of the militant pro-fascism of the Tuscan textile manufacturers was the violent reconversion crisis that was a consequence of their high unit costs and uncompetitive pricing.

In this respect, textiles were typical of Tuscan industry. Indeed, the most important by far of all Tuscan companies, Ilva, followed, though on a much greater scale, the same process. Ilva began as a modest steel company that by 1911 had obtained prominence through the formation of a trust with other firms in the sector. By 1914, the total capital of the group was already 30,000,000 lire. The real opportunities for the complex, however, were created by the war. Between 1915 and 1918 the steel production of the company nearly doubled, from an annual production of 800,000 tons to 1,300,000 tons, and in two stages in 1916 and 1918 the prewar trust was transformed into a formal merger.[22] By this time, however, steel had become only one of the activities of a diversified empire, which by the armistice had become the third industrial power in Italy, and the largest in Tuscany. From steel, Ilva had turned to the mechanical industries by building ships, weapons, and railway rolling stock. Further, the company had bought into shipping, electricity and the mining of iron, manganese and lignite. In 1918, the productive capital of the complex was valued at over 300,000,000 lire,[23] and the company employed 50,000 workers.[24] Even these vast figures (which are more intelligible if we recall that the largest company in Florence province, the Galileo, had a capital of about 3,000,000 lire)[25] do not, however, reveal the true extent and influence of this complex. Ilva, beyond its involvement in production, was also a great control centre for financial speculation, and the company bought holdings of every description throughout the Tuscan economy. As the Liberal economist Luigi Einaudi underlined, Ilva, 'instead of practicing industry, speculated on the stock exchange'.[26]

As in the case of the boom in the Prato textile industry, the feverish activity of the war years was the precursor of crisis, and was partly the cause of that crisis.[27] The expansion of companies like Ilva, though on a scale dwarfing the wool makers' growth, resembled it in its tumultuous chase for windfall profits at the expense of productive logic and rationalization. Again, no attempt was made to modernize plants, or to orient the war-time growth to the long-term requirements of peace-time Tuscany. Indeed, in the case of Ilva, no effort was made to relate the various parts of the new empire to each other, with the result that by the end of the war what had been created was not an organic whole, but a haphazard assemblage which was the polar opposite and perfect foil for Fiat, where expansion, though equally rapid and spectacular, had always been guided with a view to the long-term and to cost efficiency.[28]

The haphazard growth of Ilva, as of the wool plants and other companies, is partly explained by the managerial priorities of a new generation of flamboyant tycoons – men like Count Rosolino Orlando, Max Bondi, Arturo Luzzatto, and Cesare Fera – whose climb to control of the Ilva board room had been accomplished through sharp dealings, deception, and outright fraud that culminated in a major postwar scandal and in the exclusion of both Bondi and Luzzatto from parliament.[29] Describing the business practices of the new quadrumvirate, Attilio Odero, Count Orlando's predecessor as president until he was ousted by a shareholders' coup orchestrated by Bondi and his associates in 1917, spoke of the 'unbounded exaggeration and megalomania' of Bondi and company, and of their 'excessive desire to dominate and control', which had led to a 'fantastic accumulation of interests of every description', with harm both to Ilva and to the companies absorbed.[30]

Lest we assume that Odero was motivated solely by personal pique, we need only recall the methods employed by the new cabal as revealed by a committee appointed to investigate, on behalf of Ilva's shareholders, the financial management of the company. Reporting in December 1921, the committee found that the directors had been guilty of systematic maladministration. Since 1917 Bondi and his associates had announced to the shareholders that Ilva had embarked upon a program of naval construction, whereas in fact the new program consisted only of using company funds for stock-market speculation 'without regard for the industrial requirements of the company'. Thus, for instance, 82,000 shares of the Savona company were bought at a cost to Ilva of 30,000,000 lire – an operation that allowed Bondi to increase his share of the Ilva portfolio and to pocket enormous sums through commissions paid to his Max Bondi Bank, which acted as broker for all the transactions. Nor was the Savona adventure an isolated affair, for similar manoeuvres were carried out on an equally massive scale and with identical results with the shares of other companies such as the Ferriere Italiane, Valdarno, Forni Elettrici, and Isotta Fraschini.

At the same time, fantastic deals were struck between Ilva and the Max Bondi Bank, all of which were concluded happily for the bank as a result of very 'elastic' contracts which safeguarded the interests of the bank, if not of Ilva's shareholders. Indeed, beginning in 1918, Ilva began to underwrite the investments of the Bondi Bank. The method was simplicity itself: Ilva borrowed large sums from various credit institutions at the current commercial interest rate and then lent the money to the Bank virtually interest-free. With equal generosity Ilva made Bondi, Luzzatto, and Fera the recipients of 'grants' and overdraft facilities for millions of lire, and bore the expense of the political ventures of Bondi and Luzzatto. In simplest terms, the investigating committee suggested that the Ilva directors were committing massive embezzlement.[31]

More dispassionately, the economist R. Bachi wrote in 1919 of the inevitable results of the business practices of Ilva and Ansaldo:

The formation of these powerful groups in the steel and mechanical industries marks a great transformation in the national economy. But one cannot conclude that it makes a real and viable technical advance, because it seems that ... the transformation has taken place in a tumultuous manner, with considerable waste, and more through an excessive tendency towards expansion than for genuine economic utility. It is well known that the various branches of the new organization cannot lay claim to a sound technical structure and that such deficiencies are not the least important cause of their high [production] costs in relation to their foreign rivals. The start of the postwar period gives foundation to the suspicion that one or another of these very important companies may become a serious handicap to the national economy, and a grave menace ... .[32]

That men like Max Bondi, Arturo Luzzatto, Luigi Orlando and Guido Donegani, the tsar of Montecatini, should have risen to the leadership of Tuscan industry more or less simultaneously was not only an accident of history. There was a certain logic that it should be so. These men were the parvenus, the youngest sons of Italian capitalism. That they were concerned above all with the short term, in contrast with big industry as a whole, reflected their newness of power. It also reflected the underlying weakness of the Tuscan economy in competition with northern and foreign rivals. With unstable long-term prospects, Tuscan management was tempted to take full advantage of the speculative opportunities opened up by the war. The fact, too, that the new opportunities came largely through government contracts opened the way for a generation of managers whose perspective was that of shrewd financial dealing more than cost rationalization.[33]

The chief point for our purposes is that for an industrial structure with a series of interlocking weaknesses – in terms of its market outlets, its vulnerability to competition, its overstretched financial base, and its managerial leadership – the postwar period was, as Bachi predicted, a 'grave menace'. The postwar years were a time of crisis in any case owing to the dislocations of the war, the necessity of reconversion to a peace economy, and an international recession. For much of Tuscan industry, however, the crisis was as much structural as conjunctural, and involved the violent reassertion of those long-term limitations of the Tuscan economy which had been partly overcome by the war-time boom, but at the cost of an unstable and wasteful expansion. Moreover, just as the period of growth had been largely artificial, based on the politics of war and the bacchanalia of government contracts, so the direction in which a solution was sought was equally artificial. Instead of confronting the questions of productivity and cost efficiency, Tuscan industry sought political support for a policy of reducing wages, of restoring the flow of government contracts, and of raising a protective barrier against foreign competition. The operation implied a decisive rejection of the Giolittian system, which was founded on expansion, high profit margins, and wage concessions. Giolittism had been the political formula of the northern industrial 'establishment'. Fascism seemed to offer an alternative.

If the rallying to the fascist cause of Max Bondi, Guido Donegani, and Luigi Orlando was based in part on the vulnerable position of the Tuscan economy, there were also important political considerations which justify the metaphor of Tuscan industry as the 'weak link'. The Tuscan industrialists, that is, were particularly attracted by the assistance of the *fasci* because they were 'outsiders' in the industrial association. Confindustria remained firmly in the control of the Italian industrial élite represented by Agnelli, Alberto Pirelli, and Ettore Conti, by Fiat and the Banca Commerciale.[34] Now, the opposition within Confindustria between an 'intransigent' current led by Ansaldo and Ilva on the one hand and the 'establishment' led by Fiat should not be overstated. When confronted by the greater challenge of the labour movement, the two sides stood united. Moreover, when the recession began to bite deep in late 1920 and as the state showed itself increasingly unable to provide the guarantees for property demanded by all of industry, Confindustria as a whole moved sharply to the right and its leaders began to enter into increasingly cordial relations with the fascists. None the less, there were important differences founded on commercial rivalry and political jealousy, on contrasting personal temperament and economic outlook, on differing profit margins and political styles, and on different regional origins. Firms such as Ilva felt that their own more urgent demands for strong government intervention were short-circuited at the ministries by an industrial organization sensitive to other priorities and informed by the need to defend different interests. No longer confident of their ability to rely on Confindustria or to influence the state, the industrial 'outsiders' were more readily persuaded of the advantage of subversive self-reliance.

POLITICAL CHALLENGE

The actual evidence of the relations between heavy industry and the *fasci* is fragmentary, giving only occasional glimpses of the particular directors and companies involved. In part, the limits of the evidence are due to the discretion of the police authorities, who in their reports refer to the importance of contributions from industry but seldom mention names. Of course, the possibility that more candid documents compromising influential people were removed from the record during the regime is not to be excluded, particularly as there is a conspicuous paucity of material for such major industrial centres as Piombino and Portoferraio.

An additional factor is the discretion of industry itself. In the case of the *agrari* it was possible to discover ample evidence of their political position from lists of those enrolled in the movement; from public speeches made by leading landowners such as Serragli, Sarrochi, and Aldi Mai; from reports of the deliberations of the AAT and its branches. In the case of industry, these sources of information are generally precluded because the major industrialists seldom joined the movement or campaigned publicly on its behalf. Particularly in the case of industry, then, it would be necessary, in order to establish a more detailed picture of the collusion between the *fasci* and leading businessmen, to have access to the archives of individual companies and of the economic ministries, as well as of the Ministry of the Interior, which is so fruitful a source of information on the political preferences of farmers. Unfortunately, however, these sources have not been made available. Chance too has played a role. Large sections of the archives of the *questori* and prefects of the principal industrial centres, Livorno and Florence, were destroyed in the Second World War, while certain important press sources, including the fascist weekly *A Noi* of Livorno have been lost.

None the less, there is sufficient proof to establish a number of points. First we know that heavy industry in Tuscany, and particularly the armaments sector, provided massive financial aid to the Florence *fascio* and to the *Popolo d'Italia*. Secondly, there is direct proof of collusion with the fascists and the 'economic unions' by a number of leading Tuscan companies, including Ilva, Montecatini, the Mineraria, the Officine Galileo, and the Orlando shipyards, and such leading representatives of Tuscan capital as Max Bondi, Eduardo Rotigliano, Guido Donegani, Count Costanzo Ciano, Giuseppe and Luigi Orlando, Count Rosolino Orlando, and Luigi Pasqualini. The politics of Serragli, a leading member of the Boracifera, need little further elaboration. Moreover, the specific forms taken by the aid to fascism forthcoming from industry and the quid pro quo received in exchange suggest that fascism was seen by Tuscan industry as a means of compensating for its long-term structural weaknesses as well as of assuming the relatively more obvious task of re-establishing the control of Tuscan management over its work-force. With regard to the more immediate question of the challenge of the labour movement to the traditional powers of management over the workplace, there is no lack of documentation. Finally, the very systematic lack of certain types of evidence of industrial involvement with the fascist movement suggests certain tentative conclusions with regard to the particular nature of the pro-fascism of the Tuscan board rooms.

The actual involvement of big industry with the reaction began in Florence in the early postwar months when funds for the Citizens'

Defence Alliance and its anti-socialist militia were supplied by the armaments manufacturers. The identity of the industrial patrons of the Alliance, unlike the landlords who took part, is characteristically veiled in mystery, apart from a certain Leone Poggi, who played an active role.[35] Banchelli, however, reported that leading companies donated money in large quantities and that by the summer of 1919 the Alliance had obtained an operating fund of 1,000,000 lire.[36] Banchelli's estimate may be exaggerated, but the larger point of the deep commitment of large companies to the venture seems beyond dispute. The premises of the Alliance in Via Cavour were provided by the courtesy of the Mineraria, which had already gained a wide notoriety for its intransigent attitude to the demands advanced by its workers.[37]

It seems probable, moreover, that Ilva was involved. During the early months of the fascist movement up the autumn of 1920, Ilva was perhaps the most important patron of the *Popolo d'Italia*, and was largely responsible for Mussolini's political survival during this period of low ebb in his fortunes.[38] Certainly the *Nazione*, the Florence daily owned by Max Bondi,[39] gave considerable effort to a campaign to rally the middle classes to put a halt to the advance of socialism, and the paper devoted ample space to the Alliance and to its activities, programs, and meetings.[40] That Ilva was interested in Mussolini, and Bondi in the Alliance, is partly explained by the very unstable bases of the company's holdings and the fact that the steel industry, which was the core of Ilva's prosperity, was one of the very first sectors to be depressed, registering a sharp fall in output as early as 1919.[41] Indeed, such an explanation would also account in part for the intransigence of the Mineraria, which was largely dependent on its iron mines at S. Giovanni Valdarno.

In addition to the company interest of Ilva in the *fasci*, a personal motivation was at work involving the political ambitions of Bondi and Luzzatto, who stood in 1919 as candidates for the crumbling Liberal parties. Was it by chance that the first public political activity of the Alliance took place at that time? Certainly the idea of deploying paramilitary force as a prop to a hotly contested electoral campaign was all too congenial to Luzzatto. In his constituency in Arezzo province he hired what were squadrists in all but name to harass and assault his socialist opponents and break up their campaign rallies.[42]

The identity of the other patrons of the Alliance and its militia, which was the regional nucleus from which Tuscan squadrism evolved, cannot be determined. It is significant, however, that major industrialists had already begun to finance violent counter-revolution at such an early stage of the postwar crisis. Moreover, this industrial support was forthcoming in Tuscany not only on behalf of Mussolini and the *Popolo d'Italia* but also on behalf of an organization – the Alliance – that was to become the instrument of the violent and extremist reaction of the *agrari*. The fact, too, that industrial support was channelled to a Florentine organization established a pattern of domination by Florence that was to be a distinguishing feature of Tuscan fascism. Florence was a logical choice as the regional capital and the seat of the administrative offices of many major firms. For companies with interests scattered across the eight provinces, a centralized regional movement provided the best guarantee of an adequate protection. Once established, the position of the capital as the directing centre of the reaction proved self-reinforcing.

Although sectors of Tuscan industry had begun to organize armed self-defence, the Alliance and then the Florence *fascio* were, until late 1920, a tiny reactionary vanguard. Even the *agrari*, as we have seen, did not rally immediately to the new movement, and industry had its own motives for caution in its relations with the *fasci*. Indeed, until the autumn of 1920, fascism existed nowhere in Tuscany outside of Florence.[43] Attempts were made to establish fascist branches in a variety of centres from the middle of 1919, but these had come to nothing. The experience of Pisa, a city in the vanguard of the Tuscan reaction, is emblematic of the failure of armed patriotism to take root outside Florence before the end of 1920. The Pisa branch, founded in 1919 by Luigi Malagoli upon the shifting sands of students and veterans, lapsed rapidly into total quiescence. The city, Malagoli lamented, lacked 'men of initiative and energy', and the population lived in 'shameful apathy' and complete indifference to the social message of the *fascio*.[44] So abject was the failure of fascism at Pisa as late as September 1920 that Umberto Pasella, the national secretary of the *fasci*, charged with the still thankless task of attempting to breathe life into the Tuscan organization, exploded in frustration at his correspondents in Pisa:

I have had no news of your fascist activity. What are you doing? While from every corner of Italy there is a resurgence of fascism, you lie asleep. Is it possible that you are unable to overcome your dull apathy?[45]

What was true of Pisa, however, was equally true of the other pioneering centres of Tuscan fascism – Livorno, Piombino, and Siena. There, too, the tiny bands of enthusiasts for the cause complained until November, as the fascist organizer Persindo Giacomelli lamented, that 'we find it impossible to move'.[46]

The full extent of the failure to build the Duce's organization in the region after eighteen months of futile efforts was revealed in the first week of November 1920, when an attempt was made to summon a regional congress of the Tuscan *fasci di combattimento*. In the event, only two *fasci* apart from Florence – Pisa and Siena – were officially represented, while still unorganized groups of followers at Livorno and Piombino sent messages that two further branches were in the process of establishment. In the remainder of the eight provinces there was literally no fascist organization. As the Florentine organizers of the assembly confessed, the idea of holding an official congress had to be abandoned because of the 'tiny number of officially constituted *fasci*' and the 'insufficient number of representatives'. What took place in lieu of a congress was a simple 'exchange of ideas'.[47] The first wave of fascist expansion in Tuscany beyond the capital did not occur until after November 1920, and then took place in the major industrial centres and provincial capitals, but on Florentine initiative and under the guidance of the Florence *fascio*.

With regard to industry, the change in fascist fortunes required the development of three further premises. Of these the first was the onset of the economic recession throughout the economy from the middle of 1920. Secondly, there was the movement for workers' control culminating in the occupation of the factories. The third factor was the collapse of industrial confidence in the ability and the determination of the state to protect the besieged interests of property. It was with the rapid development of these three overlapping crises that the initial support from the most intransigent wing of Tuscan industry, represented by Ilva and the Mineraria, grew into a broad consensus of the leading members of the Tuscan Industrial Association.

Since we have already considered the long-term structural basis for the postwar crisis of Tuscan industry, we must also examine the immediate threat to managerial control in the mines, metallurgical factories, shipyards, and steel mills posed by the labour movement. The economic crisis was a major background factor which conditioned politics and encouraged counsels of parsimony to prevail in the board rooms, even leading to the first *rapprochement* between the Alliance on the one hand and Ilva and the Mineraria on the other. It was the menace to property posed by the movement of workers' control, however, which transformed wage intransigence and a diffuse sympathy for interventionism, nationalism, and the *Popolo d'Italia* into a subversive political alliance with the *fasci*.

To understand the politics of industry, one must appreciate the militancy of Tuscan labour. As in the countryside, the war in the cities had done much to politicize the working classes. There as well, a climate of popular anticipation had been created that provided a rude contrast to the worsening reality of working-class life. Wages had been devalued by the astronomical increase in the cost of living that accompanied and followed the conflict.[48] The austerity and sufferings of an unpopular war, and the introduction of militarized discipline in the factories had been borne in the expectation that the victory would bring improvements. When instead the victory ushered in a time of hunger for many, there was a reaction of anger. For the working classes, the new conditions of life are not contained only in the drastic lag between price increases and the movement of wages. A particular feature of postwar life was the housing crisis in the towns. The building trade, on the one hand, had come to a halt during the First World War while, on the other hand, the industrial companies, swollen with war-time success, bought up vast areas of the urban centres from Piombino to Arezzo, transforming homes into commercial premises. In this process they both created and profited from a new boom in urban property speculation whose effects were overcrowding and homelessness, particularly as the property boom presupposed a substantial migration to the towns to fill new jobs in industry and commerce.[49]

That the clash between mass expectation and the worsening social conditions produced a major political upheaval was due, however, to a series of further circumstances which transformed discontent and deprivation into a sense of collective injustice. The crisis in popular living standards assumed a new political significance. One important factor was the blatant social inequality between the many who had lost so much during the conflict and the war profiteers who were visibly amassing enormous fortunes and building new industrial empires. The Italian ruling class, moreover, had dangerously discredited itself by the unbridgeable gap between its honeyed pledges and the reality of the peace, by the 'empty hands' with which it emerged from the peace conference, and by the display of its own vulnerability. Further, the industrial proletariat had grown enormously in numbers and compactness during the war-time industrial expansion, while the experience of military discipline in the factories and barracks provided new bonds of solidarity. In many factories the attempt to secure workers' cooperation for the war effort had greatly strengthened and extended the very institutions – the internal committees – that were to form the basis for the factory council movement and workers' control.[50] And not least, there was the influence of the bolshevik revolution, which provided a new faith and self-confidence.

The new militancy that followed the war took on a variety of forms. We have already seen the socialist electoral victories that swept the countryside. The same was true of the industrial cities as socialist deputies and then socialist town councils were returned in the principal centres – Livorno, which was known as 'the little Russia', Piombino, Prato, Pistoia, Portoferraio, the mining towns of the Maremma and the Monte Amiata. Florence and Siena communes were held by the Liberals, but these were centres of commerce and finance, of government bureaucracy and the service sectors rather than of industry. The working class voted massively for the PSI.

Beyond the electoral challenge to Liberalism and property, the urban centres also presented a strong, if wholly spontaneous and localized, insurrectionary current. This first took expression in Tuscany, as elsewhere in the peninsula, in July 1919, when bread riots broke out in every town and city of importance. The term 'riot' accurately conveys one aspect of the movement as angry crowds stormed and looted shops and demonstrated in the streets. From the standpoint of property, however, there was a more ominous side to the movement that revealed a more conscious political purpose at work. More significant than the sacking of shops was the organized setting up of local soviets to control the distribution of goods.[51] For a few days throughout the region private enterprise was abolished in commerce. Had the PSI organized and led the movement, the consequences for property could well have been more serious and longer lasting, but the party chose instead to ignore an 'anarchic' movement it had not created, whose disorderly character it condemned, and whose spontaneous outburst it considered the antithesis of the disciplined march to socialism.[52]

The spark of rebellion, however, was not extinguished in 1919, but burst again into insurrection at Viareggio in May 1920 and at Piombino in June. Once more, the PSI stood aside while the revolts collapsed, but the uprisings in two industrial centres were a clear demonstration of popular discontent. At Viareggio a brutal display of police violence when a *carabiniere* shot and killed a man during disturbances at a football match touched off an immediate and violent reaction. A general strike was proclaimed at once, while the populace stormed the police barracks, raised barricades, and improvised a citizens' committee to take over the government of the city. In the end, the outburst came to nothing as the troops restored order, but an indication had been given of the depths of mass disaffection.[53]

The events at Viareggio were soon followed by the more violent uprising of Piombino. The announcement in June by Ilva of large-scale dismissals in the steel mills (500 men were to be laid off) led to a slow-down strike and industrial obstructionism in protest. The strike itself ended in defeat, largely as a result of the local division in the labour force between the socialists and the anarcho-syndicalists, and the failure to organize a united resistance to management. The collapse of the strike, however, was interpreted by the anarchists as a summons to action – a summons which found wide support among the steel men. A massive rebellion began that was only put down in blood by the army. Still not entirely demoralized, the steel workers demonstrated their solidarity with the men killed by calling a general strike.[54]

The movements of 1919 and the summer of 1920 were clear demonstrations of the determination of Tuscan workers to change their lot. They were all the more menacing to the Italian bourgeoisie in that they were paralleled by the display of subversion within the army, first at Fiume, and then in the Ancona mutiny of 1920; by the crumbling of the 'parties of order' in elections; and by the eruption of agrarian protest. Most directly menacing to industry, however, was the powerful movement within the factories themselves that threatened to undermine the hierarchy of the workplace and to abolish the prerogatives of management.

The movement for a revolutionary industrial democracy is most clearly identified with the factory council movement in Turin and its theoretical elaboration by the *Ordine nuovo*. By the postwar years, however, the aim of workers' control had become the heritage of the Italian labour movement as a whole, and a central preoccupation not only of Turin manufacturers but of Confindustria as a whole. For Gino Olivetti, secretary of the employers' organization, the council movement, far from being an exotic local problem of Turin, was a spreading revolutionary cancer which had come dangerously close to infecting the entire body politic. In the spring of 1920, Olivetti explained the gravity of the danger to Italian management as a whole. 'There cannot', he declared,

> exist two powers in one factory ... It is not possible, in other words, for us to tolerate within the factory the existence of a power autonomous of management which, apart from management and against its will, makes decisions and issues directives.[55]

In Tuscany we have already noted the struggle waged by internal committees in the textile industry to assume some of the traditional prerogatives of management. We have also dealt with the attempt in northwest Tuscany to expropriate the 'marble barons'. In heavy industry, where there was a longer tradition of organization and militancy, the issue of control of the place of production was raised in a more systematic and conscious fashion. This was most obvious in Florence, where there was a direct link between the metal workers of the Officine Galileo and the factory council movement in Turin, and where the socialist weekly the *Difesa* closely followed the political line of *Ordine nuovo*. Livorno, too, was a focal point in the attempt to establish democratic workers' control. There shipyard workers, engineering workers, metallurgical operatives, and dockers set up internal committees in their plants with the clear determination that they should assume the day-to-day management of production. In 1920 the Livorno workers further demanded the abolition of differential pay scales, the end of piece-rates, a ban on overtime, and the right to veto the dismissal of employees.[56]

Apart from the militantly revolutionary workers in Florence and Livorno, the question of the democratic control of industry was at the centre of the demands of the labour movement in other sectors of heavy industry, even if not always in so self-consciously subversive a way. A major example, at the heart of Tuscan enterprise, was the miners' struggle. Unfortunately, there is not enough information to follow the various phases of the contest equally well in all areas of the region. There are detailed accounts, however, of at least one crucial zone – the mineral basin of southern Tuscany, involving over 7,000 miners in Grosseto province and the Monte Amiata area of Siena province, and affecting such major companies as Montecatini, Monte Amiata, the Boracifera, and the Siele.

In this zone, where even union recognition had yet to be gained, the postwar militancy of the workers was dramatic. From the first months of 1919, the miners of the two provinces were united on the basis of a 'unitary manifesto' elaborated by the Interprovincial Miners' Federation.[57] Of the eleven points of the manifesto, a number involved the traditional trade-union question of hours, wages, and conditions of work. Even these issues were, however, unwelcome in this darkening period of the regional economy when industrial plans for reconversion to peacetime were based on low wages. Equally menacing to the employers were a number of demands intended to effect a long-term revision of the bargaining-power relation of capital and labour. Thus the unions, in an attempt to establish greater job security and to end the worst abuses, called for child labour legislation, the eight-hour day, a minimum wage guarantee, and the abolition of piece-work. The issues on which negotiations were finally shipwrecked, however, were two that potentially established effective workers' organizations and a measure of direct influence on company decision-making. These two demands were for the recognition of the miners' unions and of the Interprovincial Federation, and for the establishment of 'internal committees'. It was, in fact, the rejection on 23 June by Montecatini of the demand for union recognition which directly caused the great miners' strike that brought the extractive industry in the two provinces to a halt.[58]

The strike that began in June became the most bitter and protracted in the history of the area, lasting five months and finally ending in November with virtually total victory for the miners when the last company capitulated to the demands of the 'manifesto'.[59] Much was revealed about the nature of the struggle and the depth of the issues at stake by the fact that for both sides the November settlement was regarded as only a provisional arrangement with the substantive issues still to be decided. Above all, the agreement to set up 'internal committees' established the institutional framework for a potential industrial democracy, but left undetermined their precise powers and terms of reference. The transitory nature of the November accord was unknowingly underlined by the continuing rampant inflation: in a situation in which wage gains were so rapidly devalued, the miners were more readily concerned with the crucial question of power.

At any rate, the miners' congress held at Grosseto in February 1920 was far from content merely to register the victories of the autumn. Marino Magnani, who, together with Pietro Ravagli and Giovanni Merloni, was the leading figure of the Interprovincial Federation, stated unambiguously that the battle had just been joined. The task awaiting the movement was to determine the concrete powers of the newly established 'internal committees', whose institution was only the first step in the conquest of the mines. At the Grosseto congress the miners' movement declared a frontal assault on the power of management.

The struggle that developed in 1920 faithfully followed Magnani's orientation and the suggestion of the Grosseto congress. In June, the mercury miners of the Monte Amiata zone in a five-point memorandum demanded the 'expansion of the functions of the internal committees to include a direct voice in the control of the industry'.[60] Similarly, the miners of the Montecatini company called for the 'socialization' of the mine shafts and urged the expropriation of the owners, with the mines to be run as workers' production cooperatives.[61] With such demands the miners' movement in the middle of 1920 had in effect called for an end to private property. Understandably, Montecatini, Monte Amiata, and the Boracifera were unwilling to accept the vision outlined by the Interprovincial Federation. Italian capital was not prepared to see its principal sources of vital raw materials run as workers' cooperatives. As we shall see, the owners of southern Tuscany found in squadrism a welcome instrument for the restoration of hierarchy in the pits, the purging of the labour force, and the destruction of the labour organization.

Southern Tuscany, however, was not the only area where the issue was drawn in so limpid a manner. Though information on the specific demands of the miners' movement in other provinces is more incomplete, it is clear that parallel struggles with equally revolutionary objectives took place in the other two great mining zones of Tuscany – Elba Island and the upper Arno Valley (Arezzo) – and involved Ilva and the Mineraria, as well as a number of lesser companies. The lignite mine at Ca Maggio (near Pratovecchio) was occupied in May 1920 by the workers, and the secretary of the Arezzo Chamber of Labour wrote in triumph,

For the miners of Pratovecchio it was a success. They were the first of the 120,000 miners in Italy to take direct control of the mines.[63]

They had formed, he continued, 'the first mining soviet in Italy'.[64] Very similar was the position in the iron mines of Elba, where the miners demanded expropriation of the owners and adopted as their slogan, 'The mines to the miners!'[65]

An important feature of the movement of the miners, however, was that for all its militancy it was hopelessly divided. Not only were the miners' disputes not effectively related to the contemporary struggles of other sectors of the working class, but there was not even a reliable coordination among the various zones. The strikes in the mines of Grosseto and Siena provinces took place with little reference to the struggles in Arezzo or Livorno. Even the Interprovincial Federation of southern Tuscany was an improvised and haphazard affair. As a result, the companies affected were able to conclude separate agreements with their workers. The extreme case was that of the Boracifera, where the workers launched a movement confined to a single company. The Boracifera strike began on a different date from those in other companies and was concluded on the basis of separate terms. The idea of a united labour front was not even contemplated. Thus the miners' movement, for all its revolutionary fervour, was defused and its potential dissipated.

It was in contrast to the divided miners' strikes that the agitation of the other great category of Tuscan industrial labour – the 15,000 metallurgical workers – assumes its true significance as the high point of the postwar labour movement and as a decisive moment in the politics of industry. The metallurgical workers had a much longer experience of agitation and a far more developed organizational structure. The Tuscan metallurgical workers also had a clear strategy for the achievement of industrial democracy, and an articulated network of factory soviets. They also had the strategic advantage of large-scale factories concentrated in the most important urban centres, including Florence and Livorno. It was the struggle of the metallurgical workers, culminating in the Occupation of the Factories in September 1920, which came closest to knitting together the entire labour movement, from the railwaymen to the quarriers and from the textile workers to the men at the Officine Galileo, into a single assault on the established order. It was their struggle above all that was a watershed in the history of the regional and the Italian labour movement, as well as in the political fortunes of the *fasci*.

Since the events of the Occupation are well known and there are full accounts of the movement both nationally and in Tuscany, we need not retrace ground so familiar.[66] Here we need only underline certain major points essential to our understanding of subsequent events in the region. One such point is that the events culminating in the actual Occupation began not as an offensive on the part of the unions, but as a counter-movement of their employers. The high point of the revolutionary advance in fact had occurred during the unsuccessful Piedmont strike in April (the so-called 'sciopero delle lancette').[67] In the end, the workers of Turin, after a prolonged general strike in support of the demand for a large measure of effective control by the factory councils, had been forced to capitulate when they found themselves isolated as the PSI and the CGL refused their support. By contrast, the events of the late summer began as the first stage in the industrialists' offensive. The confrontation, in fact, began with the decision of Alfa Romeo to lock its gates.

The timing of confrontation had been chosen by the industrialists with great circumspection. The late summer of 1920 coincided with the onset of the first effects in Italy of the economic crisis, so that economic trends had begun to shift the balance of negotiating power in favour of management. Further, the April defeat had seriously depleted the resources, financial and moral, of the metal workers' union, FIOM. The locked gates in Milan found the most advanced section of the Italian labour movement already demoralized and with its leadership divided by bitter recriminations and differences of aim that proved to be the seeds of party schism. As a result, the employers were hopeful of exploiting the internal division of a movement now strategically disorientated.

If such considerations of timing governed the initial lock-out, the aims of industry with regard to the labour force were clear. Confindustria hoped to reconquer positions of power that had been grudgingly abandoned in the months of struggle. Looking beyond the central question of control in the factory, management hoped to deal a decisive blow to the socialist advance by defeating the most militant sector of the industrial work-force.

At the same time, the employers hoped, by pushing industrial conflict to an open show-down, to define a new relation with the state. Giolitti had shown himself wholly out of step with the mood of industry when, at the centre of his government program, he had put a series of fiscal reforms. Particularly unwelcome to industry were the provisions calling for the compulsory registration of stock in the name of the owner, and for a parliamentary investigation into government war-time expenditure, with the confiscation of undue profits. Each of these two reforms was estimated to bring dozens of billions of lire within the purview of the tax collector.[68] The aim, Giolitti claimed, was 'to make those who own most, pay most'.[69] Not surprisingly, Ilva, which was already in deep crisis, which was so profoundly involved in financial speculation, and which had made such handsome profits in the war, was among the first to protest.[70]

Giolittismo, as a form of Liberal rule based on wage concessions and on neutrality in industrial disputes, was no longer aceptable to business at a time when recession counselled wage retrenchment and when the working class, no longer under reformist political leadership, had adopted the goal, not of *money*, but of power. With Giolitti again in office, industry intended to compel the state to abandon its neutral stance in favour of active intervention. In a clear confrontation, some reasoned, the premier would be constrained to call in the troops to safeguard property. Giolitti himself would bury Giolittism. The lock-out was thus both a frontal assault on the labour movement and a revolt against the Giolittian exercise of Liberal rule.[71] Thus, as the workers' reply to the lock-out – occupation – began in Turin and seemed imminent in Tuscany, the Orlando brothers sent what was, in effect, an ultimatum to the prime minister:

> For about two years now, discipline within the yards has been destroyed, together with all respect for Authority and Property.
>
> Despite repeated requests for protection, the government authorities both at Livorno, and in Rome have stood aside, with the result that industry has been forced, beyond what is just, to yield to the ever-growing demands of the working class. By now it is needless to point out that the motive of the agitations is purely political, and that the aim is to overthrow the social and political order.
>
> Conditions have so deteriorated over the past months that the seizure of the plants seems imminent.
>
> In such an extremity, and faced with such an eventuality, the undersigned renews his formal request to the government authorities to move in the troops to protect the plants. Giuseppe Orlando[72]

As is well known, Giuseppe Orlando's worst fears were realized. The occupation movement, begun in response to the challenge thrown down by management, acquired its own revolutionary dynamics. Overnight the idea of workers' control was translated into reality as production continued without benefit of management under the leadership of the newly created network of factory councils and internal committees. In Tuscan terms, every factory of importance in all the major centres – Florence, Livorno, Piombino, Portoferraio, Pistoia, Viareggio, Pisa, Arezzo, S. Giovanni Valdarno – was in the control of the workers.[73] Moreover, the movement had created a class solidarity never before achieved as the metallurgical workers were supported by the rest of the working class. Throughout the region the dockers, railwaymen, tram drivers, and miners came out on strike. Indeed, when the iron mine owners attempted to boycott supplies to the occupied steel mills at Piombino, the miners occupied the pits and secured continuing production.

Finally, and this was decisive from the standpoint of industrial politics, the government refused to intervene. The Tuscan industrialists did much to pressure the government to a trial of force. We have seen the letter of Giuseppe Orlando to Giolitti. In addition, in Livorno province the

Magona d'Italia warned of international complications if Giolitti failed to act, claiming that foreign technicians were being held hostage in the factories.[74] Most significant of all, the Tuscan Industrial Association, as government inactivity continued into the middle of September, officially and unanimously voted a motion of protest against Giolitti. A resolution was passed in which a central clause was one of 'protest against the method of struggle adopted, and against the absence of the government, with harm to existing social institutions'.[75]

Nevertheless, Giolitti persisted in doing nothing, even affecting a show of nonchalance by refusing to cancel a trip abroad or to alter his standing engagements. His reasons, as he explained in his memoirs, were that he feared the possible damage to property if force was used to clear the factories. Rather than risk a trial of strength, he preferred to allow the workers' movement to exhaust itself, relying on the reformist leaders of the CGL to bring about a restoration of order.[76] In the event, Giolitti's calculations proved justified as the union hierarchy was no less terrified of revolution than the men of property. A revolution was the antithesis of the bureaucratic perspective of leaders like Baldesi, who enjoyed the position of influence and privilege the CGL already had and were unwilling to risk it on behalf of a cause that, even if it succeeded, would result in a diminution of the authority of the existing trade-union officials. Indeed, the instruments of industrial democracy – the factory councils – were explicitly intended to absorb the functions not only of management but also of the unions.[77] As a result, the CGL and FIOM officials carried out what can only be described as sabotage of the revolutionary potential of the Occupation. They threatened resignation *en masse* if the party sought to provide a unified political leadership of the struggle. They also entered into secret negotiation with the employers, concluding an agreement that registered only wage and condition improvements, relegating the crucial issues of control and democracy to an eventual parliamentary debate over the heads of the workers in a forum where the reformists were firmly in control of socialist representation, and without a specified date for the debate to begin.

With such meagre results, after the hopes and sacrifices of the days of the Occupation, the outcome can only be termed a decisive defeat for the socialist movement, and one from which it never recovered. The workers were demoralized and disillusioned, the union organization was exhausted, and the divisions within the movement had been deepened to the point where a rupture was inevitable. The initiative had passed from the workers to their opponents.

In order to comprehend the rise of fascism, however, we must understand that, from the standpoint of the Tuscan Industrial Association (AIT) in 1920, the decisiveness of the events of September was far less apparent than appears in retrospect. A victory had been won, but the war continued. Even if they had taken the initiative in the autumn confrontation, the industrialists were dismayed at the strength and unity of the Occupation movement, at the resourcefulness of the workers, and at the public display that production could continue without management. Particularly worrying was the solidarity of the working class as a whole in response to the agitation of the metallurgical workers. In Tuscany there were even signs that the struggle was being taken beyond the confines of organized labour to the non-unionized and more amorphous lower classes that had revolted in the summer of 1919 and again at Viareggio in 1920. 'Red guards' were reported by the Pisa prefect De Martino to have been formed and sent outside the factory gates into the cities. Even more ominously, they began, according to De Martino, to make 'improvised excursions into the countryside violating the rights of property'.[78] In this there was raised for the whole regional bourgeoisie the spectre of a link between industrial and agrarian protest in the forging of a single revolutionary movement. The achievement of such a single movement could not, of course, be improvised by local 'Red guards', but required a long preparation. The fact that the attempt began to be made, however, can only have confirmed men of property in their conviction that the time had come to uproot subversion at its source.

The aftermath of the movement, furthermore, provided additional cause for alarm in Tuscany. Events in Florence, for example, were far from reassuring to management. The defeat, far from leading to passive resignation, began a process of radicalization in which the workers drew their own lessons from the recent experience, and the communist wing of the PSI made major inroads in the factories of the regional capital. The leaders of the internal committee at the Galileo joined the communist faction, as did the former editors of the *Difesa*, who founded the *Azione comunista*. Then in February, the metallurgical workers of the city voted a motion of censure against the reformist leadership of FIOM, and in the union elections soon after the communists won a majority of seats on the provincial council of the union federation. In the meantime, moreover, the electoral results of the autumn did nothing to provide the reassurance that the social crisis had been resolved in favour of the 'parties of order'.

What was finally decisive about the aftermath of the Occupation, however, was the proof, as industry viewed it, that the state was no longer a reliable instrument for the defence of their interests. In September, Giolitti had stood by impassively while property had been violated. The fact that the prime minister's political calculation and his reliance on the CGL officials had proved well founded was less important than the self-confirming belief that he no longer controlled events. It would be too simple to hold that the AIT had been seized by a 'Great Terror' during the Occupation so that when the state failed to offer adequate protection its members rallied to the self-defence militia organized by the *fasci*. Italian industry, forced to make major concessions by an increasingly confident and militant union movement, had taken advantage of the first major setback of the most advanced sector of labour, and of the increasing bargaining power of management as recession began to make itself felt, to begin its own offensive to re-establish control and eliminate the threat of an Italian revolution. In its offensive, however, industry wanted the guarantee of the possibility of deploying physical force to overcome resistance. Already in May 1920, the *Toscana*, a paper tied to Guido Donegani and Count Orlando, averred:

Instead of a prime minister to occupy Montecitorio, His Majesty ought to engage a sturdy dustman to clear the piazzas.[79]

For the new role, Giolitti had been tested and found wanting. The *fasci* provided a subversive alternative.

REACTION

Until the autumn of 1920, the squads of the Alliance commanded by Zamboni, Banchelli, and Dumini had been kept in demoralizing inactivity at Florence while elsewhere in the region the armed reaction was non-existent as an effective political force. It was in the aftermath of the Occupation and the local elections that the *fasci* began their first wave of expansion. Not surprisingly, the new activity first took place in the industrial cities and provincial capitals. *Fasci* sprang up at Siena, Lucca, Livorno, Prato, Piombino, Abbadia San Salvatore, and the island of Elba. Characteristically, in almost every case the initiative in the new venture came from Florence, and the founding of most local *fasci* could be traced to a visit from the Florentine leaders.[80] This first period of success was soon to be overshadowed by the development of the movement of the *agrari*, which gave the Tuscan movement a far greater geographical extension, more stable sources of finance, and the bulk of its mass base. None the less, it is important to recall that the *fasci* began their growth outward from Florence to the other provincial capitals and industrial centres. It was as an industrial movement that fascism first developed into a regional political force, and this component remained an important source of strength. It is by examining the rallying to the reaction of the leading companies that we can appreciate the full power of the Florence *fascio*, and understand the rise of the movement in whole areas of Tuscany where the agrarian question was secondary. Fascism was industrial in Livorno and Massa-Carrara provinces, in southern Pisa province, in the zone of Monte Amiata, and in the mining areas of Arezzo and the Maremma.

The evidence of the involvement of the leading industrialists and the major companies of the region with the fascist movement, incomplete as it is, leaves little room for doubt. From the end of 1920 funds were forthcoming in large amounts from the leaders of the AIT, directed above all to the *fascio* of the capital. From Florence Umberto Banchelli reported that,

> We saw them arrive at the headquarters of the *fascio* in Piazza degli Ottaviani, those well-known faces, surly and grasping, of the former military suppliers. They were carelessly dressed and shod, but held the inevitable shiny coin of great value in their fingers; and we were forced to accept because of our need to have the means necessary to crush an evil worse than they.[81]

It was due in large measure to the conveyance of funds from landlords and industrialists in the capital that, according to the prefect Carlo Olivieri, the *fascio* in Florence had such a unique and powerful role. As he wrote to the Minister of the Interior,

> The wide favour that the fascists enjoy among the populace is due to the fact that the population has been freed by fascism from the general and unending abuses to which it had been subjected, for at least two years, at the hands of the communists.
>
> The fascists in this province are numerous and well organized as nowhere else in the Kingdom, and they are heavily supplied with funds by industrialists, property owners, and merchants.[82]

Unfortunately, the amounts given by individual businessmen have not been traced. Some of the mystery can be removed, however, by a clear demonstration of pro-fascism at Livorno following the 'legalitarian strike' of the summer of 1922, called in protest against fascist violence. On that occasion a public collection was taken to reward those who had worked as 'volunteers' to break the strike. Now, if we remember both the political purpose of the strike and the active role of the *fasci* in the recruitment of blacklegs, there is little doubt that the 10,000 lire raised were a gesture of support for the 'economic unions'. Indeed, it was just at this period that the fascist unions were beginning to achieve their first successes at Livorno. In fact, the local fascist branch and the 'Benito Mussolini' and 'Ugo Botti' action squads made donations. Alongside the local *fascio* and squads in the lists of contributors appeared the names of the foremost representatives of the Livorno industrial bourgeoisie: Count Rosolino Orlando, president of the AIT; Guido Donegani; Giuseppe and Luigi Orlando; Ezio Foraboschi, president of the Livorno Chamber of Commerce; Vittorio Chayes, president of the Associazione fra Industriali, Esercenti e Commercianti di Livorno; and the 'members' of the Unione Industriale Livornese.[83]

The political preferences of a number of major industrialists were not confined, however, to financial largesse. A few joined the movement as active militants. Edoardo Rotigliano, a leading figure at Ilva and the man chosen to represent Tuscan industry in the deliberations of Confindustria during the Occupation of the Factories, was an enthusiastic member of the Florence *fascio*.[84] Rotigliano was also deeply involved in land speculation and reaction in Pisa province. At Castiglioncello he was chairman of a company of property developers (the Società proprietari della pineta di Castiglioncello) which liberally funded the local *fascio*, with whose leaders he was reported to share a 'common faith'.[85] The involvement of Ilva in the success of fascism was also evident at Piombino, where the political secretary of the *fascio*, Antonio Pacinotti, a former lieutenant in the *arditi*, was the secretary of the Ilva shipyards.[86] The deputy director of the yards, Renato Lanza, was a member of the *direttorio* of the *fascio* at neighbouring Riotondo, together with another manager at the yards, Gino Scamiglia.[87] Still at Piombino, the director of the steel company Magona d'Italia, Arturo Piccioli, 'the arch enemy of union organization', was a fascist activist. Perhaps in deference to the difficulties of labour relations, however, Piccioli confined his fascist militancy to Florence. At Piombino he remained a Liberal.

Gino Luzzatti, the president of Monte Amiata, 'was one of the pioneers of the fascist movement in the Amiata area',[88] while one of the leading shareholders in the company, Adolfo Baiocchi, was president of the Abbadia San Salvatore *fascio*.[89] In Baiocchi's case, personal and company motives for his pro-fascist sympathies may have been inseparable, as he had also been mayor of the mining town of Abbadia until his defeat by the socialists in 1920. Prince Giovanni Ginori Conti, relative to the president of the Boracifera, Prince Giovanni Ginori Conti, was enrolled in the Florence squads.[90] The Liberal deputy, Dino Philipson, a wealthy and powerful figure in finance with close ties to industry at Pistoia, was active in the life of the Florence *fascio*, and was president and paymaster of the Pistoia fascist branch.[91] The Orlando brothers declined themselves to don black shirts, but the managers of their shipyards were among the most influential members of the fascist union movement.[92] The director of the Galileo and vice president of the AIT, Luigi Pasqualini, actively sympathized with the Florence *fascio* and encouraged the 'economic unions'.[93] Meanwhile, in the dispute we have discussed over the attempt to disarm Renato Ricci and his Carrara squadrists, Guido Donegani personally intervened with the prime minister to protect the squads and secure the revocation of the order confiscating firearms.[94]

Furthermore, if one wanted to construct an argument for the existence of a military-industrial-fascist complex in the region, no better example could be found than that of the leading role in the fascist movement of Count Costanzo Ciano.[95] Ciano was a figure of the very first rank in the Livorno *fascio*, and was fascist deputy from the city. He was also a member of the upper Livorno bourgeoisie, an admiral and graduate of the Livorno naval academy, and a man with strong personal and financial ties with Luigi Orlando. With contacts ranging deep into the military and industrial hierarchies, and yet without formal managerial responsibility, Ciano was the ideal 'front' man for the members of the AIT. Indeed, Count Ciano as fascist deputy was tireless in the corridors of parliament and of the ministries in the search for contracts, concessions, and favours for industry, and above all for the Orlando shipyards.[96]

At the same time the Tuscan Industrial Association, in agreement with the AAT, officially aided the fascist movement in one of its most important demagogic strokes to win popular support in the cities – the campaign to lower prices. In the middle of 1921, the fascists announced that they, unlike the impotent state and the blackmailing trade unions, had the solution to the problem of the soaring cost of living: they would simply patrol the shops, forcing the owners to lower the prices of goods of major necessity. The *Riscossa* loudly announced that the squads would treat any shopkeeper who put up prices 'on a par with the bolsheviks'.[97] The fascist press published lists of drastically reduced prices for goods, while the squadrists, amidst great fanfare, took to the streets to ascertain that the fascist decree was observed and to close by force any store that broke its order.[98] Obviously so clumsy an effort to stem the rising cost of goods was of little genuine or lasting efficacy. In the short term, however, prices were dramatically, if temporarily, reduced, and the fascists gained a reputation for decisiveness and action in the defence of the beleaguered consumer. What is ostensibly less clear is why the *fasci* were willing to offend the legions of anti-socialists engaged in the retail trade, and why the squads were allowed by the authorities to violate property rights and the spirit of free enterprise. The mystery is resolved, however, if one recalls that, before taking action, the *fasci* had secured the support of the Industrial and Agrarian Associations, and that these in turn had obtained the consent of the prefects and the shopkeepers' organizations.[99] In this way the AIT effectively, if not publicly, aided the fascists in one of their most important publicity campaigns.

Another longer-term and public way in which Tuscan industry actively encouraged the *fasci* was through the press. The *Telegrafo* of Livorno, and the *Nuovo giornale* and the *Nazione* of Florence – the three leading Tuscan dailies – were all closely tied to Max Bondi, and all conducted extensive propaganda campaigns on behalf of the fascist movement.[100] The editors of the Florence dailies, Carlo Scarfoglio of the *Nazione* and Athos Gastone Banti of the *Nuovo giornale* were particularly energetic. Scarfoglio from the end of the war had called for a 'resurgence' of the bourgeoisie against the perils of socialist and Catholic bolshevism.[101] And when, after the setbacks of the 'Red years' and the spectacle of impotence provided by the state, the fascists began to attack the evil at its source, the Liberal journalist in the pay of the steel industry took up the cause with enthusiasm. As the squads began their 'redemption' of town and countryside, the *Nazione* had little but praise. On the morrow of the 'events' of Ferrara, Bologna, and Lucca, the *Nazione* observed that,

Fascism is inevitably a reaction that is often bitter and violent – sometimes exaggeratedly so – but always against an emotional background of maximalist violence. It is the sharp weapon with which the middle class arms itself when it rises up against the force of destruction ... Its youth does not save it from mistakes, but it does deliver it from the boredom in which many venerable parties doze. In any event, it is another phenomenon ... of that restoration of national values which is the most comforting sign of the end of the year just past.[102]

And with the new year the papers found further cause to praise the fascists for their 'youthful energy'.[103] Scarfoglio and his paper supported the movement at every phase of its campaign against the cost of living, that 'magnificent agitation, which is conducted by the "Fasci" in a truly appealing fashion'.[104] In the spring parliamentary elections, the *Nazione* urged its readers that 'at least one fascist must emerge victorious from the polls'.[105] Moreover, when the Bonomi government in the middle of 1921 briefly showed signs of adopting tougher measures to curb squadrist violence, Carlo Scarfoglio waxed indignant in the editorial columns, taking the authorities to task, especially for Sarzana.[106] It was no unmerited accolade when the Siena fascist paper the *Scure* chose Scarfoglio and the *Nazione* as the models of the new Italian journalism that the fascists should emulate.[107]

If Tuscan heavy industry thus adopted the fascist cause as its own; if many leading representatives of the AIT enrolled in the movement; if the Industrial Association backed fascist initiatives, supplied the *fasci* with funds and shielded them from the authorities; then inevitably much was expected in return. The first and most obvious use of the squads to industry was, in the words of the *Nazione*, that of the 'sharp weapon' to excise subversion from the factories. Here, there is a parallel between town and countryside. Just as the countryside in 1921 witnessed a wave of politically motivated evictions, so in the cities a far-reaching purge of the labour force began.[108] Here economic crisis and political choice overlap. Some of the plant closures and sackings were undoubtedly a simple response to recession and the crisis of overproduction. It is crucial, however, to avoid the facile economism of the upper reaches of the GGL, who argued with Gino Baldesi that Italy was the proletariat of world industry and that, if Italian industry was to survive, the workers would have to acquiesce in fierce wage reductions and lay-offs. For Baldesi, the economy obeyed immutable laws and the working class had only to submit.[109] Such a view, in addition to its serious political consequences, prevents an understanding of events in the Tuscan cities and of the part played by the *fasci*.

A wave of factory closures swept the region from early 1921, and those who remained at work experienced wage and job insecurity, and unfavourable contracts. Part of the motivation of employers was economic. In addition, however, the industrialists had a profound political objective which was revealed in the timing of the closures and in the factory reforms that accompanied them. The industrialists used the recession to establish a new regime in the factories. Political militants were dismissed; the internal committees, factory councils, and socialist trade-union organizations abolished; and the various gains achieved in the strikes of 1919 and 1920 eliminated.[110] At the same time, where it was feasible, the workers were reclassified on the basis of innumerable categories with wage differentials for each. The purpose was to destroy the unity that had been achieved among the workers. Even the *Nuovo giornale*, the friend of property, noted in an analysis of events at the ceramics firm Richard-Ginori that the aim of the reclassifications was 'to sow confusion among the workers'.[111] In this work the *fasci* played a central role in overcoming the resistance to the new order; in providing harassment and intimidation; in recruiting the unemployed to create a new and apolitical work-force; and in creating a network of 'company unions' that were the institutional framework for industrial hierarchy, discipline, and obedience.

How this process worked is familiar from events in light industry and in the countryside. An important illustration of the usefulness of the *fasci* to heavy industry is provided in the upper Arno Valley in the iron and lignite mines near S. Giovanni. The use of the squads there by Ilva and the Mineraria to discipline the labourers was outlined by Savini, the chief of cabinet at the Ministry of the Interior. Savini wrote:

> It is reported that the local *fasci*, having intervened in the dispute, prevent the freedom of activity of the workers, making impossible any organizational action aimed at obtaining by legal means improved working conditions. There are further complaints of continuous and systematic intimidation and violence carried

out against the workers to force them to join the fascist orgnization. In the last days fascist squads seem to have kept watch at the works exit of the iron mine at S. Giovanni and to have beaten those who refused membership in the CISE.[112]

Not content with the results obtained by such means, the management in early 1922 decided on a lock-out in order to carry out a thorough purge of the mines and a restructuring of the systems of internal control. Any idea that the pit closures were dictated by economic crisis is belied by the course of events. The negotiations for the re-opening of the mines in this case were conducted exclusively with the fascist unions, whose members were offered employment with wage *increases* and improved physical conditions of work,[113] but at the price of political disarmament through membership in the fascist corporations and the abolition of the formerly militant socialist unions.

Such dealings were profitable both to industry and to Mussolini. The managers rid themselves of internal resistance to authoritarian rule in the mines as well as creating a powerful means – the 'economic unions' – for long-term repression, surveillance, and propaganda. In turn, the *fasci*, in a time of mass unemployment, gained the prestige, first of all, of having gained what the socialists could not achieve – the reopening of the pits. The *fasci* even obtained monetary benefits for the labourers, and, thanks to their contacts with the employers, won the power to distribute employment and patronage. To refuse to join the fascist unions was to be jobless. Not surprisingly, by the middle of 1922, the prefect of Arezzo reported that in the former socialist stronghold of S. Giovanni 'nearly all' of the 3,000 miners then at work had taken up membership in the fascist miners' union.[114]

Interestingly, the usefulness of the *fasci* to Ilva and the Mineraria in Arezzo province was not limited to the restoration of control over the work-force. In addition, the *fasci* took up the economic defence of Tuscan industry by lobbying the government for special concessions, tax relief, and favourable contracts. The fascist paper of Arezzo, the *Giovinezza*, openly espoused the cause of the Mineraria. After outlining the industrial crisis, the paper proposed that

> The state should in its turn help to reduce the cost of lignite, our great national product, with the reduction of freight charges, and should give even greater encouragement to these industries by accommodating them in every way, even by selling the product itself.
> It is essential that the Fascist Parliamentary Group look into the affair, in order to forestall a grave calamity that looms over our Arno Valley.[115]

Faithful to this suggestion, the fascist deputies, led by Dario Lupi, brought up in parliament the case for aid to the Mineraria and made representations to the ministries.[116] The taxpayers were asked to overcome the weaknesses of Tuscan industry by direct subsidy.

Perhaps the best opportunity to observe the mutually profitable dealings between fascism and industry was in the complex negotiations surrounding the Orlando shipyards at Livorno.[116] The affair was particularly significant because it provided the local *fascio* with its first opportunity to make inroads among the local workers. The local *fascio*, though one of the earliest to be founded, had led a difficult existence in the stronghold of the Tuscan industrial working class. As late as the summer of 1922, when the movement in many zones was consolidating its control and laying the local bases for the seizure of power, the Livorno fascists had neither effective control of the city nor a functioning union movement. The cooperation of Luigi and Giuseppe Orlando came at a crucial moment in the life of the Livorno movement.

For the Orlando brothers the affair of the closure was also an important moment – the final episode in the long process of negotiation with the Ministry of the Navy. Having been commissioned in 1916 to construct eight torpedo boats, the Orlando firm applied after the war for a re-negotiation of the terms of the contract. Pointing to the rising costs of materials and labour, the brothers applied to the Navy for 23,000,000 lire to cover the 'cost overruns'.[117] When the application was rejected at the end of 1921, the company responded by putting 1,000 workers on short-time and a three-day week. The Livorno prefect Edoardo Verdinois, himself involved at every stage of the negotiations, testified that the sole purpose of this action was to apply pressure on the government to grant the demands of the brothers.[118] Their strategy was that the decision to work short time would not only slow up defence contracts still in progress, but would also exacerbate the already serious unemployment problem in the city, thereby creating a dangerous situation for 'public order' that the government could resolve only by yielding.

Having obtained nothing in July, the shipbuilders, Verdinois reported, decided to intensify the pressure by beginning a lock-out.[119] That the purpose of the closure was to force the hand of the state was clear from the single condition laid down by Giuseppe Orlando for the reopening of the factory – receipt from the prime minister of a letter promising that the dispute with the naval ministry would be resolved 'according to the principles of equity'.[120] Naturally, the timing of the closure was not accidental, but followed the 'legalitarian strike', that last outburst of socialist militancy, which revived anxiety about the 'Red peril'.

At this point the fascists intervened. For them the occasion was a golden opportunity to extend their influence into the Livorno working class by a fulsome display of their concern for workers, their independence of the bosses, and above all, their demonstration that only they, and not the socialists, could guarantee employment. The importance the *fasci* attached to the event was underlined by the fact that their action was directed by three of their most influential leaders – Costanzo Ciano, Dino Perrone Compagni, and Giuseppe Bastianini, deputy chairman of the Partito Nazionale Fascista (PNF). The fascists began by publicly deploring the closure and declaring that their union would represent the Livorno workers in securing the re-opening of the yards.[122] Meanwhile, the fascist union organization in the city, dormant until this time, began an extensive propaganda campaign, helped by the members of the Livorno Union of Industrialists, who supplied them with funds.[123]

To dramatize the issue further, in the first week of October, Perrone Compagni issued a public ultimatum to the Orlando brothers: failing an immediate opening of the yards, the squads would march on Livorno, seize the plants, and resume production.[124] Clearly the fascist dictate cannot be taken at face value. It was hardly imaginable that the squads were to be used against one of the leading industrialists in Italy, and one known to be sympathetic to their cause. The idea seems even less plausible if we remember that Ciano himself had major interests in the Orlando yards and was closely tied to the brothers, while the managers of the yard were leading members of the Livorno *fascio* that was to direct the occupation.[125] On the other hand, as a demogogic stroke, pre-arranged with the Orlando brothers, it was brilliant.

The cleverness of the arrangement, however, did not stop there. For the company, the threat was of great value in speeding a favourable outcome in the negotiations with the state. The involvement of Admiral Ciano in the dispute was a valuable asset in the dealings with the naval ministry, and the threat of a military occupation of the city was finely calculated as political blackmail. The government, weak and vacillating, had much to fear from a major military action by the squads and was glad to avoid confrontation by yielding to the monetary demands of industry. The fears of the state authorities were given clear expression by Verdinois, who urged concession to the Orlandos to obtain a peaceful re-opening of the yards. 'I ask the government', the prefect wrote,

immediately to consider the proposal put to me by comm. [Giuseppe] Orlando. By responding to his request, we would avoid a new and most serious disruption of the public calm and without the fascist party's being able to profit thereby, as the government would only be replying to a memorandum which required a reply in the next few days. It is well to note that by the location and plan [of the city], the fascist occupation is an easy matter either by land or by sea, even leaving aside the consideration that any measures of the authorities might be frustrated by the employees [of the yards], including the highest officials, as among the managers there are active members of the *fascio*. In any case, to prevent the invasion of the

Orlando Shipyard would require a preventive occupation by at least 400 men ... Furthermore, it would be necessary to bring in all the reinforcements necessary for the city and for road blocks, as one can expect a powerful convergence of fascists from all the provinces of Tuscany.[126]

From the standpoint of the Orlando brothers, the episode was a total success. The day after receipt of the message from the Livorno prefect the Ministry of the Navy granted new defence contracts to the company and concessions over the outstanding dispute. Moreover, in separate negotiations conducted between the brothers and the PNF, a mutually agreeable settlement was reached for the re-opening of the yards with future representation of the workers to be the exclusive right of the tractable fascist unions.[127] For the employers the victory over the socialist organizations, achieved by the combination of the lengthy lock-out and the intervention of the *fascio*, was complete. Eugenio Filippi, the Livorno secretary of FIOM, even drafted a letter that was, in effect, a declaration of surrender. Taking note of the re-opening of the yard under fascist auspices, Filippi wrote that the Orlando workers,

since the long privations of the lock-out, the suppression of all effective freedoms of agitation and propaganda, and the crushing of the labour organization no longer allow any illusion about the possibility of resistance to protect the rights of labour, hereby decide:
(1) to make one last attempt to secure from management better working conditions than those announced...
(2) to submit without argument to the terms that the Orlando firm wants to impose from above ... reserving the right to take action ... as soon as the freedom and the rights of the labour organization are no longer suppressed.[128]

For the fascists, there was the immense prestige of having been seen to reopen the yards by an act of decisiveness and at odds with the bosses. Meanwhile, for the longer term, the *fasci* had gained new powers over employment in Livorno and the means to create a whole clientele system. Furthermore, at a time when Mussolini was contemplating a far bigger march than one on Livorno, he had found an opportunity to test the resolve of the state and to find it wanting.

CHAPTER 4

THE PETTY BOURGEOISIE AND THE SQUADS

A vital factor in fascist success in Tuscany was its ability to attract mass support not only in the countryside but also in the towns. Just as in the provinces, however, so too in the cities the initial appeal of fascism was very limited. Until late 1920, when the socialist assumption of power in local government directly menaced vested interests and the economic crisis began to bite, Mussolini's movement had little impact in the urban centres of the region. The first urban fascists were those who were earliest affected by the postwar social and economic dislocations and who were most deeply opposed to the defeatism and lack of patriotic fervour of the socialist party – young demobilized junior officers and students. Especially for the veterans, the *fasci* seemed a welcome contrast to a home front that was apathetic or hostile. The state made virtually no provision for the men it discharged from the army, while in the postwar economic retrenchment there were few jobs for the returning veterans and almost none that offered the status and responsibility of a war-time command. Demobilization proved a traumatic experience as the return home ended in disillusionment, hardship, and unemployment.

This experience had a subversive impact upon the rank and file of the army, upon the peasants and workers who had been conscripted into the trenches. It had a very different effect upon the élite of the newly unemployed – the young ex-officers. These were the sons of the patriotic middle classes who had volunteered, who identified with the interventionist cause, and who had grown accustomed to positions of authority. They had seen the socialist opposition to the war effort as treason, and as a vivid illustration of the dangers of the 'enemy within'. The conflict over the war, moreover, did not end with the armistice. It continued into peace-time as the PSI made responsibility for intervention, for the defeat at Caporetto, and for the hardship that ensued a major theme of post-war political propaganda. A symbolic gesture that was particularly galling to the sensibilities of former volunteers was the willingness of the PSI to include deserters among its candidates for office. The young squadrist Piazzesi, for example, recorded the outrage felt by patriotic youth at the candidacy in 1919 of the deserter Francesco Misiano for election as deputy in Turin and at the campaign in Florence of the deserter Nello Tarchiani for a post on the city council.[1]

In striking contrast to the indifference of the state and the moralizing opposition of the left, the far right from the outset lionized the veterans and especially the officers' corps, the 'aristocracy of the trenches',[2] for whom no praise was too fulsome or too florid. The Citizens' Defence Alliance and the early Tuscan *fasci* held public festivities and demonstrations in honour of the demobilized units, applauded them as they returned, and championed the practical initiatives of the veterans' association, including such ventures as the campaign to lobby employers to sack their women employees in order to hire discharged ex-combatants instead.[3] At the same time, the movement offered an immediate and practical solution to the problem of veterans' unemployment. In the creation of an armed militia the *fasci* provided scope for the skills of former officers, now to be employed in civil war against the PSI. In the squads there was the possibility of escape from tedium and economic hardship, and of renewal of the excitement, comradery, and heroism of the trenches. And all was in the name of patriotism.

It was noteworthy that war veterans, especially young ex-lieutenants and captains, made up a significant portion of the fascist membership and of the directing cadres of the movement throughout the period of the rise to power. Former enlisted men were inclined to have viewed the war as a compulsion and were likely to be of an altogether less patriotic political persuasion, while senior officers – older, better connected, and already well embarked upon their careers – were not so devoid of prospects. Where high-ranking demobilized or retired officers did join the *fasci*, they generally did so not as active squadrists or fascist organizers. Livorno was the exception. At Livorno Ciano was the fascist deputy, major general Giulio Corradi became provincial secretary of the movement,[4] and colonel Constantino Leo was an important member of the executive of the Livorno city branch.[5] More typically, generals and colonels filled honorary posts in which they lent the movement the respectability of their rank and the influence of their connections. Thus, for example, colonel Antonio Minuti was the honorary president of the Lucca *fascio*,[6] colonel Giuseppe Vertri was president of the Lari *fascio*,[7] colonel Bionaghi was a member of the electoral committee of the Florence branch,[8] and colonel Bulgarini sat on the finance committee for the Siena provincial federation.[9] Senior officers also, as we shall see, played a key role as external collaborators with fascism.[10]

Active posts within the movement and especially in the squads were generally reserved for younger and more junior men, who became the political secretaries, squad commanders, and office holders in branches throughout the region. In the towns in particular, where unemployed officers gathered in search of employment, the evidence is overwhelming. At Florence, for example, the original *fascio* in 1919 was made up 'for the very most part' of veterans.[11] Indeed, the first headquarters of the branch was the office of the Florence Veterans' Association,[12] whose president, Ferdinando Agnoletti, was for some time a leading member.[13] The involvement of demobilized officers was emphatically not just a phenomenon of 1919. Of the 14 members of the *direttorio* of the Florence *fascio* in the middle of 1921, five were former officers.[14] Of the political secretaries of the organization up to the March on Rome, four had been army captains – Italo Capanni, Carlo Pierelli, Luigi Zamboni, and Guido Carbonai.

Nor was the deep involvement of demobilized lieutenants and captains restricted to the capital. At Siena, Nazzareno Mezzetti, the former socialist and a leading figure in the fascist offensive in southern Tuscany, had obtained a commission during the war, and was the founder and leading figure in the Siena Veterans' Association.[15] In January 1921, of the six members of the *direttorio*, three had been officers – Manlio Ciliberti, the prime mover of Sienese fascism; Enrico Bruni, the political secretary; and Eufrasio Coppini.[16] In the new *direttorio* elected in the middle of 1921, the commander of the squads, Carlo Pacini, had been a captain.[17] The initial advice of Umberto Pasella to the local organizers of the Siena branch had been to make the *fascio* 'the vanguard of the section of the Veterans [Veterans' Association]'.[18]

Just as at Florence and Siena, so at Pisa the Veterans' Association was closely linked with the local fascist branch, while the president of the Association, Stefano Scotti, was an early and leading fascist.[19] Of the eight members of the *direttorio* of the Pisa *fascio* in the middle of 1921, six were ex-officers, including the political secretary, Bruno Santini, and the deputy secretary, Franco Landogno, both of whom were demobilized captains.[20]

In the same manner, the political secretaries of such important *fasci* as Livorno (Marcello Vaccari), Portoferraio (Edilio Zoni), Pontedera (Piero Marcello Pierazzi), Lari (Gino Bendinelli), Massa Marittima (Paolo Santini and Filippo Rossi), San Sepolcro (Italiano Giorni), Monterotondo (Alberto Tappari), Piombino (Antonio Pacinotti), Ravi (Umberto Marino), Lardarello (Guido Gallori), and Capannoli (Giotto Giotti) were all former lieutenants or captains.[21] Other important figures in the fascist movement from the junior ranks of the army officers' corps were Dino Castellani, the leading organizer of squadrism in Grosseto province;

Tullio Tamburini, commander of the Florence squads; Manfredo Chiostri and Italo Capanni, the first fascist deputies from Tuscany; Renato Ricci, the guiding figure of the *fasci* of Massa-Carrara; Dario Vitali, commander of the Massa-Carrara squads; Carlo Scorza, the 'boss' of Lucca; and Federigo Florio, the dominant figure in the Prato *fascio* until his death on an expedition.[22]

Beyond the commissioned officers, a number of former NCO's were particularly prominent in the Tuscan counter-revolution and deserve mention. Dino Perrone Compagni himself, the 'Grand Duke' of Tuscan fascism, had been a corporal. Amerigo Dumini, the creator of squadrism in the region and political assassin without rival, had served as a sergeant. Gennaro Abbatemaggio, a major influence in the reaction at Florence, had served as a sergeant in the *arditi*.[23] Thus the leading public figures of Tuscan fascism, the organizers of the local and provincial fascist organizations, and the commanders of the principal squads were combat-trained former officers or NCO's of the Italian army. This backbone of veteran officers stiffened the military efficiency and capacity for violence of the movement and greatly facilitated the relationship between fascism and the troops responsible for public order.

Another fruitful source of membership, particularly vital in the early months, was the student population at the universities. At Florence, Siena, and Pisa, the students contributed significantly to the strength of the reaction. Manlio Ciliberti, the first secretary of the Siena *fascio*, reported that the students were the initial nucleus of the movement in the city.[24] Indeed, Ciliberti himself was a law student, as was another of the six members of the *direttorio* in January 1921, Angelino Giandi.[25] Even in the middle of 1921 when other and more substantial groups had come forward, the university at Siena continued to play an important role in the local *fascio*. Chiurco, by then the secretary, was nearing the end of his medical studies, and the deputy secretary, Leone Ciullini, was also enrolled at the university. Giovanni Tramontano and Mario Boccini, both members of the *direttorio*, were students of medicine and law respectively, while Serafino D'Antona, another protagonist of Sienese fascism, was a young instructor in surgery.[26] The *Scure* was absolutely accurate when it reported in the autumn of 1921 that

At Siena – we must note the fact – our movement has been nourished and invigorated by the class of students. They brought us the élan of their energy and of their flourishing intellect. What is more – and this is peculiar indeed – the most active and the most resolute of all were the doctors and the medical students...[27]

Pisa presented much the same picture. From the founding of the *fascio* in April 1920, students and young instructors were prominent. In the original *direttorio* of five, two – Francesco Salinas and G. Biscioni – were enrolled in the university.²⁸ Indeed, during the summer vacation in 1920 the *fascio* lapsed into total inactivity.²⁹ The importance of student members to Pisan fascism was not, however, a product of the immaturity of the movement. At the high point of the squadrist offensive in the middle of 1921, of eight members of the executive committee elected in May, Santini, the political secretary; Andrea Mendici; and Paolo Isola were students, while Landogno was a professor in the humanities faculty.³⁰

There is no evidence that the fascists were part of a student movement as such, or that they had elaborated a program of university reforms to appeal to the particular grievances of students.³¹ To the young sons of the Tuscan bourgeoisie, however, there was much in the movement that was attractive – its cult of youth, heroism, and action; and its patriotic fervour. It also gave vent to the frustrations of an educated élite whose degrees and titles were no longer, in the straitened economic circumstances of the time, a guarantee of employment consonant with their own sense of self-importance. For students who were also war veterans – and many Sienese and Pisan fascists were, like Ciliberti and Santini, demobilized officers – the motives for pro-fascist sympathies were multiplied. For the sons of major property owners, very direct material interests were involved.

In addition to students and war veterans, the *fasci*, from the very early period of their appeal in the cities, attracted into their ranks the uprooted and idle of all social classes. The cadres of Tuscan fascism throughout our period were heavily composed of men, shiftless and unattached, for whom the counter-revolution offered employment, self-esteem, lucrative connections, and a new platform for men of broken political careers. Many influential Tuscan fascists were former revolutionary socialists who, like Mussolini, had broken with the party over the war issue and then found themselves, after the armistice, without a following. Umberto Pasella, who played a central role both nationally and in the Florence *fascio*, was of this number.³² He began his career as a socialist leader in Ferrara until he left Emilia in obscure circumstances after leading a disastrous agitation in 1910. He then established himself at Portoferraio, first as a juggler and sleight-of-hand artist, and then as an anarchist leader, until again a major political fiasco urged his departure for Florence. In the capital Pasella briefly retired from politics and became a wine merchant. With the outbreak of war, Pasella broke definitively with his revolutionary past, and made himself useful to the authorities by becoming an informer for military intelligence and denouncing his recent comrades. It was the founding of the *fasci*, however, that offered him an escape from the ruins of his political career. But Pasella was far from being alone in his political apostasy. Other foremost fascist leaders in the region were former revolutionary socialists – Alfredo Frilli,³³ Idalberto Targioni,³⁴ Dino

Castellani,[35] Bruno Frullini,[36] and Nazzareno Mezzetti.[37] Curzio Malaparte was a renegade from the Republican Party.[38]

Beyond the politically uprooted, there were the hangers-on of all classes and persuasions, upwardly mobile in aspiration, but without concrete prospects. One example of this group of *declassés* was Persindo Giacomelli, who began 1919 in search of work.[39] Giacomelli had been a crane operator at the steel mills of Piombino until 1910, when he emigrated to America. There he failed to find the golden opportunity, working as a machine operator for a printer and as a clerk in a store until he returned to his native town after the war. With a wife, two children, and wages of 11 lire a day in the spring of 1920, Giacomelli had appealed to Pasella to find him a job as a messsenger boy for the fascist central committee in Milan. By the end of the year, however, important interests began to subsidize the Piombino *fascio*, and its founder obtained a far better *sistemazione* than that of messenger boy in Milan. Soon he become a political influence to reckon with; had titles, money, and responsibility; and travelled the length and breadth of the region on expense account.

Giacomelli was far from atypical of the rising leadership of the Tuscan reaction. Dino Perrone Compagni too began the postwar period in circumstances far from satisfactory to a man on the extreme periphery of the aristocracy who insisted on being addressed as Marquis.[40] He was the descendant of a family that had once owned land, the remnants of which he lost himself in gambling debts. He enlisted in the forces in the war, and rose to the rank of corporal, though he never served at the front. Returning from the army, however, he found only unemployment for a time and then a position as a clerk in the offices of the Veterans' Association. It was only from this time that his personal fortunes began to improve, until by late 1921 he had become the most powerful politician in Tuscany, above the law and with vast resources and a private army at his command. Moreover, with his new contacts, Compagni, the 'Count of Culagna', was soon able to move into business as well and to recoup the family fortunes.

The case of Tullio Tamburini[41] was perhaps even more striking. Tamburini, originally from the countryside near Prato, had moved before the war to Florence, where he dissipated his small inheritance in a life of pleasure. Thereafter he had lived as a vagabond calligrapher who frequently slept in the open and rounded out his income by petty crime. Seeing his chance in the war, Tamburini enlisted and rose to the rank of officer, with three medals for valour, though his military career was marred by a trial for fraud. Discharged after the armistice, Tamburini found himself once again adrift in the café world of Florence, plying his prewar trades until he was rescued by his friend and associate, Dumini, and was recruited into the squads, where he rapidly established a reputation for heroic cruelty, and earned the nickname of the 'Great Club'.[42]

Pasella, Giacomelli, Compagni, Tamburini, Dumini – these were five of the foremost architects of squadrist terror and fascist 'redemption'. They were illustrative of a whole category of displaced men of ambition who found in their willingness to use violence the key to upward mobility and influence that was denied through conventional channels.

Of these five, Tamburini most nearly approached the dark criminal underworld of the provincial capitals in which the fascists also recruited. Tuscan fascism fished heavily in the troubled waters of organized crime. The usefulness of men with long experience in the use of force and few inconvenient scruples with regard to its application was evident in the work of the squads, and nowhere in Italy were such men more eagerly sought than in Tuscany, where the movement met with so little success through the traditional methods of political competition. The attractiveness of squadrism to the underworld was equally apparent, and was underlined by the police. Inspector General Di Tarsia reported from Siena, for instance, that the *fascio* was a point of convergence for large numbers of convicted criminals.[43] The reasons Di Tarsia underlined for the fascist militancy of the 'veterans of crown property' were partly psychological in that the squads offered an outlet for those who enjoyed violence.[44] More convincing was his view that membership in the *fasci* was the ideal cover for criminal activities, as it provided a 'safe conduct pass' from the police and impunity from the law.[45] Dumini, during the period of his disgrace and expulsion from the PNF during the summer of 1922, gave vivid expression to the value of the fascist membership card as the passport to judicial impunity. Recalling his past of violence, he pleaded with Michele Bianchi to reinstate him in the party:

They want me to appear before the jury as a man expelled from a party for which I committed the offence. That means a certain conviction.[46]

The most notorious representative of organized crime in Tuscan fascism was Gennaro Abbatemaggio, a leader of the Florence *fascio* and a famous *camorrista*. Born in Naples in 1883 to a skilled worker in the shipyards and a seamstress, he had ambitions far beyond the 4 lire a day his father earned. From early adolescence he moved into a life of delinquency. Finding work as a stable boy and then coachman in the employment of wealthy local families, he repeatedly organized the theft of their valuables. In 1899 he joined the camorra as a 'tough' (*piciotto*). Having passed through the standard apprenticeship as extorter, burglar, pimp, and 'fixer' of elections, he was promoted to the general staff of the

Neapolitan underworld in 1903 and earned the nickname of 'Gennaro the scoundrel' ('Gennarino 'o nfame'). Arrested and convicted for burglary, he accepted a pardon in 1910 in exchange for giving evidence for the prosecution. Thus in 1911 Abbatemaggio emerged publicly as the star witness in the great anti-camorra Cuocolo trial. Breaking the vow of silence, he exposed the inner workings of Neapolitan gang life and testified against his former associates, denouncing the 'bosses' of the camorra for theft, conspiracy, and murder.[47]

Forced to leave Naples after the trial and a further spell in prison, Abbatemaggio enlisted in the *arditi*. Demobilized after the war, he arrived in Florence and rapidly found in Mussolini's movement ample scope for his ambition, his violent skills, and his willingness to kill. On the executive committee of the Florence *fascio* he was not alone in possessing a criminal past. A colleague was Ferdinando Spinelli.[48] Another was Castellani, whom the police described as 'an individual of no sincere political convictions and of dark morality, once enrolled in the socialist party and now in the pay of the *fasci*'.[49]

For the criminal, escape from arrest and prosecution was not the only advantage of fascist membership. In addition, vast sums of money contributed by nobility and big business circulated in the tills of the movement. The point is that these funds, being secret, were not accountable, and could be easily diverted from their intended purposes by those highly placed. Indeed, in a movement with no accountability from below, in which secrecy about the precise provenance and amount of political contributions was essential, and in which convicted felons played a powerful role, the temptations to confound personal gain and political militancy were great, and the opportunities numerous. Even fascist sources indicate that the coffers of the movement were frequently plundered from within. A succession of financial irregularities punctuated the history of many of the more powerful *fasci*. One of the more clamorous of these scandals involved the well-known criminal Castellani, provincial secretary of the *fasci* in Grosseto province, who was removed from his post in the spring of 1922 when an investigation revealed, in the words of the Grosseto prefect, 'irregularity and lack of decorum with respect to the use of moneys belonging to the common fund'.[50] Similarly, at San Sepolcro the commander of the squads, Dindelli, was reported to have misappropriated large sums.[51]

Particularly at Florence, where the stakes were largest, the atmosphere of financial irregularity was heavy. So persistent were the rumours and allegations that Achille Starace personally conducted an investigation into the finances of the *fascio* in late 1921. The investigation lasted three months, but proved inconclusive as Starace found himself hampered by violent opposition at every step, and ended by having his life threatened.[52] A further and more successful investigation, in the spring of 1922, culminated in the dissolution and reconstruction of the Florence branch of the movement. The enquiry revealed a general state of maladministration and corruption, although specific allegations were carried no higher than the accountant Giorgio Cimadori, who was accused of having embezzled 1,000 lire.[53] Of all the financial scandals, however, the most famous was that of the national collection organized by the movement on behalf of the eighteen *camerati* killed on the disastrous expedition to Sarzana. The collection raised several hundred thousand lire, not one of which was received by the families intended.[54]

Furthermore, the squads themselves were ideal instruments not only for punitive expeditions but also for extortion, protection rackets, and sheer plunder. To appreciate this aspect of fascism in Tuscany, one need only read between the lines of the report of the special investigating committee under Guido Carbonai that dissolved the Florence *fascio* in the spring of 1922. The committee wrote that

Fascism must remain a movement of ideals, for the economic and moral rebirth of our nation; it must not be a band of mercenaries and pretorian guards who, for love of lucre, assassinate, rob, and plunder.
Fascism must be a movement of sacrifice and disinterestedness.
One must not join us in the hope of a paid position, or a seat on the municipal council, or a post in parliament, or in the hope of covering, with our membership card, a past of very dubious morality.
Every individual who joins us must earn his keep from his work, because, my friends, the time has ended when a group of tyrants could care for itself with the daily distribution of a few beatings.[55]

Not uncommon were the squads that, in the words of Dino Perrone Compagni, 'have acquired the habit of visiting restaurants or hotels, and of leaving without paying'.[56] In the same spirit, squadrists who travelled by rail refused to pay their fares, and threatened the lives of ticket collectors who pressed the issue. This, reported the Minister of the Interior, was not a case of isolated incidents, but had become a 'continual and systematic abuse'.[57] Alternatively, if the blackshirts needed motor vehicles for transport, they simply requisitioned them at gun-point.[58] The Florence squadrists regularly ended their outings in drunken debauches at their 'garden of Eden' – a dingy third-class hotel reserved as their private brothel.[59]

If students, ex-combatants, and 'veterans of crown property' formed the initial plebeian base of fascism in the Tuscan cities, there were other groups that became increasingly involved with the movement as the reaction gathered momentum from early 1921. These groups were a varied assortment of the urban petty bourgeoisie new to politics in Italy –

consumers and taxpayers; urban landlords and shopkeepers; clerks and lower civil servants; and the professional categories of doctors, lawyers, and engineers. Carlo Scorza reported that at Lucca it was this 'mass of the petty and middle bourgeoisie' that was the backbone of fascism – 'school teachers, professors, lawyers, engineers, doctors, officers of every description, pensioners, employees in the public and private sectors, small landlords, small industrialists'.[60] That these groups, traditionally unorganized, should have been pressed into political activism was a result, first of all, of their rapidly declining economic position. For those with fixed or slowly rising incomes, and for those with savings, the years of rapid inflation after 1915 marked a sharp decline in their standard of living. The depth of their crisis is indicated by the cost of living index, which rose above a base of 100 in 1913 to 365.8 in 1919 and 624.4 in 1920. A gram of gold cost 3.49 lire in 1913, but 5.82 in 1919 and 14.05 in 1920.[61] For white-collar employees, the mounting unemployment of the period affected them as well.

That the exasperation of these groups should have taken the political form of violent anti-socialism, however, requires some further explanation. Indeed, there were various factors which seemed to preclude the possibility of an alliance between the petty bourgeoisie and the armed reaction of the *agrari* and heavy industry. For the white-collar workers, for instance, it was their very lack of union organization that was a major influence in their declining economic position. They could be said to have had an interest in supporting unionization. Similarly, for the shopkeepers and tradesmen, their declining profits and low velocity of turnover were directly related to the falling purchasing power and living standards of the masses. For them, too, a redistribution of wealth might have had much to recommend it. Certainly, a political alliance with the ruling élites of the region was not an obvious solution to their dilemma.

In fact, the expression of hostility to advancing capitalism, to big business, and to big landed property had a deep appeal for this stratum of society. One of the premises of fascist success in winning recruits among the petty bourgeoisie was that it was not a re-edition of the established Liberal parties that were so clearly the instrument of the traditional ruling class. Fascism succeeded in part because of its newness and its claim to represent a reforming anti-capitalist populism independent of the bosses.

Nevertheless, if the rhetoric and program of the reaction included opposition to Italian capital, the practice of the *fasci* was exclusively anti-socialist. Here one contributing factor was a political error of the PSI, which failed even to attempt to appeal to the substantial grievances of these groups, so that it gratuitously alienated a social group that might have been neutralized to a greater extent. The socialist party, in its concern to preserve its proletarian identity, and in its deterministic conception of social evolution, had not developed an analysis of the class alliances necessary for an Italian revolution. As a result the working class was needlessly isolated in the postwar confrontation. The fascist solutions for the malaise of the petty bourgeoisie were facile and demagogic, but they contrasted favourably, in the view of the clerk and the grocer, with the silence of the PSI.

Beyond the errors of the PSI, however, there were very substantial reasons which led the petty bourgeoisie to see the chief threat to its position not from above but from below. One major factor which countered the possible economic arguments in favour of lower-middle-class support for a redistribution of wealth and unionization was that these strata saw the crisis facing them not only in terms of their absolute economic welfare, but also in the light of their relative social standing. The lower middle classes were profoundly conscious of enjoying a condition of comparative privilege which was threatened by the organizations of the working class and by the egalitarian principles of socialism. What enraged the petty bourgeoisie was not the existence of social hierarchy, but its own rapidly declining position in the scale.

Furthermore, the school teacher and the bank teller had no previous history of political or union activism, and enjoyed a work experience and background of socialization that stressed individual self-advancement, so that the collective and communitarian doctrines of socialism seemed menacing or at least incomprehensible. The fascists, by contrast, spoke to the consumer in his isolation and in terms that were simply understood. The fascist analysis of the crisis was simplicity itself: the high cost of food was the result of a wealthy and grasping peasant class that was holding the cities to ransom. This was the logic of the fascist agrarian program now seeking urban allies, and it appealed to the whole 'official' ideology of *mezzadria* that had never been systematically challenged and had deeply affected the thinking even of the socialists until they were faced in 1919 with the reality of mass agrarian protest. The pro-fascist press, orchestrated by Scarfoglio, attempted to mystify events in the countryside beyond all intelligibility. It was true, the *Nazione* reasoned, that the AAT was the organizing centre of the reaction, but the Agraria was the organization only of the middle strata of the countryside – the present proprietor and the small landowners.[62] And if the cause of inflation in the cities was so easily identified, the remedy was correspondingly obvious – destroy the institutions of the peasant conspiracy. In the meanwhile, the *fasci* offered to rescue the besieged consumer with their campaign to lower prices. In the major cities the *fasci* even opened stores of their own with goods at reduced cost, and set up distribution centres of charity to give olive oil and clothes free of charge to the destitute.

The barriers that divided the working class and even the most discontented sectors of the petty bourgeoisie were numerous and significant in any case. There was the deep opposition over the war issue between the patriotic middle classes, conscious of their war-time sacrifices, and the 'anti-national' PSI. There were differences as well of living style and education, of aspiration and organization – differences which linked the middle classes as a whole in opposition to the proletariat and the peasantry. A particular further source of friction between the socialist union movement and the unorganized petty bourgeoisie was the exasperation of the latter with the frequent postwar strikes, particularly in the public services. The stoppages of the post office, the trams, the railways, the hospitals, the offices of local government – all these created a degree of inconvenience which was seized upon by the right to portray a picture of socialism as synonymous with anarchy and disorder. As early as the postal strike of January 1920 when the Citizens' Defence Alliance organized volunteers to sort and distribute the mail, the social composition of those who came forward to break the strike was clear. At Lucca, for instance, the list of volunteers was composed of members of the local bar association, the Veterans' Association, and the retail traders' organization, together with clerks from a variety of local banks.[63] Not surprisingly, of course, the hand of big capital also played an encouraging role behind the scenes, as the banks gladly offered to release some of their employees for the purpose.[64] At Florence, too, one of the strike-breakers described his colleagues as 'clerks, officers, students, school teachers – the bourgeoisie, in short'.[65] On such occasions fascism donned the mantle of guarantor of order and public service.

In addition to their appeal to the petty bourgeois as consumer, to their defence of patriotic values, and to their protection of order, the fascists defended other long-term material interests of large numbers of the urban middle class – interests that were seriously menaced by the advance of socialism, and in respect of which there was little room for compromise between the two sides. Some members of the middle classes, for instance, owned small tracts of land in which they had invested their savings and which they ran on the basis of *mezzadria*. Their numbers, moreover, were swollen by the ability of some to profit from the war and to convert their money into land. The progress of rural socialism, which burdened the new owners with additional expenses on behalf of the tenants, threatened the viability of such ventures. Accordingly, small bourgeois property owners made common cause with the nobility in opposing a movement that both saw as dangerous. Urban and agrarian fascism merged.

For all those involved in the retail trade, there was also a massive competition from the socialist cooperative movement. One of the most important creations of the PSI was a network of consumer cooperatives. These cooperatives were organized and subsidized by the leagues and by the socialist-controlled local administrations. Thus the upsurge of socialist unions and of socialist electoral strength, based above all in the countryside, threatened the urban commercial classes with the possibility that a large part of the volume of their business would be removed. An indication of the threat is provided by the commune of Prato, where the socialist Cooperative Alliance had established by the middle of 1920 a network of 34 cooperatives to which 24,700 people had subscribed in a total population of 56,000.[66] It was estimated that the Cooperative Alliance had a turnover of 500,000 lire a month that was removed from private enterprise.[67] It is hardly surprising that the socialists in Prato, Pisa and elsewhere reported that the category of shopkeepers was heavily and enthusiastically organized by the fascists not only in the provincial towns and cities, but even in the villages and hamlets as well.[68] There the grocer took his stand with the landlord and the *fattore* against socialism. Moreover, the socialist paper of Pisa suggests, the reason was apparent:

The grocer is fascist because he no longer does a golden trade since the founding of the consumers' cooperative.[69]

It was this unwelcome competition that the *fasci* offered to destroy. In the province of Massa-Carrara the prefect stressed the importance of fascist violence as a means of destroying the cooperative movement:

It is reported that criminal actions of the fascists are carried out especially against the cooperatives. It seems that the tradesmen are not extraneous to the movement. By the repression of the cooperatives, which enforce price controls, they promise themselves higher profits.[70]

In this work the fascists were fully supported by the retailers' associations, which had every interest to endorse even the price campaign organized by the fascists, the AAT, and the AIT. Such a campaign enabled the merchants to compete in the short term with the cooperatives while the squads embarked upon the longer-term task of destroying the cooperatives movement root and branch. Since a number of shops were actually shut down forcibly by the blackshirts and since these shops were by definition those that defied the instructions of the tradesmen's associations, one may even suppose that the associations were not ungrateful for the chance to extend their organizational control by disciplining the renegades.

There were other major material interests of the middle classes that the *fasci* undertook to defend. For urban property owners, there were very heavy new tax burdens that had been levied by the socialist local and provincial authorities. The League of Socialist Communes, meeting after the massive socialist victories in the autumn of 1920, had adopted a series of principles deeply disturbing to those with property in the towns. In the first place, the socialist communes proclaimed that 'the Socialist administrations intend to represent the working classes exclusively' (though among the 'working classes' they included white-collar employees and technicians as well as industrial workers).[71] Going further, the communes declared that they intended to follow the principles of 'the new communist law, according to which the needs of the community stand absolutely above the right of private property'.[72]

The 'new communist law', moreover, was no mere declaration of abstract principle or intent. Using the tax powers at their disposal, the socialist local governments applied a series of new levies on urban wealth in order to finance a variety of social services and to effect a policy of redistribution. A whole range of progressive taxes was enacted – family taxes, business taxes, taxes on buildings, taxes on luxury items.[73] For example, the socialist town council of Pontedera instituted a family tax on all families with incomes in excess of 3,000 lire a year, with rates on a progressive scale from 4 per cent at the bottom to 8 per cent for incomes above 70,000 lire.[74] At the same time the Pontedera council announced that businesses with a volume of trade over 7,000 lire would be taxed progressively from a sum due of 780 lire at the lower end of the scale to 4,000 lire for businesses with a volume of trade over 35,000 lire.[75] Urban landlords, too, had been taken into consideration. A new tax was to be levied on the rent they collected, ranging from 4 per cent applied to a rent of 250 lire to 15 per cent on rents above 1,500 lire.[76] Since, clearly, there were those who fell subject to the new taxes in more than one capacity, it was obvious that a substantial portion of the incomes of the wealthy were to be used to finance initiatives for which their enthusiasm was not great – public housing, cooperatives, schools.

The urban landlord in particular had grounds to feel threatened. Not only was his wealth to be heavily taxed, but in addition the socialist-controlled local authorities carried out a series of policies that deeply encroached upon the rights of property. In Siena province, for instance, the assembled socialist communes announced in January 1921 that socialist mayors were to be empowered to requisition all buildings that were vacant or insufficiently used, to impose a rent freeze, and to prohibit by order the eviction of sitting tenants at the same time that all unions of personnel necessary for the carrying out of eviction orders – drivers, porters, messengers – were to be instructed to refuse to cooperate with such procedures.[77] Moreover, the Siena Chamber of Labour under Giulio Cavina embarked upon the organization of a tenants' league to resist evictions and to pressure the national government to requisition buildings 'in order to eliminate the outrage of seeing whole families homeless or living in hovels'.[78] Meanwhile a special requisition order was set aside for premises used as taverns, which were to be 'converted to purposes more conducive to the well-being of the people'.[79]

It was not surprising, then, that urban taxpayers' associations were formed in the major socialist-dominated communes of Tuscany for the express purpose of organizing tax resistance against the new local authorities. The specific class interests involved were apparent from the fact that among the groups officially endorsing these associations were such organizations as the Livorno Association of Building Owners and Administrators,[80] the Pisa Association of Building Owners, the Pisa Chamber of Commerce,[81] and the tradesmens' association of Prato.[82] The extent of the exasperation of the urban landlords and retailers was given by the Pisa Building Owners' Association, whose members deliberated 'in the face of this measure that disturbs the peace and of the resulting threat to paralyse the most important sources of the nation's wealth, to put up a determined resistance, and to be prepared to resort to whatever means are necessary in the struggle...'.[83] What was perhaps more interesting than the disposition to resist by 'whatever means necessary' was the fact that the taxpayers' groups joined hands with the leaders of agrarian and industrial reaction – the AAT and AIT – and that in the case of Prato at least the initiative in the new venture was directly taken by the local *fascio*.[84] In the new associations the shopkeepers and taxpayers were voting in effect to join the fascist offensive.

The support from tradesmen's and urban landlords' associations was expressed still more directly. The Florence prefect Olivieri reported that the tradesmen of the capital were among the leading contributors of funds to the local *fascio*.[85] The Prato shopkeepers' associations joined the wool manufacturers in their lock-out aimed at obtaining the dismissal of the anti-fascist police chief De Bernardis.[86] The Società fra Industriali, Commercianti ed Esercenti di Siena voted, as we have seen, to shield the Sienese squadrists from possible police action.[87] In addition, virtually wherever information is available on the social composition of the directing bodies of local *fasci* there is a heavy representation of the categories of retailers, landlords, shopkeepers and self-employed.[88]

Among the groups in the cities that enrolled in the *fasci*, special mention should be made of the railway employees. It was notable that railwaymen were in the vanguard of the Tuscan fascist movement. At Florence one of the prime movers of the second *fascio* founded in April 1920, as well as of the third and definitive *fascio* founded not many weeks later, was the railroad official Ezio Lascialfare.[89] Indeed, on the executive committee of the second *fascio* there were two other employees of the state railroads (Ezio and Mario Montanari),[90] while on the organizing committee of the third *fascio* three of the five members were railwaymen – Lascialfare, M. Montanari, and Guido Carbonai.[91] Carbonai, in particular was to assume a role of the highest importance in the Florence movement as fascist deputy, as director of the *Riscossa*,[92] and, for a time, as political secretary. Another important member of the *direttorio* of the *fascio* at the time of its maturity was Marquet Dionigi, the master of the Florence station.[93] Even in terms of numbers, the railway personnel were from the start a vital part of the reaction in Florence province. The prefect Olivieri underlined this fact in a report to the Ministry of the Interior.[94] The Florence *fascio*, composed of 3,600 members in May 1921, had a special branch for its 280 railway employees – a figure which made the railway *fascio* of the capital alone as powerful as any *fascio* in the province, apart from the capital. The railwaymens' branch was comparable in size to the *fasci* of Pistoia (350 members in May 1921) and Prato (300 members), which were among the strongholds of the reaction in Tuscany.

At Siena, the union of railway workers, founded in December 1920, was one of the first 'economic unions' in the province,[95] while in the Italian Chamber of Labour four of the eleven categories organized in fascist unions were railwaymen.[96] It was worthy of mention, too, that in the spring of 1921 two of the nine members of the *diretorio* of the Siena *fascio* worked as employees of the state railroads – Eufrasio Coppini and M. Consorti.[97]

At Pisa the fascist paper the *Idea fascista* singled out the railwaymen as one of the principal strengths on which fascist success in the province was founded. 'The victory of the Fasci', the paper told them, 'is in large measure your victory, and it is due to the large number of you'.[98] There was an official of the network in constant attendance in the *direttorio* of the Pisa *fascio* – Umberto Seisoldi until the middle of 1921,[99] when he was succeeded by Edmondo Patrizi, the Pisa station master.[100]

The active involvement of middle-level executives, represented by the station master, was apparent. The station masters of Florence and Pisa we have mentioned. In addition, the master of Arezzo station, Dante Lelli, was a leading squadrist,[101] while at Siena Coppi, the *capo gestione*, and Ferrini, master of the Asciano station, were important union organizers.[102] Further demonstrating its strength among junior executives, exemplified by the *sottocapi gestione*, the fascist union movement in October 1921 held at Pisa a regional congress of fascist *sottocapi*.[103]

The reasons that led to the fascist sympathies of railway officials were in

The petty bourgeoisie and the squads

part the usual factors that affected the middle classes — a declining economic standing, opposition to socialist lack of patriotism, and the defence of privilege. In addition, however, the railroads were the centre of a fierce class warfare of their own. The railway blue-collar workers — the manual labourers who laid the tracks, the workers who manned the depots, and, above all, the men who actually drove the trains (engineers, firemen, and brakemen) — were among the most militant sectors of the Italian working class, with one of the longest histories of organization and agitation.[104] In postwar Italy, their socialist militancy was particularly intense and menacing to the Italian ruling class. They were among the most active in support of other unions, and came out in force during the Occupation of the Factories. In addition, they conducted their own fierce struggle for wage improvements and for workers' control. In 1920, Schiavon, the most senior Tuscan railway official, faced the future with deepening gloom. Foreseeing an imminent and violent conflict, he informed his superior in Rome:

I shall deal with the question with all possible tact. But, since reasoning and persuasion are clearly unable to overcome the preconceived economic and social ideas of these hot-headed masses, or to dissuade them from a revolutionary political action which is now uncontrollable, and which even goes beyond the authority of their own leaders, we must think of preparing for the strike...

Here in Tuscany there is only a negligible and fearful minority that does not belong to the Red Union. One could say that nearly all belong to that union or sympathize with it. The last great strike increased their numbers. And loss of confidence in those who promise to support and defend them has done the rest...[105]

The chief issues, as Schiavon outlined them, were not monetary, but political. The conflict revolved around two great questions. The first was the demand of the unions that all personnel who had broken strikes in the past be dismissed. The second was for direct workers' control. The railway workers demanded to elect from among themselves the men they wanted to act as foremen and managers, and they claimed that they would obey only orders given by railroad soviets and 'depot councils'.[106] From Pisa the prefect reported at the same time that the idea was circulating of pushing the issue to a final confrontation, with the aim of 'taking possession of the railways and running them on behalf of the workers'.[107]

The lines of division in the conflict were clear. At the Florence locomotive depot, the prefect reported that on the one side were the manual labourers, firemen, and drivers, while on the other side were the foremen, the superintendent, the director of the depot, and the director's assistant.[108] Most immediately, the unions had asked for the dismissal of these men as they had not taken part in the railway strike. In the longer term, they were opposed to the unions because the unions demanded the abolition of their positions, as the traditional and rigidly hierarchical structures of command within the state-owned company were to be replaced by soviets. The *fasci* were a means of restoring discipline and hierarchy.

The organization of a violent reaction by railway employees was not simply, however, a matter of a settling of accounts within the structure of the company. In addition, there were powerful external pressures that were brought to bear upon the struggle. The railways were of vital importance to industry and commerce, and were essential to the movement of goods and supplies. As a result, industrialists and merchants were terrified of effective control of the network by workers' soviets, and stood opposed to strong unions in the sector that could cause strikes and stoppages. The press of the Liberal bourgeoisie was adamant above all that strikes in the public services were not to be tolerated. Thus, for instance, the *Rinnovamento*, the Liberal paper of Pisa, dedicated a special editorial to the railroad workers:

Strikes have immensely damaged the national economy, have raised the rate of foreign exchange, have discredited us abroad. Domestically, they have broken every sentiment of discipline and respect for the law, and they have spread distrust and discouragement among the honest citizens...

Yes, gentlemen, there will come a day – and we pray that it will not be far away – when strikes will no longer be allowed. On that day to strike will mean to lose one's job, and to be a striker will mean to be a man who has submitted his resignation. This must be, and it is indispensable that it shall be, above all in the public services.[109]

Expressing their concern for the control of transport in more tangible fashion, the business communities of major cities like Siena established regular monthly contributions on behalf of the fascist railroad unions that were pledged, in the expression of the *Scure*, to 'combat the disease' of strikes. What was particularly revealing was that, according to the same paper, the sums collected were put at the disposal of the General Inspector of Railways, who was in effect to direct the 'economic unions'.[110]

The indiscretion of the *Scure* on this point revealed another influence behind the success of the fascists in the transport sector. Industrialists and tradesmen were not the only parties interested in the maintenance of hierarchy on the railways and in the destruction of the socialist union and soviet structure. The state was also deeply concerned. In the case of the government, the reason was simple: the railways were a vital element of social control. It was indispensable that the state be able at will to deploy the *carabinieri* in force. Prime Minister Bonomi referred to the railroads as 'the most delicate public service ... on whose correct functioning is clearly based every system of control and of public order within the territory of the state'.[111] For this reason the government, as official policy, played a very active role in the violent suppression of subversion within the railway system. The state did not intend to allow the movement of troops to be dependent on the consent of workers' soviets.

The government, in the first place, had taken pains to ensure that it had established a network of informers and agents among the station personnel, the signalmen, the shunters, and the manual labourers.[112] Furthermore, already by the start of 1920 the state had taken the initiative in the recruitment and organization of what were the precursors of the railway squads and the Fascist Union of Railwaymen – armed bands of thugs to break strikes. The policy was coordinated and directed at the highest levels. Senior officials attended to the recruitment of the blacklegs.[113] The Ministries of the Interior and of Transport took care to see that they were supplied with arms and permits to carry weapons, that they were supported by the police and that they were promised substantial monetary incentives.[114] Prime Minister Nitti officially urged the prefects to cooperate with the railway officials and the industrialists, who are 'the most affected by the strike', in the organization of 'squads of volunteers'.[115]

It was this pre-existing structure, established in the first instance by the directors and managers of the state corporation and the government, and financed by industry, that was the nucleus of the fascist organization in the sector. It was this early base which explains the rapid fascist success in recruitment among railway personnel, and especially the administrative staff who were threatened by socialist subversion. In addition, with massive funds forthcoming from industry and commerce on a regular basis, the organizers of the reaction were able to recruit from the *bas-fonds* of the cities and from the ranks of the unemployed. In the January strike of 1920 'volunteers' had been brought from as far away as Naples to work in the Florence station.[116] Moreover, as the reaction established its influence, it continued to enjoy the benevolent cooperation of the directors of the railways and the ministries, who dismissed workers who resisted the fascist unions.[117]

The recruitment of 'volunteer' railwaymen from among the ranks of the unemployed illustrates one way in which the *fasci* eventually acquired a following even among some sectors of the working class. Here, however, we should be very clear about the nature of this recruitment of workers and not fall prey to the fascists' own claim that they represented the nation as a whole and stood above the claims of class particularism. In fact, as we have seen, the *fasci* acted in the name of very well-defined class interests. The fact that workers finally entered the 'economic unions' in significant numbers while a trickle even enrolled in the fascist branches does not alter the overall situation. When a worker joined the reaction, the significance of his act was that he renounced the collective interests of his class in order to protect himself. He accepted, by membership in the 'economic union', the final defeat of his class in exchange for employment and personal security. When he joined, he acted alone – not as a worker, but as an isolated individual.

Furthermore, it was absolutely apparent that, of those workers who did join the movement, virtually none achieved positions of command. The squads and the *direttori* of the important *fasci* remained securely in the hands of the middle classs. At Livorno, one of the Tuscan industrial centres, for example, the social composition of the fifteen candidates standing for election to the *direttorio* in the middle of 1921 was eloquent testimony to the exclusion of the local proletariat from influence within the organization. The candidates were:

Alberto Capitani   *sailing captain*
Vico Farulli   *tradesman*
Alessandro Fiano   *medical student*
Francesco Guerri   *professor*
Giustiniano Giustiniani   *clerk*
Nicola Lemmi-Gilly   *business-school student*
Constantino Leo   *retired army colonel*
Antonio Mancini   *doctor*
Enrico Micallef   *law student*
Piero Polese   *business representative*
Umberto Rodinis   *tradesman*
Mario Ricci   *customs official*
Ugo Sibaldi   *shipper*
Paolo Tozzi   *tradesman*
Emanuele Tron   *tradesman*[118]

The recruitment of workers began only very late in the life of the fascist organization, after the political direction had been well established by other very different interests. It was only from late 1921 – in the case of Livorno not until the summer and autumn of 1922 – that the movement began to breach the ranks of the working class in any sizeable numbers. At Lucca, the textile centre, for instance, the founder and original secretary of the *fascio*, Goffredo Pieri, disillusioned and embittered at being set aside by the rising 'duce', Carlo Scorza,[119] was explicit about the class nature of the local reaction. 'I believe I may assert', he wrote in the summer of 1921,

> that fascism here is hated by all the workers, and in fact there is not a single worker who is enrolled ... Instead there predominates the 'profiteer-clerical-monarchist' element that never takes part in any of the action ... It is well known that in our *fascio* are enrolled many war profiteers who, while we were in the trenches, starved our families.[120]

Only as the pressure of unemployment became severe, as the cost of living rose inexorably, and as fascist power began to triumph did the temptation to yield to the blandishments of the *fasci* increase. As the fascists extended their control, the powers of patronage at their disposal expanded. At the same time, the temptation to surrender grew all the greater as disillusionment with the socialist party deepened as it proved ever more incapable of defending its supporters from wage cuts, dismissals, and violence at the hands of the squads.

It was notable that the expansion of fascist appeal within the working class from late 1921 was specific. The sectors of the working class with a long experience of organization and struggle and who worked in the large-scale factories of the great industrial centres were, as a rule, the last to join the reaction. No better example, again, exists than that of Livorno with its highly organized and class-conscious proletariat of metallurgical workers, dockers, and shipbuilders, where the *fasci* were entirely isolated from the factories until the summer of 1922. More generally, and at any period until the March on Rome, there is hardly a case of a metallurgical worker, miner, or manual railway labourer who is listed in the *direttorio* of a fascist branch anywhere in Tuscany.

Where the *fasci* had greater success was in more marginal sectors of the working class whose organizations were weak or non-existent, who worked in small, often artisanal, shops, and had no experience of the great contests on behalf of the collective and communitarian goals of the Red Years – 'internal committees', union recognition, job security, democratic control. For the worker in the tiny shop, these aspirations were no part of his experience, and the sacrifice of such goals for self-protection was no great act of surrender. In the small shop the worker, furthermore, was all the more directly under the control and personal authority of the employer. That such workers may have played a significant role in some *fasci* at least is suggested by the scattered returns we have already referred to of the internal census of the movement. Thus, at Sestino (Arezzo) 13 of 50 members were classified as workers,[121] at Pozzo della Chiana (Arezzo) 20 of 50,[122] at Monciani (Arezzo) 8 of 23,[123] at Pontassieve (Florence) 16 of 33,[124] and at Sancasciano Val di Pesa (Florence) 27 of 73.[125] The mention of these towns, which had no heavy industry, is one hint of the nature of these workers. A more precise indication is provided by the listings of the occupations of members of the executives of those branches where members of the working class had obtained positions of responsibility. A first point is that of those workers who were enrolled in the fascist unions or branches, very few achieved positions of leadership. Where workers did hold posts of importance at the local level – as in the *fasci* of Peccioli (Pisa), Laiatico (Pisa), Pontedera (Pisa), Castiglioncello di

Rosignano Marittimo (Pisa), and Castellina in Chianti (Siena) – they seem not to have been industrial workers, but rather artisans and craftsmen – cobblers, blacksmiths, carpenters, chauffeurs, mechanics, gardeners, bakers.[126] The membership lists for the Grosseto *fascio* confirm this impression. At Grosseto a number of unspecified 'workers' were fascists, but equally numerous were the carpenters, bricklayers, barbers, tailors, blacksmiths.[127]

There were occasional instances as early as the end of 1920 of *fasci* in which a central nucleus was provided by miners. The two major cases were Gavorrano in the Grosseto mining zone, and Abbadia San Salvatore. Of the Abbadia example unfortunately no more is known.[128] At Gavorrano, however, it seems that special circumstances were involved and that the miners there were an atypical and marginal grouping. They were all Sardinian immigrants recruited as strike-breakers by the Montecatini company in the South like the Neapolitan railroad 'volunteers'.[129] It was noteworthy that in September 1921 the Italian Chamber of Labour, responsible for the 'economic unions' of the two major mining provinces of Siena and Grosseto, did not have a section of miners among the groups it had organized.[130] It was only from 1922 after months of mass unemployment, extended lockouts, and intense fascist pressure that the most combative and highly organized categories of the Tuscan industrial proletariat – the miners and metallurgical workers – began in desperation to take up membership in the fascist corporations.

The process by which a fascist presence was achieved within the more organized sectors of the working class is well described by the authorities in the textile city of Prato, which had been one of the strongholds of Tuscan socialism. Until the late autumn of 1921 the Prato *fascio* had achieved virtually nothing in its attempt to win recruits among the textile workers. As the crisis deepened, however, the socialist party made manifest its lack of a coherent strategy to face either the wave of dismissals and wage reductions ordered by the employers, or the outbreak of squadrism. As a result the workers, disillusioned with their party, began to opt for the security of employment held out by the 'economic unions' and the *fascio*. This movement towards the fascist organizations and the resulting collapse of socialist power in the commune proved cumulative and grew into a broad and steady stream after the total failure of the desperate autumn strike against the offensive of the manufacturers. Inspector General Di Tarsia reported in April 1922 that

Since October of last year, the working class, as a result of the long strike of the wool makers that lasted over sixty days and ended in their total defeat as they had to resume work under conditions even worse than those prevailing before the strike, have grown disgusted with their leaders. Thus it has been easy for the industrialists to cause fascism to prosper, and it has quickly achieved a terrible domination.[131]

Indeed, by January 1922, the local socialist administration had resigned, and thousands of workers had resigned from the Chamber of Labour to take up membership in the 'economic unions'.[132]

The mood of the Prato wool workers seems to have become widespread in the Tuscan working class in the course of 1921. The PSI, with its determinist and economistic analysis of the crisis, had no strategic solution except to wait. Indeed, as we have seen, much the same analysis applied to the fascist reaction, while both of the parties of the revoutionary left, PSI and PCI, disowned the spontaneously organized local resistance. As a result, the base of the party was left alone and disarmed to face the reaction. The effect on party militants was frequently one of disillusionment and despair. An anonymous police informer in Florence in the spring of 1921 reported on the morale of his socialist comrades for the benefit of the prefect, Olivieri:

The situation is excellent; the members after this movement are all disoriented and angered against the [executive] committee of the Chamber of Labour ... as well as against the socialist deputies, who have not shown their faces recently ... The communists attack Signorini and Vecchi, in such a way that there has arisen a general discontent within both the socialist and communist union and party organizations. Some will withdraw, others have already torn up their membership cards in the party and the Chamber of Labour, and want nothing more to do with them.

In short, there is such a disintegration that both the socialist and communist parties, and the union organizations, will lose 90 per cent of their members. Very few will remain, and they will be able to accomplish nothing.[133]

PART III
THE STATE

CHAPTER 5

COMPROMISE AND COLLUSION

So far we have discussed the social groups that actively joined the fascist movement. Such an elaboration is misleading, in Tuscany above all, if it conveys the impression that a large proportion of the population supported the *fasci*. In the Tuscan countryside, as we have sought to emphasize, the reaction relied for its success on the gathering of a restricted and socially heterogeneous following whose only unifying features were anti-socialism and the defence of relative privilege. That such a movement, combining as it did the material resources of the most powerful men in the region with an aroused popular base, should have become an important political force is perhaps readily comprehensible. What requires further explanation is that such a force should have risen to power, and in so brief a compass. There is a yawning gap between the early fascist expansion and the first fascist successes in the winter and spring of 1921 on the one hand and, on the other hand, the nearly complete victory of the squads over their opponents by the autumn and the conquest of state power a year later. Unaided and unabetted, the fascist movement could not have accomplished such a feat.

To understand the fascist victory then, we must go beyond an examination of the social composition of the movement to study other powerful forces that remained formally outside the movement but contributed vitally to its success. We have seen the close relationship that developed between the *fasci* and the élites of the land of Tuscan industry and of the Church. In addition, the fascist movement succeeded because it was able to mobilize the resources of the state. In this chapter we shall examine the collusion of the public authorities.

THE FALTERING OF THE CENTRAL GOVERNMENT

To understand the relations that developed between the state apparatus and the fascist movement, we must distinguish between the unabashed pro-fascism of the regional authorities in Tuscany and the hesitant and contradictory policies pursued by the national political leadership at Rome. Thus some have drawn too simple a portrait of pro-fascism in high place, branding Giolitti, for example, the John the Baptist of Mussolini. The reality is more complex.

For the Italian political leadership, in fact, too deep a sympathy for the *fasci* would have been self-defeating because the fascists were a direct challenge to the established state authority. Indeed, there is ample evidence that the two premiers who presided over the great period of fascist expansion – Giolitti and Bonomi – together with Giolitti's principal collaborator at the Ministry of the Interior, Camillo Corradini, realized some of the danger they faced and intermittently took steps to secure the repression of fascist illegality. A number of telegrams from these three men to their subordinates in Tuscany undermine any over-simple view of active pro-fascist collusion on the part of the national government. In order to avoid ambiguity on this important point, we shall quote at some length from a variety of orders sent from Rome. Thus in April 1921, Giolitti cabled Carlo Olivieri, the prefect of Florence:

The Prefect of Pisa calls to my attention that all the fascist incursions in his province originate here [i.e. at Florence]. Similarly fascist expeditions to Arezzo, Siena, and Perugia have begun from Florence. This can be tolerated no further. Take the energetic and stern measures necessary to ensure absolutely that such incursions are not repeated...[1]

Not many days later Olivieri received a further cable from the prime minister, stating:

The attempt to exert pressure so that murders may go unpunished is the most subversive action possible. Any such attempt must be prevented and, if necessary, energetically repressed.[2]

At the same time Olivieri was sent a series of dispatches from Corradini ordering him to enforce the law with impartiality and to repress fascist illegality.[3] In exactly the same spirit, the premier cabled the prefect of Arezzo in June to state that

I have been informed that the situation at San Sepolcro is deteriorating and that there have been acts of intimidation and threats to set fire to the cooperative. You must maintain order at all costs and sternly repress all violence from whatever quarter ... The Tiber Valley is also threatened by the fascist movement with violence and harassment. Act firmly. I await information. Prevent the fascists from driving about in lorries spreading panic and alarm.[4]

If these telegrams establish that Giolitti was prepared at times to order the arrest of fascists guilty of illegal violence, to direct the police to enforce the law impartially, and to repress squadrism, there is a similar stream of messages from Bonomi to the state authorities in the periphery. In August 1921, Giolitti's successor sent an urgent wire to the Florence prefecture:

I an informed that armed gangs of fascists from this city and from Prato are roaming about Pistoia committing violence against an unarmed population without encountering opposition from the local authorities. If this information is correct please take urgent measures with resolution and energy. I await a report by telegraph.[5]

Showing still greater determination, Bonomi dispatched this message to the prefects of Pisa and Florence:

It is absolutely necessary that the bloody guerrilla warfare that still breaks out here and there sporadically in various communes of this province cease immediately. I shall take harsh exemplary measures against any official who does not firmly carry out his duty in this regard ... It is in the great interest of the nation that this province no longer offer the spectacle it has long presented, and that the Government can absolutely tolerate no further.[6]

Finally, and perhaps most resolutely of all, Bonomi telegraphed the prefect of Massa-Carrara in January 1922 to inform him that:

The conditions of law and order in this province denote a revival of fascist action that is more harmful than ever. I am calling upon you personally to take energetic action to repress any attempt at violence, and to urge the authorities under you to carry out their duty with the greatest zeal. You will be held responsible for any shortcomings and failings for this Ministry will not hesitate to proceed harshly, as it firmly intends once and for all to put a stop to occurrences that are so destructive of peace and of the credit of the nation.[7]

Such examples are sufficient to show the error of the view which assumes a government conspiracy in favour of the *fasci* or postulates an identity of interest between fascism and the liberal state. Certainly neither Giolitti nor Bonomi was in any direct sense pro-fascist, and neither was prepared to accept a fascist rise to power. The difficulties involved in government policy in Rome were altogether more deep-seated and insidious.

Here one factor was simple weakness and confusion. Faced with a major economic crisis, an unstable majority in parliament, a revolutionary challenge in the provinces and a crumbling Liberal party structure, the Italian political leadership lacked the force and sense of direction necessary to pursue a firm and consistent policy. The government lived from hand to mouth, adopting a series of stop-gap and expedient measures as it followed the course of least resistance. Such vacillation was inherent in the postwar crisis, one of whose most profound aspects was that the Italian ruling class was without political leadership, and had yet to evolve a new formula for domination in the changed political circumstances. Indeed the postwar premiers – Nitti, Giolitti, Bonomi, Facta – were the very expression of a political system of Liberal rule – *giolittismo* – that was no longer viable. It was hardly surprising that government policy towards fascism was affected by the general disorientation, and that the policy was both less consistent, and frequently less firm, than the telegrams we have cited would suggest.

In particular, the Liberal leaders of postwar Italy consistently failed to deal effectively with subversion on the right because – and in this at least they were at one with the reformist socialists – they underestimated its seriousness. They held to the view that fascist violence was an 'excess' that could be pruned from the healthy trunk of the movement. Instead of seeing in squadrism the essential core of fascist practice and the embryo of a new regime, they fondly cherished the illusion that fascism was the mirror image of socialism and had therefore its own 'reformist' wing that could be 'transformed' and 'constitutionalized' according to the classical canons of Giolittian rule. In this vision there was no understanding of the way in which fascism had arisen from the very failure of Giolittism, and was by nature incompatible with the established patterns of Liberal rule. Moreover, Liberals joined the socialists in the mechanistic analysis of fascism as a mere 'reaction' that would automatically subside as the threat of revolution receded. In so grave an error there was at least the extenuation that fascism was a wholly new historical phenomenon of which there was no previous experience.

In such an 'error', however, there was also much of the far less ingenuous working of a systematic class bias. There was a continual tendency, that is, always to regard the threat of the left as the main danger of the hour while the fascists could be temporarily useful, if troublesome, allies in the struggle against the immediate and overarching menace of bolshevism. At some later date, when no longer needed, they could be discarded at will. Thus alongside and in blatant contradiction with the stern policy of anti-fascist repression that emerges from ministerial communiqués and occasionally from actual government practice as at Sarzana, where the police opened fire on the squads, the government pursued another and altogether more ambiguous line of action with far-reaching consequences. This other policy was to punish above all any signs of sympathy towards the left within the government bureaucracy while yielding to pressure from provincial notables that a blind eye should be turned to local connivance with the *fasci*, or at least refusing to defend provincial law enforcement officers who sought to maintain the impartiality of the law against squadrism.

In this other 'soft' policy was reflected the unwillingness of a weak government to alienate the traditional holders of local power. Mirrored in it was the class interest of a Liberal regime that, while not pro-fascist, as the fascists were both an embarrassment and a threat, still found in the extreme right a political force with which a measure of accommodation could be found, and which could on occasion prove extremely useful. This policy at times led to the gross violation of the putative neutrality of the state, and the official policy of repressing fascist 'extremism'. A particularly clear example we have discussed was government policy towards the railroads, where the state actively cooperated with the establishment of armed squads.

To the extent that the government adopted this policy of accommodation with the reaction (which it did inconsistently as it lurched again and again towards sterner action when fascist violence grew especially bloody, when alarm grew at the extent of fascist power, or when provincial state authorities showed signs of going far beyond the limits of government toleration and acted in open defiance of directives from Rome), it would not be correct to hold that Liberal Italy finally succumbed to irresistible fascist force. It would be more accurate to say that it committed suicide. The Liberal state, that is, directly contributed to the fascistization of its own provincial apparatus. Pro-fascist collaboration and subversion, in the absence of firm direction and consistent resistance from Rome, rapidly enveloped the state machine in the Tuscan provinces. By 1922 the process had become all but irreversible as the political and social crisis acquired the added dimension of a crisis of the articulation of the state. Rome, that is, lost the ability to impose its will on its provincial officials. The March on Rome was preceded by a slow and almost unnoticed process in which the PNF acquired control of the provinces.

In Tuscan terms, at least, the foundations for the 'soft' policy towards the reaction were laid during the revolutionary crisis of 1920, well before the establishment of the fascist movement as an effective political force in the region. In 1920, that is, in the Tuscan provinces it became axiomatic that the task of the state authorities, if not to repress the socialist movement outright, was at least to make its life difficult even though, as we have seen, socialist activity generally was conducted on a strictly legalitarian basis. Thus everywhere in the agricultural strikes of 1920 the Tuscan prefects made it their function – with government acquiescence – to guarantee the 'right to work' of strike-breakers, while frequently the police did what they could to harass the strikers. In all of this, of course, little pretence was made of preserving the neutrality of the law, and in this fashion the premises were quietly established for official benevolence towards the reaction. This the Ministry at Rome did nothing to counter.

Similarly, still in 1920, the Ministry of the Interior made it clear to its dependencies that to adopt an attitude of strict neutrality on the social question could be fatal to a career in the government bureaucracy. This message was clearly put forward in November when the government removed from his post the prefect of Grosseto, Dario Gutierrez, a man with no socialist sympathies, but one who earned the displeasure of the local notables by his refusal to follow the sanctioned practice of Tuscan prefects of favouring the provincial ruling class. Gutierrez seems to have been guilty of a strict impartiality both during the electoral campaign, when he refused to use the resources of the prefecture to influence the ballot, and during the agricultural strikes when he did little to encourage strike-breaking. These failings were bitterly resented by the landlords, and Count Alfredo di Frassineto, then president of the AAT, protested strongly to the government about the conduct of the prefect and the police under his command.[8]

Most unpardonably, during the occupation of the great *latifondi* of the province during the agrarian agitation, the prefect issued a series of decrees assigning land to the peasants.[9] On this issue the Grosseto prefect found not only the landlords of the province and the AAT ranked against him, but also the General Confederation of Agriculture, which appealed to have his 'illegal' and 'unjust' measures rescinded, and, by implication, to have him removed.[10] In the event, the government yielded to pressure and replaced Gutierrez with Antonio Boragno and then Raffaele Rocco, both men more attuned to the needs of property. For the socialist paper of Grosseto, there was little mystery about the affair. The *Risveglio* commented,

The forces of the bourgeoisie have omitted nothing in their campaign to undermine the man who refuses to be their instrument.[11]

If in 1920 the premises for unabashed state partiality were established, in 1921 a series of government measures made the position dramatically clearer. The most famous of these, of course, was Giolitti's decision in the spring of 1921 to form a grand 'National Bloc' as a sort of anti-socialist 'united front' of the right in which the fascists were included. This decision reveals much of the attitude of Rome towards the reaction, and at the time, of course, provided the fascists with a new and badly needed claim to legitimacy just at the moment when squadrist violence was reaching its height. Within the government apparatus such a major decision was inevitably taken as a cue, as an indication of the direction the political wind was blowing, and as a warning that the fascists had powerful allies and were to be treated with care.

Any effects such a decision may have had on the Tuscan authorities were rapidly and heavily underscored by a series of further measures that dramatically demonstrated that to attempt to apply the law to the fascists was to risk one's career. The decisions that made the position unmistakable were the cashiering betweeen mid 1921 and early 1922 of a series of high Tuscan officials who attempted to curb fascist violence. The first of the purges occurred in June at the expense of Achille De Martino, the prefect of Pisa, who was replaced by the infamous Pietro Frigerio. As prefect of Rovigo, Frigerio had gained a wide notoriety as 'the fascist prefect *par excellence*'.[12] Soon after taking up his post, in fact, the new prefect of Pisa made a public speech in which he proclaimed fascism 'a necessary dyke against the arrogant encroachments of bolshevism'.[13] As at Grosseto, so at Pisa the change of prefect seemed, to the local socialists, readily explicable. De Martino, claimed *L' Ora nostra*, 'is going because he is no friend of the fascists'.[14]

In September it was the turn of the prefect of Siena, Federico Masino. Here the political significance of the change was especially evident as the new appointee was the undisguised *filofascista* Mauro Michele Bertone. Indeed, in this case there is the testimony of Masino himself that his removal was a direct yielding to fascist pressure. 'Today', wrote Masino, 'I have been informed that Marquis Dino Perrone Compagni ... is doing his best in Rome to obtain my transfer.'[15] And in February came the dismissal of the Prato police chief De Bernardinis, who was replaced by Captain Micheli, a man put forward by the paymasters of the local *fascio*.[16] Of all the transfers, this was perhaps the most blatant, as the Florence prefect Vincenzo Pericoli himself made clear.[17] In both cases what impressed government officials was that the state had yielded to blackmail and refused to support its functionaries against the *agrari* and the *fascisti*.

Yet again the government yielded to pressure at Massa-Carrara, where the prefect, who tried to curb the squads commanded by Ricci and Fabbricotti was, as we have seen, sabotaged by the prime minister. Nor did the government enhance its reputation for resolution in May 1921, when Perrone Compagni was able with impunity openly to threaten to lay siege to the Pisa prefecture. At that time De Martino, still prefect, cabled Corradini at the Ministry of the Interior that

Marquis Perrone, the General Secretary of the Fasci in Tuscany, has telephoned me from Florence ... to declare peremptorily that if by midnight tomorrow the fascists arrested at Capannoli and held at Pontedera prison are not released, then not less than 10,000 fascists ... will march on Pisa to lay siege to the Prefecture and take it over.[18]

In this fashion, by weakness and indecision, as well as by a willingness to compromise with the reaction, the Liberal political leadership set in motion the process of the dissolution of its own authority. The fascists, the *agrari*, and the industrialists were allowed to colonize the upper reaches of the Tuscan state hierarchy. When sporadically throughout 1921, and then more urgently at the eleventh hour, the need was felt to check the tendency and to curb squadrist power and fascist terror, the process had proceeded too far, and there was a serious problem of where to discover, at the provincial level, officials prepared to give and carry out the necessary orders against the fascists. The reaction had been allowed to capture the state machine from within, and the writ of central government no longer ran securely in the eight provinces. Certainly the limited administrative orders that Giolitti and his successors sought to issue were unlikely to be effective in a context in which provincial officials had learned to their cost that Rome had neither the will nor the authority to back them in their implementation. To follow the injunctions of Rome was to expose oneself to the reprisals of the local men of power, while to wink at the deeds of the *fasci* was to risk little.

THE POLITICAL ACTIVISM OF THE ARMED FORCES, MAGISTRATES, AND PREFECTS

The ambiguous attitude of the central government towards the *fasci* accelerated a process that was already well under way in the provinces for other reasons. In Tuscany perhaps more than anywhere in the peninsula, the power of the state was massively employed by the provincial authorities – police, *carabinieri*, magistrates, and prefects – in open and active support of the fascist movement. It was common in Italy at this period for the government officials in the periphery to assist the cause of social reaction through collusion. What was notable in Tuscany was the wholehearted alliance between state power and fascism. It was this alliance which made the civil war in the eight provinces uneven from the start and gave the fascists a force far in excess of their number. In Tuscany a vital aspect of the victory of social reaction was the assistance of what can only be termed a counter-revolution by the regional 'forces of order'.

The factors which led to such a massive sympathy with the fascist cause on the part of the authorities, from the prefect in some provinces to the lowest *carabiniere*, were many. To begin, we should make a distinction between, on the one hand, the troops of the regular conscript army, who reflected the Italian society from which they were drawn, and, like that society, were tainted with subversive 'new ideas' as the army mutiny at Ancona in the middle of 1920 made clear; and, on the other hand, the men and officers of the security forces – police, *guardie regie*, and, above all, *carbinieri*. The latter were professional volunteer soldiers whose conceptions of patriotism and the social order were far different from those of the conscript peasants and workers. The conscripts retained an organic bond with the class from which they had been seconded and to which they returned after the armistice. The police and *carabinieri*, by contrast, even if they were of working-class origin, were fully cut off from the society of which they had been a part by long years in distant barracks and an intense apprenticeship in the virtues of hierarchy and discipline. The *carabiniere* in particular, like his civilian counterpart in Tuscan rural society, the *fattore*, had been carefully recruited on the basis of his political reliability and his identification, not with the class from which he came, but with the condition to which he aspired. The police forces, it should not be forgotten, were paid, trained, and indoctrinated to defend law and order, and the law embraced the existing structure of property and class. Inherent in the profession of *carabiniere* was the defence of the status quo, and not by chance had he become the popular symbol of a repressive social order.

For these reasons, there had long been a natural and reciprocal diffidence between even the lowest ranks of the security forces and the socialists. This diffidence was transformed into open aversion after the armistice when the unpatriotic war-time 'shirkers' were held to be the chief cause and sole beneficiaries of the astronomical inflation of which the police, as non-unionized public employees, were victims; and when socialist demonstrations and strikes, together with the whole series of spontaneous riots and uprisings of 1919 and 1920, caused very real hardship, long hours, and physical danger for the police.

In the case of the officers and the men who commanded them – the *questori*, prefects, and magistrates – the reasons for antipathy to the socialist cause were multiplied. These were men who came from the middle classes or, in the case of many senior officials, even from the upper reaches of the bourgeoisie and aristocracy, and they shared the usual hostility of their class to the collectivist and egalitarian goals of socialism. The PSI, moreover, had deeply offended the caste spirit of the officers' corps by its anti-war propaganda and its call for a full investigation into the conduct of the war and the responsibility for the defeat at Caporetto. In personal terms, too, the élite of the army and the state bureaucracy had nothing to gain from below, whereas men of power in the region – industrialists, landlords, merchants – could be instrumental in making or breaking a career.

In any case, there were often material interests to defend. Ranking officers sometimes had close and mutually profitable relations with military suppliers, as we noted in the case of Admiral Ciano, and came almost naturally to share the views of their clients with regard to the social question. Similarly, the power of the prefect was bound up with his ability to reward and punish through his control of ample powers of patronage and it was in his interest to cultivate good relations with important local employers. Some officials were also landlords or had direct interests in business, and were not in a position to observe a strict neutrality on such issues as expropriation and nationalization. A clear example of such conflicts of interest was the case of Cinotti, the public prosecutor of Siena, who was an important local landlord and could hardly have been expected to administer even-handed justice against a political movement that acted to defend the prerogatives and control of property.[19] To be sure, Cinotti exercised his authority with a consistency of pro-fascist bias that earned him censure for 'lack of energy' and 'deficient action' from the prime minister himself.[20] It was no surprise when in early 1922 one police inspector reported to Rome:

At Siena the judicial authorities ... need to demonstrate a more effective and energetic activity.
 I categorically exclude the possibility that the public prosecutor there is the man best suited for such a task.[21]

The point is that Cinotti was far from exceptional, even in Siena province. At Piancastagnaio, for instance, the public prosecutor, Gino Bandi, was the nephew of the major landowner and patron of squadrism, Filippo Pellegrini.[22] There was ample justification for Bonomi to complain of the 'lack of energy' of the entire Sienese judiciary.[23]

There were, furthermore, frequent personal bonds that linked the fascist reaction to the upper reaches of the provincial bureaucracy, and made it unlikely that the full rigour of the law would be applied to squadrists. The *questore* of Lucca, Carlo Grazioli, for instance, had a young son, Fabbrizio, who was enrolled in the local *fascio*.[24] At Massa, the daughter of the *questore*, Piano, moved extensively in fascist circles,[25] while the deputy *questore*, Giustiniani, had a son who was an active member of the *fascio* and he himself was reportedly tied to the inner circles of the local reaction by sentimental bonds.[26] Still at Massa, the wife of deputy police commissioner Pisacane was the cousin of the commander of the local squads, and the couple was on close terms of friendship with the principal fascists of the city; and deputy commissioner Iorio had a son who was a squadrist.[27] At Siena the son of the *questore*, Rostagno, was an active fascist.[28]

The various interests leading men of property and high state officials had in common were sufficient to guarantee a certain sympathy with the fascist cause, and a willingness, perhaps, to turn a blind eye when possible to the deeds of the squads, as well as a propensity to harass the socialists and energetically repress the *arditi del popolo*. What converted this general sympathy into active collusion was, in addition to the ambiguity of policy at Rome, the feeling on the part of the state officials in the periphery that they had lost control of events. The political calculations that applied at the provincial level in areas where socialist power was greatest were different from those that obtained in the national capital. For senior Tuscan officials responsible for the preservation of the 'public order', the *fasci* were – after the great agrarian strikes of 1920, the Occupation of the Factories, the display of impotence and uncertainty of the government, and the collapse of the Liberal parties in the local elections – all that stood between them and the abyss of social anarchy or the creation of a new social order in which their privileges and positions would be swept aside. The police, the *carabinieri*, and the prefects saw themselves in 1920 imminently in danger of being engulfed by the great socialist current that they were powerless to control. The reports arriving at the Ministry of the Interior from the Tuscan provinces, and above all from the great centres of agrarian unrest, sounded a loud cry of alarm.

D'Eufemia, the prefect of Siena, 'the Reddest province in Tuscany', was perhaps the most explicit. In the spring of 1920 he wrote of living in 'terrible anxiety', explaining that

This Prefecture does not have at its disposal adequate and sufficient means to face the necessities of this critical moment.[29]

Outlining the situation more fully in June, the anxious D'Eufemia reported that

The security forces at my disposal are minimal in relation to the needs of the entire province. The troops ... are hardly sufficient for the defence of their own barracks, the prisons, and the public buildings. The detachments of the RR.CC are all reduced to two or three men even in the centres of greatest unrest.[30]

Facing a situation in which they felt their vital interests in peril and themselves impotent, the authorities in Siena province viewed the fascists, in the words of the *sottoprefetto* at Montepulciano, as 'allies against a common enemy'.[31]

Interestingly, it was this feeling (i.e. that the *fasci* – patriotic, hierarchical, and committed to the protection of private property – were not a subversive movement undermining the state, but the only means, in a revolutionary situation, of restoring the authority of the forces of order) which the police inspectors and prefects themselves stressed in accounting for the collaboration of the state authorities with the movement. Thus, still from Siena, Inspector General Gaudino reported:

... the real thing to underline is the tendency of the RR.CC – and perhaps all the armed forces – to sympathize with fascism. This tendency is founded, as far as the *carabinieri* are concerned, on the good will that the fascists have shown, and continue to show, for them, respecting them, defending them, and praising their action, unlike the subversives who have always abused and mistreated them. The tendency is founded on the concept – according to their lights – that the fascists are the defenders of order ... And their action, furthermore, nearly always uncertain, irresolute, and little energetic towards the fascists, is the result, not only of their feelings, but also of their trepidation, of their fear that ... they would do badly to face difficult situations ... without precise directives and with a marked shortage of force.[32]

Such an attitude, and such an explanation of police pro-fascist conduct were far from confined to the single province of Siena. From Pisa, as we have noted, Frigerio considered fascism a 'necessary dyke'. Even from the relative calm of Lucca, prefect Gennaro Di Donato noted with alarm in 1921 that the security forces available were 'totally inadequate even for normal duties'[33] and it was to this lack of manpower to deal with the socialist threat that he attributed the pro-fascist sympathies of the troops at his command.[34] At Florence, Olivieri in 1920 had complained bitterly about the 'special, very dangerous, conditions of this province'[35] and the shortage of troops, and by the spring of 1921 he revealed his belief that the propaganda of the extremists was 'confronted only by the powerful and audacious rise of fascism'.[36]

On the part of police officers in the field who faced a danger they considered imminent, there seems to have been a further attitude of deep resentment to the vacillating politicians and bureaucrats who gave orders from their desks at Rome to maintain law and order against both left and right of the political spectrum, but failed to provide the detailed policy guidelines, the men, and the equipment to make such a policy practicable. To police officers with such a view, the very orders to repress fascist violence came to be regarded not as a resolute indication of policy, but as a cynical attempt by frightened bureaucrats at Rome to pass responsibility onto their hapless subordinates. Thus one Tuscan police commissioner, who for obvious reasons remained anonymous, gave full expression in the pages of the *Nuovo giornale* to the contempt he felt for his superiors. In a letter full of subversive implications, he wrote,

In my fifteen years of service I have never read ... a circular with precise instructions for the maintenance of law and order. All the circulars contain the same stereotyped phrases: 'The law must be defended at all cost!', 'Obedience to the law must enforced upon everyone!' But how and with what means are never made clear.

It is useless to fool ourselves with regard to orders! All the heads of governments are the same! Giolitti, Orlando, Salandra, Nitti, Bonomi, monarchists, radicals, liberals, democrats – all the same.

From their pens come forth nothing but vague and uncertain dispositions that unsay what they say, and are always questionable. They are, in short, directives that avoid any and every responsibility, to the embarrassment of those who must carry them out.

To this I should add that the prefects in turn do their best further to confuse the issue, as they always give orders from their desks and have no understanding of what it is to do duty in the piazza, or of what constitutes crowd psychology.[37]

Not surprisingly, an important factor in determining the cordiality with which officials regarded the reaction was the strength of the socialist challenge. There was a rough correlation in Tuscany between the degree of agrarian unrest and the persistence of reports of complicity by the authorities, with Siena, the famous 'Red' province, being at one end of the spectrum with the most blatant and brutal spectacle of reactionary political militancy on the part of the authorities, and Lucca at the other. Another influence on the degree of active state involvement was the success of the reaction in turning the flank of socialist subversion by conventional political means. The same considerations which prompted Tuscan fascism to rely particularly heavily on violence and military tactics also persuaded the police and the military to provide more substantial support for the squads. It was partly for this reason that some authorities at the time drew a clear distinction between the record of state functionaries in Tuscany and that of their counterparts even in other provinces where the postwar civil struggle was most bitterly contested. 'The characteristic feature of the events in Tuscany', wrote Palmiro Togliatti,

> consists in the substitution of the power and the military force of the state for the fascist organization in the war against the men and the associations of the proletariat.
>
> Such a substitution did not take place in Emilia in so complete and striking a fashion. Solidarity there was, as there has always been ... but it is here ... that the state has revealed itself in brutal fashion.[38]

So brutal and pervading was the involvement of the state in the armed reaction that the socialist Giovanni Zibordi wrote from Pisa that

> Nearly everywhere in the areas overrun by fascism the working class has found itself confronted with two enemies – the fascists and the armed forces of the state.[39]

It was for this reason too that *Avanti*! singled out Siena province in all of Italy as 'the most hit by the criminality of the *fasci*, owing to the open collusion of the security forces'.[40]

Finally, the willingness of certain local state officials to attempt in difficult circumstances to enforce ministerial directives and the law against the fascists can be seen to have been influenced by a sense that their careers were being favourably considered in Rome. It was not only by chance that among the Tuscan prefects those assigned to the most influential and prestigious posts – Livorno and Florence – were the most 'ministerial', and that the prefect at the regional capital, Carlo Olivieri, was the most Giolittian of prefects.[41] Conversely, men relegated to the less powerful posts were more tainted with right-wing subversion. This relationship, of course, also worked the other way around, as the most vital posts were those most under scrutiny from Rome, and the Ministry of the Interior was likely to send to such a delicate post as Florence only men it felt able to rely upon. None the less, there are indications that a positive feeling of resentment against the ministry was a contributing factor in the pro-fascist subversion of more than one senior Tuscan official. Certainly, at Siena the local press accounted in part for the notorious pro-fascism of the prefect Bertone by his bitter feeling that his career was being undermined by assignment to a sleepy post like Siena, a province from which his predecessor, Masino, had complained of rusting away in idleness.[42] Of Bertone the *Paese* reported that

The new prefect yearns to avenge himself against Bonomi, who from Piacenza demoted him to Siena.[43]

As the *Bandiera socialista* put it, Bertone

works and acts contrary to the orders of the central government. Prefect Bertone is an eager man who dares to say, 'I care nothing for the government. Here I am in command.'[44]

If such was the attitude of state officials at Siena, how much worse was the problem of morale at Grosseto, the traditional place of punishment and exile for state officials who had fallen into disfavour.[45] The effects of being sent to such a post were reported by the prefect of Grosseto, who informed the Ministry of the Interior that the commanding officers of the *carabinieri* in the province, Major Masi and Captain Piccaluga,

consider their posting to Grosseto a punishment and have no other thought or concern than that of hastening their transfer. Nor do they refrain from making their feelings known, even in public.
  They have therefore little love for their duty, and very little interest in cooperating with the police in various necessary assignments.[46]

It was hardly on such officials that the state could rely for an energetic defence against fascist subversion.

Whatever the motivations, the fact of massive collaboration with fascism by the Tuscan state officials is beyond dispute, and can be readily established from police reports themselves.[47] Throughout 1921 and 1922, the files of the Ministry of the Interior are filled with accounts of the 'excessive tolerance', 'passivity', 'insufficient energy', and 'deficient action' that characterized the conduct of Tuscan law-enforcement officials towards the *fasci*. The police and *carabinieri* arrested and punished the socialists, but refused to interfere with the violent work of the squads, while magistrates took pains not to convict young men of the right. At the height of squadrist activity in Arezzo in the spring of 1921, Inspector General Paolella reported that punitive expeditions were

> neither prevented nor dissuaded nor checked by the Authorities, who have frequently disregarded them and have almost always shown no concern. Chambers of Labour, Case del Popolo, socialist clubs, and consumers' cooperatives have been sacked and burned, and there have been bloody clashes.[48]

Concerning himself broadly with Florence at the same period, Olivieri pointed out that

> the troops, the *carabinieri*, the *regie guardie*, city hall, and the magistrates wholly sympathize with the fascists.[49]

With more explicit reference to the police and the RR.CC in the San Miniato zone, the Florence prefect noted that their action

> shows itself in all circumstances insufficient and ineffective. Nearly always the police either stand by inactively while the fascists systematically carry out their acts of vandalism and pillage, or they take note of the *fait accompli*.[50]

With regard to the judges, there is considerable evidence that they sabotaged proceedings against those few unlucky fascists who happened to be arrested, though there is no evidence that they went further, either by joining the squads in their work or by enrolling in the *fasci*. Procrastination, delay, obstructionism, the acquittal in defiance of all evidence – these were the weapons the judges wielded in defence of social reaction. From Grosseto, for instance, inspector Paolella informed Rome that

> The local magistrates ... are also inclined to fascism, and, although they avoid public displays, they give proof of their sympathies in the exasperating slowness with which they carry out investigations.[51]

Another police inspector made the same point in Lucca province. As he explained in the middle of 1922

> The judicial authorities, until recently and with rare exceptions, were not very prompt in carrying out penal proceedings against persons accused of crimes of violence in the political struggle.
> Even recently, moreover, not a few trials have ended in acquittals that have caused amazement.[52]

As we have seen, the sympathy obtaining between the fascists and the judiciary was so great that the movement became a haven for convicted criminals who found in fascist membership a promise of impunity for a life of crime. Some individual magistrates were even willing to expound upon their political partiality in interviews with investigators from the Ministry of the Interior. At San Miniato, for example, the investigating magistrate Alfonso Borrelli deplored fascist excesses, but confessed to a deep appreciation of the role of the *fasci* in halting revolution. In his view, moreover,

> The dominant note of fascist excesses is violence against things; that of communist excesses is the thirst for blood.[53]

Borrelli's colleague at San Miniato, the public prosecutor Oscar Muzi, made no greater attempt to assume a posture of neutrality. 'As for the fascists', Inspector General Lutrario reported of Muzi after an interview,

> he declared that the public conscience disapproved of some excesses, but finds a justification for them, both in their youthful enthusiasm and in the need to reply with energy to the arrogance of communism.[54]

If such a clearly partisan position on the part of the judiciary was expressed in a pronounced bias with which the law was applied, the pro-fascism of the armed forces – the regular army, the police, and the *carabinieri* – took an altogether more active and violent shape. The 'forces of order' from the bottom to the very top of the regional chain of command played a direct part in the success of squadrism. The army and police often joined the fascist movement in open defiance of the law against political affiliation. They led and accompanied punitive expeditions, and supplied the fascists with transport, weapons, and ammunition. The prevailing state of affairs within the military quickly became apparent to Ezio Lascialfare, the former railroad employee and founder of the second Florence *fascio*, who attended the Lucca military academy for non-commissioned and reserve officers in 1920–1. With considerable satisfaction Lascialfare let Pasella know of his activities:

> I am at the NCO cadet school in Lucca, and I need hardly tell you that my activity as a fascist is not at an end. On the contrary, the adjutant major, Lieutenant Orazio Carrara, when he discovered that I was a fascist, asked me to form a clandestine *fascio* among the cadets. After several agreements among ourselves, through the effort alone of the excellent and valiant Lieutenant Carrara, the secret *fascio* was formed with the membership of 300 of the 370 cadets. From this you can see the fruitful propaganda carried on by our lieutenant.[55]

Lascialfare, however, was guilty either of naivety or of an excess of discretion in attributing the success of the highly illegal *fascio* to the initiative alone of the valiant Lieutenant Carrara. In fact, the initiative was sponsored and protected by the very highest military authorities, both at the academy and at the regional military command at Florence. The commanding officer of the Lucca academy, Colonel Bottini, gave every encouragement to the new organization[56] while the regional army headquarters sanctioned the activity and defended the venture from disciplinary measures. Indeed, parallel initiatives took place at the Livorno naval academy[57] and at the cadet school for *carabinieri* at Florence under the command of Colonel Giuseppe Palizzolo de Ramione, himself a landowning member of the aristocracy. Colonel Palizzolo was particularly eloquent in the defence of the fascist militancy of the *carabiniere* cadets under his command. 'Everyone', he wrote,

> agreed with the view that, during the tumults and the barricades of February and March, when all of Florence applauded the work of the fascists; saw them hasten into danger in order to re-establish law and order, which had been overturned by communist elements; watched them uphold the Fatherland; and heard them shout '*Long live the carabinieri!*' when our troops, who until then had known only the jeers of the raging mob, marched by, they [i.e. cadets] believed in good faith that it was a patriotic duty to be with them.[58]

Camillo Corradini was not, however, content to place responsibility for the political conduct of the troops with their immediate superiors alone. The under-secretary at the Ministry of the Interior correctly outlined the pro-fascist collusion at the supreme Tuscan commands in Florence. As he stressed in a message to the Minister of War,

> I have been informed that the enrolment of officers and men in the *fasci* has occurred with the consent of the army corps command. The command has argued simplistically that regulations forbid the participation of officers in subversive associations, but that this association is not subversive, but patriotic, and is therefore not among those which officers are forbidden to join. A number of officers ostentatiously display the insignia of the association and, I repeat, many officers as a matter of common knowledge take part ... in fascist punitive expeditions ... All this takes place with never a correction or disciplinary action by the military authorities of the army corps, which does not investigate, punish, or repress this purely political activity which is carried out by criminal means.[59]

The most cursory examination of the reports received from the Tuscan provinces during this period confirms Corradini's observations at every point. From the very earliest cases of fascist violence the hand of the military and police authorities is transparently evident. One of the early and less bloody squadrist enterprises, for instance, was the attempt to prevent the seating in February 1921 of the socialist-dominated provincial council of Florence at the Palazzo Medici-Riccardi. Naturally, on this occasion, after the events of Bologna, Ferrara, and Lucca, and after open threats by the Florence squads, the authorities were not unaware of the possibility of disorders, and on the day of the meeting the building was cordoned off with troops outside and teemed with police inside. The mystery, then, was how a band of fascists succeeded in entering the building, raising the *tricolore*, sacking offices, disrupting the proceedings, and then vanishing again without being apprehended, particularly as a number of the fascists were already well known and were even identified by journalists present at the time.[60] The explanation, of course, as Olivieri himself concludes, was that 'the fascists succeeded in entering the Provincial Hall because of the lack of opposition they encountered from the police and particularly because of the open sympathy of the officers and men of the 69th Infantry Division'.[61]

In addition, the crushing of the rebellion in the working-class neighbourhoods of Florence after the murder of Spartaco Lavagnini was a clear instance of close cooperation between the army and the squads. The regular army and the blackshirts crushed the revolt together, and afterwards paraded, still together, through the streets exhibiting the 'trophies' they had claimed in reprisal raids against the homes of socialist party militants.[62] Much the same occurred almost contemporaneously at Siena, where a furious resistance by the workers at the Casa del Popolo was put down by the cannon and machine guns of 200 troops, who then stood aside and watched as the squads plundered the building and set it alight.[63]

From that time, as the reaction began to gather momentum, the evidence is almost endless. At Cerreto Guidi (Florence) the *commissario prefettizio* Franceschi forced all municipal employees to join the *fascio*.[64] At Barberino di Mugello (Florence) the socialists were arrested *en masse* by the police and beaten in their cells before being released.[65] A refinement of this procedure was adopted at Empoli, where socialists arrested by the *carabinieri* were delivered directly to the squadrists for punishment.[66] In the zone of Volterra the socialist deputy Modigliani reported that the *carabinieri* trained young squadrists, including convicted felons, in the use of firearms.[67] In Siena the commander-in-chief of the *carabiniere* division, Major Calcaterra, openly and publicly declared himself to be 'ultra-fascist'.[68] In Pitigliano (Grosseto) the commander of the local *carabinieri* station gave the fascists a free rein to commit 'every sort of violence and threat against the citizens'.[69] From Pisa province even Frigerio admitted simply that 'the *carabinieri* and the army are openly and partisanly for the fascists',[70] and a number of officers on active duty were officially enrolled in the *fascio*.[71] Similarly, the Livorno fascist branch included among its 'active elements' regular naval and artillery officers.[72] In the commune of Prato the troops of the *carabinieri* regularly joined the squads in their actions.[73] At Seravezza (Lucca) the Minister of the Interior complained in the autumn of 1921 of 'systematic violence' against the workers. 'There are complaints of the inertia of the *carabinieri* and of their stubborn complicity with fascist elements'.[74] At Lucca the *fascio* was founded largely on the initiative of Colonel Umberto Minuti,[75] and the collusion between the authorities and the fascists was such that the prefect Di Donato reported:

As for the elements composing the security forces, while I can count on the investigating agents, I have reservations about the RR.CC, who have not always fulfilled their duty when it was a question of acting against the fascists and their sympathizers.

With regard to the army contingent, it is made up mainly of the soldiers of the school for reserve officers and NCO's. These are nearly all fascists...[76]

The most extensive evidence, however, as well as the most revealing with respect to the involvement of the very highest police and military authorities, emerges from the investigations carried out by the Ministry of the Interior into the circumstances surrounding three of the most violent squadrist exploits in this entire period of bloody civil war – the expeditions to Grosseto, Roccastrada, and Foiano della Chiana. Police reports on these events revealed unmistakably that the fascist work of terror was carried out with the knowledge, the approval, and the assistance at all levels of the Tuscan military and police hierarchies.

Perhaps the point of departure here should be the military occupation by 1,000 armed squadrists in June 1921 of Grosseto, until then the socialist stronghold of southern Tuscany and the capital of a province where until then the indigenous forces of reaction were virtually nonexistent as an effective political force. It was for this very reason that fascists converged from all over Tuscany to institute a 'night of the long knives' during the night of 29 to 30 June, leaving 55 people dead and 16 wounded, and the major socialist headquarters and the homes of party militants sacked.[77] The mere fact that trains and lorries filled with armed fascists were able to converge upon the city from centres throughout the region (Florence, Siena, Livorno, Lucca, Chiusi, Montepulciano, Arezzo, Foiano della Chiana) and then to invade the city and wage pitched battles with the socialists without once encountering police resistance and without a single arrest being made or a weapon confiscated is itself a clear indication of the attitude of the authorities. There is in addition, however, the direct testimony of Inspector General Paolella, who arrived at Grosseto during the small hours of the night and described his experience. 'The city' he reported,

> teemed with squads and fascists who boldfacedly displayed weapons of every description. At the entrance to the city I noted three fascists armed with army rifles amicably chatting with a patrol of *carabinieri*. I immediately took command and neither to the prefect, Boragno, nor the *questore*, Frasca, did I hide my surprise at the abnormal state of affairs, and particularly at the deplorable inactivity and complicity of the police forces. They replied that the commander of the division of *carabinieri*, Major Mario Duboin, had ordered his men to adopt this course of action... I gave precise orders during the night that those responsible for criminal action be disarmed and arrested. But despite my instructions not one arrest was carried out and no weapons were confiscated.[78]

Paolella's arrival during the fascist occupation of Grosseto was only a part of a long period of acquaintance by the inspector of the collaboration of the authorities with the *fasci* and of the sabotage of his own efforts to restore order and a semblance of impartiality. Not long after the events of Grosseto, Paolella conducted an investigation into the frightful slaughter at Roccastrada, where the fascists had set fire at random to peasant cottages, burned ricks, and indiscriminately shot those they encountered, killing ten and wounding others.

As usual, the fascists had picked their target well as Roccastrada was a major socialist stronghold where the peasants had organized a production cooperative and which had been the scene of armed resistance to an earlier fascist raid.[79] As usual also, Paolella found that the *carabinieri* had been present in force before the end of the fascist exploit, but had not intervened, even though they outnumbered the squadrists by 85 to 46. In fact, among the blackshirts on the occasion was an official of the Prefecture, a certain Rocco di Rienzi.[80] Not only had the *carabinieri* been guilty at the time of criminal negligence, but afterwards the regional commander-in-chief of the RR.CC, General Leopoldo Ferré, 'whose pro-fascist sympathies are well known, especially in Florentine circles', when informed of the facts, 'tended to excuse them, and, not rarely, even to justify them'.[81] As a result, although he was able to identify those responsible for the massacre, which was led and directed by Dino Castellani, secretary of the Grosseto *fascio*, and had arrest warrants issued against them, the warrants were never carried out and Castellani remained at large, and even continued his political activity undisturbed.

Indeed, almost the only practical effect of his efforts was that Paolella's life was threatened.[82] In the inspector's own words,

Of the collusion and support of the *carabinieri* in the recent disorders in the Maremma I have had clear proof. Nearly every order I gave was communicated to the fascists, which created a very hostile atmosphere around me, so much so that I was threatened with a punitive expedition. It is sufficient to note that of thirty-three arrest warrants personally issued by me in all secrecy, only four were executed.

And, as for the army, as an instance of its attitude, I shall point out that during the abnormal situation at Grosseto I was compelled to have the commander of the garrison rebuked because at the end of the exercises the captain of the detachment used to have his men march across the city singing *Giovinezza*.[83]

To Paolella's account we need only add that the captain of the Grosseto *carabiniere* detachment, Bavaresco, was in fact a fascist closely associated with the local commander of the squads, Valentino Adami, and that several officers of the command of the Grosseto army headquarters were enrolled in the *fascio*. Indeed, one of them, Filippo di Gennaro, was reported to be a member of the *direttorio* of the *fascio* at Civitavecchia.[84] Furthermore, the famous General Ferré exposed his views not only to

Paolella, but even to the High Command of the military police. In a report on the conduct of the *carabinieri* in Pisa province, he resolutely defended his subordinates by denying all allegations of their collusion with the fascists as falsifications fabricated by interested parties with ulterior motives. So upright were the *carabinieri* at Pisa, in fact, that Ferré concluded his report with the statement, 'I have, therefore, no proposals to submit to the High Command.'[85]

Leopoldo Ferré was not, however, the only commanding officer in the region prepared to protect his subordinates from disciplinary action for their political activism on behalf of the counter-revolution. The regular army commander-in-chief in Tuscany, General Giacomo Ponzio, was similarly inclined. Reporting in 1922 on the conduct of the *carabinieri* in Siena province, where, if anything, the complicity of the military police with fascism was even more blatant than in Pisa, General Ponzio pronounced the troops free of all blame and denied the need for further disciplinary measures. At the end of his statement, Ponzio summarized,

After what has been said above, it is superfluous to insist that the action of the *carabinieri* in Siena province is guided by the necessary impartiality and calm, and that the force carried out its mission of enforcing the law upon all with full rectitude, for which reason this General Command sees no need for further measures...[86]

Yet more evidence revealing the behaviour of the police forces, and linking the highest military authorities in the region to the reaction, emerged in the wake of the squadrist raids on Foiano della Chiana of 12 and 17 April 1921. Again, the official investigation on behalf of the Ministry of the Interior was entrusted to Paolella. Reporting on the events which had occurred, he wrote:

In their various expeditions, the fascists have made an ostentatious display of arms and large quantities of munitions – arms and munitions which are certainly furnished by military personnel, not a few of whom are enrolled in the movement.

The incursion at Foiano in fact was led by Captain Giuseppe Figino who commanded the detachment of the 70th Infantry Division on police duty at Arezzo, and took with him two model 91 rifles from the barracks and gave them to the fascists.

But I am informed even by army circles that most of the arms and munitions come from the arsenals of Perugia and Florence, and particularly the latter city.[87]

Perhaps the most important point to emerge from this statement is the fact that the *fasci* were regularly supplied with weapons from the military arsenals at Florence. Specifically on the Foiano expedition, the fascists had been issued, the Minister of War Rodinò confirmed, with 50 rifles and the requisite ammunition from the arsenal of the 19th Artillery Regiment on the authority of the lieutenant colonel in command.[88] Still with reference to the 19th Artillery Regiment, the major Florence squadrist Bruno Frullini noted,

Certain objects belonging to the 19th Regiment went in vast numbers to join the books in the basement of the Gonnelli shop.

Every now and then I made a small withdrawal, which served magnificently for our action and for our expeditions.[89]

It was this ready supply of military equipment, and the presence of trained officers to direct its use which gave the fascists such a decisive advantage over the unarmed socialists and *popolari*. Moreover, the fact that the sources of weapons were the army arsenals of the capital served effectively to strengthen the power of the Florence *fascio* as the directing centre of the regional fascist offensive. Most importantly, the massive collusion of the authorities with fascism helped to set the movement on the road to Rome.

CONCLUSION

Tuscan fascism began as a small band of anti-socialist vigilantes in the murky backwaters of Florentine politics in 1919 and 1920. In 1921, in the wake of the attempt by the left to overturn the existing structures of power, Mussolini's movement expanded dramatically and in geometric progression throughout the region. Imitating methods first tested in Trieste, Ferrara, and Bologna, the Tuscan fascists destroyed the socialist and Catholic unions as effective political forces before the end of the year. In the process the *fasci di combattimento* acquired a mobilized political following, a powerful paramilitary organization, substantial sources of finance, and a thick network of party branches. In 1922 the Tuscan fascists were in a position to sieze local power and to lay the local foundations for the October *coup d'état*.

The meteoric rise of the extreme right was no accident or 'parenthesis' in Tuscan history. Such a description could be applied accurately to fascism in the South of Italy. In the Mezzogiorno, with the exception of Apulia, fascism was a sickly and transplanted growth, an offshoot of the success of the movement elsewhere. Fascism had no deep bases in the structure of southern Italian society. There was large-scale unrest south of Rome during the postwar crisis, but it rapidly petered out. The South gave rise to a series of spontaneous and unorganized protests – land occupations, demonstrations, and riots – that presented no genuine challenge to overturn the social order. There was no need for squadrism.

Tuscany was entirely different. In the eight provinces fascism achieved a dynamism that was surpassed, if at all, only in Emilia. The revolutionary right in Tuscany waged a victorious civil war against the mass parties of the left. In the process it developed its own distinct leadership, program, and organizational structures. Far from waiting for the tide of events elsewhere to tip the local situation in their favour as southern fascist leaders did, the Tuscan *ras* exploited the strength of the movement in the region to aid their comrades in other regions.

Just as in the North, therefore, so too in Tuscany fascism was an integral part of the development of the society. Immediate circumstances contributed to its appeal – war-time divisions, demobilization, economic recession – but they are not adequate to explain its strength and the specific social groups it recruited. Fascism was not a mere product of outraged patriotism; a psychological escape from the tensions of unemployment and 'mass society'; a violent expression of the insecurities unleashed by the conversion of the economy to peace-time production after the industrial boom of the war; or a simple counter-revolution. All of these factors played a part, but none is sufficient to explain the success of Dino Perrone Compagni and his squads.

For this purpose it is essential to explore the long-term tensions embedded in the structures of the society. Most important of all was the conflict between landlord and tenant, which had a long pre-history. The intensity of the conflict and the specific issues of contention are intelligible only in the context of the whole crisis of traditional *mezzadria*. Fascism in this sense arose in the Tuscan countryside as a violent means of repressing the stresses generated by the modernization of Tuscan agriculture.

The encompassing of the former Grand Duchy within first a national and then a world market necessitated the rationalization of production in order to withstand the competition of more advanced agricultural systems. Such rationalization had a major effect on class relationships as well as upon crop rotations, investment levels, and machinery. In the new commercial *mezzadria* the authority of the landlord declined, the occasions for conflict between lord and peasant multiplied, and the established methods of containing and defusing grievances from below were overwhelmed. In this already highly charged context, 'accidental' or externally imposed circumstances such as recession and the war-time promises of the state raised the simmering discontent of the sharecroppers into an all-out assault on the power of the landlords in 1919 and 1920. Fascism re-imposed hierarchy, authority, and the rights of property.

For this reason the Tuscan example does not refute the link between fascism and the modernization of agriculture so apparent in the more highly developed and more frequently studied sectors of farming in the Po Valley. On the fully modernized and capitalist farms of Ferrara, Rovigo, Ravenna, Cremona, and Bologna provinces the modern world visibly entailed the destruction of peasant society altogether. Here a clearly capitalist class structure emerged in the form of leaseholding farmers at one pole of the social scale and the mass of proletarianized day labourers at the other. The Po Valley fascist bosses such as Italo Balbo and Dino Grandi acted in the interest of a developing agrarian capitalism. They preserved profit, labour discipline, and managerial authority from the necessity of making fundamental concessions to the rural trade unions. In the North, agrarian fascism, as Barrington Moore so fruitfully suggested and a variety of local studies have confirmed, was related to the tensions of modernization.

Tuscany, the heartland of the apparently traditional *mezzadria*, appears to undermine such an approach. Upon closer inspection, however, the contradiction is dispelled. *Mezzadria* remained the legal form of the contract between landlord and tenant, but the effective content of the social relationship involved grew ever more to resemble the northern Italian bond between farmer and rural proletarian. Tuscan fascism, no less than fascism in Emilia, enabled property owners and managers to suppress the class conflicts generated by modernization.

Nevertheless, the fact that in Tuscany capitalist development took place through the commercialization of an existing peasant society rather than through its replacement by a more fully developed rural capitalism did produce important traits specific to central Italy. Because it developed in a context of relative occupational homogeneity among those who worked the land, fascism was far less able in Tuscany than in the 'classic' provinces of the North to attract a popular following. The Tuscan fascists were unable to exploit the contrasting interests of day labourers and intermediate peasants in order to divide one group against another. Whereas northern Italian fascism operated with substantial claims to be a populist movement of the right, the *fasci* to the south of the Apennines were unambiguously the instruments of the landlords.

This distinguishing feature led in turn to two other salient aspects of the movement. The first was the degree of the reliance on terror. Violence, however, was an intrinsic part of fascist practice everywhere, and squadrism can be understood on no other terms. The distinction is that in Tuscany fascism consisted during the postwar years of little other than systematic repression and intimidation. The movement made little effort, as it did in the North, to recruit a broadly based following. The Tuscan *fasci* were not prepared to elaborate programs or to debate ideas. Fascism attracted intellectuals, but what they brought to the cause was the acceptance of the vision prophetically described by the futurist Ardengo Soffici. In his novel *Lemmonio Boreo*, Soffici, himself a future squadrist, portrayed a venomous modern Don Quixote bent on ridding his country of subversives and parasites. Putting his books away with the view that discussion and persuasion were useless and too late, Lemmonio Boreo set about silencing his enemies with fists, clubs, and dogs. Only in the use of dogs and in the absence of lorries and rifles did Soffici fail to foretell the actual practice of the Florence squads.

In addition to an overwhelming reliance on violence, the peculiarities of the Tuscan social structure imposed on fascism a marked centralization in the regional capital. Florence played a role unparalleled in any other region in the development of the *fasci*. The capital directed the activities of branches throughout the eight provinces of the region, and the Florence squads, led by the élite 'La Disperata', played a leading role in 'punitive expeditions' everywhere in Tuscany.

Such was the extent of the part played by the capital that a problem of interpretation arises. An important theme in the literature of the rise of fascism in Italy is the division between 'agrarian' and urban or industrial fascism. Fascism in the countryside was more extreme, more violent, and more broadly based. The problem in relation to Tuscany is that urban squadrists from the capital played the decisive part in the destruction of agrarian socialism. If the grocer and the clerk from Florence were the leading figures in the spreading of terror to rustic Foiano della Chiana and Roccastrada, how valid is it to describe the agrarian question as central to fascism? What is the purpose of stressing the crisis of *mezzadria*? Would it not be more useful to describe Tuscan fascism as a product of the urban petit-bourgeoisie?

The problem with such a view is that the petit-bourgeoisie – the white-collar employee, the retailer, and the clerk – did not constitute an independent political force. There were, of course, specific grievances that helped to drive this sector of society, which the fascist theorist A. Lanzillo termed the 'twilight zone' of Italian political life, into politics. They were united, for example, by anti-socialism, patriotism, a shortage of prospects in a straitened economy and the insecurity of inflation. On the other hand, the lower middle classes were too amorphous to have created a political movement of their own. When they joined fascism, they were participating in a political force whose social agenda was set by more powerful interests.

Still more importantly, the role of the urban petit-bourgeoisie suggests the multifaceted impact of the agrarian question. The Tuscan experience suggests that any rigid distinction between 'urban' and 'agrarian' fascism is untenable. In Florence, Siena, and Pisa, for instance, the agrarian interests of the urban population were extensive. Many professionals, traders, and employees of town hall had long invested their savings in the purchase of smallholdings that they ran on the basis of *mezzadria*, even with just a single *podere* and a single tenant family. For them the socialization of the land and the rise of unionization were a direct threat. For employers in the building and textile trades, the work-force they confronted was composed of peasants, and was represented by the farm workers' union. For everyone in the towns, rising prices seemed to be deeply affected by the agitations of the *mezzadri*. At the same time, it was the votes of newly politicized sharecroppers that returned socialist local administrations that raised such thorny urban issues as tax reform and tenants' rights, and menaced the existing distribution of municipal contracts, permits, and licences. The cities, in Mao Tse-tung's famous phrase, seemed indeed to be surrounded by the countryside, and the petty bourgeoisie made common cause with the landlord in crushing the peasant threat.

A more telling difficulty is posed by industry. Unlike the pattern that predominated at the national level, Tuscan industry and Tuscan agriculture took up a common fascist militancy. Tuscan industrialists showed few of the hesitations of the national leaders of Confindustria in coming to terms with Mussolini. On the contrary, leading industrialists in every sector embraced fascism openly in its most violent form.

This behaviour on the part of Tuscan big business was exceptional. For some sectors of industry the explanation again suggests the interdependence of industrial and agrarian capitalism. For the pasta-maker, the textile entrepreneur, and the chemical manufacturer, agrarian unrest and peasant unionization directly affected their interests. They depended on agriculture for labour, raw materials, and a market. Important members of their boards of directors were landlords directly involved in the contest for control of the land.

Although valid as a significant factor in explaining the behaviour of some sectors of industry, the idea of the convergence of interests between town and countryside does not apply to all of Tuscan manufacturing. The shipbuilders of Livorno, the steel producers of Piombino and Portoferraio, and the marble quarriers of Massa-Carrara were far removed from a direct dependence on the countryside. Their pro-fascism was none the less intense, and challenges any notion that fascism cannot be industrial as well as agrarian.

The conclusion in relation to the experience of one region is that the decisive motor force in the emergence of fascism was the agrarian question. The success of the movement, however, was founded on its ability to attract other and more contingent interests pushed into political activism by the fear of socialism, the pride of patriotism, and the tensions of an economy in crisis. Tuscan fascism, although rooted above all in the countryside, did not defend just the interests of a single class. It represented instead a constellation of social interests that had in common the horror of Italian bolshevism, the loss of confidence in the state, and the willingness to use violence to defend order, property, and hierarchy.

NOTES

I PARTNERSHIP AND LOVE

1 In 1930, according to the agricultural census, there were about 4,100 *fattorie* in Tuscany of an average size of just over 200 hectares. The actual distribution according to size was the following:

Under 100 hectares		100 to 300 hectares		Over 500 hectares	
number	area	number	area	number	area
2,361	40,186 ha	1,318	297,907 ha	442	499,705 ha

Ministero per la Costituente, *Rapporto della commissione economica: agricoltura*, 2 vols. (Rome, 1946–7), vol. I, p. 21

It should be noted that the size of the *fattoria* provides little indication of the concentration of landownership in Tuscany, as the property of a single landlord very often included a number of *fattorie*, sometimes located in several provinces.

The number of *poderi* per *fattoria* varied enormously, but was seldom fewer than ten. Angelo Camparini and Mario Bandini, *Rapporti fra proprietà impresa e mano d'opera nell'agricoltura italiana: Toscana* (Rome, 1930).

The total cultivated area of Tuscany in 1939 was 2,162,753 hectares: Osservatorio di Economia Agraria per la Toscana, *L'economia agraria della Toscana* (Rome, 1939), p. 49.

2 Quoted in Ernesto Ragionieri, 'La questione delle leghe e i primi scioperi dei mezzadri in Toscana', *Movimento operaio*, 7 (1955), p. 454.

Much the same hope of introducing *mezzadria* into industry had been expressed in 1836 by Marquis Capponi, who declared:

I am of the opinion that if a solution is ever to be found to the grand question, as it regards the working classes, and if in manufactures the plan is ever to be discovered of better reconciling the interest of the workman with that of the employer, it will be in approximating the manufacturing system to that which is pursued in agriculture under the denomination of mezzeria ... (Quoted in John Bowring, *Report on the Statistics of Tuscany, Lucca, the Pontifical, and the Lombardo-Venetian States, with a Special Reference to their Commercial Relations* (London, 1837), in British Parliamentary Papers, 1839, vol. XVI (165), p. 43.)

For a similar view that *mezzadria* was 'the application of a natural law to agriculture' and the same wish that 'the spirit of *mezzadria* must be gradually

extended to other forms of human activity', see Ildebrando Imberciadori, *Per la storia della mezzadria* (Florence, 1941), p. 17.
3 Quoted in Carlo Pazzagli, *L'agricoltura toscana nella prima metà dell'800* (Florence, 1973), p. 429.
   Of all the statements of the political effectiveness of *mezzadria* as a source of political stability, perhaps the most famous is that of Sidney Sonnino, who wrote:
   In *mezzadria* there is a large class of cultivators of conservative views who are directly interested in the keeping of the peace, who are the enemies of all disorder, and who are the watchful upholders of law and order. Even in those moments when [elsewhere] ... every political action of the authorities is made uncertain and weak, in Tuscany opposition has never found support ... because it is opposed by the peasants, who themselves cooperate in the work of repression. ('La mezzeria in Toscana', in Leopoldo Franchetti, *Condizioni economiche ed amministrative delle province napoletane* (Florence, 1875), p. 214.
4 A. Giovannini, 'I funerali della mezzeria', *Messaggero del Mugello*, 28 March 1920.
5 *Ibid.* For a more recent defence of the 'official' view of *mezzadria*, see the interview with Baron Luigi Ricasoli in Ministero per la Constituente, *Rapporto della commissione economica*, II, pp. 146–53. See also James Aguet, *La terra ai contadini* (Rome, 1920), pp. 82–6.
6 My account of traditional mezzadria and of the developments which profoundly changed it is based above all on the following:
   Accademia R. Economico-agraria dei Georgofili, *Atti*
   Bastogi, G. A., *Una scritta colonica* (Florence, 1903)
   Fattore toscano
   Giorgetti, Giorgio, 'Agricoltura e sviluppo capitalistico nella Toscana del'700', *Studi storici*, 9 (1968), pp. 742–84
   Giunta per la Inchiesta Agraria, *Atti*, vol. III, fasc. 1: *La Toscana agricola: Relazione sulle condizioni dell'agricoltura e degli agricoltori nella IX circoscrizione (provincie de Firenze, Arezzo, Siena, Lucca, Pisa e Livorno)* (Rome, 1881)
   Istituto Nazionale di Economia Agraria, *Inchiesta sulla piccola proprietà coltivatrice formatasi nel dopoguerra*, 15 vols., (Rome, n.d.), esp. vol. by Bandini, *La Toscana*, and vol. by Giovanni Lorenzoni, *L'ascesa del contadino italiano nel dopoguerra* (Rome, 1938)
   Rapporti fra proprietà, impresa e mano d'opera nell'agricoltura italiana, 18 vols., esp. vol. by Comparini and Bandini, *La Toscana*
   Ministero per la Costituente, *Rapporto della commissione economica*
   Mirri, Mario, 'Mercato regionale e internazionale e mercato nazionale capitalistico come condizione dell'evoluzione interna della mezzadria in Toscana', in Istituto Antonio Gramsci, *Agricoltura e sviluppo del capitalismo* (Rome, 1970), pp. 393–428
   Mori, Giorgio, 'La mezzadria in Toscana alla fine del XIX secolo', *Movimento operaio*, 7 (1955), pp. 479–510
   La Valdelsa dal 1848 al 1900: sviluppo economico, movimenti sociali e lotta politica (Milan, 1957)
   Osservatorio di Economia Agraria per la Toscana, *L'economia agraria della Toscana* (Rome, 1939)
   Pazzagli, Carlo, *L'agricoltura toscana*
   Petrocchi, Bernardino, *L'agricoltura nella provincia di Firenze* (Florence, 1927)

Radi, Luciano, *I mezzadri: le lotte contadine nell'Italia centrale* (Rome, 1962)
Ragionieri, Ernesto, 'La questione delle leghe e i primi scioperi dei mezzadri in Toscana', *Movimento operaio*, 7 (1955), pp. 454–8
Sereni, Emilio, *Il capitalismo nelle campagne, 1850–1900* (Turin, 1948)

7 On the landowners' use of *stime*, see Giorgetti, *Agricoltura*, p. 749; and Reginaldo Cianferoni, 'I contadini e l'agricoltura in Toscana sotto il fascismo', in Unione Regionale delle Province Toscane, *La Toscana nell'Italia unita, 1861–1945* (Florence, 1962), pp. 390–1 n.21.
8 Quoted in R. Cianferoni, 'I contadini e l'agricoltura', p. 387. Luciano Radi succinctly summed up the opposition of class interests between lord and tenant with respect to the size of the *podere*: 'whereas the total saleable production per unit area of land increased as the size of the *podere* decreased, production per unit of labour increased as the size of the *podere* increased' (*I mezzadri*, p. 88).
9 Quoted in Luciano Radi, *I mezzadri: le lotte contadine dell'Italia centrale* (Rome, 1962), p. 239.
10 Frank McArdle, *Altopascio: A Study in Tuscan Rural Society, 1587–1784* (Cambridge, 1978), ch. 3.
11 On peasant overwork under the traditional system of *mezzadria* see Pazzagli, *L'agricoltura toscana*.

The socialist Carolo Scarperi also wrote in 1930:
> The *mezzadro* has no set hours nor legal protection, and in the summer season he works up to twenty hours a day. His children and his women come under the terms of no child labour laws or protective legislation. The maintenance of the *podere* imposes the mobilization of the entire family without regard even for the infirmities of its members. ('Il mezzadro si ribella', *Difesa*, 24 July 1920).

The fascist paper of Lucca, the *Intrepido*, took pains to emphasize that the ability to squeeze the utmost labour from the entire peasant family was the great benefit of *mezzadria*. In systems of wage labour, children, the aged, the ill, and the disabled were lost to the economic system. In *mezzadria*, by contrast, these forces too were set in motion – and at no cost to the landlord! The aged and the sick were put to work guarding the haystacks, and small children were set the lighter chores in the fields, about the house, or in the animal sties. Thus,
> It is from this free provision of forces that are minimal but always in motion that the landlord and the *mezzadro* make a profit. The former is freed from having to pay for those small services while for the latter the convalescent, the old man, and the child cease to be completely unproductive and a burden. Weekly articles signed 'L. M.', 'Il problema agrario', *Intrepido*, 28 May 1922.

12 Quoted in Bowring, *Report on the Statistics*, pp. 42–3.
13 Mario Tofani, 'I mezzadri nell'Italia centrale', in Ministero per la Costituente, *Rapporto della commissione economica*, vol. II, p. 476; C. Passerini, *Redditi di contadini e di operai* (Verona, 1938); Giorgetti, *Agricoltura*.
14 'Ai contadini', *Difesa*, 31 May 1900.
15 *L'assicurazione e la legislazione sociale* (Florence, 1898).
16 *Ibid.*, pp. 3–4.
17 *Ibid.*, p. 11.
18 *Ibid.*, Mazzini returned to the theme in 1912. See *Assistenza, previdenza ed assicurazioni sociali* (Florence, 1912).
19 Quoted in Mori, *La Valdelsa*, p. 25.
20 'The erroneous self-sufficing principle', declared Capponi, 'pervades every-

thing, even to the extent that a single field should produce everything, that one man should do everything; there is no such thing as division of labour – no intermediate branch of occupation.' Quoted in Bowring, *Report*, p. 42.

21 Arthur Young had noted in 1796 that the soil of Tuscany tended to be of poor quality in the valleys as well as in the hills:
Almost all the hills are composed of tufa or of a mixture of clay and loam; they are therefore hardly suitable for tilling. And the valleys, being either formed or changed by the rivers that bathe them, must necessarily be of low fertility as these rivers carry with them the arid bits of earth that they took from the hills. *Voyage en Italie*, trans. François Soulés (Paris, 1796), p. 246.

The principal exceptions to the general infertility of the Tuscan soil were the Arno Valley, the Elsa Valley, and – above all – the Chiana Valley, the traditional 'granary of Tuscany'.

22 Referring to the previous investment of capital immobilized in terrace cultivation and farm buildings, Capponi stated in 1836 that,
Under these two heads Tuscany presents a peculiarity completely characteristic, and the immense expenses incurred ... create great difficulties in the way of adopting any other mode of cultivation, even should the system pursued become ruinous. Quoted in Bowring, *Report on the Statistics*, p. 43.

23 On *mezzadria* as an obstacle to the rationalization of agricultural production, see Giorgetti, Agricoltura, Mirri, 'Mercato', and J. C. L. Simonde de Sismondi, *Tableau de l'agriculture toscane* (Geneva, 1801), pp. 207–19.

24 In this analysis of the conditions of Tuscan *mezzadri*, the fascist paper of Lucca, the *Intrepido*, reported that poaching was so widespread that during the harvest season the tenant families slept in the fields, preferably armed with hunting rifles, to guard the crop. *Intrepido*, 9 July 1921.

This aspect of rural social relations was conveyed by the traditional Tuscan proverbs: 'Tra mal d'occhio e l'acqua cotta, il padrone non gliene tocca' (Between crop disease and the water boiling in the peasant's kitchen, the landlord never sees his share); and 'Cento scrivani non guardano un fattore e cento fattori non guardano un contadino' (A hundred accountants are not enough to keep watch on a *fattore*, and hundred *fattori* are not enough to keep watch on a peasant). Giuseppe Giusti, *Raccolta di proverbi toscani* (Florence, 1913), pp. 8 and 18.

25 'Impressioni di agricoltura toscana', *Fattore toscano* 24 November 1912. On the position of the *fattore*, see Bastogi, *Una scritta colonica*, pp. 40–52.

26 'La figura morale e giuridica degli agenti rurali (fattori, sottofattori, guardie campestri, garzoni, ecc.)', *Bandiera rossa – Martinella*, 6 January 1921.

27 This is the description of Lambruschi in the middle of the nineteenth century. Quoted in Pazzagli, *L'agricoltura toscana*, p. 410.

28 On the role of patronage and paternalism in central Italian *mezzadria*, see Sydel F. Silverman, 'Patronage and Community-Nation Relationships in Central Italy', *Ethnology*, 4 (1965), pp. 172–90; and *Three Bells of Civilization: The Life of an Italian Hill Town* (New York and London, 1975), pp. 87ff.

On the importance of paternal aid, the accounts of the landlord Ferdinando Vai for his *fattoria* of Mulinaccio near Prato (Florence province) are eloquent. For the single year May 1912 to May 1913 in the records of the 35 *poderi* which made up the estate, there is a host of such entries as '255.38 lire – produce administered for food'; '10 lire – cash given to Paolo Sizzi for his needs'; '100 lire – cash advanced to Francesco Vangi to buy wheat'; '70 lire –

cash given to Augusto Biancalani on the occasion of the death of his wife'; and '30 lire – cash given to Giovacchino Becocci on the occasion of the illness of his father and son'. ASP, AVR, Filza 421 ('Mulinaccio: conti colonici dal giugno 1912 al 31 maggio 1913').

29 On the importance of lordly paternalism as a factor in Tuscan social stability, see below, pp. 23–4 and note 56.

On the continuing direct involvement of the landowners in the region with the affairs of their estates even in the early decades of the twentieth century, see Bandini, *La Toscana* in Istituto Nazionale di Economia Agraria, *Inchiesta*, p. 20.

30 Quoted in Bastogi, *Una scritta colonica*, p. 37.

31 For Weber's use of the concept of traditional or patriarchal authority, see Max Weber, *Economy and Society* (New York, 1968), 3 vols., pp. 212–17, 237–41, 1006–10. See also H. H. Gerth and C. Wright Mills, eds., *From Max Weber: Essays in Sociology* (London, 1948), pp. 78–9, 245–7, 295–301.

32 'Della condizione degli agricoltori in Toscana', *Biblioteca dell'economista*, series 2, vol. II (Turin, 1860), p. 549.

33 *Atti del Parlamento Italiano*, Camera dei Deputati, Legislatura XXV, Sessione 1919–20, Discussioni, VII, p. 6576.

34 For estimates of the size of the sharecropping family, see pp. 27–8.

35 Sismondi, 'Della condizione degli agricoltori', pp. 551–2.

36 Giorgetti, *Agricoltura*, pp. 749–50.

37 On the traditional authority of the *capoccia* (or *reggitore*) within the *mezzadro* family as recognized in law, see Raffaele Cognetti De Martiis, 'La famiglia colonica e la consuetudine', *Rivista di diritto agrario*, II (1932), p. 199.

On the institutions of the tenant family and the *capocciato* the central work is Mario C. Ferrigni, *Il capoccia nella mezzeria toscana: appunti di diritto civile* (Florence, 1901). See also Bastogi, *Una scritta colonica*, esp. pp. 52–9; and Sismondi, *Tableau de l'agriculture toscane*, pp. 100–1.

38 See 'Disdetta di colonia', 14 October 1915, ASP, AVR, Filza 110, fasc. 2, sottofasc. 'Mulinaccio: disdetta – Giovacchino Becocci'.

39 See 'Disdetta di colonia', 16 October 1915, ASP, AVR, Filza 110, fasc. 2, sottofasc. 'Mulinaccio: disdetta – Pietro Fioravanti'.

40 Ferrigni, *Il capoccia*, p. 26.

In much the same spirit, Gino Sarrocchi, in a speech to the Chamber, termed the *capocciato* a 'rigid and miserly authority'. *Atti del Parlamento Italiano*, Camera dei Deputati, Legislatura XXV, Sessione 1919–20, Discussioni, VII, p. 6579.

41 Karl Marx, 'The Eighteenth Brumaire of Louis Bonaparte', in Karl Marx and Frederick Engels, *Selected Works* (Moscow, 1962), vol. I, p. 334.

42 Bowring, *Report on the Statistics*, p. 42.

43 The socialist paper of Florence wrote at the turn of the century of the Tuscan peasants 'who, by living in cottages dotted across the countryside, are kept from contact with other peasants and with the workers in the towns'. 'Ai contadini', *Difesa*, 12 May 1901.

44 Quoted in Pazzagli, *L'agricoltura*, pp. 414–15. Similarly, the Bastogi pact declared that

It will not be tolerated that members of the tenant family should frequent markets and fairs without good cause known to the Proprietors or their agents, as it will not be allowed that they should attend taverns and wine bars, where vice is practised, and where there is gaming, which is the ruin of families. It will be equally and severely

prohibited for the tenant to go hunting, with whatever means, on the estate or off it. ...
   Should the tenant lend himself to a dissolute and scandalous life, whether for offences against the law or against morals, the Proprietors shall have the right to seek the immediate termination of the contract. (*Una scritta colonica*, p. 137.)
45 Mori, *La Valdelsa*, p. 17.
46 On the Italian fiscal system as a means of primitive accumulation, see Rosario Romeo, *Breve storia della grande industria in Italia* (Rocca Sancasciano, 1972, first edn 1961), ch. 2.
   For an account of the specific measures employed, see the sections on finance in Epicarmo Corbino, *Annali dell'economia italiana*, 4 vols. (Città di Castello, 1931–8)).
47 *Le recenti agitazioni agrarie e i doveri della proprietà* (Rome, 1907), pp. 39–40.
48 On the crisis of *mezzadria* and the role in that crisis played by transoceanic competition and the tariff war, see Mori, 'La mezzadria'. On the longer-term importance of the relation between Tuscan *mezzadria* and the international market, see Mirri, 'Mercato'.
   On the price oscillations of wheat and corn in particular from 1851 to 1914, see Ministero per la Costituente, *Rapporto della commissione economica*, vol. I, pp. 478–80 and 480–1.
49 On the introduction of industrial crops in Italy the standard work is Vittorio Peglion, *Le nostre piante industriali: canapa, lino, bietola da zucchero, tabacco, ecc.* (Bologna, 1919). There is also much information in the chapter on agriculture in each volume of Corbino, *Annali dell'economia italiana*.
   On the introduction of tobacco in the Chiana Valley, see Ciro Marchi, 'La coltivazione del tabacco in Valdichiana', Accademia dei Georgofili, *Atti*, *1908*, quinta serie, vol. I, disp. 3a, pp. 283–360. The importance of sugar beet in the Tuscan economy is stressed in the article 'La coltivazione delle barbabietole', *Giovinezza*, 19 March 1922. More generally for a detailed discussion of the crop systems in every agricultural zone of Tuscany, cf. Camparini and Bandini, *Rapporti fra proprietà impresa e mano d'opera*.
50 Giunta per la Inchiesta Agraria, *Atti*, vol. III, fasc. 1: *La Toscana agricola*, p. 276. An example of the timing and nature of the transformations which occurred is provided by the *fattoria* of Fibbiana in the commune of Montelupo (Florence province) belonging to Camilla Durazzo Mannelli-Riccardi. This *fattoria* was transformed in 1890 with the introduction of the new industrial crops, including sugar beet; a quadrennial rotation system; and mechanical equipment. From 1903 modernized fruit cultivation also began with the intensive cultivation of pears and peaches. See Isidoro Valdelsani, 'Liete impressioni di agricoltura toscana: la Fattoria di Fibbiana', *Fattore toscano*, 31 January 1913.
51 Giunta per la Inchiesta Agraria, *Atti*, vol. III, fasc. 1: *La Toscana agricola*, pp. 271–8; Ministero d'Agricoltura, Industria e Commercio, *Notizie intorno alle condizioni dell'agricoltura negli anni 1878–1879* (Rome, 1881).
52 Istituto Nazionale di Economia Agraria, *Inchiesta sulla piccola proprietà coltivatrice formatasi nel dopoguerra* (Rome, n.d.), p. 86.
53 Telegram of Sottoprefetto Cassini to Ministero dell'Interno. Direzione Generale della Pubblica Sicurezza, 12 July 1922, ACS, PS (1922), b. 45, fasc. Arezzo, sottofasc. 'agitazione agraria', n. 731. See also Mori, *La Valdelsa*, pp. 69–70.
54 'Applicabilità del contratto d'impiego ai fattori', *Fattore toscano*, 7 May 1914.

55 Guicciardini, *Le recenti agitazioni agrarie* (Rome, 1907); Pier Francesco Serragli, 'Le agitazioni dei contadini e l'avvenire della mezzeria', reprinted in *La mezzadria negli scritti dei Georgofili*, II (Bologna, 1935), esp. pp. 186–90.

For another example of the advocacy of a renewed lordly paternalism, see the article by the landlord Vittorio Racah, 'La mezzadria e i doveri del proprietario', *Fattore toscano*, 15 February 1913. Racah argued for: a 'return to the land' by absentee proprietors; action by the owners to improve the education and technical knowledge of the peasants; the use of an even and impartial, but firm and never familiar, manner with tenants; the improvement of peasant housing; the provision of medicines by the lords to the tenants in the event of sickness; aid to the tenants in years of poor harvests; the avoidance by the lords of open political preferences; and the maintenance on the estates of a correct balance between the size of the *poderi* and the size of the peasant families.

As a further example of the importance attached by the lords to paternalism as an antidote to agrarian unrest, the leading landlord, T. Pestellini, Serragli's successor as president of the Tuscan Agrarian Association, later emphasized the declining involvement of the Tuscan landlords with their estates as a major cause of the social upheavals which had occurred in the region. In this respect Pestellini contrasted Tuscany with the relative calm in the countryside of the Marches and Umbria, where the landowners were less given to absenteeism, and delegated less of their authority to the *fattori*. Mario Tofani, 'La mezzadria nell'Italia centrale', in Ministero per la Costituente, *Rapporto della commissione economica*; II, p. 474.

For absenteeism on the part of the landowners as an underlying cause of agrarian agitation, cf. also J. Aguet, pp. 54–5. On the increasing absenteeism in Tuscany, cf. Bastogi, *Una scritta colonica*, p. 35.

56 Emilio Sereni, *La questione agraria nella rinascita nazionale italiana* (Rome, 1946, pp. 192–3.
57 Guicciardini, *Le recenti agitazioni*; Mori, *La Valdelsa*, pp. 244–5.
58 Ministero per la Costituente, *Rapporto della commissione economica*, I, p. 218. On the increased burden of expenses falling to the tenant, cf. also Giovanni Perini, 'La mezzadria in Toscana e la revisione del patto colonico', *Messaggero del Mugello*, 22 June 1919; and Guicciardini, *Le recenti agitazioni*, p. 31.
59 Expenses for machinery figured in the debit columns of many of the tenant accounts as an item of still strictly limited proportions, e.g. 10.87 lire on the Pelagio *podere* for 'repair of machines', 4.15 lire at Pelagio-Sacchi; 7.10 lire at Pianaccio; 5.02 lire at Piani; 10.88 lire at Poggiale; and 7.75 lire at Poggio.
60 In 1884 an official medical report on the health conditions of *mezzadri* at Montaione in the commercializing Elsa Valley reported:
The diet, in general, is a mixture of wheat and corn, with a few potatoes, beans, vegetables, and milk. There is also considerable fruit, particularly figs and cherries. Most drink water and little wine ... and there are many cases of pellagra. Moreover, in the last twenty years there have been at least three epidemics of scarlet fever of considerable severity, at least two very serious epidemics of diphtheria, more frequent outbreaks of German measles of mild impact; at least two epidemics of smallpox and at least three of typhus with serious outcome.

Moreover, the report noted that the standards of both nutrition and sanitation were declining. Quoted in Mori, *La Valdelsa*, pp. 198–9.
61 See the weekly articles signed 'L.M.', 'Il problema agrario: condizioni fisiche,

igieniche e sanitarie dei lavoratori della terra', *Intrepido*, 4 June 1922 – 6 August 19212.
62 'L. M.', 'Il problema agrario', *Intrepido*, 9 July 1922 and 16 July 1922.
63 On the diet of *mezzadri*, see 'L. M.', 'Il problema agrario', *Intrepido*, 25 June 1922.
64 'L. M.', 'Il problema agrario', *Intrepido*, 2 July 1922.
65 'L. M.', 'Il problema agrario', *Intrepido*, 18 June 1922.
66 Francesco Niccolai, 'La Fratellanza Colonica Toscana', *Messaggero del Mugello*, 30 October 1921.
67 Giulio Alvi, 'I proprietari terrieri al bivio', *Messaggero toscano*, 2 March 1920.
68 For central Italy (Tuscany, Umbria, and the Marches) and Lazio together the total number of emigrants per year rose from 7,334 in 1876 to 27,486 in 1896, and 121,481 in 1913: Commissariato Generale dell'Emigrazione, *Annuario statistico della emigrazione italiana dal 1876 al 1925* (Rome, 1926), p. 10. From Tuscany alone, in 1876–7, 297 people departed for every 100,000 inhabitants, as compared with 1330 per 100,000 in 1913–14 (*ibid.*).

Interestingly, the Georgofili themselves pointed out that the chief causes of the outward emigration from the region were the increasing combined burden of taxation from the state and indebtedness to the lords. Mortgage debts in Tuscany were reported to be higher than in any other region of Italy. Conte Donato Sanminiatelli, 'Sulla emigrazione rurale, specialmente dalla Toscana e sulla opportunità di moderarla col favorire l'incremento della piccola possidenza', Accademia dei Georgofili, *Atti*, 1912, quinta serie, vol. IX, disp. Ia, pp. 217–19.
69 Osservatorio d'Economia Agraria per la Toscana, *L'economia agraria*, p. 85 and p. 85n.

For a study of the variations in size of sample *poderi* from several *fattorie* in Siena province, see Ugo Sorbi, 'Ampiezza poderale e densità colonica dal 1880 al 1947 in alcune aziende agrarie della Toscana', *Rivista di economia agraria*, 5 (1950), pp. 371–424. The tendency that Sorbi reports is neither uniform nor massive in the *poderi* he examines, but his evidence does point towards a general secular trend towards a reduction in size, at least from the second half of the nineteenth century. As he writes, 'There has been a tendency towards a diminution in the average area of the *podere*' (*ibid.*, p. 421).
70 W. K. Hancock, *Ricasoli and the Risorgimento in Tuscany* (London, 1926), pp. 12–14. Capponi simply suggests a range in size of the traditional family from 6–8 members at one extreme to 20–25 members at the other. Bowring, *Report on the Statistics*, p. 41.
71 Osservatorio d'Economia Agraria per la Toscana, *L'economia agraria*, p. 85 and p. 85n.
72 *Ibid.*, p. 75.
73 *Rapporti fra proprietà impresa e mano d'opera*, p. 19.
74 'I funerali della mezzeria', *Messaggero toscano*, 28 March 1920.

Writing of a later period, but referring to the same process of disintegration of the sharecropping family both in size and as a moral unit, Mario Tofani observed,

Many of the needs of the category of *mezzadri* are particularly felt by the young, who have occasion more easily than their elders to compare their living conditions with those of the city workers. A contributing factor in making this comparison more unfavourable is the organization of the *mezzadro* family, which still maintains its traditional patriarchal character, particularly with regard to family administration, which is almost exclusively the prerogative of the *capoccia*.

> For this reason ... there is a widespread sense of discontent among the younger members of the family. This discontent is largely due to their economic subjection to the head of the family, and it is reflected as well in the relations between the family and the landlord. ('La mezzadria nell'Italia centrale', vol. II, p. 476.)

Cf. also Alessandro Martelli, *La questione del bracciantato agricolo nella Toscana* (Florence, 1921), pp. 11–12, and Istituto Nazionale di Economia Agraria, *Monografie di famiglie agricole: I mezzadri di Val di Pesa e di Chianti* (Rome, 1931), pp. 10–12.

75 On the importance of household industry to the sharecropping family economy, see Simonde de Sismondi, 'Della condizione degli agricoltori in Toscana, pp. 551–2, and 'La mezzadria nell'Italia centrale', vol. II, p. 476.

Cf. also Alessandro Martelli, *La questione del bracciantato agricolo nella Toscana*, pp. 11–12.

76 Tofani has pointed out that the economy of the *podere* has long been less closed than has sometimes been thought, and has indicated some of the established links that had long existed between land and the market:

> In the hill *poderi*, whose economy is based on olive oil and wine production, it is a normal thing, especially in the case of *poderi* belonging to the same *fattoria*, to have the exchange of olive oil and wine, through the landlord, for wheat. These are what we may call internal exchanges taking place within the *fattoria*. But market prices undoubtedly affect them, in as much as the relative prices – that is, the relation between the price of wheat on the one hand and of olive oil and wine on the other – make the exchanges more or less advantageous for one of the two parties.
>
> On the *poderi* in the valleys instead, or even on extensive *poderi* of the hills and mountains which produce only cereal crops and livestock, the autonomy of the peasant family with regard to food, and in particular wheat, may be complete. But the relations of the *poderi* with the market are not lessened, because animal husbandry may have a notable importance, and there may be the cultivation of industrial crops, while, on the other hand, even the production of wheat may be greater than the needs of the family ... 'La mezzadria nell'Italia centrale', vol. II, p. 480.

77 On the changing relations between *fattoria* and *podere*, see Giorgetti, 'Agricoltura e sviluppo capitalistico', p. 757, though I would suggest that this transformation takes place much later than Giorgetti sometimes indicates – certainly not before the very last decade or two of the nineteenth century. Carlo Pazzagli's definitive study of *mezzadria* in the first half of the nineteenth century *L'agricoltura toscana*, is conclusive proof that it had not taken place at that time. Cf. also Mario Mirri, 'Mercato regionale', pp. 398–9.

For further evidence of the nature and timing of this transformation, see also the articles cited in notes below.

78 On the new role of the *fattori*, see, for example, 'Esame di conscienza', *Fattore toscano*, 7 April 1914: G. Gastone Bolla, 'Applicabilità del contratto d'impiego ai fattori', *Fattore toscano*, 7 May 1914; 'Impressioni di agricoltura toscana', *Fattore toscano*, 24 November 1912; Ferruccio Morganti, 'I tre casi', *Fattore toscano*, 22 May 1913; and 'Chi siamo e cosa vogliamo', *Fattore toscano*, 22 May 1914.

79 As Emilio Sereni describes the transformation,
> The process of capitalistic evolution of the *fattoria* is always tied to a process of immiseration and genuine expropriation of the large mass of *mezzadri* ... In such cases ... a completely different economic and social reality is hidden under the old juridical cover. The *colono*, now deprived of the basic means of production, has become in fact a semi-proletarian. (*La questione agraria nella rinascita nazionale italiana*, pp. 190–5.)

Notes to pages 30–34   219

On the proletarianization of the *mezzadri*, cf. also Radi, *I mezzadri*, pp. 69ff; and Sereni, *Il capitalismo nelle campagne*, pp. 327ff.
80 Bastogi, *Una scritta colonica*, pp. 71–149.
81 *Ibid.*, pp. 107ff.
82 *Ibid.*, p. 115.
83 *Ibid.*, p. 115.
84 *Ibid.*, p. 124.
85 *Ibid.*, p. 107.
86 *Ibid.*, pp. 116–18. On the opposition of the tenants to the changes introduced in the agriculture, Mario C. Ferrigni also writes that 'the tenant puts up a tenacious and constant opposition to crop innovation, and above all to the introduction of the so-called industrial crops which replace the food crops', *Il capoccia nella mezzeria toscana*, p. 22.
87 On the contract of *camporaiolato* (semi-proletarianized sharecropping), see Ministero per la Costituente, *Rapporto della commissione economica*, vol. I, pp. 260–3; Camparini and Bandini, *Rapporti fra proprietà impresa e mano d'opera*, pp. 18–20; and Mario Tofani, 'Piccole imprese di contadini compartecipanti in Toscana', *Rivista di economia agraria*, 6 (1931), pp. 299–341. For the first appearance of *camporaioli* in the Elsa Valley in the middle of the nineteenth century, see Mori, *La Valdelsa*, pp. 71–2. On the *mezzaioli*, see Camparini and Bandini, *Rapporti fra proprietà impresa e mano d'opera*, pp. 22–4.
89 Tofani, 'La mezzadria nell'Italia centrale', p. 478.
  On the process by which the *pigionali* were formed, see also Giorgetti, *Agricoltura*, pp. 751–2, and Camparini and Bandini, *Rapporti fra proprietà e mano d'opera*, pp. 19–20.
90 Camparini and Bandini, *Rapporti fra propietà impresa e mano d'opera*, p. 19.
91 'I problemi dell'agricoltura toscana e le sue esigenze di sviluppo', *Rivista di economia agraria*, 16 (1961), no. 4, p. 19.
92 On the role of *braccianti* in the various zones of Tuscan agriculture, see Camparini and Bandini, *Rapporti fra proprietà impresa e mano d'opera*.
93 Comparing figures for the agricultural population of Tuscany in 1881 and 1921, we find that the agricultural population of the region rose, according to the census of 1881 and corrected figures for the 1921 census, from 578,401 to 924,946. *Censimento della popolazione del regno*, 1881, vol. III, table 3; Arrigo Serpieri, *La guerra e le classi rurali italiane* (Bari, 1930), p. 461. If we adopt the initial figures of 461,545 provided by the Giunta per la Inchiesta Agraria, the difference is even more pronounced (*Atti*, vol. iii, fasc. 1: La Toscana agricola, p. 121).
94 Camparini and Bandini, *Rapporti fra proprietà impresa e mano d'opera*, p. 12.
95 *Un comune socialista: Sesto fiorentino* (Rome, 1953), pp. 177–86. On the decline of religious observance in the Elsa Valley, see Mori, *La Valdelsa*, p. 245.
96 General accounts of the war years which have influenced the discussion here are: Piero Melograni, *Storia politica della grande guerra* (Bari, 1969); Giuseppe Prato, *Il Piemonte e gli effetti della guerra sulla sua vita economica e sociale* (Bari, 1925); and Arrigo Serpieri, *La guerra e le classi rurali italiane* (Bari, 1930).
97 On the war-time policies of the state concerning agriculture, see Melograni,

Storia politica; Serpieri, La guerra; Mario Silvestri, Isonzo 1917 (Turin, 1965), pp. 9–40. See also 'Lo stato e la terra', Avanti! 20 January 1917.
 98 Ennio De Simone, 'Cattolici, mezzadri e proprietari in provincia di Firenze nel primo dopoguerra', Bollettino dell'Archivio per la storia del movimento sociale cattolico in Italia, 18 (1983), pp. 52–3.
 99 Serpieri, La guerra, p. 219.
100 On the congress of socialist local administrators, see Avanti! 17, 18, 19 April 1916.
    A specific commune where the mayor outlined in detail the effects of the war upon the ability of the local administration to provide services is Gravina in Apulia. See the 'relazione morale' by Giuseppe Musacchio, 'Tornata del 21 febbraio 1919', Archivio Comunale di Gravina, Deliberazioni del Consiglio Comunale, 1919.
101 See, for instance, De Simone, 'Cattolici, mezzadri e proprietari', pp. 61–3; and Mario Toscano, 'Lotte mezzadrili in Toscana nel primo dopoguerra, 1919–1922', Storia contemporanea, 9 (1978), p. 879.
102 Conditions on the Isonzo front are vividly described in Silvestri, Isonzo 1917.
103 Carlo Scarpini, 'Il mezzadro si ribella', Difesa, 24 July 1920. Antonio Gramsci also describes this process:
    Selfish individualistic instincts were weakened, a common united spirit was formed … a habit of social discipline was born; the peasant conceived of the state in its complex enormity, in its measureless power, in its intricate construction … Bonds of solidarity were created that otherwise only tens of dozens of years of historical experience and of continuous struggle could have created. In four years, in the mud and slaughter of the trenches, a spiritual world was formed, ready to take shape in enduring and dynamic social institutions. (Giansiro Ferrata and Niccolo Galo, eds., 2000 pagine di Gramsci (Milan, 1964), vol. I, p. 405).
104 An important article on the relationship between the war and the issue of land is Antonio Papa, 'Guerra e terra, 1915–1918', Studi storici, 10 (1969), pp. 3–45.
105 On the presentation of the Russian revolution by the Italian socialist movement, see 'Lo svolgimento della rivoluzone russa', Avanti! 1 April 1917; F. Ciccotti, 'I contadini nella rivoluzione russa', Avanti! 10 April 1917; 'Cernoff e la riforma agraria', Avanti!, 8 September 1917.
106 'L'arrivo a Torino dei delegati del "Soviet"', Avanti!, 6 August 1917; 'Il "Soviet" in Italia', Avanti!, 1 August 1917; 'Salutiamo la Rivoluzione russa', Avanti!, 11 August 1917.
107 See Papa, 'Guerra e terra'. For a sample of reports on initiatives to inform the peasants of their right to the land, see Massimo Samoggia, 'Il diritto dei contadini alla terra', Avanti!, 14 March 1917; and 'L'Adunanza del Consiglio Nazionale della Federazione dei Lavoratori della Terra', Avanti!, 24 and 25 April 1917.
108 On the background to the occupations in Lazio, see Report of Prefect of Rome to Ministero dell'Interno, Direzione Generale della Pubblica Sicurezza, ACS, PS (1920), b. 99, fasc. Roma: agitazione agraria (invasioni di terreni).
    On the occupations during the war, see 'Per la requisizione delle terre incolte', Avanti!, 14 September 1916; 'Il Congresso di Frascati', Avanti!, 21 September 1916; 'L'Ufficio della Federazione Lavoratori della Terra', Avanti!, 1 January 1917; and 'Per la legge sugli usi civici nel Lazio', Avanti!, 22 May 1917.
109 In 1920, the Tuscan countryside achieved a national primacy, Arrigo Serpieri

reports, as a greater percentage (27.84 per cent) of the agricultural population took part in strikes there than in any other region of Italy. Emilia had a comparative figure of 24.12 per cent, followed by Umbria (21.77 per cent) and Apulia (10.8 per cent). *La guerra e le classi rurali italiane* (Bari, 1930).
110 'Le leghe dei contadini in Toscana', *Difesa*, 12 January 1902.
111 On these first strikes of *mezzadri* in Tuscany, see Francesco Guicciardini, *Le recenti agitazioni*; Lando Magini, *Gli scioperi dei mezzadri nel circondario di Montepulciano* (Siena, 1902); Mori, 'La mezzadria in Toscana', *La Valdelsa*, p. 479; and Radi, *I mezzadri*, pp. 102–9. For contemporary press accounts, see 'I mezzadri fiorentini', *Avanti!*, 10 August 1906, and 'Lo sciopero dei mezzadri a Sesto Fiorentino', *Avanti!*, 20 and 22 September 1906.
112 Carlo Scarpini, 'Il mezzadro si ribella', *Difesa*, 24 July 1920.
113 'Movimento febbrile', *Bandiera rossa – Martinella*, 8 November 1919.
114 *Vita nuova*, 19 October 1919.
115 For enumerations of the peasant demands, see 'La riforma del patto colonico', *Nazione*, 3 October 1919; 'Richiesta per la riforma del patto colonico', *Vita nuova*, 5 October 1919; 'L'agitazione per la riforma del patto colonico', *Nuovo giornale*, 3 October 1919; and Pier Francesco Serragli, 'Le agitazioni dei contadini e l'avvenire della mezzeria', reprinted in *La mezzadria negli scritti del Georgofili*, vol. II (Bologna, 1935), pp. 156–8.
116 For a discussion of the reaction of the Tuscan landowners to each of the peasants' demands by the then vice-president of the Tuscan Agrarian Association, see Serragli, 'Le agitazioni dei contadini', pp. 161–7.
117 Romeo, *Breve storia*.
118 Serpieri, *La guerra*, p. 106.
119 *Ibid.*, p. 219. For this point see also the following list of agricultural prices:

Prices of some principal agricultural products, 1915–1921
(expressed in lire per quintal)

Year	Current prices	Constant-value (1945) prices	Current prices	Constant-value (1945) prices
	Wheat		Rye	
1915	40	3,133	34	2,663
1916	38	2,267	35	1,889
1917	43	1,563	37	1,345
1918	56	1,352	48	1,159
1919	69	1,528	57	1,263
1920	90	1,519	73	1,232
1921	115	2,119	87	1,603
	Barley		Oats	
1915	27	2,115	30	2,350
1916	29	1,565	30	1,619
1917	37	1,345	33	1,200
1918	48	1,159	42	1,014
1919	57	1,263	60	1,329
1920	73	1,232	87	1,468
1921	85	1,566	95	1,751

	Corn		Sugar beet	
1915	29	2,272	2.45	192
1916	29	1,565	2.80	151
1917	31	1,127	3.95	143
1918	40	966	9.50	229
1919	49	1,085	9.50	194
1920	64	1,080	11.50	304
1921	90	1,659	16.50	252
	Broad beans		Haricot beans	
1915	29	2,272	42	3,290
1916	31	1,673	53	2,861
1917	42	1,527	113	4,107
1918	49	1,183	273	6,593
1919	68	1,506	154	3,411
1920	139	3,346	198	3,342
1921	129	2,377	178	3,280
	Olive oil		Wine	
1915	167	13,081	36	2,820
1916	204	11,012	78	4,210
1917	295	10,723	79	2,872
1918	375	9,056	104	2,512
1919	450	9,967	186	4,120
1920	767	12,947	227	3,832
1921	954	17,601	201	3,708

Source: Ministero per la Costituente, *Rapporto della commissione economica: agricoltura*, vol. I (Rome, 1947), table 13, pp. 518–19.

120 Romeo, *Breve storia*, p. 126. On the economic position of the landlords, see also Riccardo Bachi, *L'Italia economica nel 1920: annuario della vita commerciale, industriale, agraria, finanziaria e della politica economica* (Città di Castello, 1921), p. 300.
121 For the text of the new pact agreed upon in the Mugello, see 'I nuovi patti colonici', *Messaggero del Mugello*, 9 November 1919.
122 Ministero per la Costituente, *Rapporto della commissione economica*, vol. II, p. 143.
123 Quoted in Carlo Rotelli, 'Lotte contadine nel Mugello, 1919–1922', *Il movimento di liberazione in Italia*, 24 (1972), no. 107, pp. 39–64.
124 *Nuovo giornale*, 1 November 1921.
125 The demand for the recognition of *consigli di fattoria* was among the demands that the Siena Chamber of Labour intended to advance in the strike of 1920 for inclusion in the regional pact. Telegram of Prefetto D'Eufemia to Ministero dell'Interno, Direzione Generale della Pubblica Sicurezza, 27 June 1920, ACS, PS (1920), b. 60, fasc. Siena, sottofasc. 'agitazione agraria', n. 677.

On the importance of the *consigli de fattoria* in the Siena countryside, see also Telegram of D'Eufemia to Ministero dell'Interno, n.d., ASS, AGP, Filza

n. 171, Cart. di Ins. 51. It was in part the avoidance of such revolutionary demands by the most advanced sections of the rural labour movement that the Tuscan Agrarian Association (AAT) hoped to gain by its proposal for a unified regional pact.

126 'La gigantesca battaglia dei coloni toscani', *Difesa*, 15 July 1920.

The prefect of Arezzo also saw the question of direction of the estates as the central issue in the landlords' intransigence in the summer of 1920: telegram of Giannoni to Ministero dell'Interno, Direzione Generale della Pubblica Sicurezza, 27 June 1920, ACS, PS (1920), b. 46, fasc. Arezzo, sottofasc. 'agitazione agraria', n. 890.

127 These were the economic demands, for instance, of the *braccianti* at Monteroni d'Arbia in Siena province in the summer of 1920: telegram of Prefetto di Siena to Ministero dell'Interno, Direzione Generale della Pubblica Sicurezza, 30 August 1920, ACS, PS (1920), b. 60, fasc. Siena, sottofasc. 'agitazione agraria'.

128 *La questione del bracciantato agricolo*, p. 6.

129 *Ibid.*, p. 4.

130 For examples of the landlords' demand that the government institute a broad program of public works, see Martelli, *ibid.*; 'Per i lavori pubblici nel circondario di S. Miniato', *Nazione*, 13 August 1921; 'Per la disoccupazione nei centri agricoli', *Nazione*, 27 January 1921; 'La spina del bracciantato', *Nazione*, 13 May 1920. Similarly, P. F. Serragli as vice-president of the Tuscan Agrarian Association, took up the question at the congresses of the Association at Florence in 1920 and at Pisa in 1921. See *Nuovo giornale*, 1 December 1920 and 30 October 1921, and 1 November 1921.

131 As one example of the zeal for government repression shown by the Tuscan landowners, and landlords of the S. Miniato area (Florence province) sent the following telegram to the Minister of the Interior:
Meeting landlords S. Miniato area discuss extremely serious problem unemployment, strongly protest acquiescence of Government towards imposition violence, workers monopoly against local landowners. Demand exemplary repression of guilty, effective upholding law and order, protection of private property. Reprinted in 'Per la disoccupazione nel circondario di S. Miniato', *Nazione*, 28 February 1920.

132 'Gli interessi degli agricoltori toscani difesi nel Convegno di ieri a Firenze', *Nuovo giornale*, 1 December 1920; 'La decisione del grande convegno agrario', *Nazione*, 1 December 1920.

133 *Ibid.*

134 For census figures for the agricultural population, see below Chap. 2, n. 19.

135 Martelli, *La questione del bracciantato agricolo*.

136 That the decision of the AAT to agree to a single unified regional pact was essentially a manoeuvre to buy time was admitted by Giovanni Marchi, director of *Terra nostra*, the official paper of the Florence branch of the Association, in an interview with *Nuovo giornale*. Explaining the landlords' initiative, Marchi said,
The motives underlying the decision of the Tuscan Agrarian Association to take the initiative of the unified regional pact arose from the preparations for a great general strike that the socialist organizers of the various provinces were making for the threshing season ...

It was then that the Agrarian Association, aware of the dangers that a vast agitation would have created – an agitation in which the landlords would have found themselves isolated, commune by commune – decided to form a 'united front' of resistance. At the same time, in order to avoid needless harm to production, the landlords decided to call

the directing body of the Federterra to negotiations to draw up a Regional pact...
Then according to you, the initiative of the unified pact was a pretty clever manoeuvre?
Most clever!
Nuovo giornale, 20 July 1920.

137 On the actions of the police to protect the 'right to work' (*libertà di lavoro*), see Telegram of Prefetto di Arezzo, Giannoni, to Min. Int., Dir. Gen. PS, 6 July 1920, ACS, PS (1920), b. 46, fasc. Arezzo, sottofasc. 'agitazione agraria', n. 881. In this regard, Giannoni wrote,
For this purpose agreements were made with the local branch of the Tuscan Agrarian Association, with which it was decided to proceed with threshing, in the areas where there is a danger of violence such as the Chiana Valley, by zones or in rotation in order to install a fixed guard duty in each locality.
See also Telegram of Giannoni to Min. Int., Dir. Gen. PS, 10 July 1920, ACS, PS (1920), b. 46, fasc. Arezzo, sottofasc. 'agitazione agraria'; and Telegram of Prefetto di Siena to Min. Int., Dir. Gen. PS, 30 October 1919, ACS, PS (1919), b. 45, fasc. Siena, n. 1066.

138 *Avanti!* 10 July 1920. For a similar estimate, see Prefetto di Siena D'Eufemia, Telegram to Min. Int., Dir. Gen. PS, 27 June 1920, ACS, PS (1920), b. 60, fasc. Siena, sottofasc. 'agitazione agraria', n. 677.

139 The text of the regional pact signed on 6 August 1920 is in *Nazione*, 8 August 1920.

140 'Riassunto delle disposizioni principali per l'assicurazione dei coloni contro gli infortuni del lavoro', *Bollettino mensile della Associazione Agraria di Prato*, 6 February 1919.

141 'Norme per l'assicurazione obbligatoria per invalidità e vecchiaia dei coloni, personale di fattoria, ecc.', *Bollettino della Associazione Agraria di Prato*, 8 April 1921.

142 The concern of the AAT throughout this period can be traced in the *Bollettino dell'Associazione Agraria Toscana*, which made the question of welfare payments for *mezzadri* one of its major themes. See also the *Bollettino dell'Associazione Agraria di Prato* for these years.

143 'In tema di assicurazioni sociali', *Bollettino dell'Associazione Agraria Toscana*, 1 October 1922.

144 'L'assicurazione contro gli infortuni in agricoltura', *Difesa agricola*, 14 October 1922.

145 'La rivincita dello Stato', *Resto del Carlino*, 20 November 1919.

146 On this congress, see 'Il convegno agrario di Rimini', *Resto del Carlino*, 31 August 1920; reprinted in *Emilia*, 3 (1951), pp. 232–6.

147 Ibid.

148 'I risultati delle elezioni amministrative', *Resto del Carlino*, 26 November 1920.

149 *Bandiera rossa – Martinella*, 31 October 1920. The six communes not won by the PSI were: Siena, Radda, Gaiole, S. Cascian dei Bagni, Radicofani, and Castelnuovo Berardenga. See also Ugo Giusti, *Le correnti politiche italiane attraverso due riforme elettorali, dal 1909 al 1921* (Florence, 1922), pp. 32–3. In Pisa province the PSI won 26 of 42 communes. *Ora nostra*, 13 November 1920.

150 *Bollettino dell'Associazione Agraria Toscana*, 8–25 August 1921.

151 Arrigo Serpieri, 'Le sperequazioni tributarie', *Resto del Carlino*, 20 November 1921.

152 'La sovrimposta sui terreni', *Nazione*, 14 April 1921.
   In Grosseto province the landlords estimated in 1921 that they were obliged to pay over 300 lire per hectare in surtaxes alone: 'Il convegno nazionale agrario per la questione dei tributi locali', *Resto del Carlino*, 25 September 1921.
   On the importance attached by landowners to the new taxes, see 'L'assemblea dei proprietari terrieri contro l'aumento delle imposte fondiarie degli E.L.', *Nazione*, 24 June 1921. The question was dwelt upon at length by Serragli at two congresses of the AAT. See *Nazione*, 1 December 1920 and 30 October–1 November 1921.
153 *Bollettino dell'Associazione Agraria Toscana*, 14 July 1921.
154 During the early agricultural strikes of 1920, the Prefect of Arezzo reported, for example, that 'the most excited peasants engaged in some violence against the *agenti di beni* or *fattori*'. Telegram of Giannoni to Min. Int., Dir. Gen. PS, 23 February 1920, ACS, PS (1920), b. 46, fasc. Arezzo, sottofasc. 'agitazione agraria'. Then, during the larger strikes in May, Giannoni elaborated on the acts of violence committed at the expense of the *fattori*: some *fattori* were forced to march carrying the red flag, and there were clashes here and there between socialists and peasants who sought to continue work. As a general statement, however, Giannoni himself concluded that such incidents were 'not serious and in any case are unavoidable in economic conflicts of this kind'. Telegram of Giannoni to Min. Int., Dir. Gen. Pubblica Sicurezza, 22 May 1920, ACS, PS (1920), b. 46, fasc. Arezzo, sottofasc. 'agitazione agraria'.
155 This was the description of the province given by Police Inspector General L. Gaudino. Cf. Report to Direttore Generale della PS, 20 November 1921, ACS, PS (1921), b. 86A, fasc. Siena, p. 2.
156 Report of Prefetto D'Eufemia to Min. Int., Dir. Gen. PS, 26 July 1920, ACS, PS (1920), b. 60, fasc. Siena, sottofasc. 'agitazione agraria'.
157 On the financing of the *fasci* by the Agrarian Association in Florence province see Telegram of Prefetto di Firenze, Pericoli, 11 April 1922, ACS, PS (1922), b. 71B, fasc. Firenze (1), n. 1210.
   From Prato, Ispettore Generale della Pubblica Sicurezza Tarsia reported of the AAT that:
   The entire membership of this association... belongs to the *fascio*. In fact, information received leads to the certain conclusion that the Association, which now has about 600 members, the most important producers of the area, and which is extremely powerful both politically and financially, finances the *fascio*, which has become its support and its defence. Report of Ispettore Generale della Pubblica Sicurezza Di Tarsia, 'Situazione politica nei riguardi dell'ordine pubblico', to Min. Int., Dir. Gen. PS, 7 April 1922, ACS, PS (1922), b. 71B, fasc. Prato, p. 1.
   Similarly, from Chiusi (Siena province), the prefect reported that the local *signori* had established a semi-voluntary system of taxation among themselves to finance the local *fascio*. Prefetto Masino to Min. Int., Dir. Gen. PS. 27 June 1921, ACS, PS (1921), b. 86A, fasc. Siena, n. 860.
   Alternatively, there is evidence that major landlords also hired the squads privately without the mediation of the AAT. An example appears to have been Filippo Pellegrini at Piancastagnaio (Siena). Cf. Letter of on. Bisogni to on. Bevioni, 22 July 1921, ACS, PS (1921), b. 64A, fasc. Siena, sottofasc. 'agitazione agraria'.
   Again, it is hardly a coincidence that the finance committee of the fascist

provincial organization in Siena included among its five members the major landlords Count Idalberto Scroffa and Count Curzio Ugurgeri. Giorgio Alberto Chiurco, *Storia della rivoluzione fascista* (Milan, 1972), vol. III, p. 452.

More generally, on the financing of the national fascist movement by the Agrarian Associations through regular official systems of internal self-taxation, see Sereni, *La questione agraria*, p. 229; Ferdinando Cordova, 'Le origini dei sindacati fascisti', *Storia contemporanea*, 1 (1970), pp. 973–5; C. I. W. Seton-Watson, *Italy from Liberalism to Fascism* (London, 1967), p. 599n.

158 The *Solco*, the official paper of the Siena branch of the AAT, referred to the blackshirts as 'our fascists'. *Messaggero del Mugello*, 10 July 1921.
159 Sarrocchi, for example, took part at dedications of fascist standards at Roccastrada and Follonica. See *Ombrone* 23 October and 13 November 1921. He also made public speeches on behalf of the Siena *fascio* and took part in pro-fascist demonstrations. See *Popolo di Siena*, 18 December, 1920.

Gino Aldi Mai officiated at the dedications of the standards of the *fasci* of Grosseto, Follonica, Manciano, and Casteldelpiano. See *Ombrone*, 13 November 1921, 25 December 1921, and 15 October 1921. See also Chiurco, *Storia della rivoluzione fascista*, vol. III, p. 389.
160 *Atti del Parlamento Italiano*, Camera dei Deputati, Legislatura XXV, Sessione 1919–21, Discussioni, IX, p. 8501.
161 *Ibid.*, pp. 8498–501. also 'Le cause e le responsabilità dei conflitti in Toscana', *Corriere della sera*, 9 March 1921.
162 *Atti del Parlamento Italiano*, Camera dei Deputati, Legislatura XXV, Sessione 1919–21, Discussioni, IX, pp. 8498–501.
163 On relations between the AAT and the fascist unions, see below, pp. 62–9.
164 On Pierazzi's leading roles in the fascist movement in Grosseto province, see Prefetto di Grosseto to Min. Int., PS, 26 May 1921, ACS, PS (1925), b. 97 ('costituzione dei fasci'), fasc. Grosseto, n. 605; Telegram of Prefetto Boragno to Min. Int., PS 30 April 1921, ACS, PS (1921), b. 79A, fasc. Grosseto, n. 539; 'L'imponente adunata a Grosseto', *Riscossa* 1 October 1921; and Chiurco, *Storia della rivoluzione fascista*, vol. III, p. 389.
165 Letter of Prefetto di Grosseto, Rocco to S.E. il Sottosegretario di Stato per l'Interno, 4 September 1921, ACS, PS (1921), b. 79A, fasc. Grosseto, sottofasc. Roccastrada, n. 637. Cf. Chiurco, *Storia della rivoluzione fascista*, vol. III, p. 535.
166 Report of Ispettore Generale di PS Paolella to Direttore Generale di PS, 27 April 1921, ACS, PS (1921), b. 75A, fasc. Arezzo.
167 *Dovere*, 9 April 1921.
168 For Count Girolomo Piccolomini's positions in the AAT, see *Vedetta senese* 16 November 1920, and *Era nuova*, 7 July 1921. For mention of his participation in the Siena squads, see Chiurco, *Storia della rivoluzione fascista*, vol. II.
169 *Ibid.*, vol. III, p. 453.
170 On the fascist activities of Angelo Tiezzi, see *ibid.*, vol. III, p. 454, and vol. IV, pp. 15 and 174.
171 *Ibid.*, vol. III, p. 453. For mention of Rolando Bocchi Bianchi's position in the AAT, see *Era nuova*, 9 June 1921.

172 Report of Prefetto De Martino to Min. Int., PS, 12 June 1921, ACS, PS (1925), b. 98, fasc. Pisa ('costituzione dei fasci').
173 Libertario Guerrini, *Il movimento operaio empolese dalle origini alla guerra di liberazione* (Florence, 1954), pp. 249–50; *Giovinezza*, 15 May 1921.
174 Guerrini, *Il movimento operaio*, p. 251.
175 *Ibid.*, pp. 20–9, 239–40.
176 Chiurco, *Storia della rivoluzione fascista*, vol. III, p. 233.
177 Bruno Frullini, *Squadrismo fiorentino* (Florence, 1933), pp. 121–2, 295–6.
178 *Ibid.*, p. 55.
179 For lists of Tuscan squadrists, cf Chiurco, *Storia della rivoluzione fascista*, vol. I, pp. 290ff.
180 Frullini, *Squadrismo fiorentino*, pp. 290–4.
181 For a partial list of members of the Alliance, see Chiurco, *Storia della rivoluzione fascista*, vol. III, pp. 339–40.
182 Hubert Corsi, *Le origini del fascismo nel Grossetano* (1919–1922) (Rome, 1973), pp. 169–70. Cf. also p. 160.
183 *Vedetta senese*, 4 April 1921.
184 Telegram of Pericoli, 11 April 1922, ACS, PS (1922), b. 713, fasc. Firenze (1), n. 1210.
185 Giovanni Marchi, 'Il liberalismo e Mussolini', *Fiamma*, 19 November 1921. For other articles asserting the identity of aims between Liberalism and fascism, see Alberto Giovannini, 'Fascisti e liberali', *Fiamma*, 20 October 1921; L. L. Lombardi, 'Liberalismo e fascismo', *Rinnovamento*, 26 August 1922; and 'Destra Nazionale', *Fiamma*, 11 February 1922.
186 'Destra Nazionale', *Fiamma*, 11 February 1922.
187 'La riscossa fascista', *Fiamma*, 30 April 1921. Cf. 'La morte della rivoluzione', *Fiamma*, 1 January 1921.
188 'Il fascismo e la patria', *Rinnovamento*, 29 January 1921.
189 On the founding of the AAT, see *Corriere mugellano*, 20 April 1919; *Unità cattolica*, 15 April 1919.
190 Mario Tofani notes of central Italy,
   It is true that there is not always an exact correspondence between property and estate. But although it is rather rare, especially in Tuscany, for a single estate to be organized on the property of more than one owner, the opposite occurs frequently – namely that several estates, or *fattorie* belong to a single landlord. The result is a notable concentration of landownership, as is easy to observe from a direct knowledge of the holdings of certain families, particularly families of the old nobility, whose lands extend for thousands and tens of thousands of hectares. 'La mezzadria nell'Italia centrale', in Ministero per la Costituente, *Rapporto della commissione economica*, vol. II, pp. 472–3.
   For a consideration of the concentration of landownership in each agricultural zone of Tuscany, see Camparini and Bandini, *Rapporti, fra proprietà impresa e mano d'opera*, vol. III, fasc. I: *La Toscana agricola*. For consideration by provinces, see Osservatorio di Economia Agraria per la Toscana, *L'economia agraria della Toscana*, p. 49.
   Generalizing for comparative purposes, the Ministry for the Constituent Assembly in 1945 gave the following division by area:

	Holding (percentage)		
	Small	Medium	Large
North	45.7	37.9	16.4
Centre	44.2	32.2	23.6
South	59.1	29.1	11.8

Ministero per la Costituente, *Rapporto della commissione economica*, vol. I, p. 52. Cf. also pp. 138–9.

191 Istituto Nazionale di Economica Agraria, *Inchiesta sulla piccola proprietà*, p. 20.
192 *Ibid.*
193 'Il convegno agrario toscano', *Unità cattolica*, 29 October 1931.
194 *Nuovo giornale*, 1 December 1920.
 By its Pisa congress of October 1921 the AAT claimed a membership of 12,000 representing a taxable income of 13,000,000 lire: *Messaggero toscano*, 30 October 1921 and 1 November 1921.
195 'Violenza', *Messaggero del Mugello*, 8 February 1920.
196 Mario Piazzesi, *Diario di uno squadrista toscano, 1919–1922* (Rome, 1980), p. 55.
197 Quoted in Roberto Cantagalli, *Storia del fascismo fiorentino* (Florence, 1973), p. 54.
198 *Ibid.*, pp. 54–64; Amerigo Dumini, *Diciasette colpi* (Milan, 1967), p. 15.
199 The AAT was divided into 3 categories of members – landowners; bailiffs (fattori), and peasants – thereby ensuring that the largest potential membership group (the peasants) would be constitutionally guaranteed a minority influence: see 'La secessione degli agenti rurali dall'Associazione Agraria Toscana', *Difesa agricola*, 15 March, 1922.
200 For reports on this congress, see *Nazione*, 1 December 1920, and *Nuovo giornale*, 1 December 1920.
201 'Il Risveglio degli agricoltori', *Nazione*, 4 December 1920.
202 *Nuovo giornale*, 1 December 1920.
203 'Il risveglio sovversivo nelle campagne', *Difesa agricola*, 5 November 1921.
204 The landlords' paper, *Difesa agricola* (25 March 1922), reported:
 From the first moment we were little persuaded of the practicability of this mingling with the same organization of categories whose interests could become opposed ...
 Effectively, the third category – that of the peasants – has never shown signs of life within the Association. The many enrolments have served to fill the rosters; but they have never opened the way to a direct agreement over contracts, nor have they prevented the numerous strikes that have troubled Tuscany ...
205 *Messaggero toscano*, 1 November 1921.
206 Chiurco, *Storia della rivoluzione fascista*, vol. III, pp. 308–9.
207 *Ibid.*, vol. III, p. 535.
208 This point is clearest of all in Siena and Grosseto provinces where Chiurco, the leader of the squads in both provinces and provincial secretary of the Siena *fasci*, was also the chief fascist union organizer.
209 Giulio Cavina, the former secretary of the Siena Chamber of Labour and socialist deputy, reported that in Siena province the fascist unions, in order to retain their hold on the agricultural workers, were pressed at times to make

economic demands, and threatened to use the strike weapon – a course of action not always well received by the *agrari* affected. See 'Il conflitto agrario-fascista in provincia di Siena', *Avanti!* 9 September 1922. See 'Aspetti della lotta di classe: la biscia morde il ciarlatano', *Avanti!* 10 September 1922.

At Poggibonsi (Siena) the fascists actually occupied the estate of Ilario Montesi in order to compel him to hire unemployed labourers enrolled in the fascist organization. Chiurco, *Storia della rivoluzione fascista*, vol. IV, p. 171.

210 *Scure*, 25 September 1921.

Similarly the *fascio* of Sovicille (Siena) had received assurances from the local landlords of 'help and assistance on behalf of our members'. Letter of Direttorio of *fascio* of Sovicille to Sigg. Proprietari del Comune di Sovicille, 10 May 1922, ASS, AGP, Filza 181, Cart. di Ins. 49.

For the program of the first fascist unions in Tuscany, see *Era nuova*, 13 January 1921 and 4 February 1921.

In Siena province as well the landlords announced that they would hire only workers who produced proof of membership in the fascist unions. Letter of Bonelli, Segretario Provinciale della Federterra to Prefetto di Siena, 25 October 1921, ASS, AGP, Filza 174, Cart. di Ins. 31.

211 Prefetto Masino to Min. Int., Dir. Gen. PS 20 July 1921, ACS, PS (1921), b. 86A, fasc. Siena, n. 978.
212 Giacomo Lambroso, 'I sindacati nazionali', *Riscossa*, 26 February 1921.
213 Cf. 'Sindacalismo fascista', *Difesa*, 18 February 1922.
214 Emilio Papasogli, 'La via maestra', *Riscossa*, 10 September 1921.
215 'I fascisti toscani alla prova di fronte al Sindacalismo Nazionale', *Riscossa*, 5 August 1922.
216 *Era nuova*, 13 January 1921.
217 *Ibid*.
218 Carlo Romagnoli, Idalberto Targioni, Eugenio Chiti, and Salvadori, 'Il primo congresso della Corporazione dei Sindacati Nazionali', *Riscossa*, 10 June 1922.
219 For the text of the communiqué of the Camera del Lavoro Italiana of Siena, see *Era nuova*, 23 February 1922.
220 *Era nuova*, 13 October 1921.
221 Francesco Niccolai, 'La Fratellanza Colonica Toscana', *Messaggero del-Mugello*, 30 October 1921.
222 'Un sindacato autonomo di mezzadri aderenti ai fasci a Montepulciano', *Riscossa*, 26 February, 1921.
223 *Era nuova*, 13 October 1921; *Difesa agricola*, 14 January 1922.

Marquis Bichi Ruspoli Forteguerra was a member of the central committee of the Siena sub-section of the AAT. See *Vedetta senese*, 16 November 1920.

224 See, for example, L. Magini, 'Ai contadini', *Difesa agricola*, 6 August 1921; and *Difesa agricola*, 5 November 1921.
225 *Difesa agricola*, 5 November 1921.
226 For the text of the new pact, see *Difesa agricola*, 2 December 1922.

2 THE APPEAL OF THE RIGHT

1 'I padroni della ferocia squadrista', *Rinascita*, 29 (1972), p. 20.

2 On the class basis of northern fascism, see my article, 'On the Social Origins of Agrarian Fascism in Italy', *European Journal of Sociology*, 13 (1972), pp. 268–95. The chief sources on which I have relied for my account are: Luigi Arbizzani, 'Lotte agrarie in provincia di Bologna nel primo dopoguerra', in Renato Zangheri, ed., *Le campagne emiliane nell'epoca moderna* (Milan, 1957), pp. 283–332; Paul Corner, *Fascism in Ferrara, 1915–1925* (Oxford, 1974); Barrington Moore, Jr, *Social Origins of Dictatorship and Democracy: Lord and Peasant in the Making of the Modern World* (Boston, 1966); Luigi Preti, *Le lotte agrarie nella valle padana* (Turin, 1955); Mario Vaini, *Le origini del fascismo a Mantova* (Rome, 1961); F. Pittorru, 'Origini del fascismo ferrarese', *Emilia*, 3 (1951), pp. 293–8; and Rinaldo Salvadori, 'Il dopoguerra e le origini del fascismo nel mantovano', *Rivista storica del socialismo*, 1 (1958), pp. 285–309; Anthony Cardoza, *Agrarian Elites and Fascism: The Province of Bologna, 1901–1926* (Princeton, 1983); Alice A. Kelikian, *Town and Country under Fascism: The Transformation of Brescia, 1915–1926* (Oxford, 1986); and Alessandro Roveri, *Le origini del fascismo a Ferrara, 1918–1921* (Milan, 1974).

3 Carlo Scarpini, 'Il mezzadro si ribella', *Difesa*, 24 July 1920.

4 Renato Zangheri, 'Introduction to Renato Zangheri, ed., *Le campagne emiliane nell'epoca moderna* (Milan, 1957), p. lxxxviii.

5 On the adoption of the slogan, 'Land to the peasants!' See Report of Prefetto di Siena to Min. Int., Dir. Gen. PS, 23 September 1919, ACS, PS (1919), b. 45, fasc. Siena, sottofasc. 'agitazione agraria', n. 741; and Telegram of Prefetto di Siena to Min. Int., Dir. Gen. PS, 1 July 1920, ACS, PS (1920), b. 60, fasc. Siena, sottofasc. 'agitazione agraria', n. 621.

Alternatively the socialist slogan was 'Land to those who work it!' ('la terra a chi la lavora'). Report of Prefetto di Siena D'Eufemia to Camillo Corradini, 12 August 1920, ASS, AGP, Filza 170, Cart. di. Ins. 29 ('Partiti politici e ordine pubblico').

Mori suggests that the tendency in practice of socialists in Tuscany to modify the agrarian program of the PSI was not new in the postwar period, but had been one of the problems encountered from the beginning by party activists in the Tuscan countryside (*La Valdelsa*, pp. 247–52).

6 Giovanni Droandi, 'Il nuovo patto colonico e le sue consequenze: schema di azione socialista', *Falce*, 5 June 1920.

7 Telegram of Prefetto di Siena D'Eufemia to Min. Int., Dir. Gen. PS, 1 July 1920, ACS, PS (1920), b. 60, fasc. Siena, sottofasc. 'agitazione agraria', n. 621.

8 Telegram of D'Eufemia to Min. Int., Dir. Gen. PS, 26 July 1920, ACS, PS (1920), b. 60, fasc. Siena, sottofasc. 'agitazione agraria'.

9 Report of D'Eufemia to Camillo Corradini, 12 August 1920, ASS, AGP, Filza 170, Cart. di Ins. 29 ('Partiti politici e ordine pubblico').

10 See below, Chap. 3.

11 See article signed 'A.V.', 'Lo stato dei sindacati', *Ordine nuovo*, 6 March, 1921.

12 For examples of this aspect of fascist propaganda, see the articles cited below, note 26.

13 For a discussion of *imponibile di mano d'opera* and *collocamento di classe*, see Barbadoro, 'Problemi e caratteristiche storiche del movimento sindacale italiano', *Rivista storica del socialismo*, 6 (1963), pp. 248–52; Preti, *Le lotte agrarie*, pp. 385–9; and Zangheri, *Le campagne emiliane*, pp. xxxviii ff.

14 D'Eufemia reported that in the strike of 1920 the Siena Chamber of Labour planned to present for inclusion in the regional pact a demand for *consigli di fattoria* 'which [the Leagues] would want to have in charge of the technical direction of the agricultural estates'. Telegram of Prefetto di Siena D'Eufemia to Min. Int., Dir. Gen. PS, 27 June 1920, ACS, PS (1920), b. 60, fasc. Siena, sottofasc. 'agitazione agraria', n. 677.

15 'I fatti di Toscana: lezioni del passato da non dimenticare', *Ordine nuovo*, 8 March 1921. Cf. also Palmiro Togliatti, 'L'esempio di Firenze', *Ordine nuovo*, 11 March 1921.

For another contemporary account of the rapidity of the socialist collapse in Bologna, see 'Dal massimalismo al fascismo; la trasformazione politica di Bologna', *Corriere della sera*, 31 January 1921.

16 On the Florence uprising of 27 February to 3 March 1921, see Report of Prefetto Olivieri to Min. Int., Dir. Gen. PS, 6 March 1921, ACS, PS (1921), b. 78A. fasc. 1, n. 869; and Report of Olivieri to Min. Int., Dir. Gen. PS, 10 March 1921, ACS, PS (1921), b. 78A, fasc. 1, n. 869.

See also *Nuovo giornale*, 2–3 March 1921; *Resto del Carlino*, 1, 2 and 3 March 1921; G. A. Chiurco, *Storia della rivoluzione fascista*, vol. III, pp. 91–8; and *Era nuova*, 28 February to 5 March 1921, which reported that in the fighting 18 were killed, over 300 wounded, and 700 arrested.

17 In Siena in early March a pitched battle was fought between the local socialists on the one hand and the *carabinieri* and fascists on the other that was won only through the use of artillery and machine guns. After the battle it was reported that the *carabinieri* and fascists together stormed the Casa del Popolo, sacked it, and set if aflame. See *Vedetta senese*, 5 and 9 March 1921.

For reporting of events at Pisa, cf. *Messaggero toscano*, 3 March 1921. On Empoli and Pontedera, see *Messaggero toscano*, 4 March 1921; on San Giovanni Valdarno, see *Messaggero toscano*, 25 March 1921; and on Livorno, see *Messaggero toscano*, 15 April 1921, 20 July 1921, and 21 July 1921. Accounts of these events are also to be found in other major regional papers.

18 Palmiro Togliatti, 'L'esempio di Firenze', *Ordine nuovo*, 11 March 1921.

The evidence for Togliatti's statement suggests that resistance in the Tuscan countryside took four forms:

(1) sporadic, scattered acts of individual self-defence and retaliation against the squadrists;

(2) large-scale uprisings and pitched battles fought by peasants in such agricultural centres as Pontedera and Foiano della Chiana. For the events at Pontedera, see *Messaggero toscano*, 4 March 1921. For the battle at Foiano della Chiana, see Chiurco, *Storia della rivoluzione fascista*, vol. III, pp. 195–7; and *Corriere della sera*, 18 and 19 April 1921.

(3) the more organized opposition of the non-party anti-fascist resistance movement known as the *arditi del popolo*. The *arditi del popolo*, of course, were no merely Tuscan movement, but it was notable that the organization was especially strong in the Pisan plain, where it caused considerable concern to the authorities. The prime minister himself expressed alarm at the 'persistent activity' of the *arditi del popolo* in Pisa province. Telegram of Bonomi to Prefetto di Pisa, 24 October 1921, ACS, PS (1922), b. 59, fasc. Pisa ('Associazione arditi del popolo'), n. 26005.

In the countryside of Pisa province, the local socialist party organizations – led by the socialist deputy, Giuseppe Mingrino; the socialist mayor of Cascina, Giulio Guelfi; the socialist league and cooperative leader, Priano Cappellini; and Giuglielmo Bacci – took an active part in setting up workers' and peasants' defence squads, and the prefect reported in the summer of 1921 that the movement was rapidly gaining ascendancy over the working masses of town and countryside, with over 300 men organized into defence brigades at Pisa, 200 at Pontedera, and 200 at Cascina, in addition to 500 at Piombino. See Telegrams of Prefetto Frigerio to Min. Int., Dir. Gen. PS, 18 July 1922, ACS, PS (1922), b. 59, fasc. Pisa ('Associazione arditi del popolo'); and 14 August 1921, ACS, PS (1922), b. 59. Pisa ('Associazione arditi del popolo'), ns. 1229, 1230 and 1231. See also Report of Generale Leopoldo Ferré to Comando Generale dell'Arma dei Carabinieri Reali, 'Inchiesta sull'azione dell'Arma nella provincia di Pisa', 31 July 1921, ACS, Ministero dell'Interno, Gabinetto di S. E. Bonomi, Ordine Pubblico (1921–22), b. 5, fasc. 56 (Pisa).

(4) passive political resistance. Actual military resistance proved less enduring than the passive refusal of the Tuscan peasants to be recruited into the fascist unions or to pass over in discouragement into the fascist political organizations. One of the long-standing complaints of the Tuscan fascists was that of the 'apathy' and 'indifference' of the Tuscan peasant to fascist persuasion. Thus Idalberto Targioni, as late as August 1922, reported from Florence province, that

Fascism has been victorious in winning over all social classes, including the industrial proletariat and the artisans, but it has not yet succeeded in conquering the *braccianti* and the peasants, except in meagre numbers. 'I fascisti toscani alla prova di fronte al Sindacalismo Nazionale', *Riscossa*, 5 August 1922.

19 The Tuscan agricultural population of 924,946 was, according to corrected figures for the 1921 census, thus subdivided:

proprietors	188,051
leaseholders	18,669
sharecroppers	540,458
contract labourers	22,656
day labourers	155,112

Serpieri, *La guerra e le classi rurali*, p. 361.

This contrasts with the following figures for Emilia:
total agricultural population	112,528
proprietors	251,312
leaseholders	116,318
sharecroppers	366,116
contract labourers	22,579
day labourers	356,203

Ibid.

20 My discussion of small new peasant proprietorship is based primarily on Istituto Nazionale di Economia Agraria, *Inchiesta sulla piccola proprietà coltivatrice formatasi nel dopoguerra*, 15 vols. (Rome, n.d.).
21 For comparative regional minimum unemployment figures, see below, note 83.
22 'L'esempio di Firenze', *Ordine nuovo*, 11 March 1921. For a discussion of the

history of the expansion of the fascist movement in Tuscany, see below, chap. 6.
23 Frullini, *Squadrismo fiorentino*, pp. 271–2.
24 For the speech by De Ambris at the Milan Congress in May 1920, see 'La Il Adunata fascista. Le relazioni: il problema agricolo', *Popolo d'Italia*, 21 May 1920.
25 *Ibid.*
26 On the fascist agrarian program during this period, see among others Mussolini's articles 'Fascismo e terra', *Opera omnia*, 36 vols. (Florence, 1951–63), vol. XVI, pp. 170–3; 'Da provincia rossa a provincia fascista. Il fascismo e il problema terriero nel ferrarese', *Opera omnia*, vol. XVI, pp. 229–30; 'Il fascismo e i rurali', *Gerarchia*, 1 (1922), pp. 237–43. See also Gaetano Polverelli, 'Il fascismo e la soluzione del problema agrario', *Popolo d'Italia*, 11 May 1921; and Polverelli, 'La posizione del fascismo di fronte alla questione agraria', *Intrepido*, 6 February 1921.
27 Quoted in Franco Catalano, *Potere economico e fascismo: la crisi del dopoguerra, 1919–1921* (Milan, 1964).
28 'Il fascismo e i rurali', *Gerarchia*, 1 (1922), p. 240.
29 Gaetano Polverelli, 'Il fascismo e la soluzione del problema agrario', *Popolo d'Italia*, 11 May 1921.
30 Fabio Pittorru, 'Origini del fascismo ferrarese', *Emilia*, 3 (1951), p. 295.
32 'Il fascismo e i rurali', *Gerarchia*, 1 (1922), p. 24.
33 Idalberto Targioni, 'I doveri del contadino', *Riscossa*, 15 April 1922.

For the fascist agrarian program elaborated in Florence province, see above all the series of articles by Targioni, 'I doveri del contadino', *Riscossa* 8 and 15 April 1922, 13 May 1922, 3 June 1922, 24 June 1922, and 12 August 1922. See also Umberto Odett, 'Il fascismo ed i contadini toscani', *Riscossa*, 22 January 1921; Carlo Romagnoli, 'L'agricoltura in Toscana', *Giovinezza*, 18 June 1922; Idalberto Targioni, 'La parola dei fascisti ai grandi e piccoli proprietari della terra', *Giovinezza*, 27 November 1921; Idalberto Targioni, 'Dedicato ai proprietari della terra ed ai contadini', *Giovinezza*, 15 May 1921; Idalberto Targioni, 'Democrazia rurale. Torniamo alla terra', *Giovinezza*, 26 May 1921.
34 Idalberto Targioni, 'I doveri del contadino', *Riscossa*, 15 April 1922.
35 Idalberto Targioni, 'La parola dei fascisti ai grandi e piccoli proprietari della terra', *Giovinezza*, 27 November 1921.

Similarly, the Tuscan fascist movement at its regional congress in March 1921 adopted the slogan, 'The land to those who make it produce the most in the interest of themselves and of the community!' ('Il Convegno regionale dei Fasci toscani', *Intrepido*, 23 March 1921). See also 'A chi la terra?', *Intrepido*, 29 October 1921.
36 'Dopo il Congresso', see *Riscossa*, 26 March 1921.
37 Idalberto Targioni, 'Ritorniamo alla terra', *Giovinezza*, 15 May 1921.
38 Idalberto Targioni, 'Democrazia rurale. Torniamo alla terra', *Giovinezza*, 26 May 1921.
39 'L. M.', 'A chi la terra?' *Intrepido*, 29 October 1921.
40 'L'Italia agricola', *Intrepido*, 24 December 1921.
41 'L'Italia agricola', *Intrepido*, 31 December 1921, 7 January 1922, 14 January 1922.
42 Early in the nineteenth century, Cosimo Ridolfi had written in criticism of the Tuscan landlords that

We have wanted them [i.e. the *fattori*] to come from a poor and subjected class in order to pay them little. Only out of pride have we looked for *fattori* who had obtained from school not some real achievement but only some diploma that would make us forget their background. We have demanded of them a base and humiliating service, and we have not given them our trust, save in an excess of lightness ...
Quoted in Bastogi, *Una scritta colonica*, p. 46.

43 This was the practice, for instance, of Ferdinando Vai at his *fattoria* of Mulinaccio in 1912. ASP, AVR, Filza 110, fasc. 2, sottofasc. 'Fattoria del Mulinaccio: domande per il posto di agente (1912)'.

44 See Letter of Ferdinando Vai to Sottofattore Vincenzo Bagnai, 3 January 1927, and Letter of Vincenzo Bagnai to Ferdinando Vai, 5 January 1927, ASP, AVR, Filza 110, fasc. 2, sottofasc. 'Richiesta di matrimonio da parte del sottofattore Vincenzo Bagnai (1927)'.

45 *Ibid.*

46 On the association of *fattori*, see above, Chap. 1. With regard to the insecurity of the post, one *fattore* reported:
With a little money that he slaps into the purse of this man [i.e. the *fattore*], the boss makes him act, makes him go to market, makes him defend his property. And then?
  At the smallest error in accounting, farewell! On the road you will encounter many of these disappointed men ... who, once sacked, are reduced to the roughest and most difficult trades. 'La figura morale e giuridica degli agenti rurali (fattori, sottofattori, guardie campestri, garzoni, ecc.)', *Bandiera rossa – Martinella*, 6 January 1921.

  So precarious was the position of the *fattore* that there was a long-standing joke that he was 'non fattore, ma fatto a ore' (not a proper bailiff but an overseer hired by the hour). See article signed 'Il Fattore', 'Esame di coscienza', *Fattore toscano*, 7 April 1914. On this point see also Ferruccio Morganti, 'I tre casi', *Fattore toscano*, 22 May 1913.

47 The census of 1911, for example, reported that there were 4,277 *fattori* in Tuscany. Ministero di Agricoltura, Industria e Commercio: Direzione Generale della Statistica e del Lavoro, *Censimento della popolazione del Regno d'Italia al 10 giugno 1911* (Rome, 1915), vol. v, table 7. It should be noted, however, that this figure does not include the *fattore*'s assistants, the *sottofattori*, and guards.

48 On the importance of the *fattore* as the hero of fascist rural mythology, see Francesco C. Rossi, ed., 'Contadini della Toscana', *Itinerari*, 7 (1960), esp. pp. 450–1 and 468ff.

49 On the *gruppi di competenza*, see Alberto Aquarone, 'Aspirazioni technocratiche del primo fascismo', *Nord e Sud*, 52 (1964), pp. 109–28.

50 This and preceding quotation: *Scure*, 18 March 1922.

51 'La secessione degli agenti rurali dall'Associazione Agraria Toscana', *Difesa agricola*, 25 March 1922.

52 I. Targioni, 'I doveri del contadino', *Riscossa*, 3 June 1922.

53 *Ibid.*

54 *Ibid.*

55 'L'Agraria in Toscana e la situazione dei coloni bianchi e rossi', *Ordine nuovo*, 17 October 1921.

56 Prefect Olivieri to Minister of Agriculture and Minister of the Interior, 9 February 1921, ACS, PS (1921), b. 59A, fasc. Firenze.
  The firm determination of the Agrarian Association to use eviction as an instrument of policy emerges also from the following telegram from T. Pestellini, the president of the AAT, to the prime minister:

This Association in a meeting today of all the representatives from the Tuscan region has decided that if a decree is issued extending agrarian contracts, then all existing sharecropping pacts will be denounced and all wage labourers will be sacked, because it is felt that it would be useless to tolerate the expense of estates that cannot be entrusted to tenants of our choice. Telegram of Pestellini to Presidente Consiglio Ministri, 22 February 1922, ACS, PS (1922), b. 45B, fasc. Firenze, sottofasc. 'agitazione agraria'.

57 In March 1921 the hon. Bosi, socialist deputy from Siena, announced in the Chamber that, 'There are thousands and thousands of eviction notices that have been given by way of reprisal': *Atti del Parlamento Italiano*, Camera dei Deputati, Legislatura xxv, Sessione 1919–21, Discussioni, I, p. 8765. Cf. also *ibid.*, p. 8766.

58 *Ora nostra*, 12 August 1921.

59 *Nuovo giornale*, 1 December 1920.

Giovanni Carrara, in his study of *mezzadria*, reports that this policy of reducing the size of the *podere* and awarding portions, known as *stralci*, to landless *braccianti* was much followed in this period in zones of mixed tenure of *mezzadria* and *bracciantato*. *Il contratto di mezzadria* (Urbino, 1936), p. 18.

60 *Atti del Parlamento Italiano*, Camera dei Deputati, Legislatura xxv, Sessione 1919–21, Discussioni, x, p. 8774.

61 *Ibid.*, pp. 8773–4.

62 Giovanni Lorenzoni, *L'ascesa del contadino italiano nel dopoguerra*, in Istituto Nazionale di Economia Agraria, *Inchiesta sulla piccola proprietà formatasi nel dopoguerra* (Rome, 1938), vol. xv.

63 Istituto Nazionale di Economia Agraria, *Inchiesta sulla piccola proprietà*, pp. 76–7.

64 Lorenzoni, *L'ascesa del contadino*.

65 On the origins of small property after the war, see *Ibid*; Istituto Nazionale di Economia Agraria, *Inchiesta sulla piccola proprietà*; and Serpieri, *La guerra e le classi rurali*.

66 For comparative prices of agricultural products, see above, Chap. 1, note 119.

67 Lorenzoni, *L'ascesa del contadino*, p. 180.

68 Report of Ispettore Generale L. Gaudino to Direttore Generale della Pubblica Sicurezza, 20 November 1921, ACS, PS (1921), b. 86A. fasc. Siena, p. 2.

69 See 'I piccoli proprietari si organizzano', *Dovere*, 12 June 1920; Prefetto di Siena D'Eufemia to Min. Int., Dir. Gen. PS (1920), b. 60, fasc. Siena, sottofasc. 'agitazione agraria'.

On the opposition of small peasant proprietors to the Leagues during the strikes of 1920 in Pisa province, see also Telegram of Prefetto De Martino to Min. Int. Dir. Gen. PS, 12 July 1920, ACS, PS (1920), b. 56, fasc. Pisa, sottofasc. 'agitazione agraria', n. 1772.

70 Prefetto di Siena D'Eufemia to Min. Int., Dir. Gen. PS, 26 July 1920, ACS, PS (1920), b. 60, fasc. Siena, sottofasc. 'agitazione agraria'.

71 Report of Ispettore Generale della Pubblica Sicurezza Di Tarsia, 'Situazione politica nei riguardi dell'ordine pubblico', to Min. Int., Dir. Gen. PS, 7 April 1922, ACS, PS (1922), b. 71B, fasc. Prato, p. 2.

72 'Ai contadini!'', *Scure*, 10 April 1920.

73 For the distribution of small peasant proprietorship in every agricultural zone of Tuscany, see Istituto Nazionale di Economia Agraria, *Inchiesta sulla piccola proprietà*.

74 Quoted in Pittorru, 'Origini del fascismo ferrarese', p. 294. For a report of a similar enthusiasm of the head of the Agrarian Association, Vico Mantovani, see 'Il comm. Mantovani a Cento', *Resto del Carlino*, 10 May 1921.

With respect to the diffusion of small peasant proprietorship as a strategy to combat subversion in the countryside, perhaps the most complete statement of all is that of the Lazio landlord James Aguet, *La terra ai contadini*. Aguet accepts in full the argument that peasant proprietorship is economically backward, but urges it for 'reasons of a social and political nature' (pp. 48–9). As he puts it,

> The principle of 'land to the peasants' is the demonstration of a wise and prudent political understanding ... Thus to guarantee the peasant a plot of land means to transform this man into a patriot jealous of the welfare of his country, ready for any sacrifice to preserve its independence and prosperity (pp. 56–7). On the effectiveness of the fascist land program in Ferrara province, see Corner, *Fascism in Ferrara*, pp. 157ff.

75 'La terra ai contadini', *Scure*, 1 May 1921.

On the conscious choice of Ferrara as a model for Sienese fascism, see 'A Ferrara', *Scure*, 15 March 1921; and 'Il fascismo nelle campagne', *Scure*, 1 May 1921. See also 'Per Ferrara fascista', *Scure*, 2 May 1922.

76 'La terra agli operai', *Rinnovamento*, 3 September 1921 and 21 October 1922.

77 Report of Ispettore Generale L. Gaudino to Direttore Generale della Pubblica Sicurezza, 20 November 1921, ACS, PS (1921), b. 86A, fasc. Siena, pp. 1–2.

78 See 'Ai contadini', *Scure* 1 May 1921; and 'Attività fascista', *Scure* 15 May 1921.

79 Telegram of Prefetto di Pisa to Min. Int., Dir. Gen. PS, 28 June 1920, ACS, PS (1920), b. 56, fasc. Pisa, sottofasc. 'agitazione agraria', n. 1253.

80 Umberto Odett, 'Il fascismo ed i contadini toscani', *Riscossa*, 22 January 1921.

As an example of the importance attached to the family by a leading Tuscan fascist, see Carlo Scorza, *Brevi note sul fascismo – sui capi, sui gregari* (Florence, 1930), pp. 3, 11. For Scorza the four cardinal principles in which the fascist must believe are God, Country, Family, and Life.

81 Giovanni Droandi, 'Il nuovo patto colonico e le sue conseguenze: schema di azione socialista', *Falce* 5 June 1920.

82 Report of Ispettore Generale Paolella to Direttore Generale della Pubblica Sicurezza, 27 April 1921, ACS, PS (1921), b. 75A, fasc. Arezzo.

83 Comparative figures contrasting Tuscany with the northern region of Emilia, Lombardy, and Veneto in terms of their yearly minimum numbers of unemployed are:

	1919	1920	1921
Tuscany	17,130	43,284	37,823
Emilia	74,780	131,974	148,665
Lombardy	32,247	110,816	135,248
Veneto	57,103	117,897	105,226

Renzo De Felice, *Mussolini il fascista*, 2 vols. (Turin, 1966–8), vol. I, p. 143n.

84 See above Chap. 1.

85 Cf., for example, the notices 'Ufficio del Lavoro', *Giovinezza* (Arezzo), 4

December 1921 and 11 December 1921. The Camera del Lavoro Italiano of Siena also ran an Ufficio del Lavoro. See *Era nuova*, 23 September 1921, and Chiurco, *Storia della rivoluzione fascista*, vol. III, p. 309.
86 *Idea fascista*, 23 April 1922.
87 Letter of Bonelli, Segretario Provinciale della Federterra to Prefect of Siena, 25 October, 1921, ASS, AGP, Filza 174, Cart. di Ins. 31.
88 Letter of Gaetano Danesi to Segreterio Generale dei Fasci, 7 September 1921, ACS, MRF, parte 1, b. 105, fasc. San Piero a Ponti, n. 4.
89 'Movimento sindacale fascista', *Idea fascista*, 9 April 1922 (emphasis added).
90 Quoted in Luigi Arbizzani, 'Lotte agrarie in provincia di Bologna nel primo dopoguerra', in Renato Zangheri, *ed.*, *Le campagne emiliane*, p. 331.
91 See the following articles by Gino Baldesi: 'Serenamente', *Difesa*, 21 May 1921; 'Disarmare', *Difesa*, 25 June 1921; and 'La Verità', *Difesa*, 6 August 1921.
92 Gino Baldesi, 'I due estremi si toccano', *Difesa*, 18 May 1921, and 'Le due minaccie', *Difesa*, 14 May 1922.
93 On the *arditi del popolo*, see Ferdinando Cordova, *Arditi e legionari dannunziani* (Padua, 1969), esp. pp. 83–113.
94 On this point, see Corner, *Fascism in Ferrara*, chap. 6. S. J. Woolf mentions the importance of small, agriculturally based industry in the rise of fascism. *European Fascism* (London, 1968), p. 46.
95 On the predominance of women in the textile industry in Lucca province, see Prefetto Di Donato to Ministero per il Lavoro e la Previdenza Sociale, Direzione Generale del Lavoro, 12 August 1921, ASLU, AGP, Filza 200, fasc. Anno 1921 ('Partiti politicis'), n. 1182.
96 Corradino Calamai, *L'industria laniera nella provincia di Firenze* (Florence, 1927).
97 *Ibid.*
98 Ugo Cuesta, 'Le industrie pratesi nella morsa della crisi', *Nuovo giornale*, 3 July 1921.
99 *Ibid.*
100 Edoardo Ugolini, 'I vampiri della lana', *Lavoro*, 22 May 1920.
101 For analysis of the origins and nature of the crisis of the Prato wool industry, see 'Il dopoguerra: l'industria laniera', *Lavoro*, 21 December 1918 and 25 January 1919; 'La crisi a Prato e gli industriali', *Lavoro*, 28 May 1921. See also Ugo Cuesta, 'Le industrie pratesi nella morsa della crisi', *Nuovo giornale*, 3 July 1921; Ugo Cuesta, 'La crisi dell'industria laniera', *Nuovo giornale*, 6 July 1921.
102 'Il vero significato dello sciopero', *Patria*, 11 November 1919.
103 'Siamo noi, padroni di noi stessi?', *Patria*, 21 December 1919.
104 See the series of articles entitled 'La questione dei "Consigli di fabbrica"', *Patria*, 28 March, 25 April, 2 May, and 9 May 1920.
105 'L'agitazione agraria nel Pratese', *Nazione*, 4 December 1920.
106 On the course of the strike, see *Lavoro* through the autumn of 1921, and for its outcome, see 'Dopo lo sciopero dei lanieri', *Lavoro*, 26 November 1921.
107 'Lo sciopero degli operai lanieri', *Patria*, 4 September 1921.
108 *Patria*, 19 February 1922.
109 For the text of the resolution adopted by the Prato taxpayers, see ACP, Miscellanea, Filza Ministeri 1922, fasc. 1.

110 'Il PPI e gli scioperi', *Patria*, 29 February 1920.
111 'La falsa strada del PPI', *Patria*, 29 August 1920.
112 Report of Ispettore Generale Di Tarsia, 'Situazione politica nei riguardi dell'ordine pubblico', to Min. Int., Dir. Gen. PS, 7 April 1922, ACS, PS (1922), b. 71B, fasc. Prato.
113 Maria Luisa Florio, *Federico Guglielmo Florio nella vita e nell'opera* (Sancasciano Val di Pesa, n.d.), pp. 67, 84.
114 *Ibid*. On the support of the Prato industrialists for fascism, see also Report of Prefetto di Firenze Pericoli to Min. Int., Dir. Gen. PS, 28 July 1922, ACS, PS (1922), b. 71B, fasc. Prato, n. 1694; and Telegram of Pericoli to Min. Int., Dir. Gen. PS, 11 April 1922, ACS, PS (1922), b. 71B, fasc. Firenze (1), n. 1210. In the latter Pericoli pointed out that the Prato fascists were 'the genuine expression of the mean local industry', which 'has it in mind to prevent the existence and resurgence of any working-class organization whatsoever'.
115 Report of Ispettore Generale Di Tarsia, 'Situazione politica nei riguardi dell'ordine pubblico', to Min. Int., Dir. Gen. PS 7 April 1922, ACS, PS (1922), b. 71B, fasc. Prato.
116 *Patria*, 5 June 1921.
 With nearly 500 workers, the Lanificio Calamai was the third in size among the 102 Prato wool companies. Calamai, *L'industria laniera*, pp. 86–7.
117 Rosangela Degl'Innocenti Mazzamuto, *Le lotte sociali e le origini del fascismo a Prato, 1919–1922* (Prato, 1974), document 32, p. 195.
118 Report of Ispettore Generale Di Tarsia, 'Situazione politica nei riguardi dell'ordine pubblico', to Min. Int., Dir. Gen. PS, 7 April 1922, ACS, PS (1922), b. 71B, fasc. Prato.
 On this incident see also Telegrams of Prefetto Pericoli to Min. Int., Dir. Gen. PS, 18 February 1922, ACS, PS (1922), b. 71B, fasc. Prato, n. 3798 and n. 3836.
119 'La violenza e la legge', *Patria*, 30 January 1921.
120 'Intorno alla violenza', *Patria*, 12 February 1922. On the reaction of the paper to fascist violence, see also 'Il fascismo', *Patria*, 16 January 1921; 'La violenza e la legge', *Patria*, 30 January 1921; 'Resurrezione', *Patria*, 24 April 1921; 'Liberalismo immortale', *Patria*, 1 and 22 January 1922.
121 Report of Ispettore della Pubblica Sicurezza (signature indecipherable) 'Provincia di Lucca – condizioni dello spirito pubblico', to S. E. il Ministro dell'Interno, 20 August 1922, ACS, PS (1922), b. 74, fasc. Lucca, sottofasc. Lucca.
122 Maria Carla Morganti writes, 'Numberless were the strikes fought by the organized workers, and every firm, no matter how small, had its own contestation' ('Lotta economica e tensioni sociali nel dopoguerra a Lucca, 1919–1922', unpublished B.A. thesis, University of Pisa, Faculty of Political Science, 1974).
123 *Ibid*.
124 Morganti, 'Lotta economica', pp. 284–5.
125 Report of Di Donato to Min. Int., Dir. Gen. PS, 2 May 1922, ACS, PS (1922), b. 74, fasc. Lucca, sottofasc. Lucca, n. 884.
126 Report of Ispettore della Pubblica Sicurezza (signature indecipherable), 'Provincia di Lucca – condizioni dello spirito pubblico', to S. E. il Ministro

dell'Interno, 20 August 1922, ACS, PS (1922), b. 74, fasc. Lucca, sottofasc. Lucca. For Pietrasanta, see Morganti, 'Lotta economica', p. 274.
127 Carlo Scorza, *Brevi note sul fascismo – sui capi, sui gregari* (Florence, 1930), pp. 77–80. Scorza's sociology at this point, however, is obscure and misleading. Particularly mystifying is his description of small industry as an 'intermediate' force of mediation in the great conflict between capital and labour.
128 Morganti, 'Lotta economica'.
129 *Dovere*, 8 January 1921.
130 For information on the San Sepolcro *fascio*, see Report of G. B. Marziali to Piero Bolzon, Vice-Segretario dei Fasci, n.d., ACS, MRF, parte 1, b. 106, fasc. San Sepolcro, n. 17, 7 pages. For the membership of the *direttorio*, see *ibid.*, pp. 1–2.
131 Telegram of Prefetto Limongelli to Min. Int., Dir. Gen. PS, 9 June 1921, ACS, PS (1921), b. 75A, fasc. Arezzo, n. 731.
  Marziali also described both Fosco Buitoni and Valentino Dindelli as 'violent by nature and therefore excellent fascists yesterday, but very bad fascists today'. Report of G. G. Marziali to Piero Bolzon, n.d., ACS, MRF, parte 1, b. 106, fasc. San Sepolcro, n. 17, p. 4.
132 Letter of on. Luigi Bosi to Merloni, 28 April 1922, ACS, PS (1922), b. 65, fasc. Arezzo, sottofasc. San Sepolcro.
133 *Ibid.*
134 Telegram of Prefetto Alfonso Limongelli to Min. Int., Dir. Gen. PS, 9 June 1921, ACS, PS (1921), b. 75A, fasc. Arezzo, n. 731. See also Telegram of Prefetto Limongelli to Min. Int., Dir. Gen. PS, 6 July 1921, ACS, PS (1921), b. 75A, fasc. Arezzo, n. 731.
135 Marziali reported, for instance, that the commander of the San Sepolcro squads, Dindelli, used the blackshirts to force men from the town to promise to marry his sister, 'who ... is the field where many have pastured and continue to pasture, more or less illicitly'. Report of G. B. Marziali to Piero Bolzon, n.d., ACS, MRF, parte 1, b. 106, fasc. San Sepolcro, n. 17.
136 *Ibid.*, pp. 2–4. In addition to its activities in the town, the *fascio* also reportedly practised extortion from the peasants in the surrounding countryside (*ibid.*, p. 4).
137 The Arezzo fascist paper *Giovinezza* reported that fascism in the Tiber Valley was largely dependent on the San Sepolcro *fascio*, 'the most important *fascio* in the Tiber Valley': 'La situazione dei Fasci nella provincia di Arezzo', *Giovinezza* (Arezzo), 27 November 1921.
138 Ernesto Ragionieri, *Un comune socialista: Sesto fiorentino* (Rome, 1953), pp. 205ff.
139 The brick-maker Nestore Fontani, for instance, was the delegate of the fascist unions of Poggibonsi (Siena) at the interprovincial congress of Economic Unions belonging to the Camera del Lavoro Italiana held at Siena in October 1921. *Era nuova*, 13 October 1921.
140 Guerrini, *Il movimento operaio empolese*.
141 Letter of Serpieri, Presidente della Società fra Industriali, Commercianti ed Esercenti di Siena e Provincia to Prefetto di Siena, 15 May 1922, n. 1182, ASS, AGP. Filza 181, Cart. di Ins. 31.
142 ACS, MRF, parte 1, b. 104, fasc. Pozzo della Chiana, n. 1.
143 ACS, MRF, parte 1, b. 106, fasc. Sestino, n. 1.

144 ACS, MRF, parte 1, b. 103, fasc. Modigliana, n. 1.
145 ACS, MRF, parte 1, b. 104, fasc. Pontassieve, n. 1.
146 ACS, MRF, parte 1, b. 104, fasc. Premilcuore, n. 6.
147 ACS, MRF, parte 1, b. 105, fasc. Sancasciano Val di Pesa, n. 1.
148 ACS, MRF, parte 1, b. 106, fasc. Seggiano, n. 1.
149 See below, Chap. 6.
150 In 1913 there were in the province of Massa-Carrara 777 quarries employing a work-force of 12,340 men. In addition, directly linked to the marble industry were some 154 saw mills and 140 laboratories employing respectively 1984 and 2,980 workers. Camera di Commercio e Industria di Carrara, 'Memoriale a S. E. il Presidente del Consiglio dei Ministri', 31 August 1917, ASM, Archivio del Commissariato di PS di Carrara, b. 53 (1920), Cat. A4, fasc. 'Derville – Ditta francese; occupazione cave'.
151 Telegram of Prefetto Nicola De Bernardinis to Min. Int., 23 October 1920, ACS, PS (1920), b. 80, fasc. Carrara ('movimento anarchico'), n. 23487. Cf. also Telegram of Prefetto Palmieri, 21 March 1921, ACS, PS (1920), b. 80, fasc. Carrara ('movimento anarchico'), n. 331.

On the origins of fascism at Carrara, see Antonio Bernieri, 'La nascita del fascismo a Carrara', in Unione Regionale delle Provincie Toscane, *La Toscana nel regime fascista, 1922–1939* (Florence, 1971), vol. II, pp. 677–97.
152 For the text of the contract signed on 10 April 1920, by representatives of the Chamber of Labour and of the Federazione Industriali del Marmo, see ACS, PS (1920), b. 53, fasc. Massa e Carrara, sottofasc. 'agitazione marmisti'.
153 *Ibid.*, pp. 679–80.
155 'Il fascismo in Lunigiana', *Paese*, 29 March 1922.
156 See Mori, *La Valdelsa*. On the personal direction of the company by Donegani during the strikes and disputes of 1922, see Telegram of Prefetto Berti to Min. Int., Dir. Gen. PS 8 August 1922, ACS, PS (1922), b. 47A, fasc. Massa, sottofasc. 'agitazione minatori e marmisti', n. 167.
157 For the text of the contract signed on 13 November 1922 by the Società Marmifera Nord Carrara and the Sindacati Nazionali, cf. the appendix to Report of Prefetto Berti to Min. Int., Dir. Gen. PS, 18 November 1922, ACS, PS (1922), b. 47A, fasc. Massa, sottofasc. 'agitazione minatori e marmisti', n. 167.
158 Report of Ispettore Generale della PS Paolella, 26 January 1922, ACS, PS (1922), b. 75B, fasc. Massa, sottofasc. Carrara (1).

On the furnishing to the *fasci* in the province of Massa-Carrara of 'means of every description' by the Carrara industrialists, see Telegram of Prefetto Berti to Min. Int. Dir. Gen. PS, 6 July 1922, ACS, PS (1922), b. 47a, fasc. Massa, sottofasc. 'ordine pubblico – richiesta di rinforzi', n. 690.
159 Report of Prefetto Berti, 'Carrara: situazione locale' to Min. Int., Dir. Gen. PS, 28 May 1922, ACS, PS (1922), b. 74, fasc. Lucca, sottofasc. Seravezza, n. 13R.
160 Telegram of Berti to Min. Int., Dir. Gen. PS, 10 July 1922, ACS, PS (1922), b. 75B, fasc. Massa, sottofasc. Carrara (2), n. 4800.
161 Lyttelton, *The Seizure of Power*, p. 168.
162 Chiurco, *Storia della rivoluzione fascista*, vol. I, p. 300.
164 Telegram of Questore di Lucca Grazioli to Min. Int., 9 May 1921, ASM, Archivio del Commissariato di PS, b. 55 (1921), fasc. 'Lotta fra fascisti e communisti', sottofasc. 'Forte dei Marmi: fascisti di Carrara', n. 560.

165 Chiurco, *Storia della rivoluzione fascista*, vol. 1, p. 300.
  At Carrara Dell'Amico was reported to be *caposquadra*: 'Un'altra domenica di conflitti', *Corriere della sera*, 19 July 1921.
166 'Cenno sommario dei fatti avvenuti nel Comune di Carrara dal 19 marzo al 26 luglio 1921', ASM, Archivio del Commissariato di PS di Carrara, b. 55 (1921), fasc. 'Scioperi'.
166 Telegram of Prefetto Giuseppe Grignolo to Min. Int., Dir. Gen. PS, 20 July 1921, ACS, PS (1921), b. 60B, fasc. Massa, sottofasc. 'disoccupazione'.
168 Telegrams of Ispettore Generale della PS Paolella to Min. Int., Dir. Gen. PS, 16, 18, and 20 January 1922, ACS, Ministero dell'Interno. Gabinetto di S. E. Bonomi. Ordine Pubblico (1921–2),. b. 4, fasc. 43 (Massa-Carrara).
169 Telegram of Bonomi to Prefetto di Carrara, 25 January 1922, ACS, Ministero dell'Interno. Gabinetto di S. E. Bonomi. Ordine Pubblico (1921–2), b. 4, fasc. 42 (Massa-Carrara).

3 BIG BUSINESS AND MUSSOLINI

1 For my account of the politics of heavy industry nationally I have relied above all on the following:

> Mario Abrate, *La lotta sindacale nella industrializzazione in Italia 1906–1926* (Turin, 1967)
> Valerio Castronovo, *Agnelli* (Turin, 1971)
>   'La grande industria: giochi interni e linea di fondo', *Il Ponte*, 26 (1970), pp. 1198–221.
> Renzo De Felice, *Mussolini il rivoluzionario* (Turin, 1965)
>   *Mussolini il fascista*, 2 vols. (Turin, 1966–8)
> Daniel Guérin, *Fascisme et grand capital* (Paris, 1945)
> Piero Melograni, 'Confindustria e fascismo tra il 1919 e il 1925', *Il Nuovo osservatore*, 6 (1965), pp. 835–73
> Roland Sarti, *Fascism and the Industrial Leadership in Italy, 1919–1940: A Study in the Expansion of Private Power under Fascism* (Berkeley, 1971)

2 Valerio Castronovo, *La stampa italiana dall'Unità al fascismo* (Bari, 1973), p. 271.
3 On the financing of fascism by heavy industry, see De Felice, *Mussolini il rivoluzionario*, *passim*; De Felice, *Mussolini il fascista*, *passim*; Renzo De Felice, 'Primi elementi sul finanziamento del fascismo dalle origini al 1924', *Rivista storica del socialismo*, 22 (1964), pp. 223–53; and Castronovo, *La stampa italiana*, pp. 255–73.
4 Agostino Lanzillo, *Le rivoluzioni del dopoguerra: critiche e diagnosi* (Città di Castello, 1922), esp. pp. 255–6.
  On the contrast between agrarian and industrial fascism, see also De Felice, *Mussolini il fascista*, vol. 1, esp. chap. 2; and Preti, *Le lotte agrarie*, p. 449.
5 Nicos Poulantzas, *Fascisme et dictature* (Paris, 1970), Chap. 1.
6 For a brief history of the company in the form of a report by Donegani to the shareholders, see 'Montecatini', *Nazione*, 13 October 1925. See also *Gazetta di Lucca*, 4 May 1921.
7 'I discorsi degli onorevoli, Sarrochi e Donegani', *Nazione*, 5 April 1924.
8 See 'Montecatini', *Nazione*, 28 April 1923 and 2 April 1924.
9 Giorgio Mori, 'Materiali, temi ed ipotesi per una storia dell'industria nella regione toscana durante il fascismo', in Unione Regionale delle Province

Toscane, *La Toscana nel regime fascista, 1922–1939* (Florence, 1971), pp., 143–5.
10 *Ibid.*, p 134; and Società Boracifera di Lardarello, *Bilancio al 31 dicembre 1913* (Florence, 1914).
11 *Ibid.*, pp. 132, 134, 171.
12 Società Magona d'Italia, *Bilancio 1934* (Florence, 1935), and *Battaglie fasciste*, 21 February 1925.
13 For the development of Tuscan industry, see Giorgio Mori, 'L'industria toscana fra gli inizi del secolo e la guerra di Libia', in Unione Regionale delle Province Toscane, *La Toscana nell'Italia unita*, pp. 219–331; and 'Materiali, temi ed ipotesi', pp. 109–309.

For a survey of industry in Florence province, see Camera di Commercio e Industria di Firenze, *Statistica industriale: Notizie sulle condizioni industriali della Provincia di Firenze. Anno 1911* (Florence, 1911).
14 For an analysis of the state of Tuscan industry in this period, see Mori, 'Materiali, temi, ed ipotesi', esp. pp. 126–72.
15 On the expansion of Ilva, see above, pp. 127–30.

On the war-time expansion of Montecatini, see Alberto Caracciolo, 'La grande industria nella prima guerra mondiale', in Caracciolo, ed., *La formazione dell'Italia industriale* (Bari, 1969), pp. 213–14. For information on Guido Donegani, see *Gazzetta di Lucca*, 4 May 1921.
16 Mori, 'Materiali, temi ed ipotesi', pp. 142–3.
17 On the position of Ginori Lisci, see *ibid.*, pp. 132, 134, 171.
18 *Ibid.*, pp. 133–4, 141, 144, 170.
19 *Ibid.*, pp. 132, 137.
20 See Alberto Caracciolo, 'La grande industria nella prima guerra mondiale', in Caracciolo, ed., *La formazione dell'Italia industriale*, pp. 163–219.
21 See above, pp. 107–8.
22 Riccardo Bachi, *L'Italia economica nel 1918, annuario della vita commerciale, agraria, finanziaria e della politica economica* (Città di Castello, 1919), pp. 140–1.
23 *Ibid.*, p. 141.
24 Adrian Lyttelton, *The Seizure of Power* (London, 1973), p. 206.
25 Giuliano Procacci and Giovanni Rindi, 'Storia di una fabbrica: le Officine Galileo di Firenze', *Movimento operaio*, 6 (1954), p. 23.
26 'Industria e speculazione', *Corriere della sera*, 8 May 1921. See also 'La situazione dell'Ilva', *Corriere della sera*, 11 May 1921.
27 On the Prato textile industry, see above, pp. 100ff.
28 For contrasting descriptions of the war-time expansion of Ilva and Ansaldo on the one hand and Fiat on the other, cf. Bachi, *L'Italia economica nel 1919 ...* (Città di Castello, 1920), pp. 140–5.

See also Caracciolo, 'La grande industria nella prima guerra mondiale', pp. 211–13 and 198–201.
29 On the unscrupulous business practices of Bondi, Fera, Orlando, and Luzzatto, as well as the exclusion of Bondi and Luzzatto from parliament, see 'L'assalto allo Stato: Luzzatto e Bondi diffidati e contestati', *Dovere*, 11 February 1921; 'I pescecani alla sbarra', *Dovere*, 19 February 1921; 'Le elezioni Bondi e Luzzatto annullate', *Dovere*, 26 March 1921; 'Lo Stato, L'Ilva e il Deputato', *Dovere*, 2 July 1921; and 'Il programma navale dell'Ilva', *Dovere*, 16 July 1921.

30 Quoted in 'Il programma navale dell'Ilva', *Dovere*, 16 July 1921.
31 For the text of the report of the committee of investigation, see 'Le gravi risultanze dell'inchiesta sull'Ilva', *Corriere della sera*, 13 December, 1921. See also 'La discussione all'assemblea dell'Ilva', *Corriere della sera*, 14 December, 1921.
32 Bachi, *L'Italia economica nel 1918*, p. 142.
33 On the weaknesses of the Tuscan steel industry, see Bachi, *L'Italia economica nel 1918*, pp. 140–5; Bachi, *L'Italia economica nel 1920*; Rosario Romeo, *Breve storia della grande industria in Italia*, pp. 79, 122–4, 126–9; Guido Albertelli, 'Le insidie dei siderurgici', *Critica sociale*, 30 (1920), no. 11, pp. 71–2; and 'Ancora su le insidie dei siderurgici', *Critica sociale*, 30 (1920), no. 11, pp. 165–71; Gino Luzzatto 'Siderurgia e socialismo', *Critica sociale*, 30 (1920), no. 7, pp. 101–4; Dante Piccioli, 'L'industria siderurgica italiana veduta da vicino', *Critica sociale*, 30 (1920), no. 18, pp. 281–9.
34 On the opposition of interests within Confindustria between the 'establishment' and the 'outsiders', see Lyttelton, *The Seizure of Power*, pp. 206–8. See also Paolo Arvati, 'Giacinto Menotti Serrati fra il biennio rosso e la crisi del massimalismo (1919–1922)', *Movimento operaio e socialista*, 18 (1972), no. 4, p. 61.
35 Cantagalli, *Storia del fascismo fiorentino*, pp. 54–64.
36 Umberto Banchelli, *Le memorie di un fascista*, p. 7.
37 Cantagalli, *Storia del fascismo fiorentino*, pp. 54, 63–4.
   On the particular intransigence of the Mineraria in the Valdarno area, see Letter of Prefetto di Arezzo to Min. Int., Dir. Gen. PS, 8 June 1919, ACS, PS (1919), b. 38, fasc. Arezzo, n. 397.
38 Castronovo, *La stampa italiana*, pp. 255–73.
39 *Ibid.*, pp. 243–4.
40 Announcements of meetings appeared frequently. For examples in 1919, see *Nazione*, 9 and 30 July, 17 August, 6 and 9 October, 1919.
41 Italian national production of iron, measured in tons per annum, exhibited the following trend:

    1913   603,116
    1915   679,970
    1916   946,604
    1917   998,632
    1918   694,677
    1919   465,655
    1920   389,966

   Bachi, *L'Italia economica nel 1920*, p. 212.
42 'I mazzieri del Valdarno', *Risveglio*, 12 November 1919.
43 In June 1920 Umberto Pasella reported that there were only three *fasci* operating in Tuscany – at Florence, Pisa, and Livorno. Letter to P. Giacomelli, 17 June 1920, ACS, MRF, parte, 1, b. 104, fasc. Piombino, n. 8.
   Closer inspection reveals, however, that the Livorno *fascio* existed chiefly on paper and had to be established anew in November 1920. See Telegram of Zamboni to CC dei Fasci, 18 November 1920, ACS, MRF, parte 1, b. 103, fasc. Livorno, cart. 1, n. 38; and Letter of Paolo Pedani to Pasella, 20 November 1920, ACS, MRF, parte 1, b. 103, fasc. Livorno, cart. 1, n. 40.
   Similarly, the Pisa *fascio*, although not formally dissolved, lapsed into total inactivity until November, when there began the 'Pisan fascist renaissance'.

See Letters of Luigi Malagoli to Segretario Generale dei Fasci, 20 September and 13 November 1920, ACS, MRF, parte 1, b. 104, fasc, Pisa, n. 26 and n. 29.
44 Letters of Luigi Malagoli to Umberto Pasella, 29 April and 5 May 1920, ACS, MRF, b. 104, fasc. Pisa, n. 7 and n. 9.
45 Letter to Luigi Malagoli, 17 September 1920, ACS, MRF, b. 104, fasc. Pisa, n. 22.
46 Letter to Umberto Pasella, 12 June 1920, ACS, MRF, b. 104, fasc. Piombino, n. 9.
47 'Verbale del Convegno dei Rappresentanti dei Fasci della Toscana', 5 November 1920, ACS, MRF, b. 102, fasc. Firenze, cart. 2, n. 137.
48 Average daily wages in Italy during the war were:

1913	3.54 lire
1916	4.03 lire
1917	4.90 lire
1918	6.04 lire

This compares with a cost of living index (1913 = 100), which ran:

1913	100
1915	132.7
1916	199.7
1917	306.3
1918	409.1

Gwyn A. Williams, 'Proletarian Forms', *New Edinburgh Review*, special issue on Gramsci, n.d., vol. I, p. 62. The substance of this article is included in the book *Proletarian Order* (London, 1975).
49 The extent of the halt in the construction industry, which was a major factor in the postwar shortage of accommodation, is given by the number of new rooms made available as dwellings in Florence between 1913 and 1922:

1913	4,432
1914	1,702
1915	1,292
1916	1,265
1917	689
1918	281
1919	145
1920	233
1921	87
1922	981

Mori, 'Materiali, temi ed ipotesi', p. 153n.

For an examination of the causes of the crisis, see dott. Cantore, 'La crisi delle abitazioni', *Libertà*, 11 June 1921; 'Il grave problema delle abitazioni', *Giovinezza* (Arezzo), 27 November 1921; 'Il problema delle abitazioni e la crisi dell'industria edilizia', *Dovere*, 3 December 1921.
50 Gwyn Williams, 'Proletarian Forms', pp. 64–5.
51 On these events in Florence, see 'Firenze insorge contro gli affamatori del popolo', *Difesa*, 4 July 1919; 'Il popolo di Firenze ha pronunziato il suo inesorabile verdetto', *Difesa*, 5 July 1919; and 'Il proletariato affida all'azione diretta la tutela del diritto alla vita', *Difesa*, 12 July 1919.

For reports on the course of the uprisings throughout Tuscany, see, for instance, *Nuovo giornale*, 4–12 July 1919.

52 Luigi Cortesi, *Il socialismo italiano tra riforme e rivoluzione, 1892–1921* (Bari, 1969), pp. 709–11.
53 For police reports on the events on the events at Viareggio, see ACS, PS (1921), b. 60B, fasc. Viareggio, *passim*. For a brief published account, see Ivan Tognarini, 'Toscana: crisi siderurgica e potere in fabbrica', *Il ponte*, 26 (1970), pp. 1335–7.
   See also 'Viareggio in rivolta', *Corriere della sera*, 4 May 1920, and 'La fine dei disordini a Viareggio', *Corriere della sera*, 5 May 1920.
54 On the events at Piombino, see Ugo Cuesta, 'La situazione a Piombino', *Nuovo giornale*, 12 June 1920; Mario Malan, 'Una giornata di violenze e di saccheggi a Piombino', *Nuovo giornale*, 27 June 1920; and 'Scene di saccheggio a Viareggio', *Corriere della sera*, 27 June 1920. See also Tognarini, 'Toscana: crisi siderurgica', pp. 1337–41.
55 *Ordine nuovo*, 15 May 1920.
56 A careful study of the struggle for workers' control in Livorno is provided by Tobias Abse, 'The Political Struggle in Livorno, 1918–1922: The Rise of Fascism in a Socialist Stronghold', unpublished Ph.D. thesis, Cambridge University, 1983, Chap. 4.
57 For the eleven points of the manifesto, see *Risveglio*, 13 April 1919.
58 On the start of the strike, see *Risveglio*, 6 July 1919.
59 For announcement of the first victories of the strikers, see *Risveglio*, 13 July 1919.
   The terms of the settlement with the Società Antimonifera are reported in *Risveglio*, 17 August 1919. On the settlement with Carlo Marchi and Co. see *Risveglio*, 10 August 1919. The last company to capitulate was the Siele. The settlement there is reported in *Risveglio*, 30 November 1919.
60 'Il Congresso dei minatori a Grosseto', *Risveglio*, 22 February 1920.
61 *Risveglio*, 20 June 1920.
62 *Risveglio*, 29 August, 1920.
63 *Falce*, 5 June 1920.
64 *Ibid*.
65 Letter of Rappresentanti degli operai degli stabilimenti siderurgici di Piombino e Portoferraio, nonche dei minatori dell'Elba, accompagnati dal Segretario della Camera del Lavoro di Piombino, Elba e Maremma, 12 March 1920, ACS, PS (1920), b. 56, fasc. Pisa, sottofasc. 'disoccupazione'.
   See also Prefetto Gasperini to Min. Int., Dir. Gen. PS, 2 June 1921, ACS, PS (1921), b. 60A, fasc. Livorno, sottofasc, 'minatori', n. 913.
66 On the Occupation of the factories at the national level, see Paolo Spriano, *L'occupazione delle fabbriche* (Turin, 1964); Castronovo, *Agnelli*, chap. 3; and Gianni Bosio, 'L'occupazione delle fabbriche e i gruppi dirigenti e di pressione del movimento operaio', *Il ponte*, 26 (1970), pp. 1136–90.
   On Tuscany more particularly, see Tognarini, 'Toscana: crisi siderurgica'; Alfonso Preziosi, 'L'occupazione degli Alti forni di Portoferraio', *Movimento operaio e socialista*, 17 (1971), no. 1, pp. 45–56; and Procacci and Rindi, 'Storia di una fabbrica' esp. pp. 27ff.
67 On this strike, see Giuseppe Maione, 'Il biennio rosso: lo sciopero delle lancette, Marzo-Aprile 1920', *Storia contemporanea*, 3 (1972), pp. 239–304. See also Castronovo, *Agnelli*, pp. 223–9.
68 For examination of the fiscal program of the Giolitti government, see *Nuovo giornale*, 10, 15, 16, 17, 18, 22, 24, 25, 28, 29, 30, 31 July and 1 August 1920.

69 Quoted in *Nuovo giornale*, 16 July 1920.
70 Castronovo, *Agnelli*, p. 235.
71 On the lock-out as a revolt against Giolittian Liberalism, see *ibid.*, pp. 240–3.
72 Letter of Giuseppe Orlando to Presidente del Consiglio dei Ministri e Ministro dell'Interno, 2 September 1920, ACS, PS (1920), b. 74, fasc. Livorno ('agitazione metallurgici').
73 For extended reports on the course of the Occupation in Tuscany, see the September issues of *Nuovo giornale* and *Nazione*.
74 Telegram of Prefetto De Martino to Min. Int., Dir. Gen. PS, 13 September 1920, ACS, PS (1920), b. 75, fasc. Pisa ('agitazione metallurgici').
75 *Nazione*, 16 September 1920.
76 As Giolitti explained two years later:
> From the outset I had a firm and clear conviction that experience would teach the workers that they could not obtain their objectives ... As I saw it, the episode was repeating ... the analogous situation of 1904, which had roused such fear and then revealed itself as inept ... Accordingly, I let the experiment develop up to a certain point, in order to convince the workers that it was impossible for them to succeed and to prevent the agitators from being able to blame others for their failures.
>
> At the time, I was blamed for not having employed the police to make the law respected and to prevent the violation of private property ... But even admitting that I could have had the factories occupied by the police before the workers could seize them ... I should then have found myself in the awkward position of having almost the entire police force ... shut up in the factories ... this would in fact have been playing into the hands of the revolutionaries, who asked for nothing better.
>
> On the other hand, if after the occupation I had called for the police forces to eject the workers from the factories, bloodshed and conflict would have been the result, with the added probability that the workers before giving way would have wrecked their strongholds. Giovanni Giolitti, *Memoirs of my Life*, trans. Edward Storer (London, 1923), pp. 437–8.

77 The opposition between the councils and the unions was clearly explained in the article 'Sindacati e consigli', *Ordine nuovo*, 12 June 1920. For the *Ordine nuovo*, the unions had been a precious conquest of the working class that had extended the rule of law to the tyranny of the work-place. The task of the revolution, and therefore also of the councils, however, was to break the bonds of industrial legality in order to overturn the fundamental relations of power.
78 Quoted in Tognarini, 'Toscana: crisi siderurgica', pp. 1352–3.
79 Quoted in *ibid.*, p. 1334.
80 On the special role of the Florence *fascio* as the organizing centre of fascism throughout the region, the prefects provided ample testimony. From Pisa, for example, De Martino wrote of Florence as the 'epicentre' of the fascist movement throughout Tuscany, and claimed that the Florence *fascio* provided the 'excessive and violent thrust' to the fascist reaction in the whole region. Telegrams of De Martino to S. E. Corradini, Sottosegretario Interni, 17 May 1921, ACS, PS (1921), b. 83B, fasc. Pisa (1), n. 19137; and to S. E. Giolitti, n.d., ACS, PS (1921), b. 83B, fasc. Pisa (1), n. 14246.

Similarly, from Lucca province, Di Donato reported that fascism in the Nievole Valley 'has always been under the direct influence of the fascist organizations of Florence province'. Telegram to Min. Int., Dir. Gen. PS, ACS, PS (1922), b. 74, fasc. Lucca, sottofasc. Lucca. The organization of the Lucca *fascio* was the work of Gennaro Abbatemaggio of Florence. Letter of Questore di Lucca Grazioli to Ispettore Generale della PS Luigi Gaudino, 21 December

1920, ACS, PS (1921), b. 79B, fasc. Lucca. See also Letter of Goffredo Pieri to Cesare Rossi, 7 November 1920, ACS, MRF, parte 1, b. 103, fasc. Lucca, n. 14.
  The founding of the Arezzo *fascio* had been undertaken by Dino Perrone Compagni and Manfredo Chiostri of the Florence organization. Report of Ispettore Generale della Pubblica Sicurezza Paolella to Direttore Generale della Pubblica Sicurezza, 27 April 1921, ACS, PS (1921), b. 75A, fasc. Arezzo.
  The definitive establishment of the Livorno *fascio* in November 1920 took place on the initiative of the Florence fascists Zamboni, Lascialfare, and Galardini. Letter of Zamboni to Umberto Pasella, 18 November 1920, ACS, MRF, parte 1, b. 102, fasc. Firenze, cart. 2, n. 176. See also *Telegrafo*, 18 November 1920.
  The setting up of the fascist branch at Grosseto was accomplished by Dino Castellani, who had been dispatched by the Florence leadership in the middle of 1921 for the purpose. Telegram of Ispettore Generale della PS Paolella to Min. Int., Dir. Gen. PS, 4 July 1921, ACS, PS (1921), b. 79A, fasc. Grosseto; and Report of Paolella, 'Conflitti a Grosseto e Provincia', 4 August 1921, ACS, PS (1921), b. 79A, fasc. Grosseto.
81 Umberto Banchelli, *Le memorie di un fascista, 1919–1922* (Florence, 1922), p. 35. dell'Interno,
82 Letter to Ministro dell'Interno, 21 April 1921, ACS, PS (1921), b. 78A, fasc. 1, n. 12211. The Prefect of Pisa described Florence as the 'epicentre' of Tuscan fascism. Telegram of De Martino to S. E. Corradini, 17 May 1921, ACS, PS (1921), b. 83B, fasc. Pisa (1), n. 19137.
83 For lists of contributions, see *Telegrafo*, 9 August to 18 September 1922.
84 Banchelli, *Le memorie di un facista*, p. 32; Tognarini, 'Toscana: crisi siderurgica', p. 1355; Edoardo Savino, *La nazione operante* (Milan, 1928), p. 258; Chiurco, *Storia della rivoluzione fascista*, vol. III, p. 233.
85 Chiurco, *Storia della rivoluzione fascista*, iii, p. 233.
86 Letter of Pacinotti to Umberto Pasella, 26 February 1921, ACS, MRF, parte 1, b. 104, fasc. Piombino, n. 25.
87 Prefect di Pisa to Min. Int., Dir. Gen. PS, 10 February 1922, ACS, PS (1925), b. 98, fasc. Pisa ('costituzione dei fasci').
88 Savino, *La nazione operante*, p. 691.
89 Prefetto Masino to Min. Int., Dir. Gen. PS, 8 February 1921, ACS, PS (1925), b. 98, fasc. Siena ('costituzione dei fasci'), n. 163. See also Masino to Min. Int., Dir. Gen. PS, 20 July 1921, ACS, PS (1921), b. 86A, fasc. See Siena, n. 978.
90 Chiurco, *Storia della rivoluzione fascista*, vol. I, p. 357.
91 Telegram of Prefetto Olivieri to Min. Int., Dir. Gen. PS, 31 January 1921, ACS, PS (1925), b. 96B, fasc. Firenze ('costituzione dei fasci'), n. 405. See also Banchelli, *Le memorie di un fascista*, pp. 40–1; and Frullini, *Squadrismo fiorentino*, p. 118.
92 Telegram from Prefetto di Livorno Verdinois, 8 October 1922, ACS, PS (1922), b. 46, fasc. Livorno: disoccupazione.
93 Procacci and Rindi, *Storia di una fabbrica*, pp. 44–6.
94 Letter of Guido Donegani to S. E. Ivanoe Bonomi, Presidente del Consiglio, 20 January 1922, ACS, Min. Int. Gabinetto di S. E. Bonomi. Ordine Pubblico (1921–2), b. 4, fasc. 43 (Massa-Carrara). On this affair, see above, p. 149–50.
95 For two fascist hagiographies of Ciano, see Domenico Cavagnari, 'L'ammira-

glio d'armata Costanzo Ciano: il marinaio e l'eroe della Grande Guerra', *Liburni civitas*, 12 (1939), pp. 97–110; and Roberto Farinacci, 'Costanzo Ciano fascista', *Liburni civitas*, 12 (1939), p. 111–15.

96 See Luigi Einaudi, *Cronache economiche e politiche di un ventennio* (Turin, 1961), vol. VI, pp. 971–2.
97 'Caro viveri', *Riscossa*, 19 February 1921.
98 On the lowering of prices, see Piazzesi, *Diario di uno squadrista toscano*, pp. 169–70.
99 For the public statement issued by the AAT in support of the campaign to lower prices, see 'Un appello dell'Associazione Agraria a tutti gli agricoltori' *Nazione*, 22 June 1921. On the action taken by the AAT, the AIT, the mayor of Florence, and the shopkeepers' organizations on behalf of the campaign, see 'La crisi del commercio e la necessità del ribasso dei prezzi', *Nazione*, 10 June 1921; 'Di fronte all'ineluttabile fenomeno del ribasso', *Nazione*, 12 June 1921; 'Il problema del ribasso dei prezzi', *Nuovo giornale*, 12 June 1921; and 'Il primo successo dell'agitazione contro il caro-vita', *Nuovo giornale*, 18 June 1921.

On this campaign, see also Banchelli, *Le memorie di un fascista*, pp. 44–9.
100 On the control of the *Nazione*, *Telegrafo*, and *Nuovo giornale* by Ilva, see Valerio Castronovo, *La stampa italiana dall'Unità al fascismo*, pp. 243–4.

The *Nuovo giornale* was bought by Max Bondi in February 1919 for 1,400,000 lire: 'Cronaca fiorentina', *Unità cattolica*, 7 February 1919.

In 1921 the *Nuovo giornale* and *Nazione* received 1,875,000 lire directly from Ilva. *Ora nostra*, 13 January 1922.
101 For Scarfoglio's articles to rally the 'working bourgeoisie', see, among others, 'Lo stato morale della borghesia', *Nazione*, 20 November 1919; 'Intesa morale ed unione economica', *Nazione*, 21 November, 1919; 'Pratica del movimento dei lavoratori borghesi', *Nazione*, 22 November 1919; 'Difesa del borghese', *Nazione*, 1 November 1919. See also Carlo Mannucci, 'La rivoluzione della classe media', *Nazione*, 8 January 1920.
102 Aldo Bonelli, 'Il bilancio di un anno', *Nazione*, 1 January 1921.

At the same time the *Telegrafo* attributed all responsibility to the socialists and declared of fascism that,

It is only a matter of defence. It does not matter if this defence is sometimes disproportionate to the gravity of the offence. It is a defence that is becoming holy ... Romolo Caggese, 'Dopo Bologna ...', *Telegrafo*, 29 November 1920. See also *Telegrafo*, 23 November 1920.
103 *Nazione*, 18 June 1921.
104 'La disciplina dei "Fasci" nella lotta', *Nazione*, 17 June 1921.
105 'Il discorso Rosadi', *Nazione*, 12 May 1921.
106 'Giunti all'inevitabile', *Nazione*, 26 July 1921.
107 See 'Carlo Scarfoglio', *Scure*, 29 July 1922.
108 The prefect of Pisa, for instance, reported from Piombino that known political subversives were systematically purged in the dismissals. Prefetto di Pisa to Min. Int., Dir. Gen. PS, 15 June 1922, ACS, PS (1922), b. 49, fasc. Pisa: disoccupazione, n. 736.
109 Tognarini, 'Toscana: crisi siderurgica', p. 1332.

The view of passive submission to the objective economic laws of the crisis was far from being a purely personal view held by Baldesi. At the depth of the crisis in the spring of 1921, the Florence Chamber of Labour offered this advice, which deserves to be quoted at length:

Comrades! Workers! ... A painful, agonizing crisis has burst upon us all, and especially on those whose living depends on their work alone.

The national union organization and the Industrial Central Committee are studying – we do not know with what success – the means to face this repetition of a phenomenon rooted in the bourgeois economy and foreseen, moreover, by all those who have lived ... in the world of reality.

It is in respect of this reality that we address all those, the soldiers of labour, who are part of our organization in order that, in the discipline of a faith based on the highest sense of humanity and justice, they may be able to wait calmly for the present difficulties to be overcome.

Many were and are impatient, and believe that voluntaristic deeds and the daring of a few can shorten the laborious march of the proletariat. In their impatience they are led to ruinous anger and impetuous outbursts from which no one gains.

How shall we deal with the crisis? How shall we overcome this period? ...

It is up to us today to give our view, however modest, which is an encouragement to a more precise understanding of the present situation and an appeal for calm.

May everyone remain quietly at his post ... trusting in the unfailing social process and demonstrating thereby that the work-force is the force of intelligence. (Circular of 16 April 1921 of the Giunta Esecutiva della Camera del Lavoro di Firenze, attached to Telegram of Prefetto Olivieri to Min. Int., Dir. Gen. PS, 29 April 1921, ACS, PS (1921), b. 89B, Cat. 5, Partito Socialista, fasc. 2, sottofasc. Firenze, n. 1645.)

110 The political motivation behind the closures was frequently expressed quite clearly by the government authorities in their reports and even by the industrialists themselves. A case in point is the closing of the Galileo in April 1921. The Florence prefect Carlo Olivieri considered political conflict within the plant a major cause of the shut-down. Indeed, the immediate cause of the disturbances caused by the workers (to which the lock-out was a prompt reply) was the attempt of management to purge the labour force by dismissing political activists. See Telegrams of Olivieri to Min. Int., Dir. Gen. PS, 15 March 1921 and n.d., ACS, PS (1921), b. 59A, fasc. Firenze (1). See also Letter of Olivieri to Min. Int., Dir. Gen. PS, 16 March 1921, ACS, PS (1921), b. 59A, fasc. Firenze (1).

The managers of the Galileo, subsequently seeking in court the authority to denounce the existing labour contract and replace it with another, underlined labour indiscipline as the chief reason for their action. The three 'unfavourable conditions' facing the company were, in the view of management, 'internal disorder', 'the fight of labour against capital', and 'the low productivity of the workers'. See 'Una grave decisione degli Amministratori della "Officine Galileo"', *Nuovo giornale*, 5 April 1921.

A particularly blatant instance of this misrepresentation was uncovered by the *Nuovo giornale* in an investigation of events at the Richard-Ginori plant at Sesto Fiorentino. There the factory was closed with the usual public complaints about declining profits and workers' productivity. In fact, however, official company records revealed that profits and productivity were not only high but rising, and that dividends to shareholders were being increased: 'Una nostra inchiesta', *Nuovo giornale*, 2 February 1922. This example does not, of course, disprove the obvious fact that many industries were in crisis, but it does indicate that the employers' offensive was more concerned with *control* than with simple calculations of profit.

111 'Una nostra inchiesta', *Nuovo giornale*, 2 February 1922.

112 Capo Gabinetto Savini to Prefetto di Arezzo, 14 December 1921, ACS, PS (1921) b. 75A, fasc. Arezzo, sottofasc. S. Giovanni in Valdarno, n. 31151.

113 Prefect Limongelli reported that;
The workers' organization CISE, having examined the situation of the industry and the difficult circumstances of the workers, sought and obtained from the directors of the mines improved wages and conditions of work for all the workers now employed in the pits. (Telegram to Min. Int., Dir. Gen. PS 21 December 1921, ACS, PS (1921), b. 75A. fasc. Arezzo, sottofasc. S. Giovanni in Valdarno.)
This example is not meant to imply that wage increases were the rule. Clearly the reverse was true. The point is merely to indicate that the strictly economic dimension was secondary and could even be sacrificed to expediency in the struggle to achieve political domination.
114 Prefetto Enrico Cavalieri to Min. Int., Gabinetto, 19 August 1922, ACS, PS (1922), b. 42, fasc. Arezzo, sottofasc. disoccupazione, n. 856; and Telegram of Cavalieri to on. Ministero dei Lavori Pubblici, 16 October 1922, ACS, PS (1922), b. 42, fasc. Arezzo, sottofasc. 'disoccupazione', n. 15704.
115 'La Società Mineraria e il Valdarno', *Giovinezza* (Arezzo), 11 December 1921.
116 *Giovinezza* (Arezzo), 30 April 1922.
117 For a brief account of the affair of the Orlando yards, see Angelo Tasca, *Nascita e avvento del fascismo* (Bari, 1971), vol. II, pp. 481–2 n. On fascism at Livorno, see Abse, 'The Political Struggle in Livorno'.
118 See 'La vertenza fra lo Stato e il Cantiere Orlando', *Telegrafo*, 22 September 1922; and 'La vertenza fra il Cantiere Orlando e il Governo', *Telegrafo*, 26 September 1922.
119 Telegram of Verdinois to Min. Int., Dir. Gen. PS, 9 January 1922, ACS, PS (1922), b. 46, fasc. Livorno: disoccupazione, n. 26.
For a partial account of the events at Leghorn, see Einaudi, *Cronache economiche e politiche*, vol. VI, pp. 898–900.
120 For an extended account of the events of the lock-out see Telegram from Verdinois, 8 October 1922, ACS, PS (1922), b. 46, fasc. Livorno: disoccupazione.
121 *Ibid.*
122 For the manifesto of the Federazione dei Sindacati Economici, see *Telegrafo*, 29 September 1922.
123 See above, p. 148–9.
124 For the text of the letter of Perrone Compagni, see *Telegrafo*, 9 October 1922. See also ACS, MRF, parte, 1, b. 103, fasc. Livorno, carte. 5, n. 324.
125 Telegram from Prefetto Verdinois, 8 October 1922, ACS, PS (1922), b. 46, fasc. Livorno: disoccupazione.
126 *Ibid.*
127 For the text of the agreement between the Cantiere Orlando and the PNF, see *Telegrafo*, 14 October 1922.
128 For the letter of Filippi, see *Telegrafo*, 12 October 1922.

4 THE PETTY BOURGEOISIE AND THE SQUADS

1 *Diario di uno squadrista toscano*, pp. 87–91.
2 De Felice, *Mussolini il rivoluzionario*, p. 473.
3 For examples of the attention of the Citizens' Defence Alliance to the returning veterans, see the manifestos of the Alliance on the occasions of the return of the 19th Artillery Regiment and the 84th Infantry Regiment and the 84th Infantry Regiment, *Nazione*, 30 July 1919 and 17 August 1919.

An instance of the demand of the Veterans' Association that women employees be sacked is provided by the section of the Associazione Combattenti at Monsummano (Lucca province), which voted a resolution stating, 'We want the immediate dismissal of women ... minors, and shirkers from government employment.' (Ordine del Giorno of 9 April 1922, ASLU, Filza 204, fasc. 'agitazioni', n. 103). Similar resolutions were voted by the ANC at Borgo a Mozzano, Villa Basilica, Fornaci di Barga, and Viareggio in Lucca province. See ASLU, *ibid.*

The attitude of the *fasci* had already been clearly expressed by the fascist paper of Lucca, which wrote,

We do not want to be called antifeminists, but we absolutely cannot allow that men full of intelligence and vitality should be subjected to unemployment when we see that in many offices, businesses, and so on many girls are taking up posts that should be given to the veterans. Let them be cared for first..., 'La disoccupazione', *Intrepido*, 23 January 1921.

4 Chiurco, *Storia della rivoluzione fascista*, vol. IV, p. 29.
5 Report of Commissione Esecutiva Provvisoria to Segretario Generale dei Fasci, 1 June 1921, ACS, MRF, b. 103, fascio Livorno, cart. 2, n. 106, p. 4.
6 Letter of Goffredo Pieri to Cesare Rossi, 7 November 1920, and Letter of Della Maggiora to U. Pasella, 28 December 1920, ACS, MRF, b. 103, fasc. Lucca, n. 14 and n. 27.
7 Report of Prefetto Frigerio, 21 July 1921, ACS, PS (1925), b. 98, fasc. Pisa ('costituzione de fasci').
8 Chiurco, *Storia della rivoluzione fascista*, vol. III, p. 233.
9 *Ibid.*, vol. IV, p. 452.
10 See below, Chap. 5.
11 Letter of Pietro Carrer to Segretario dei Fasci, 30 June 1919, ACS, MRF, b. 103, fasc. Firenze, cart. 1, n. 2.
12 *Ibid.*
13 On the role of Agnoletti in the *fascio* as an ally of Dumini, see Letter of Luigi Zamboni to Segretario Politico Generale, 3 December 1920, ACS, MRF, b. 102. fasc. Firenze, cart. 2, n. 181.
14 For information on the members of the executive committee of the Florence *fascio* elected at this time, see Telegram of Olivieri to Min. Int., Dir. Gen. PS, 18 June 1921, ACS, PS (1925), b. 96B, fasc. Firenze ('costituzione dei fasci'), n. 2180.
15 For biographical information on N. Mezzetti, see *Fiamma*, 14 May 1921.
16 Letter of *fiduciario* of Siena *fascio*, Angelino Guroli, to CC dei Fasci, 19 January 1921, ACS, MRF, b. 106, fasc. Siena, n. 61.
17 Letter of G. A. Chiurco and D. Bernardinis to CC dei Fasci, 7 April 1921, ACS, MRF, b. 106, fasc. Siena, n. 70.
18 Letter of Umberto Pasella to Adolfo Pieri, 14 September 1919, ACS, MRF, b. 106, fasc. Siena, n. 4.
19 Letter of Luigi Malagoli to Umberto Pasella, 29 April 1920, ACS, MRF, b. 104, fasc. Pisa, n. 7.
20 De Martino to Min. Int., Dir. Gen. PS, 2 May 1921, ACS, PS (1925), b. 98, fasc. Pisa ('costituzione dei fasci'), n. 728.
21 For information on the political secretaries of these *fasci*, see:
    Livorno – Report of the Commissione Esecutiva del Fascio di Livorno to Segretario Politico Generale, 1 June 1921, ACS, MRF, b. 103, fasc. Livorno, cart. 2, n. 106.

For Portoferraio – Chiurco, *Storia della rivoluzione fascista*, vol. III, pp. 258–60.

For Pontedera – Prefetto di Pisa to Min. Int., Dir. Gen. PS, 9 November 1921, ACS, PS (1925), b. 98, fasc. Pisa ('costituzione dei fasci'), n. 1979.

For Lari – Report of Prefetto Frigerio, 21 July 1921, ACS, PS (1925), b. 98, fasc. Pisa ('costituzione dei fasci').

For Massa Marittima – Letter of Direttorio del Fascio di Massa Marittima to CC dei Fasci, 5 December 1921, ACS, MRF, b. 103, fasc. Massa Marittima, n. 4.

For San Sepolcro – Report of G. B. Marziali to Piero Bolzon, n.d., ACS, MRF, b. 196, fasc. San Sepolcro, n. 7.

For Monterotondo – Chiurco, *Storia della rivoluzione fascista*, vol. III, pp. 388–9.

For Piombino – ACS, MRF, b. 104, fasc. Piombino, n. 18.

For Ravi – Chiurco, *Storia della rivoluzione fascista*, vol. III, pp. 389–90.

For Lardarello – Prefect De Martino to Min, Int., Dir. Gen. PS, 2 May 1921, ACS, PS (1925), b. 98, fasc. Pisa ('costituzione dei fasci'), n. 917.

For Capannoli – Report of Prefetto di Pisa, 1 July 1921, ACS, PS (1925), b. 98, fasc. Pisa ('costituzione dei fasci').

22 For information on the military background of Dino Castellani, see Telegram of Ispettore Generale di PS Paolella to Min. Int., Dir. Gen. PS, 4 July 1921, ACS, PS (1921), b. 79A, fasc. Grosseto.

For biographical information on Tullio Tamburini, see Banchelli, *Le memorie di un fascista*, pp. 72–6.

On Chiostri and Capanni, see Cantagalli, *Storia del fascismo fiorentino*; and Savino, *La nazione operante*, pp. 183 and 174.

On Renato Ricci, see Chiurco, *Storia del fascismo fiorentino*, vol. II, pp. 124–5.

For the role of Dario Vitali, see Telegram of Prefetto Berti to Min. Int., Dir. Gen. PS, 20 September 1921, ACS, PS (1922), fasc. 1, sottofasc. Massa e Carrara: Congresso fasci della provincia, n. 1522.

On the importance of F. G. Florio and his squad 'Della Morte', see Florio, *Federico Guglielmo Florio*; and Degl'Innocenti Mazzamuto, *Le lotte sociali*, pp. 153–5. The founding secretary of the Prato *fascio* was captain Falconi, an officer of the Prato Veterans' Association (*ibid.*, p. 120).

23 For biographical information on Perrone Compagni and Dumini, see Cantagalli, *Storia del fascismo fiorentino*, pp. 154 and 16–17 respectively.

On Abbatemaggio's military career, see Letter of Goffredo Pieri to Cesare Rossi, 7 November 1920, ACS, MRF, b. 103, fasc. Lucca, n. 14, p. 1.

24 Letter of Ciliberti to Umberto Pasella, 4 May 1920, ACS, MRF, b. 106, fasc. Siena, n. 19. Ciliberti also mentions workers as a second group of importance in the initial life of the Siena *fascio*. I have no further evidence on this point.

25 Letter of Guroli to CC dei Fasci, 19 January 1921, ACS, MRF, b. 106, fasc. Siena, n. 61.

26 Letter of G. A. Chiurco and D. Bernardini to CC dei Fasci, 7 April 1921, ACS, MRF, b. 106, fasc. Siena, n. 70. See also *Era nuova*, 7 April 1921.

27 'F. G.', 'Il nostro movimento', *Scure*, 11 September 1921.

28 Letter of Luigi Malagoli to Umberto Pasella, 29 April 1920, ACS, MRF, b. 104, fasc. Pisa, n. 7.

29 Letter of Pasella to Malagoli, 17 September 1920, ACS, MRF, b. 104, fasc. Pisa, n. 22.
30 De Martino to Min. Int., Dir. Gen. PS, 8 June 1921, ACS, PS (1925), b. 98, fasc. Pisa ('costituzione dei fasci'), n. 2252.
   Bruno Frullini stresses the role of students throughout the history of the Florence *fascio*, underlining in particular the contribution of the young squadrists Alessandro Pavolini, Carlo Nannetti, Raffaele Manganiello, and Piero Sacchi, (*Squadrismo fiorentino*, p. 273).
31 Lyttelton, *The Seizure of Power*, pp. 56–7.
32 For biographical information on Pasella, see Banchelli, *Le memorie di un fascista*, pp. 69–72; and Tasca, *Nascita e avvento del fascismo*, vol. I, pp. 163–4.
33 On the socialist past of Alfredo Frilli, see ACS, PS (1922), b. 65, fasc. Arezzo, sottofasc. 'agitazione pel trasloco dell'ispettore scolastico Frilli'.
34 See above, p. 64.
35 For information on Castellani's socialist past, see Report of Ispettore Generale di PS Paolella to Min. Int., dir. Gen. PS, 'Conflitti a Grosseto e provincia', ACS, PS (1921), b. 79A, fasc. Grosseto.
36 For Bruno Frullini's former membership of the PSI, see Letter of Luigi Zamboni to Segretario Politico Generale dei Fasci, 30 November 1920, ASC, MRF, b. 102, fasc. Firenze, cart. 2, p. 173.
37 See above, p. 64.
38 For some biographical information on Malaparte, see A. J. De Grand, 'Curzio Malaparte: The Illusion of the Fascist Revolution', *Journal of Contemporary History*, 7 (1972), pp. 73–89.
39 For Giacomelli's outline of his own background and prospects, see his letters to Umberto Pasella, 4 and 7 April 1920, ACS, MRF, b. 104, fasc. Piombino, n. 4 and n. 6.
40 For biographical information on Perrone Compagni, see Cantagalli, *Storia del fascismo fiorentino*, p. 154.
41 For biographical information on Tamburini, see Cantagalli, *Storia del fascismo fiorentino*; and Banchelli, *Le memorie di un fascista*, pp. 72–6.
42 Letter of Commissione Straordinaria Incaricata della Ricostituzione del Fascio to Michele Bianchi, 15 May 1922, ACS, MRF, b. 102, fasc. Firenze, cart. 3, n. 236.
43 Quoted in Letter from Ministero dell' Interno (signature indecipherable) to Prefetto di Siena, 10 June 1922, ASS, AGP, Filza 81, n. 14950.
44 *Ibid.*
45 *Ibid.*
46 Letter of Dumini to Bianchi, 15 July 1922, ACS, MRF, b. 102, fasc. Firenze, cart. 3, n. 288.
47 On the criminal connections of Abbatemaggio, see article 'I fascisti', *Grido della rivolta*, 6 November 1920.
   Abbatemaggio's career in the underworld is revealed in his own testimony at his trial in July 1910 and then at the Cuocolo trial throughout 1911. The best published source is *Mattino* of Naples throughout these months. Important articles for his biography are: 'La giornata in tribunale: processo Abbatemaggio', *Mattino*, 20–21, 21–22, 24–25 July 1910; 'La preparazione allo svolgimento del processo Cuocolo', *Mattino*, 28–29 December 1910; 'La confessione di Gennaro Abbatemaggio', *Mattino*, 29–30 January 1911; 'La

confessione Abbatemaggio', *Mattino*, 30–31 January 1911; and 'Il processo Cuocolo', *Mattino*, 12–13, 21–22, and 25–26 March 1911.
48 Telegram of Olivieri to Min. Int., Dir. Gen. PS, 18 June 1921, ACS, PS (1925), b. 96B, fasc. Firenze ('costituzione dei fasci'), n. 2180.
49 Report of Ispettore Generale di PS Paolella to Min. Int., Dir. Gen. PS, 'Conflitti a Grosseto e provincia', 4 August 1921, ACS, PS (1921), b. 79A, fasc. Grosseto.
50 Prefetto Rocco to Min. Int., Dir. Gen. PS, 6 March 1922, ACS, PS (1922), b. 73B, fasc. Grosseto, sottofasc. Grosseto.
51 Report of G. B. Marziali to Piero Bolzon, n.d., ACS, MRF, b. 106, fasc. San Sepolcro, n. 17, pp. 3–4.
52 Banchelli, *Le memorie di un fascista*, pp. 84–6.
53 'Risultati dell'inchiesta a carico del Rag. Giorgio Cimadori del Fascio di Firenze', 18 July 1922, ACS, MRF, b. 104, fasc. Firenze, cart. 4, n. 301.
54 Cantagalli, *Storia del fascismo fiorentino*, pp. 276–7.
55 Report of Carbonai, Molinari, and Poggi of the Commissione Straordinaria Incaricata della Ricostituzione del Fascio, n.d., ACS, MRF, b. 102, fasc. Firenze, cartella 3, 216. See also 'La ricostituzione', *Riscossa*, 29 April 1922.
56 Circular of Dino Perrone Compagni to the provincial secretaries of the PNF, 15 September 1922, ACS, MRF, b. 103, fasc. Livorno, carte. 5, n. 294.
57 Quoted in Telegram of Prefetto di Massa e Carrara to Signor Commissario di PS di Carrara, 18 August 1921, ASM, Archivio del Commissariato di PS di Carrara, b. 55 (1921), fasc. 'Scioperi', sottofasc. 'Circa viaggi irregolari di comitive di fascisti', n. 1450.
58 Telegram of Questore di Massa to Sig. Comm. di PS di Carrara, 26 June 1921, ASM, Archivio del Commissariato di PS di Carrara, b. 55 (1921), fasc. 'Scioperi', sottofasc. 'Sequestri di autoveicoli ad opera fascisti'.
59 Piazzesi, *Diario di uno squadrista toscana*, pp. 164–5.
60 Carlo Scorza, *Brevi note sul fascismo*, p. 79.
61 Prato, *Il Piemonte*, p. 184; De Felice, *Mussolini il rivoluzionario*, p. 434; Roberto Vivarelli, *Il dopoguerra in Italia e l'avvento del fascismo* (Naples, 1967), vol. I, p. 359n.
62 'Il risveglio degli agricoltori', *Nazione*, 4 December 1920. According to the *Nazione*, 'Large landed property in Tuscany is exceptional'.
63 For the list of postal volunteers drawn up for the prefect of Lucca, see ASLU, AGP, Filza 192 (1920–1), fasc. 'Movimenti rivoluzionari'.
64 See Letter of De Faloppio of the Credito Italiano, Succursale di Lucca, to Segretario Generale del Comune di Lucca, 16 January 1920, ASLU, *ibid.*; and Letter of Direttore de Monte dei Paschi di Siena, Sede di Lucca, n.d., ASLU, *ibid.* See also Letter of Fandini, Presidente del Consiglio dell'Ordine degli Avvocati presso la Corte di Lucca, to Sig. Prefetto della Provincia di Lucca, 18 January 1920, ASLU, *ibid.*
65 Piazzesi, *Diario di uno squadrista toscana*, p. 59.
66 'La cooperazione nel pratese', *Lavoro*, 8 May 1920.
67 *Ibid.*
68 'Fascismo e mortadella', *Ora nostra*, 8 July 1921.
69 *Ibid.*
70 Quoted in Telegram of Prefetto di Massa e Carrara to Signori Sottoprefetti, Signor Commissario di PS Carrara, Comando della Direzione dei RR.CC, Massa, 2 May 1921, ASM, Archivio del Commissariato di PS Carrara, b. 55

(1921), fasc. 'Lotta fra fascisti e communisti', sottofasc. 'Obbligo avviso partenze di fascisti', n. 867.
71 'Norme per comuni socialist', *Bandiera rossa – Martinella*, 17 December 1920.
72 *Ibid.*
73 On the measures adopted by the socialist communes, see 'Il congresso provinciale senese dei comuni socialisti', *Bandiera rossa – Martinella*, 1 January 1921; 'Il convegno nazionale a Milano dei comuni socialisti', and 'Il convegno dei rappresentanti comunali degli interessi proletari', *Avanti*! (Piedmont edition), 2 and 3 December 1920. See also Bachi, *L'Italia economica nel 1920*, p. 365–72.
74 See *Ora nostra*, 7 January 1921.
75 *Ibid.*
76 *Ibid.*
77 'Il congresso provinciale senese dei comuni socialisti', *Bandiera rossa – Martinella*, 1 January 1921.
78 *Vedetta senese*, 23 September 1921.
79 'Il congresso provinciale senese dei comuni socialist', *Bandiera rossa – Martinella*, 1 January 1921.
80 On the tax strike organized at Livorno by the Associazione Proprietari e Amministratori di Fabbricati under Francesco Mugnai, see *Telegrafo*, 9 August 1922. For the report drawn up in protest by the Association, see Associazione Livornese fra Proprietari e Amministratori di Fabbricati contro Comune di Livorno', ACS, PS (1922), b. 74, fasc. Livorno: Inchiesta eseguita dall'Ispettore Generale di PS Lutrario, allegato xx. According to the latter the commune of Livorno had voted for 1921 a surtax on buildings and land of 3,195,108.85 lire.
81 On the organization of a tax strike at Pisa by the Unione fra i Proprietari di Fabbricati di Pisa e Provincia and by the Camera di Commercio di Pisa, see 'I proprietari di fabbricati contro le vessazioni fiscali', and 'Contro le vessazioni fiscali', *Rinnovamento*, 7 January 1922 and 17 June 1922. Significantly, the initiative was supported by the Pisa section of the AAT, whose president, G. R. Cerrai, played an active part.
82 *Patria*, 19 February 1922.
83 *Patria*, 19 February 1922. See also Ordine del giorno dei contribuenti di tutto il territorio pratese, 13 February 1922, ACP, Filza Ministeri 1922, fasc. 1.
84 *Ibid.*
85 Letter of Carlo Olivieri to Ministro dell'Interno, 21 April 1921, ACS, PS (1921), b. 78A, fasc. 1, n. 12211.
86 Telegrams of Prefetto Pericoli to Min. Int., Dir. Gen. PS, 18 February 1922, ACS, PS (1922), b. 71B, fasc. Prato, n. 3798 and n. 3836.
87 See above, p. 114.
88 See below, pp. 257–8. For the social composition of various *fasci* in Pisa province, see ACS, PS (1925), b. 98, fasc. Pisa ('costituzione dei fasci'), *passim*. In June 1921 the *direttorio* of the Florence *fascio* contained the following members:
   Carlo Pirelli   *ex army captain, 'benestante'*
   Marquet Dionigi   *station master, central Florence station (S. Maria Novella)*
   G. B. Marziali   *ex army captain*

Giacomo Lumbroso *ex army lieutenant, student*
Raffaello Faccioli *'benestante'*
Umberto Banchelli *tradesman*
Guido Carbonai *ex army captain, railway employee*
Amerigo Dumini *'benestante'*
Ferdinando Spinelli *'possidente'*
Luigi Sebregondi *'possidente'*
Pietro Rosai *'possidente'*
Pasquale Lazzeri *'possidente'*
Raffaello Manganiello *medical student*
Giorgio Angiolo Cimadori *engineer*

Telegram of Prefetto Olivieri to Min. Int., Dir. Gen. PS, 18 June 1921, ACS, PS (1925), b. 96B, fasc. Firenze ('costituzione dei fasci'), n. 2180.
89 Letter from Lascialfare to CC dei Fasci, 29 June 1920, ACS, MRF, b. 102, fasc. Firenze, cart. 1, n. 98.
90 Cantagalli, *Storia del fascismo fiorentino*, pp. 108ff.
91 Letter of Lascialfare to CC dei Fasci, 29 June 1920, ACS, MRF, b. 102, fasc. Firenze, cart. 1, n. 98.
92 Telegram of Valle to Min. Int., Dir. Gen. PS, 2 September 1921, ACS, PS (1922), fasc. 1, sottofasc. Firenze ('federazione provinciale fascista'), n. 3027.
93 Telegram of Olivieri to Min. Int., Dir. Gen. PS, 18 June 1921, ACS, PS, (1925), b. 96B, fasc. Firenze ('costituzione dei fasci'), n. 2180. See also Savino, *La nazione operante*, pp. 223–4.
94 Telegram of Olivieri to Min. Int., Dir. Gen. PS, 26 May 1921, ACS, PS, (1925), b. 96B ('costituzione dei fasci'), n. 619.
95 *Fiamma*, 11 December 1920.
96 *Scure*, 11 September 1921.
97 Letter of G. A. Chiurco and D. Bernardini to CC dei Fasci, 7 April 1921, ACS, MRF, b. 106, fasc. Siena, n. 70.
98 'Ai ferrovieri fascisti', *Idea fascista*, 13 August 1922.
99 Prefetto De Martino to Min. Int., Dir. Gen. PS, 8 June 1921, ACS, PS (1925), b. 98, fasc. Pisa ('costituzione dei fasci'), n. 2252; and De Martino to Min. Int., Dir. Gen. PS, 31 March 1921, ACS, *ibid*.
100 Prefetto di Pisa to Min. Int., Dir. Gen. PS, 16 September 1921, ACS, PS (1925), b. 98,. fasc. Pisa ('costituzione dei fasci'), n. 3182.
101 Dante Lelli took part in the famous expedition to Foiano della Chiana on 17 April 1921. Cantagalli, *Storia del fascismo fiorentino*, pp. 207–8.
102 *Era nuova*, 20 September 1921.
103 Prefetto di Pisa to Min. Int., Dir. Gen. PS, ACS, PS (1921), b. 69A, fasc. Pisa ('agitazione ferrovieri'), n. 3705. In the railroad hierarchy, *capo gestione* and *sottocapo gestione* were the ranks immediately below station master.
104 On the militancy of the railway workers, see Giuliano Procacci, *La lotta di classe in Italia all'inizio del secolo XX* (Rome 1970), pp. 32–4.
105 Letter of Schiavon to on. Sig. Amministratore Generale, 25 March 1920, ACS, PS (1920), b. 70, fasc. Firenze ('agitazione ferrovieri'), n. 3629.
106 *Ibid*. On the central importance of the first demand, see also Telegram from Schiavon to Amministratore Generale, 27 March 1920, ACS, *ibid*., n. 232.
107 Prefetto di Pisa to Min. Int., Dir. Gen. PS, 15 March 1920, ACS, PS (1921), b. 69A, fasc. Pisa ('agitazione ferrovieri'), n. 555.

108 Telegram of Prefetto Camillo De Fabritiis to Min. Int., Dir. Gen. PS, 19 March 1920, ACS, PS (1920), b. 70, fasc. Firenze ('agitazione ferrovieri'), n. 1256.
109 'Ai signori ferrovieri', *Rinnovamento*, 26 June 1920. For examples of the violent attacks of the Liberal press on strikes in the public services especially, see, among others, the articles 'L'inutile prova', *Nuovo giornale* 9 April 1920; 'Follie', *Nuovo giornale*, 21 December 1920; and 'La questione del caroviveri', *Nazione*, 13 May 1919.
110 'Pro ferrovieri fascisti', *La Scure*, 8 January 1922.
111 I. Bonomi to S. E. l'on. Avvocato Giulio Rodino, Ministro della Giustizia e Affari di Culto, 17 August 1921, ACS, PS (1922), b. 59, fasc. Arditi del Popolo: affari generali.
112 Report of Sig. Palumbo, n.d., ACS, PS (1921), b. 69A, cat. D2, fasc. 1 ('agitazione ferrovieri: affari generali').
113 Letter of Schiavon to on. Sig. Amministratore Generale, 25 March 1920, ACS, PS (1920), b. 70, fasc. Firenze ('agitazione ferrovieri').
114 Telegram of Sottosegretario di Stato (signature indecipherable) to Ministero Trasporti Marittimi e Ferroviari, 26 January 1920, ACS, PS (1921), b. 69A, cat. D2, fasc. 1 ('agitazione ferrovieri: affari generali'). The undersecretary of state wrote: 'I request that you take measures to ensure that the volunteers who replace the striking railwaymen be given permits to go armed ...'.
On the monetary rewards offered, see 'I ferrovieri fedeli saranno premiati', *Unità cattolica*, 23 January 1920. For the plans of the *carabinieri* in Lucca province to break any eventual strike on the railways by providing armed escorts to protect the 'right to work' of volunteers, see Orders of Major Zanardi, il Comandante della Divisione Reali Carabinieri di Lucca to Comando delle Compagnie RR.CC. di Lucca Interne e Esterne, 17 December 1921, ASLU, AGP, Filza 192, fasc. Comandi militari.
115 Telegram of Nitti to Prefetti del Regno, 14 June 1920, ASS, AGP, Filza 171, Cart. di Ins. 51, n. 12699. See also Telegram of Nitti to Prefetto di Siena, n.d., ASS, *ibid.*, n. 10997.
116 'Cronaca fiorentina', *Unità cattolica*, 27 January 1920.
117 *Telegrafo*, 18 and 21 August 1922.
118 ACS, MRF, b. 103, fasc. Livorno, cart. 2, n. 115.
Other *fasci* in other provincial capitals present a similar picture. Thus the *direttorio* of the Pisa *fascio* in September 1921 was composed of the following:
Galliano Baldini   *infantry lieutenant*
Franco Landogno   *ex army officer, professor in the faculty of humanities*
Camillo Betti   *engineering student*
Edmondo Patrizi   *station master, Pisa station*
Agenore Serchiani   *infantry lieutenant*
Armando Nuti   *cattle merchant*
Pietro Bergonzi   *officer in the reserves*
Corrado Perraymod   *ex army captain*
Prefetto di Pisa to Min. Int., Dir. Gen. PS, 16 September 1921, ACS, PS (1925), b. 98, fasc. Pisa ('costituzione de fasci'), n. 3182.
In April 1921 the *direttorio* of the Siena *fascio* was made up of:
Mario Boccini   *lawyer*
Duilio Bernardini   *post-office employee*

L. Giunti   *customs guard*
M. Consorti   *railway employee*
E. Coppini   *railway employee*
Serafino D'Antona   *surgeon*
Alfredo Moggi   *lawyer*
Carlo Pacini   *ex army captain, clerk*
D. Testi   *warehouse agent*
Giovanni Tramontana   *university student*
G. A. Chiurco   *medical student*
Leone Ciullini   *student*
Manlio Ciliberti   *law student*
Nello Bernardini   *clerk*

Letter of G. A. Chiurco and D. Bernardini to CC dei Fasci, 7 April 1921, ACS, MRF, b. 106, fasc. Siena, n. 70. See also *Era nuova*, 7 April 1921.

In October 1921 the *direttorio* of the Grosseto *fascio* was made up of:
Agostino Adami   *engineer*
Dino Andriani   *secretary of the Grosseto branch of the Agrarian Association*
Bruno Saletti   *mechanic*
Gino Berti   *clerk*
Giuseppe Saletti   *brick-layer*
Francesco Stellini   *railway employee*

Prefetto di Grosseto to Min. Int., Dir Gen. PS, 14 October 1921, ACS, PS (1925), b. 97, fasc. Grosseto ('costituzione dei fasci'), n. 932.

119 The fascist paper of Lucca referred to Scorza as 'our Duce'. Cf. *Intrepido* 19 March 1922.
120 Letter of Goffredo Pieri to Segretario Generale dei Fasci, 11 July 1921, ACS, MRF, b. 103, fasc. Lucca, n. 46/1–2.
121 ACS, MRF, b. 106, fasc. Sestino, n. 1.
122 ACS, MRF, b. 104, fasc. Pozzo della Chiana, n. 1.
123 ACS, MRF, b. 103, fasc. Moncioni, n. 1.
124 ACS, MRF, b. 104, fasc. Pontassieve, n. 1.
125 ACS, MRF, b. 105, fasc. Sancasciano Val di Pesa, n. 1.
126 See respectively, for Peccioli, Prefetto di Pisa to Min. Int., Dir. Gen. PS, 1 July 1921, ACS, PS (1925), b. 98, fasc. Pisa ('costituzione dei fasci'); for Laiatico, Prefetto di Pisa to Min. Int., Dir. Gen. PS, 9 July 1921, ACS, *ibid.*; for Pontedera, Prefetto di Pisa to Min. Int., Dir. Gen. PS, 9 November 1921, ACS, *ibid.*, n. 1979; for Castiglioncello di Rosignano Marittimo, Prefetto di Pisa to Min. Int., Dir. Gen. PS, 6 September 1921, ACS, *ibid.*; and for Castellina in Chinati, Prefetto Masino to Min. Int., Dir. Gen. PS, 8 March 1921, ACS, *ibid.*, n. 163.
127 For the list of members of the Grosseto *fascio*, see Corsi, *Le origini del fascismo nel grossetano*, pp. 169–70 n.
128 In November 1920 Manlio Ciliberti reported from Abbadia S. Salvatore the establishment of the 'first nucleus in Italy of fascist miners and metallurgical workers': Letter of Ciliberti to Cesare Rossi, 22 November 1920, ACS, MRF, b. 106, fasc. Siena, n. 40.
129 See Telegram of Prefetto di Grosseto to Min. Int., Dir. Gen. PS, 3 May 1921, ACS, PS (1925), b. 97, fasc. Grosseto ('costituzione dei fasci'), n. 519; and Report of Ispettore Generale di PS (signature indecipherable), 2 May 1922,

ACS, PS (1922), b. 73B, fasc. Grosseto, sottofasc. Grosseto, p. 4.

The socialist deputy Giovanni Merloni testified in 1920 in parliament to the recruitment by Montecatini of Sardinian blacklegs to break the miners' strike at Gavorrano, Boccheggiano, and Ribolla. *Atti del Parlamento Italiano*, Camera dei Deputati, Legislatura XXV, Sessione 1919–20, Discussioni, v, pp. 5082–3.

130 *Scure*, 11 September 1921.
131 Report of Ispettore Generale della PS Di Tarsia, 'Situazione politica nei riguardi dell'ordine pubblico', to Min. Int., Dir. Gen. PS, 7 April 1922, ACS, PS (1922), b. 71B, fasc. Prato, pp. 2–3.
132 Roberto Piccioli, 'Nuovi incidenti a Prato', *Nuovo giornale*, 13 January 1922.
133 Telegram of Olivieri to Min. Int., Dir. Gen. PS, 6 March 1921, ACS, PS (1921), b. 89B, cat. K5 'Partito socialista', fasc. 2, sottofasc. Firenze.

5 COMPROMISE AND COLLUSION

1 Giolitti to Olivieri, 23 April 1921, ACS, PS (1921), b. 78A, fasc. 1, no. 1329.
   On this occasion of the burning down of the premises of the typographers of the socialist paper *Difesa*, Giolitti cabled Olivieri:
   I am amazed that the security forces have not acted rigorously to prevent the devastation of the typographical premises of the paper *Difesa*. The authors of the fire must be arrested and handed over to the proper judicial authority. Proceed immediately to an investigation in order to determine who is responsible for the inaction of the police.
   (Telegram of 27 January 1921, ACS, PS (1921), b. 78A, fasc. 1.)
2 Giolitti to Prefetto di Firenze, 27 April 1921, ACS, PS (1921), b. 78A, fasc. 1, n. 9798.
3 See Telegrams of Corradini to Prefetto di Firenze, 24 and 26 May 1921, ACS, PS, (1921), b. 78A, fasc. 1, n. 12449.
4 Giolitti to Prefetto di Arezzo, 14 June 1921, ACS, PS (1921), b. 75A. fasc. Arezzo, n. 13825.
5 Bonomi to Prefetto di Firenze, 5 August 1921, ACS, PS (1921), b. 78A, fasc. 2.
6 Bonomi to Prefetti di Pisa and Firenze, n.d., ACS, Ministero dell'Interno, Gabinetto di S. E. Bonomi. Ordine Pubblico (1921–2) b. 5, fasc. 56 (Pisa), n. 17202.
7 Ministro dell'Interno to Prefetto di Massa-Carrara, 11 January 1922, ACS, Ministero dell'Interno, Gabinetto di S. E. Bonomi. Ordine Pubblico (1921–2), b. 4. fasc. 43 (Massa-Carrara).
8 Letter of di Frassineto to Min. Int., Dir. Gen. PS, 11 July 1920, ACS, PS (1920), b. 52, fasc. Grosseto, sottofasc. 'agitazione agrari', n. 2138.
9 Telegram of Gutierrez to Min. Int., Dir. Gen. PS, 12 November 1920, ACS, *ibid.*, n. 15611.
10 Letter of Donini to Sig. Comm. Vigliani, 29 October 1920, ACS, PS (1920), b. 52, fasc. Grosseto, sottofasc. 'agitazione agraria', n. 2516. See also Letter of Consigliere Delegato of the AAT to S. E. Il Ministro dell'Interno, 21 October 1920, ACS, *ibid.*, n. 247.
11 'Il retroscena di un provvedimento', *Risveglio*, 14 November 1920.
   For an article denying the interpretation of the events given by the *Risveglio*, but actually making it seem all the more plausible in view of the extreme hostility expressed towards Gutierrez, see 'Ma che retroscena!', *Ombrone*, 20 November 1920.

12 'Il prefetto se ne va', *Ora nostra*, 24 June 1921.
13 Telegram of Bonomi to Frigerio, 9 July 1921, ACS, PS (1921), b. 83B, fasc. Pisa (2), n. 15940.
14 'Il prefetto se ne va', *Ora nostra*, 24 June 1921.
15 Letter of Masino to Savini, 2 August 1921, ACS, Ministero dell'Interno, Gabinetto di S. E. Bonomi. Ordine Pubblico (1921–2), b. 6, fasc. 66 (Siena).
16 On this episode, see Telegrams of Prefetto Pericoli to Min. Int., Dir. Gen. PS, 18 February 1922, ACS, PS (1922), b. 71B, fasc. Prato, n. 3798 and n. 3836. See also Report of Ispettore Generale Di Tarsia to Min. Int., Dir. Gen. PS, 7 April 1922, ACS, *ibid.*, esp. p. 11.
17 *Ibid.*
18 Telegram of De Martino to S. E. Corradini, 26 May 1921, ACS, PS (1921), b. 83B. fasc. Pisa (1), n. 20122.
19 'Ripresa fascista nel senese', *Paese*, 17 September 1921.
20 Letter of Bonomi to Ministro della Giustizia, 15 December 1921, ACS, Ministero dell'Interno, Gabinetto di S. E. Bonomi. Ordine Pubblico (1921–2), b. 6, fasc. 66 (Siena).
21 Report of Ispettore Generale di PS (signature indecipherable) to Direttore Generale della PS, 17 March 1922, ACS, PS (1922), b. 83, fasc. Siena, sottofasc. Chiusi.
22 Prefetto di Siena to Min. Int., Dir. Gen. PS, n.d., ACS, PS (1921), b. 64A, fasc. Siena, sottofasc. 'agitazione agraria'.
23 Letter of Bonomi to Ministro della Giustizia, 15 December 1921, ACS, Ministero dell'Interno, Gabinetto di S. E. Bonomi. Ordine Pubblico (1921–2), b. 6, fasc. 66 (Siena).
24 Letter of Prefetto Di Donato to Min. Int., Dir. Gen. PS, 8 April 1922, ACS, PS (1922), b. 74, fasc. Lucca, sottofasc. Lucca, n. 652.
25 Letter to on. Modigliani, 5 May 1922, ACS, PS (1922), b. 74, fasc. Lucca, sottofasc. Seravezza.
26 Letter of Modigliani, n.d. (but probably 21 December 1921), ACS, Ministero dell'Interno, Gabinetto di S. E. Bonomi. Ordine Pubblico (1921–2), b. 4, fasc. 43 (Massa), p. 5.
27 *Ibid.* On the ties linking the police authorities at Massa to the *fascio* see Report of Ispettore Generale di PS Secchi to Min. Int., Dir. Gen. PS, 9 November 1921, ACS, *ibid.*; and Telegram of Savini, Capo Gabinetto, Ministero dell'Interno, to Prefetto di Massa, 26 November 1921, ACS, *ibid.*
28 Report of Ispettore Generale L. Gaudino to Min. Int., Dir. Gen. PS, 20 November 1921, ACS, PS (1921), b. 86A, fasc. Siena, p. 3. see also 'Ripresa fascista nel senese', *Paese*, 17 September 1921.
29 Report of Prefetto di Siena to Min. Int., Dir. Gen. PS, n.d., ASS, AGP, Filza 171, Cart. di Ins. 51; and Prefetto di Siena to S. E. Alberto La Pegna, 19 April 1920, ASS, *ibid.*
30 D'Eufemia to Min. Int., Dir. Gen. PS, 30 June 1920, ACS, PS (1920), b. 60, fasc. Siena, sottofasc. 'agitazione agraria'.
31 Report to Comm. Gaudino, Ispettore Generale di PS, n.d., ASS, AGP, Filza 174, Cart. di Ins. 31, n. 159.
32 Report of Ispettore Generale L. Gaudino to Direttore Generale della PS, 20 November 1921, ACS, PS (1921), b. 86A, fasc. Siena.

For precisely the same explanation, stressing the humiliation of the police forces during the period of socialist ascendancy and underlining their lack of

men and equipment, cf. Report of Ispettore Generale di PS (signature indecipherable), 15 September 1921, to Direttore Generale della PS, ACS, PS (1921), b. 86A, fasc. Siena.
33 Telegram of Prefetto Di Donato to Min. Int., Dir. Gen. PS, 23 July 1921, ACS, PS (1921), b. 79A, fasc. Lucca, n. 1080
34 Letter of Di Donato to S. E. il Presidente del Consiglio dei Ministri, 23 April 1921, ACS, PS (1921), b. 79B, fasc. Lucca, n. 516.
35 Report of Olivieri to Camillo Corradini, 6 March 1921, ACS, PS (1921), b. 78A, fasc. 1. The Florence prefect wrote,
 I have always insisted on the special, very dangerous, conditions of the Province in order to have reinforcements of *guardie, carabinieri*, and police officers. The Ministry has been unable to grant my requests, but now it is my duty to declare that it would be a dangerous error if with the repression that has taken place we were to be left with the means we had before.
 The only way to maintain law and order, especially at this time, is to preserve among the masses that impression of force that the Authorities have shown very clearly ... But to keep up that impression the means are indispensable – means that I do not have and that the Ministry must, at all costs, provide.
 The *Sottoprefetto* at S. Miniato, Lungarini, expressed a similar exasperation with the Ministry of the Interior and a similar alarm about the dangerous situation he faced. 'The events which have taken place', he wrote in January 1921,
 have confirmed my view ... of the conditions of the area, conditions which recent occurrences have made still more serious. The requests I made before were modest, but ... the Ministry has done nothing to enable me to face the gravity of the situation, which has not been appreciated as it should have been. (Report of Lungarini to Olivieri, 31 January 1921, ACS, PS (1921), b. 78A, fasc. 2.)
36 Report of Olivieri to Camillo Corradini, 6 March 1921, ACS, PS (1921), b. 78A, fasc. 1.
37 'L'ordine pubblico e la polizia', *Nuovo giornale*, 25 October 1921.
38 'L'esempio di Firenze', *Ordine nuovo*, 11 March 1921.
39 'Fascismo e rivoluzione militare', *Ora nostra*, 17 February 1922. Zibordi did not apply this analysis to Tuscany alone, but it is significant that a Tuscan socialist paper should have had this analysis.
40 'La criminale azione dei fasci e delle autorità in Provincia di Siena', *Avanti!* (Rome edition), 29 July 1921.
41 Olivieri was a 'Giolittian' prefect in more than one sense. In his case, it seems that the dilemma of the national government was duplicated on the regional level. Olivieri began his tour of duty at Florence in late 1920 by believing that the fascists were a political force that could be useful in countering the force of socialist subversion. He continued in this belief until the period of the great squadrist offensives in the spring of 1921, when he realized that he had underestimated the danger of the movement. At that time he began to attempt to curb fascist violence and to urge his subordinates to enforce the law with greater impartiality, only to discover, like the prime minister, that by then open sympathy for fascism had become deeply entrenched in the state apparatus and was not easily uprooted by orders and decrees from above.
 For a clear expression of Olivieri's early sympathy towards the fascists and his belief that they were useful in the struggle against socialism, see Olivieri's report to Camillo Corradini, 6 March 1921, ACS, (1921), b. 78A, fasc. 1. For an instance of his initial inclination to shield his pro-fascist subordinates from disciplinary action and investigation, his reaction to the destruction of the

typographical premises of the socialist weekly *Difesa* in January 1921 is instructive. On that occasion Giolitti was distressed to discover that the police had neither intervened to prevent the occurrence nor apprehended the guilty parties afterwards. Olivieri offered the bland and unconvincing explanation that there was no blame to be attributed to the police: the *carabinieri* dispatched to the scene of the offence had simply arrived too late because their truck had broken down. See his telegram in reply to Giolitti's query, 6 February 1921, ACS, PS (1921), b. 78A, fasc. 1. For extensive evidence of Olivieri's attempt from the spring of 1921 to reverse the trend and halt fascist illegality, which had assumed alarming proportions, see ACS, PS (1921), b. 78A, fasc. 1, *passim*.

At Livorno the attitude of the two prefects who directed police activities during the period of fascist expansion, Gasperini and Verdinois, seems to have been one of passive sympathy. They were unwilling to repress the movement and were prepared to turn a blind eye on occasion to its deeds, but they were not prepared to condone massive and subversive violence. For an instance of Gasperini's attempt to defend his subordinates against allegations of pro-fascist collusion, see Letter of Gasperini to Presidente del Consiglio dei Ministri, 20 March 1921, ACS, PS (1921), b. 79B, fasc. Livorno, n. 554. For a more candid expression of the sympathy of Verdinois with the local *fascio*, see Letter of Verdinois to Min. Int., Dir. Gen. PS, 26 May 1922, ACS, PS (1922), b. 74, fasc. Livorno (1), n. 1600. Verdinois referred to Marcello Vaccari as 'a valiant man who took part in our war and who is hated by the communists because he is a fascist'.

The Livorno socialists had reason to complain of the conduct of the authorities. See, for example, Telegram of Modigliani to S. E. Giolitti, 19 March 1921, ACS, PS (1921), b. 79B, fasc. Livorno, n. 9068; and Report of the Sindaco di Livorno Mondolfi to Ispettore Lutrario, 12 May 1922, ACS, PS (1922), b. 74, fasc. Livorno (1). Interestingly, Modigliani and Mondolfi point to the 'scandalous impotence' and 'deferential courtesy' of the authorities towards the fascists, who were certain of legal impunity, but do not regard the Livorno officials as actively taking part in punitive expeditions.

42 Of his post at Siena Masino wrote,
I care strangely little about staying at Siena. On the contrary ... I would be glad to have a post of greater importance as, being used to working a great deal, here I feel that I am rusting away. (Letter to Savini, 2 August 1921, ACS, Ministero dell'Interno, Gabinetto di S. E. Bonomi, Ordine Pubblico (1921–2), b. 6, fasc. 66 (Siena).

43 'Ripresa fascista nel senese', *Paese*, 17 September 1921.

44 'Soprusi e rappresaglie contro i lavoratori di Siena', *Bandiera socialista*, 15 January 1922.

45 Corsi writes that
The State had always been disinterested in the Maremma, and Grosseto was remembered only as a warning to negligent officials who were very often posted there as punishment. *Le origini del fascismo nel grossetano*, pp. 71–2.

46 Telegram of Prefetto di Grosseto to Min. Int., Dir. Gen. PS, 10 August 1922, ACS, PS (1922), b. 46, fasc. Grosseto ('ordine pubblico'), n. 386.

47 As far as possible, I have tried to use, as evidence of the conduct of government officials, official state documents. Naturally, however, there were also contemporary press reports of police partiality too numerous to list here. In addition to those articles cited elsewhere in the notes to this chapter, some of the most representative articles on the complicity of the state with fascism

from the socialist and communist press are: 'Sfratto', *Azione comunista*, 13 August 1921; 'Il fascismo: autorità e istituzioni di Stato', *Difesa*, 9 April 1921; 'la città di Grosseto occupata e terrorizzata', *Ordine nuovo* 11 March 1921; and *Era nuova*, 2 February 1921.

48 Report of Ispettore Generale di PS Paolella to Direttore Generale della PS, 27 April 1921, ACS, PS (1921), b. 75A, fasc. Arezzo.

49 Letter of Carlo Olivieri to Min. Int., Dir. Gen. PS, 21 April 1921, ACS, PS (1921), b. 78A, fasc. 1, n. 12211.

In precisely the same spirit Inspector General Luigi Gaudino wrote from the capital that Florence is 'fascist in its soul' and sympathized with the movement, 'including a large part of the Judges, the Army, the Regie Guardie, and the Carabinieri'. Report 'Incidenti tra popolari e fascisti a Firenze', 14 July 1921, ACS, PS (1921), b. 59A, fasc. 14.

50 Telegram to Sottoprefetto di S. Miniato and to Comandante Divisione Esterna dei RR.CC, 17 June 1921, ACS, PS (1921), b. 59A, fasc. 2.

Similarly, at Livorno the socialist mayor Mondolfi complained that the fascists were assured of the 'deferential courtesy of the authorities and of the certainty of impunity'. Report to Ispettore Generale della Pubblica Sicurezza Lutrario, 12 May 1922, ACS, PS (1922), b. 74, fasc. Livorno (1). The socialist deputy Modigliani also denounced the 'scandalous impotence of the authorities towards fascism'. Telegram to S. E. Giolitti, 19 March 1921, ACS, PS (1921), b. 79B, fasc. Livorno, n. 9068.

51 Report of Ispettore Generale Paolella to Min. Int., Dir. Gen. PS, 'Conflitti a Grosseto e Provincia', 4 August 1921, ACS, PS (1921), b. 79A, fasc. Grosseto.

52 Report by Ispettore di PS (signature indecipherable), 'Provincia di Lucca – condizioni dello spirito pubblico', to S. E. il Ministro dell'Interno, 20 August 1922, ACS, PS (1922), b. 74, fasc. Lucca, sottofasc. Lucca.

As for Siena province, Inspector General Gaudino declined to question directly the objectivity and impartiality of the magistrates. None the less, he did observe a marked tendency to delay the bringing of fascists to trial. 'Judicial proceedings', he wrote,

were slow, long, almost inert in the conducting of trials. And since for long periods there is no outcome with respect to the many indictments that have been made, particularly against the fascists, one has the impression that Justice never succeeds in punishing those who are missing. (Report of Ispettore Generale L. Gaudino to Direttore Generale della PS, 20 November 1921, ACS, PS (1921), b. 86A, fasc. Siena, p. 5.)

Similarly Bonomi himself as prime minister complained of the 'lack of energy' and 'deficient action' of the judiciary in Siena, and made special reference to the public prosecutor. Bonomi to Ministro della Giustizia, 15 December 1921, ACS, Ministero dell'Interno, Gabinetto di S. E. Bonomi, Ordine Pubblico (1921–2), b. 6, fasc. 66 (Siena).

53 Quoted in Report of Ispettore Generale di PS A. Lutrario, 'Le condizioni generali della sicurezza pubblica nel circondario di S. Miniato. Le manifestazioni dello spirito pubblico circa la lotta tra fascisti e sovversivi', 16 July 1921, ACS, PS (1921), b. 78A, fasc. 2.

54 *Ibid.*

55 Letter of Lascialfare to Pasella, 14 December 1920, ACS, MRF, b. 103, fasc. Lucca, n. 16.

56 Letter of Prefetto di Lucca Di Donato to S. E. il Presidente del Consiglio dei Ministri, 23 April 1921, ACS, PS (1920), b. 79B, fasc. Lucca, n. 516.

Colonel Bottini even published a letter to his cadets in the fascist paper of

Lucca. See 'Ai miei allievi', *Intrepido*, 17 April 1921.
57 The fascist nucleus at the Livorno Naval Academy is mentioned in Frullini, *Squadrismo fiorentino*, p. 73.
58 Report of Palizzolo, 18 June 1921, ACS, PS (1921), b. 78A, fasc. 2.
59 Camillo Corradini to Ministro Guerra, 27 May 1921, ACS, PS (1921), b. 75A, fasc. Arezzo.
60 For a press account of the event, see *Nuovo giornale*, 22 February 1921.
61 Telegram to Min. Int., Dir. Gen. PS, 21 February 1921, ACS, PS (1921), b. 78A. fasc. 1, n. 5695. See also report of Olivieri to Min. Int., Dir. Gen. PS, 23 February 1921, ACS, *ibid.*, n. 767.

  The commanding officer of the 69th Infantry Division was Colonel Pizzarelli, who was another possible example for a theory of a fascist-military-industrial complex, as he cultivated close relations not only with fascists in Florence province, but also in Lucca province, as well as with important military suppliers. See Report of Prefetto di Lucca to Min. Int., Dir. Gen. PS, 24 April 1922, ASLU, Filza 202, fasc. Agitazione fascista a Altopascio, n. 783.
62 See Chiurco, *Storia della rivoluzione fascista*, vol. III, pp. 96–8.
63 'Gravissimo conflitto a Siena', *Resto del Carlino*, 5 March 1921. Cf. also Chiurco, *ibid.*, vol. III, pp. 110–13. The troops were commanded by Major Calcaterra. Cf. also *Vedeta senese*, 5 and 9 March 1921.
64 Letter of Olivieri to Sottoprefetto di S. Miniato and to Comandante Divisione Esterna dei RR.CC, 19 May 1921, ACS, PS (1921), b. 78A, fasc. 2.
65 Letter of Olivieri to Questore di Firenze and to Comandante Divisione Interna dei Reali Carabinieri, 20 May 1921, ACS, PS (1921), b. 78A, fasc. 2.
66 Letter of Olivieri to Sottoprefetto di S. Miniato and to Comandante la Divisione Esterna dei RR.CC, 19 May 1921, ACS, PS (1921), b. 78A, fasc. 2.
67 Telegram of Modigliani to Ecc. Corradini, 6 April 1921, ACS, PS (1921), b. 83B, fasc. Pisa (1).
68 'Appunti', 20 November 1921, ACS, Ministero dell'Interno, Gabinetto di S. E. Bonomi. Ordine Pubblico (1921–2), b. 6, fasc. 66 (Siena). See also Letter from Ministry of the Interior (signature indecipherable) to Prefetto di Siena, 10 June 1922, ASS, AGP, Filza 181, Cart. di Ins. 31, n. 14950.
69 Telegram of Capo Gabinetto, Mi. Int., to Prefetto di Grosseto, 21 November 1921, ACS, Min. Int., Gabinetto di S. E. Bonomi. Ordine Pubblico (1921–2), b. 3, fasc. 37 (Grosseto).
70 Telegram to Bonomi, 12 July 1921, ACS, PS (1921), b. 83B, fasc. Pisa (2), n. 1084.
71 Telegram of Prefetto De Martino to S. E. Giolitti, 21 April 1921, ACS, PS (1921), b. 83B, fasc. Pisa (1), n. 14246.
72 Letter of L. Zamboni to Umberto Pasella, 18 November 1920, ACS, MRF, b. 102, fasc. Firenze, cart. 2, n. 176.
73 Report of Ispettore Generale della PS Di Tarsia, 'Situazione politica nei riguardi dell'ordine pubblico', to Min. Int., Dir. Gen. PS, 7 April 1922, ACS, PS (1922), b. 71B, fasc. Prato, esp. pp. 10–14.
74 Telegram to Prefetto di Lucca, 2 September 1921, ACS, PS (1921), b. 79B, fasc. Lucca, n. 21148.
75 Letter of Questore di Lucca Grazioli to Ispettore Generale di PS Luigi Gaudino, 21 December 1920, ACS, PS (1921), b. 79B, fasc. Lucca.
76 Letter to S. E. il Presidente del Consiglio dei Ministri, 23 April 1921, ACS, PS (1921), b. 79B, fasc. Lucca, n. 516.

In Florence province alone in the autumn of 1921, the cabinet of the prime minister listed the following places as among those in which the authorities of the Pubblica Sicurezza or the *commissari prefettizi* and *commissari regi* were 'notoriously in the hands of the fascists or of the *agrari*': Incisa, Rignano, and the Upper Arno Valley 'in general'; Barberino di Mugello, Carmignano, Carcheri, and Ginestra in the commune of Lastra a Signa; Capraia, Montelupo, Agliana; Bottegone in the commune of Pistoia; 'etc.' See 'Pro-memoria' of October 1921, ACS, Min. Int., Gabinetto di S. E. Bonomi. Ordine Pubblico (1921–2), b. 2, fasc. 32 (Firenze).

77 For an account of the occupation of Grosseto by the fascists written by the prefect at the time, see Boragno, 'Relazione sui fatti accaduti in Provincia di Grosseto', 15 August 1921, ACS, PS (1921), b. 79A, fasc. Grosseto.

Far from intervening as the trainloads and trucks of fascists converged on Grosseto, the police and *carabinieri* were reported to have applauded as they went by. See Mario Molan, 'Tregua a Grosseto dopo la furia della guerriglia civile', *Nuovo giornale*, 2 July 1921.

78 Report of Ispettore Generale Paolella to Min. Int., Dir. Gen. PS, 'Conflitti a Grosseto e provincia', ACS, PS (1921), b. 79A, fasc. Grosseto.

79 On the events at Roccastrada, see ACS, PS (1921), b. 79A, fasc. Grosseto, sottofasc. Roccastrada, *passim*.; and unsigned article, 'Dal paese più terrorizzato', n.d., ACS, Min. Int., Gabinetto di S. E. Bonomi. Ordine Pubblico (1921–2), b. 3, fasc. 37. See also Corsi, *Le origini del fascismo*, pp. 149–56.

For a fascist account of events at Roccastrada by the deputy Manfredo Chiostri, see 'L'inchiesta fascista sui fatti di Roccastrada', *Corriere della sera*, 29 July 1921. Chiostri made no attempt to deny the outrages commited, but explained them away as due to the fear of the squadrists of being massacred in a hostile environment.

80 Telegram of Bonomi to S. E. il Ministro Tesoro, 30 July 1921, ACS, PS (1921), b. 79A, fasc. Grosseto, n. 17917.

81 Report of Paolella, 'Conflitti a Grosseto e provincia', ACS, PS (1921), b. 79A, fasc. Grosseto.

82 Ibid.

83 Ibid.

84 'I carabinieri e il fascismo', *Paese*, 10 August 1921.

85 Report of Leopoldo Ferré to Comando Generale dell'Arma dei Carabinieri Reali, 'Inchiesta sull'azione dell'Arma nella provincia di Pisa', 31 July 1921, ACS, Min. Int., Gabinetto di S. E. Bonomi. Ordine Pubblico (1921–2), b. 5, fasc. 56 (Pisa).

Such a report is particularly revealing if we recall that when Dino Perrone Compagni threatened in May 1921 to march on the Pisa Prefecture, the prefect De Martino reported in alarm that he could not rely on the troops at his command to act against the fascists and requested massive reinforcements. See Telegram of De Martino to S. E. Corradini, 26 May 1921, ACS, PS (1921), b. 83B, fasc. Pisa (1), n. 20122.

86 Report of Il Generale di Corpo d'Armata Comandante Generale Giacomo Ponzio, 'Azione dell'Arma nella provincia di Siena', to Min. Int., Dir. Gen. PS, 30 June 1922, ACS, PS (1922), b. 83, fasc. Siena (1), n. 14950.

87 Report of Paolella to Direttore Generale di PS, 27 April 1921, ACS, PS (1921), b. 75, fasc. Arezzo.

88 Letter of Rodino to S. E. il Presidente del Consiglio dei Ministri, 12 May 1922, ACS, PS (1921), b. 75A, fasc. Arezzo, n. 62. See also Cantagalli, *Storia del fascismo fiorentino*, pp. 207–8.
89 *Squadrismo fiorentino*, pp. 261–2.

BIBLIOGRAPHY

ARCHIVAL SOURCES

Archivio Centrale dello Stato, Rome (ACS)
  Series of Documents:
  Ministero dell'Interno: Direzione Generale della Pubblica Sicurezza, Divisione Affari Generali e Riservati (1914–26) (PS)
  Ministero dell'Interno: Direzione Generale della Pubblica Sicurezza, Divisione Affari Generali e Riservati (1903–49) (PS) (1903–49)
  Ministero dell'Interno: Gabinetto di S. E. Bonomi, Ordine Pubblico (1921–1922)
  Mostra della Rivoluzione Fascista (MRF)
Archivio Comunale di Prato, Prato (ACP) Miscellanea
Archivio di Stato di Livorno, Livorno (ASLI)
  Questura: Archivio segreto
Archivio di Stato di Lucca, Lucca (ASLU)
  Archivio di Gabinetto della Prefettura di Lucca (AGP)
Archivio di Stato di Massa, Massa (ASM)
  Archivio di Commissariato di PS di Carrara (ACPS)
Archivio di Stato di Prato, Prato (ASP)
  Archivio Vai Rurale (AVR)
Archivio di Stato di Siena, Siena (ASS)
  Archivio di Gabinetto della Prefettura di Siena: Affari di Gabinetto (AGP)

PRESS SOURCES

Amico del popolo, Prato
Avanti!, Milan and Rome editions
Azione comunista, Florence
Azione democratica, Cortona
Bandiera del popolo, Pistoia
Bandiera rossa – Martinella, Siena
Bandiera socialista, Siena
Battaglie fasciste, Florence
Corriere della sera, Milan
Corriere mugellano, Borgo S. Lorenzo
Difesa, Florence

Difesa agricola, Siena
Dovere, Arezzo
Era nuova, Siena
Falce, Arezzo
Fattore toscano, S. Miniato, then Florence
Fiamma, Siena
Gazzetta di Lucca, Lucca
Giovinezza, Arezzo
Giovinezza, Empoli
Grido della rivolta, Florence
Idea fascista, Pisa
Intrepido, Lucca
Lavoro, Prato
Libertà, Florence
Messaggero del Mugello, Borgo S. Lorenzo
Mattino, Naples
Nazione, Florence
Nuovo giornale, Florence
Ombrone, Grosseto
Ora nostra, Pisa
Ordine nuovo, Turin
Osservatore romano, Rome
Paese, Rome
Patria, Prato
Popolo d'Italia, Milan
Popolo di Siena, Siena
Popolo pistoiese, Pistoia
Resto del Carlino, Bologna
Rinnovamento, Pisa
Riscossa, Florence
Risveglio, Grosseto
Scure, Siena
Serchio, Lucca
Soviet, Naples
Telegrafo, Livorno
Terra, Florence
Unità cattolica, Florence
Vedetta senese, Siena
Vita nuova, Empoli
Vita del popolo, Arezzo

PARLIAMENTARY PAPERS

Atti parlamentari

PERIODICALS OF THE PERIOD

Accademia R. Economico-agraria dei Georgofili, *Atti*
Bollettino dell'Associazione Agraria Toscana
Comunismo

Critica sociale
Gerarchia
Iconoclasta!

ARTICLES AND BOOKS

Abràte, Mario. *La lotta sindacale nella industrializzazione in Italia, 1906–1926* (Turin, 1967)
Abse, Tobias. 'The Political Struggle in Livorno, 1918–1922: The Rise of Fascism in a Socialist Stronghold' (Unpublished Ph.D. thesis, Cambridge University, 1983)
Accati, Luisa. 'Lotta rivoluzionaria dei contadini siciliani e pugliesi nel 1919–1920', *Il Ponte*, 26 (1970), pp. 1263–93
Aguet, James. *La terra ai contadini* (Rome, 1920)
Agulhon, Maurice. *The Republic in the Village* (Cambridge, 1982)
Alatri, Paolo. 'L'Italia dal liberalismo al fascismo', *Studi storici*, 10 (1968), p. 192–210
  Le origini del fascismo (Rome, 1962)
Albertelli, Guido. 'Ancora su le insidie dei siderurgici', *Critica sociale*, 30 (1920), no. 11, pp. 165–71
  'Le insidie dei siderurgici', *Critica sociale*, 30 (1920), no. 5, pp. 71–2
Albertini, Luigi. *Venti anni di vita politica*, 5 vols. (Bologna, 1950–3)
Aquarone, Alberto. 'Aspirazioni tecnocratiche del primo fascismo', *Nord e Sud*, 52 (1964), pp. 109–28
  L'organizzazione dello stato totalitario (Turin, 1965)
Are, Giuseppe. *L'industrializzazione in Italia (1861–1900)* (Bologna, 1977)
Arendt, Hannah. *The Origins of Totalitarianism* (London, 1958)
Arfe, Gaetano. *Storia del socialismo italiano, 1892–1926* (Turin, 1965)
Arlacchi, Pino. *Mafia, Peasants and Great Estates: Society in Traditional Calabria* (Cambridge, 1983)
Arvati, Paolo. 'Giacinto Menotti Serrati fra il biennio rosso e la crisi del massimalismo (1919–1922)', *Movimento operaio e socialista*, 18 (1972), no. 4, pp. 37–100
Attal, Salvatore. 'Il fascismo livornese', *Liburni civitas*, 5 (1932), pp. 291–7
Bachi, Riccardo. *L'Italia economica nel 1918: annuario della vita commerciale, agraria, finanziaria e della politica economica* (Città di Castello, 1919)
  L'Italia economica nel 1919: annuario della vita commerciale, agraria, finanziaria e della politica economica (Città di Castello, 1920)
  L'Italia economica nel 1920: annuario della vita commerciale, industriale, agraria finanziaria e della politica economica (Città di Castello, 1921)
  L'Italia economica nel 1921: annuario della vita commerciale, industriale, agraria, finanziaria e della politica economica (Città di Castello, 1922)
Balbo, Italo. *Diario 1922* (Milan, 1932)
Banchelli, Umberto. *Le memorie di un fascista, 1919–1922* (Florence, 1922)
Bandettini, Pierfrancesco. *La popolazione della Toscana dal 1810 al 1959* (Florence, 1961)
Banfield, Edward C. *The Moral Basis of a Backward Society* (Glencoe, Ill. 1958)
Barbadoro, Idomeneo. 'Problemi e caratteristiche storiche del movimento sindacale italiano', *Rivista storica del socialismo*, 6 (1963), pp. 227–95

Bardellini, Giuseppe. 'Il fascismo nel ferrarese', *Critica sociale*, 53 (1961), pp. 279–81
Barsanti, Danilo. *Castiglione della Pescaia: Storia di una comunità dal XVI al XIX secolo* (Florence, 1984)
Bassi, Enrico. 'I fatti di Palazzo d'Accursio', *Critica sociale*, 53 (1961), pp. 153–5.
 'La lotta agraria nel bolognese nel 1920', *Critica sociale*, 54 (1962), pp. 73–4
Basso, Lelio. *Gaetano Salvemini: socialista e meridionalista* (Manduria, 1959)
Bastogi, G. A. *Una scritta colonica* (Florence, 1903)
Bernieri, Antonio. 'Il fascismo a Carrara tra il 1919 e il 1931', *Movimento operaio e socialista*, 10 (1964), no. 2, pp. 105–19
 'La nascita del fascismo a Carrara', in Unione Regionale delle Province Toscane, *La Toscana nel regime fascista, 1922–1939* (Florence, 1971)
Biblioteca Storica Toscana. *Agricoltura e società nella maremma grossetana dell'800* (Florence, 1980)
Bonomi, Ivanoe. *La politica italiana dopo Vittorio Veneto* (Turin, 1955)
Bosio, Gianni. 'L'occupazione delle fabbriche e i gruppi dirigenti e di pressione del movimento operaio', *Il Ponte*, 26 (1970), pp. 1136–90
Bowring, John. *Report on the Statistics of Tuscany, Lucca, the Pontifical, and the Lombardo-Venetian States, with a Special Reference to their Commercial Relations* (London, 1837), in British Parliamentary Papers, 1839, vol. XVI (165)
Briggs, John W. *An Italian Passage: Immigrants to Three American Cities, 1890–1930* (New Haven, 1978)
Broglio, Francesco Margiotta, ed. *La Chiesa del Concordato* (Bologna, 1977)
Brunori, Ernesto. *Mezzadria in crisi* (Padova, 1961)
Calamai, Corradino. *L'industria laniera nella provincia di Firenze* (Florence, 1927)
Camera di Commercio ed Arti di Livorno. *Elenco delle principali industrie esistenti nella provincia di Livorno* (Leghorn, 1908)
Camera di Commercio ed Arti di Pisa. *Relazione sull'andamento agricolo, commerciale e industriale della provincia di Pisa nell'anno 1906* (Pisa, 1908)
 Relazione sull'andamento agricolo, commerciale e industriale della provincia di Pisa nell'anno 1914 (Pisa, 1915)
Camera di Commercio e Industria di Firenze. *Statistica industriale: Notizie sulle condizioni industriali della Provincia di Firenze, Anno 1911* (Florence, 1911)
Camera di Commercio e Industria di Livorno. *Movimento del commercio e della navigazione del porto di Livorno negli anni 1921, 1922, 1923* (Leghorn, 1925)
 Il porto di Livorno nell'anno 1924 (Leghorn, 1925)
Cammett, John, M. *Antonio Gramsci and the Origins of Italian Communism* (Stanford, 1967)
Camparini, Angelo, and Bandini, Mario. *Rapporti fra proprietà impresa e mano d'opera nell'agricoltura italiana: Toscana* (Rome, 1930)
Cantagalli, Roberto. *Storia del fascismo fiorentino* (Florence, 1973)
Caponi, Claudio. 'I cattolici pratesi e le lotte agrarie, 1920–1922', *Archivio storico pratese*, 45 (1969), pp. 3–99
 Leghe bianche e lotte agrarie nel pratese, 1918–1922 (Prato, 1972)
Caracciolo, Alberto, ed. *La formazione dell'Italia industriale* (Bari, 1969)
 Il movimento contadino nel Lazio, 1870–1922 (Rome, 1952)
 L'occupazione delle terre in Italia (date and place of publication not indicated)

Cardoza, Anthony. *Agrarian Elites and Italian Fascism: The Province of Bologna, 1901–1926* (Princeton, 1983)
Carocci, Giampiero. *Giolitti e l'età giolittiana* (Turin, 1971)
Carrara, Giovanni. *Il contratto di mezzadria* (Urbino, 1936)
Castronovo, Valerio. *Agnelli* (Turin, 1971)
  'La grande industria: giochi interni e linea di fondo', *Il Ponte*, 26 (1970), pp. 1198–221
  La stampa italiana dall'Unità al fascismo (Bari, 1973)
Casucci, Costanzo. *Il fascismo: antologia di scritti critici* (Bologna, 1961)
Catalano, Franco. *Potere economico e fascismo: la crisi del dopoguerra, 1919–1921* (Milan, 1964)
Cavagnari, Domenico. 'L'ammiraglio d'armata Costanzo Ciano: il marinaio e l'eroe della Grande Guerra', *Liburni civitas*, 12 (1939), pp. 97–110
Cervetto, Arrigo. 'Dopoguerra rosso e le orgini del fascismo nel novarese', *Rivista storica del socialismo*, 2 (1959), pp. 604–37
Chabod, Federico. *A History of Italian Fascism* (London, 1963)
Chiurco, G. A. *Fascismo senese* (Siena, 1923)
  Storia della rivoluzione fascista, 5 vols. (Milan, 1972)
Cianferoni, Reginaldo, 'I contadini e l'agricoltura in Toscana sotto il fascismo', in Unione Regionale delle Province Toscane, *La Toscana nell'Italia unita, 1861–1945* (Florence, 1962)
Ciuffoletti, Zeffiro. 'L'introduzione delle macchine nell'agricoltura mezzadrile toscana dall'Unità al fascismo', *Annali dell'Istituto Alcide Cervi*, 2 (1980), pp. 101–20
Clark, Martin. *Antonio Gramsci and the Revolution that Failed* (New Haven, 1977)
  'Italian Squadrism and Contemporary Vigilantism', *European History Quarterly*, 18 (1988), pp. 33–50
Clough, Shepard B., and Livi, Carlo. 'Economic Growth in Italy: An Analysis of the Uneven Development of the North and South', in Barry E. Supple, ed., *The Experience of Economic Growth: Case Studies in Economic History* (New York, 1963)
Clough, Shepard B. *The Economic History of Modern Italy* (New York, 1964)
Cognetti de Martiis. 'La famiglia colonica e la consuetudine', *Rivista di diritto agrario*, 11 (1932), pp. 194–200
Cohen, Jon S. 'The 1927 Revaluation of the Lira: A Study in Political Economy', *The Economic History Review*, 25 (1972), pp. 642–54
Colapietra, Raffaele. *Napoli tra dopoguerra e fascismo* (Milan, 1962)
Colarizi, Simona. *Dopoguerra e fascismo in Puglia, 1919–1926* (Bari, 1971)
Colletti, Lucio. *Ideologia e società* (Bari, 1972)
Colombi, Arturo. 'Squadrismo agrario', *Emilia*, 3 (1951)
Commissariato Generale dell'Emigrazione, *Annuario statistico della emigrazione italiana dal 1876 al 1925* (Rome, 1926)
Comune di Grosseto: Società Storica Maremma. *Campagne maremmane tra '800 e '900* (Grosseto, 1983)
Conti, Ettore. *Dal taccuino di un borghese* (Milan, 1946)
Coppa, Frank J. 'Economic and Ethical Liberalism in Conflict: The Extraordinary Liberalism of Giovanni Giolitti', *The Journal of Modern History*, 42 (1970), pp. 191–216

Coragnari, Domenico. 'L'ammiraglio d'armata Costanzo Ciano', *Liburni civitas*, 12 (1939), pp. 97–110

Corbino, Epicarmo. *Annali dell'economia italiana*, 5 vols. (Città di Castello, 1931–8)

Cordova, Ferdinando. 'Le origini dei sindacati fascisti', *Storia contemporanea*, 1 (1970)

Arditi e legionari dannunziani (Padua, 1969)

Corner, Paul. *Fascism in Ferrara, 1915–1925* (Oxford, 1974)

Corradini, Enrico, *Discorsi nazionali* (Rome, 1916)

La marcia dei produttori (Rome, 1916)

Corsi, Hubert. *Le origini del fascismo nel grossetano, 1919–1922* (Rome, 1973)

Cortesi, Luigi. *Le origini del partito comunista italiano: il PSI dalla guerra di Libia alla scissione di Livorno* (Bari, 1972)

Il socialismo italiano tra riforme e rivoluzione, 1892–1921 (Bari, 1969)

Croce, Benedetto. *A History of Italy, 1871–1915* (Oxford, 1929)

Davis, John, A., ed. *Gramsci and Italy's Passive Revolution* (London, 1979)

Deakin, F. W. *The Brutal Friendship: Mussolini, Hitler and the Fall of Italian Fascism* (London, 1962)

De Felice, Franco. *L'agricoltura in Terra di Bari* (Bari, 1971)

'L'età giolittiana', *Studi storici*, 10 (1969), pp. 114–90

De Felice, Renzo. *Le interpretazioni del fascismo* (Bari, 1969)

Mussolini il fascista, 2 vols. (Turin, 1966–8)

Mussolini il rivoluzionario (Turin, 1965)

'Primi elementi sul finanziamento del fascismo dalle origini al 1924', *Rivista storica del socialismo*, 22 (1964), pp. 223–53

Degl'Innocenti Mazzamuto, Rosangela, *Le lotte sociali e le origini del fascismo a Prato, 1919–1922* (Prato, 1974)

De Grand, Alexander J. 'Curzio Malaparte: The Illusion of the Fascist Revolution', *Journal of Contemporary History*, 7 (1972), pp. 73–89

Italian Fascism: Its Origins and Development (Lincoln, 1982)

The Italian Nationalist Movement and the Rise of Fascism in Italy (Lincoln, 1978)

De Grazia, Victoria. *The Culture of Consent: Mass Organization of Leisure in Fascist Italy* (Cambridge, 1981)

Del Carria, Renzo. *Proletari senza rivoluzione: storia delle classi subalterne italiane dal 1860 al 1950*, 2 vols. (Milan, 1966)

De Rosa, Gabriele. *Il partito popolare italiano* (Bari, 1972)

Storia del movimento cattolico in Italia (Bari, 1966)

De Simone, Ennio 'Cattolici, mezzadri e proprietari in provincia di Firenze nel primo dopoguerra', *Bollettino dell'Archivio per la storia del movimento sociale cattolico in Italia*, 18 (1983), pp. 39–78

Dorso, Guido. *La rivoluzione meridionale* (Rome, 1945)

Dumini, Amerigo. *Diciasette colpi* (Milan, 1967)

Einaudi, Luigi. *La condotta economica e gli effetti sociali della guerra italiana* (Bari, 1933)

Cronache economiche e politiche di un ventennio (Turin, 1961)

Faina, Gianfranco. *Lotte di classe in Liguria dal 1919 al 1922* (Genoa, 1965)

Farinacci, Roberto. 'Costanzo Ciano fascista', *Liburni civitas*, 12 (1939), pp. 111–15

Squadrismo: dal mio diario della vigilia, 1919–1922 (Rome, 1934)

Storia della rivoluzione fascista (Cremona, 1937)
Fermi, Laura. *Mussolini* (Chicago, 1961)
Ferrata, Giansiro, and Galo, Niccolo, eds., *200 pagine di Gramsci* (Milan, 1964)
Ferrigni, Mario C. *Il capoccia nella mezzeria toscana: appunti di diritto civile* (Florence, 1901)
Finer, Herman. *Mussolini's Italy* (New York, 1965)
Florio, Maria Luisa. *Federico Guglielmo Florio nella vita e nell'opera* (Sancasciano Val di Pesa, n.d.)
Foerster, Robert. *The Italian Emigration of our Time* (Cambridge, Mass., 1919)
Forgacs, David, ed. *Rethinking Italian Fascism* (London, 1986)
Francassini, Tomaso. *A Prato dal'19 al'22: Cronistoria di una città toscana* (Prato, 1931)
Francini, Mario. *Primo dopoguerra e origini del fascismo a Pistoia* (Pistoia, 1970)
Fried, R. C. *The Italian Prefects: A Study in Administrative Politics* (New Haven, 1963)
Friedrich, Carl J., and Brzezinsky, Z. *Totalitarian Dictatorship and Autocracy* (Cambridge, Mass., 1965)
Fromm, Erich, *Fear of Freedom* (London, 1960)
Frullini, Bruno. *Squadrismo fiorentino* (Florence, 1933)
Gaeta, Franco. *Nazionalismo italiano* (Naples, 1965)
Germino, Dante Lee. *The Italian Fascist Party in Power: A Study in Totalitarian Rule* (Minneapolis, 1959)
Gerschenkron, Alexander. *Economic Backwardness in Historical Perspective* (Cambridge, Mass., 1966)
Gerth, H. H., and Mills, C. Wright, eds. *From Max Weber: Essays in Sociology* (London, 1948)
Giachetti, Cipriano. *Fascismo liberatore* (Florence, 1922)
Giolitti, Giovanni. *Memoirs of My Life*, trans. Edward Storer (London, 1923)
Giorgetti, Giorgio. 'Agricoltura e sviluppo capitalistico nella Toscana dell '700', *Studi storici*, 9 (1968), pp. 742–84
Giorgi, Enzo. *La meccanizzazione agroicola in Toscana* (Florence, 1955)
Giunta per la Inchiesta Agraria, *Atti*, vol. III, fasc. 1: *La Toscana agricola: Relazione sulle condizioni dell'agricoltura e degli agricoltori nella IX circoscrizione (provincie di Firenze, Arezzo, Siena, Lucca, Pisa e Livorno)* (Rome, 1881)
Giusti, Giuseppe. *Raccolta di proverbi toscani* (Florence, 1913)
Giusti, Ugo. *Le correnti politiche italiane attraverso due riforme elettorali, dal 1909 al 1921* (Florence, 1922)
Gramsci, Antonio. *Quaderni del carcere*, 4 vols. (Turin, 1975)
Grassi, Fabio. *Il tramonto dell'età giolittiana nel Salento* (Bari, 1973)
Grieco, Ruggero, 'La rivisione dei fitti agrari in Italia' *Lo Stato operaio*, 1 (1927), pp. 421–8
Grifone, Pietro. *Il capitale finanziario in Italia* (Turin, 1971)
Grossi, Paolo. *An Alternative to Private Property: Collective Property in the Juridical Consciousness of the Nineteenth Century* (Chicago, 1981)
Gruppo di Studo sulla Resistenza nelle Campagne Toscane. *I contadini toscani nella resistenza* (Florence, 1976)
Guérin, Daniel. *Fascisme et grand capital* (Paris, 1945)
Guerrini, Libertario. *Il movimento operaio empolese dalle origini alla guerra di liberazione* (Florence, 1954)

Gui, Luigi. *Il partito popolare italiano e i patti agrari* (Rome, 1956)
Guicciardini, Francesco. *Le recenti agitazioni agrarie e i doveri della proprietà* (Rome, 1907)
Hancock, W. K. *Ricasoli and the Risorgimento in Tuscany* (London, 1926)
Hobsbawm, E. J. *Primitive Rebels: Studies in Archaic Forms of Social Movement in the Nineteenth and Twentieth Centuries* (Manchester, 1959)
Horowitz, Daniel. *The Italian Labor Movement* (Cambridge, Mass., 1963)
Hughes, H. Stuart. *The United States and Italy* (Cambridge, Mass., 1965)
Imberciadori, Ildebrando. *Per la storia della mezzadria* (Florence, 1941)
Istituto Antonio Gramsci. *Agricoltura e sviluppo del capitalismo* (Rome, 1970)
Istituto Centrale di Statistica. *Sommario di statistiche storiche italiane* (Rome, 1958)
Istituto Centrale di Statistica e Ministero per la Costituente. *Compendio delle statistiche elettorali italiane dal 1848 al 1934*, 2 vols. (Rome, 1946–7)
Istituto Nazionale di Economia Agraria. *La distribuzione della proprietà fondiaria in Italia: Relazione generale*, 2 vols. (Rome, 1926)
  Inchiesta sulla piccola proprietà coltivatrice formatasi nel dopoguerra, 15 vols. (Rome, n.d.)
  Monografie di famiglie agricole: I mezzadri di Val di Pesa e di Chianti (Rome, 1931)
  Rapporti fra proprietà, impresa e mano d'opera nell'agricoltura italiana, 18 vols. (Rome, n.d)
Joll, James. *Intellectuals in Politics* (London, 1960)
Jemolo, Arturo Carlo. *Church and State in Italy, 1850–1950* (Oxford, 1960)
Kautsky, Karl. *La questione agraria* (Milan, 1971)
  La via al potere (Bari, 1969)
Kelikian, Alice A., *Town and Country under Fascism: The Transformation of Brescia, 1915–1926* (Oxford, 1986)
Kertzer, David, I. *Family Life in Central Italy, 1880–1910: Sharecropping, Wage Labor and Coresidence* (New Brunswick, 1984)
Kirkpatrick, Ivone. *Mussolini: A Study in Power* (New York, 1964)
Kornhauser, William. *The Politics of Mass Society* (London, 1960)
Lanzillo, Agostino. *Le rivoluzioni del dopoguerra: critiche e diagnosi* (Città di Castello, 1922)
Lenin, V. I. *Teoria della questione agraria* (Rome, 1972)
Levi, Carlo. *Christ Stopped at Eboli* (New York, 1947)
Lipset, Seymour Martin. *Political Man* (London, 1966)
Lorenzoni, Giovanni, *L'ascesa del contadino italiano nel dopoguerra*, in Istituto Nazionale di Economia Agraria, *Inchiesta sulla piccola proprietà formatasi nel dopoguerra* (Rome, 1938), vol. xv
Luzzatto, Fabio. 'I contratti agrari in Italia al principio del secolo XIX secondo l'inchiesta condotta da Filippo Re', *Rivista di diritto agrario*, 11 (1932), pp. 145–70
Luzzatto, Gino. 'Siderurgia e socialismo', *Critica sociale*, 30 (1920), no. 7, pp. 101–4.
Lyttelton, Adrian. 'Fascism in Italy: The Second Wave', *Journal of Contemporary History*, 1 (1966), pp. 75–100
  The Seizure of Power: Fascism in Italy, 1919–1929 (London, 1973)
McArdle, Frank. *Altopascio: A Study in Tuscan Rural Society, 1587–1784* (Cambridge, 1978)

Maccianti, Guido. *I contadini della Valdelsa* (Castelfiorentino, 1903)
Magini, Lando. *Gli scioperi dei mezzadri nel circondario di Montepulciano* (Siena, 1902)
Maione, Giuseppe. 'Il biennio rosso: lo sciopero delle lancette, marzo–aprile 1920' *Storia contemporanea*, 3 (1972), pp. 239–304
Mannheim, Karl. *Ideology and Utopia* (London, 1966)
Marabini, Andrea. 'La mezzadria in Italia', *Lo Stato operaio*, 10 (1936), pp. 145–54 and 219–28
Martelli, Alessandro. *La questione del bracciantato agricolo nella Toscana* (Florence, 1921)
Martelli, Marcello. 'Origini e sviluppo della mezzadria in provincia di Reggio Emilia' *Rivista di economia agraria*, 12 (1957), pp. 532–44
Martini, Mario Augusto. *Le agitazioni dei mezzadri in provincia di Firenze* (Florence, 1921)
  La mezzadria toscana nel momento presente (Florence, 1910)
Marx, Karl. 'The Eighteenth Brumaire of Louis Bonaparte', in Karl Marx and Frederick Engels, *Selected Works* (Moscow, 1962)
Mazzini, Carlo Massimiliano. *L'assicurazione e la legislazione sociale* (Florence, 1898)
  Assistenza, previdenza ed assicurazioni sociali (Florence, 1912)
Mazzoni, Nino. *Lotte agrarie nella vecchia Italia* (Milan, 1946)
Megaro, Gaudens. *Mussolini in the Making* (Boston, 1938)
Melograni, Piero. 'Confindustria e fascismo tra il 1919 e il 1925', *Il Nuovo osservatore*, 6 (1965), pp. 835–73
  Storia politica della grande guerra (Bari, 1969)
Melograni, Piero, ed. *Corriere della sera, 1919–1943* (Rocca San Casciano, 1965)
Messeri, Andrea. *Socialismo e struttura di classe: L'organizzaione locale del PSI nel biennio rosso* (Bologna, 1978)
  La mezzadria negli scritti dei Georgofili, 1833–1939, 2 vols. (Bologna, 1934–5)
Ministero di Agrocoltura, Industria e Commercio, *Notizie intorno alle condizioni dell'agricoltura negli anni 1878–1879* (Rome, 1881)
Ministero di Agricoltura, Industria e Commercio: Direzione Generale della Statistica e del Lavoro, *Censimento della popolazione del Regno d'Italia al 10 giugno 1911* (Rome, 1915)
Ministero per la Costituente, *Rapporto della commissione economica: agricoltura*, 2 vols. (Rome, 1946–7)
Mirri, Mario. 'Mercato regionale e internazionale e mercato nazionale capitalistico come condizione dell'evoluzione interna della mezzadria in Toscana', in Istituto Antonio Gramsci, *Agricoltura e sviluppo del capitalismo* (Rome, 1970), pp. 393–428
Missori, Mario. *Governi, alte cariche dello stato e prefetti del regno d'Italia* (Rome, 1973)
Modona, Neppi. *Sciopero, potere politico e magistratura, 1870–1920* (Bari, 1969)
Molinelli, Raffaele. *Per una storia del nazionalismo italiano* (Urbino, 1966)
Moore, Barrington, Jr. *Social Origins of Dictatorship and Democracy: Lord and Peasant in the Making of the Modern World* (Boston, 1966)
Norandi, Rodolfo. *Storia della grande industria in Italia* (Turin, 1966)
Morganti, Maria Carla. 'Lotta economica e tensioni sociali nel dopoguerra a Lucca, 1919–1922' (Unpublished B.A. thesis, University of Pisa, Faculty of Political Science, 1974).

Mori, Giogio. *La Valdelsa dal 1848 al 1900: sviluppo economico, movimenti sociali e lotta politica* (Milan, 1957)
   'La mezzadria in Toscana alla fine del XIX secolo', *Movimento operaio*, 7 (1955), pp. 479–510
Muratore, Rosario. 'Il dopoguerra rosso e le origini del fascismo nel novarese'. *Rivista storica del socialismo* 2 (1959), pp. 604–37
Mussolini, Benito. *L'agricoltura e i rurali:discorsi e scritti di Benito Mussolini* (Rome, 1932)
   Opera omnia, 36 vols. (Florence, 1951–63)
Nenni, Pietro. *Storia di quattro anni, 1919–1922* (Rome, 1946)
Neufeld, Maurice F. *Italy: School for Awakening Countries* (Ithaca, NY, 1961)
Neumann, Sigmund. *Permanent Revolution* (London, 1965)
Nolte, Ernst. *Three Faces of Fascism* (London, 1965)
Osservatorio di Economia Agraria per la Toscana, *L'economia agraria della Toscana* (Rome, 1939)
Palla, Marco. *Firenze nel regime fascista, 1929–1934* (Florence, 1978)
Pampaloni, Umberto. 'Variazioni e tendenze del patto fiorentino di mezzadria negli ultimi cento anni', *Rivista di economia agraria*, 12 (1957), pp. 172–96
Papa, Antonio. 'Guerra e terra, 1915–1918', *Studi storici*, 10 (1969), pp. 3–45
Paris, Robert. *Histoire du fascisme en Italie* (Paris, 1963)
Passerini, C. *Redditi di contadini e di operai* (Verona, 1938)
Pazzagli, Carlo. *L'agricoltura toscana nella prima metà dell'800* (Florence, 1973)
Peglion, Vittorio. *Le nostre piante industriali: canapa, lino, bietola da zucchero, tabacco, ecc.* (Bologna, 1919)
Pesce, Giovanni. *La marcia dei rurali* (Rome, 1929)
Petrocchi, Bernardino. *L'agricoltura nella provincia di Firenze* (Florence, 1927)
Piazzesi, Mario. *Diario di uno squadrista toscano, 1919–1922* (Rome, 1980)
Piccioli, Dante. 'L'industria siderurgica italiana veduta da vicino' *Critica sociale*, (1920), no. 18, pp. 281–9
Piore, Michael. *Birds of Passage: Migrant Labour and Industrial Societies* (Cambridge, 1974)
Pittorru, Fabio. 'Origini del fascismo ferrarese', *Emilia*, 3 (1951), pp. 293–8
Poulantzas, Nicos. *Fascisme et dictature* (Paris, 1970)
Prato, Giuseppe. *Il Piemonte e gli effetti della guerra sulla sua vita economica e sociale* (Bari, 1925)
Preti, Luigi. *Le lotte agrarie nella valle padana* (Turin, 1955)
Preziosi, Alfonso, 'L'occupazione degli Alti Forni di Portoferraio', *Movimento operaio e socialista*, 17 (1971), no. 1, pp. 45–56
Procacci, Giovanna. 'Italy: From Interventionism to Fascism, 1917–1919', *Journal of Contemporary History*, 3 (1968), pp. 153–76
Procacci, Giuliano. 'Appunti in tema di crisi dello stato liberale e di origini del fascismo', *Studi storici*, 7 (1965), pp. 221–39
   'Geografia e struttura del movimento contadino della valle padana nel suo periodo formativo, 1901–1906' *Studi storici*, 6 (1964), pp. 41–121
   La lotta di classe in Italia all'inizio del secolo XX (Rome, 1970)
Procacci, Giuliano, and Rini, Giovanni. 'Storia di una fabbrica: Le Officine Galileo di Firenze', *Movimento operaio*, 6 (1954), pp. 5–49
Radi, Luciano. *I mezzadri: le lotte contadine nell'Italia centrale* (Rome, 1962)
   Un comune socialista: Sesto fiorentino (Rome, 1953)

Ragionieri, Ernesto. 'La questione delle leghe e i primi scioperi dei mezzadri in Toscana', *Movimento operaio*, 7 (1955), pp. 454–78

Repaci, A. *La marcia su Roma: mito e realtà* (Rome, 1963)

Rigola, Rinaldo. *Storia del movimento operaio italiano* (Milan, 1946)

Risaliti, Renato. *Il movimento socialista a Pistoia durante la prima guerra mondiale* (Pistoia, 1970)

Rizzo, Franco. 'Appunti per una storia del nazionalismo', *Nord e sud*, 3 (1956), pp. 100–15

Roberts, D. *The Syndicalist Tradition and Italian Fascism* (Chapel Hill, 1979)

Rocca, Massimo. *Come il fascismo divenne una dittatura* (Milan, 1952)

Rochat, Giorgio. *L'esercito italiano da Vittorio Veneto a Mussolini, 1919–1925* (Bari, 1967)

Romagnoli, Luciano. 'Problemi e prospettive dell'alleanza tra braccianti e mezzadri in Romagna', *Emilia*, 3 (1951), pp. 283–7

Romeo, Rosario. *Breve storia della grande industria in Italia* (Rocca Sancasciano, 1972, first edn 1961)
Risorgimento e capitalismo (Bari, 1970)

Rossi, Cesare. *Mussolini com'era* (Rome, 1947)

Rossi, Ernesto. *I padroni del vapore* (Bari, 1955)

Rossi, Francesco C., ed. 'Contadini della Toscana', *Itinerari*, 7 (1960)

Rossi-Doria, Manlio, 'The Land Tenure System and Class in Southern Italy', *American Historical Review*, 64 (1958)

Rotelli, Carlo. 'Lotte contadine nel Mugello, 1919–1922', *Il movimento di liberazione in Italia*, 24 (1972), no. 107, pp. 39–64

Roth, Jack J. 'The Roots of Italian Fascism: Sorel and Sorelismo' *Journal of Modern History*, 39 (1967), p. 30–45

Roveri, Alessandro. *Le origini del fascismo a Ferrara, 1918–1921* (Milan, 1974)

Salomone, A. W. *Italy in the Giolittian Era: Italian Democracy in the Making, 1900–1914* (Philadelphia, 1960)

Salvadori, Rinaldo. 'Il dopoguerra e le origini del fascismo nel mantovano', *Rivista storica del socialismo*, 1 (1958), pp. 285–309

Salvatorelli, Luigi. *Nazionalfascismo* (Turin, 1923)

Salvatorelli, Luigi, and Mira, Giovanni. *La storia d'Italia nel periodo fascista* (Turin, 1964)

Salvemini, Gaetano, *The Fascist Dictatorship in Italy* (New York, 1967)
Opere (Milan, 1961)
Scritti sulla questione meridionale (Turin, 1955)

Santarelli, Enzo. *Aspetti del movimento operaio nelle Marche* (Milan, 1956)
Le origini del fascismo, 1911–1919 (Urbino, 1963)
'Il processo del corporativismo: elementi di transizione storica', *Critica marxista*, 10 (1972), no. 4, pp. 20–39
Storia del movimento e del regime fascista, 2 vols. (Rome, 1967)

Sarti, Roland. *Fascism and the Industrial Leadership in Italy, 1919–1940: A Study in the Expansion of Private Power under Fascism* (Berkeley, 1971)
'Fascist Modernization in Italy: Traditional or Revolutionary?', *American Historical Review*, 74 (1970), pp. 1029–46

Savino, Edoardo. *La nazione operante* (Milan, 1928)

Schmidt, Carl T. *The Plough and the Sword: Labor, Land, and Property in Fascist Italy* (New York, 1938)

Schneider, Herbert, and Clough, Shepard. *Making Fascists* (Chicago, 1929)

Schneider, Jane and Peter. *Culture and Political Economy in Western Sicily* (Chicago, 1979)
Scorza, Carlo. *Brevi note sul fascismo – sui capi, sui gregari* (Florence, 1930)
Sechi, Salvatore. *Dopoguerra e fascismo in Sardegna* (Turin, 1969)
Sereni, Emilio. *Il capitalismo nelle campagne, 1860–1900* (Turin, 1948)
  La questione agraria nella rinascita nazionale italiana (Rome, 1946)
Serpieri, Arrigo. *La guerra e le classi rurali italiane* (Bari, 1930)
  La politica agraria in Italia (Piacenza, 1925)
  Studi sui contratti agrari (Bologna, 1930)
Serragli, Pier Francesco. 'Le agitazioni dei contadini e l'avvenire della mezzeria', reprinted in *La mezzadria negli scritti del Georgofili*, vol. II (Bologna, 1935), pp. 156–8
Seton-Watson, Christopher I. W. *Italy from Liberalism to Fascism* (London, 1967)
Silone, Ignazio. 'La società italiana e il fascismo: una vecchia inchiesta sul PNF', *Tempo presente*, 12 (1969), pp. 857–71
Severini, Carlo. 'Il sindacalismo fascista', *Liburni civitas*, 5 (1932), pp. 357–65
Silverman, Sydel, F. 'An Ethnographic Approach to Social Stratification: Prestige in a Central Italian Community', *American Anthropologist*, 68 (1966), pp. 899–921
  'Patronage and Community-Nation Relationships in Central Italy' *Ethnology*, 4 (1965), pp. 172–90
  Three Bells of Civilization: The Life of an Italian Hill Town (New York and London, 1975)
Silvestri, Claudio. *Dalla redenzione al fascismo: Trieste, 1918–1922* (Udine, 1959)
Silvestri, Mario. *Isonzo 1917* (Turin, 1965)
Smith, Denis Mack. *Italy: A Modern History* (Ann Arbor, 1959)
  Mussolini (London, 1981)
Simonde de Sismondi, J. C. L. 'Della condizione degli agricoltori in Toscana', *Biblioteca dell'economista*, series 2, vol. II (Turin, 1860), pp. 543–66
  Tableau de l'agriculture toscane (Geneva, 1801)
Snowden, Frank M. 'On the Social Origins of Agrarian Fascism in Italy', *European Journal of Sociology*, 13 (1972), pp. 268–95
  Violence and Great Estates in the South of Italy: Apulia, 1900–1922 (Cambridge, 1986)
Società Boracifera di Lardarello, *Bilancio al 31 dicembre 1913* (Florence, 1914)
Società Masina d'Italia, *Bilancio 1934* (Florence, 1935)
Soffici, Ardengo. *Opere*, 7 vols. (Florence, 1959–68)
Sonnino, Sidney. 'La mezzeria in Toscana', in Leopoldo Franchetti, *Condizioni economiche ed amministrative delle province napoletane* (Florence, 1875), pp. 177–223
Sorbi, Ugo. 'Ampiezza poderale e densità colonica dal 1800 al 1947 in alcune aziende agrarie della Toscana', *Rivista di economia agraria*, 5 (1950), pp. 371–424
Spriano, Paolo. *L'occupazione delle fabbriche* (Turin, 1964)
  'I padroni della ferocia squadrista', *Rinascita*, 29 (1972), pp. 20–1
  Storia del partito comunista, 5 vols. (Turin, 1967–75)
Sturzo, Luigi. *Italy and Fascismo* (London, 1926)
  Storia del partito popolare italiano, 3 vols. (Bologna, 1956)

Tannenbaum, Edward R. 'The Goals of Italian Fascism', *American Historical Review*, 74 (1969), pp. 1183–205
Tarrow, Sidney G. *Peasant Communism in Southern Italy* (New Haven, 1967)
Tasca, Angelo. *Nascita e avvento del fascismo* (Bari, 1971); trans. as *The Rise of Italian Fascism* (New York, 1966)
Thayer, John, A. *Italy and the Great War: Politics and Culture, 1870–1915* (Madison and Milwaukee, 1964)
Tofani, Mario. 'I mezzadri nell'Italia centrale', in Ministero per la Costituente, *Rapporto della commissione economica: agricoltura*, 2 vols. (Rome, 1946–7), vol. II
  'La mezzadria dell'Italia centrale nelle sue origini e nella situazione attuale', *Rivista di economia agraria*, 18 (1963), pp. 120–30
  'Piccole imprese di contadini compartecipanti in Toscana', *Rivista di economia agraria*, 6 (1931), pp. 299–341
  'I problemi dell'agricoltura toscana e le sue esigenze di sviluppo', *Rivista di economia agraria*, 16 (1961), pp. 5–43
Togliatti, Palmiro. *Lezioni sul fascismo* (Rome, 1970)
Tognarini, Ivan. 'Toscana: crisi siderurgica e potere in fabbrica', *Il ponte*, 26 (1970), pp. 1325–58
Toscano, Mario. 'L'evoluzione del contratto di mezzadria in Toscana tra dopoguerra e fascismo, 1919–1922', *Annali della Fondazione Luigi Einaudi*, 12 (1978), pp. 439–93
  'Lotte mezzadrili in Toscana nel primo dopoguerra, 1919–1922', *Storia contemporanea*, 9 (1978), pp. 877–950
Tranfaglia, Nicola. 'Dalla neutralità italiana alle origini del fascismo', *Studi storici*, 10 (1969), pp. 335–87
Travaglini, Carlo M. *Il dibattito sull'agricoltura romana nel secolo XIX (1815–1870)* (Rome, 1981)
Ungari, Paolo. *Alfredo Rocco e l'ideologia giuridica del fascismo* (Brescia, 1963)
Unione Regionale delle Provincie Toscane. *La Toscana nell'Italia unita, 1861–1945* (Florence, 1962)
  La Toscana nel regime fascista, 1922–1939 (Florence, 1971)
Vaini, Mario. *Le origini del fascismo a Mantova* (Rome, 1961)
Valeri, Nino. *Da Giolitti a Mussolini* (Milan, 1967)
Vausard, Maurice. *L'Intelligence catholique dans l'Italie du XXe siècle* (Paris, 1921)
Vigezzi, Brunello, ed. *Dopoguerra e fascismo: politica e stampa in Italia, 1919–1925* (Bari, 1965)
Villari, Pasquale. 'Il capitalismo agrario in Italia', *Studi storici*, 8 (1966), pp. 471–513
Vivarelli, Roberto. 'Benito Mussolini dal socialismo al fascismo', *Rivista storica italiana*, 79 (1967), pp. 433–59
  'Bonomi e il fascismo in alcuni documenti inediti', *Rivista storica italiana*, 62 (1960), pp. 147–57
  Il dopoguerra in Italia e l'avvento del fascismo (Naples, 1967)
  Il fallimento del liberalismo: studi sulle origini del fascismo (Bologna, 1981)
Weber, Eugene. *Peasants into Frenchmen: The Modernization of Rural France, 1870–1914* (London, 1979)
Weber, Max. *Economy and Society*, 3 vols. (New York, 1968)
Webster, Richard. *Christian Democracy in Italy, 1860–1960* (London, 1961)

Industrial Imperialism in Italy, 1908–1915 (Berkeley, 1975)
Woolf, S. J. *European Fascism* (London, 1968)
Young, Arthur. *Voyage en Italie*, trans. Francois Soulés (Paris, 1796)
Young, W. Hilton. *The Italian Left: A Short History of Political Socialism in Italy* (London, 1949)
Zangheri, Renato, ed. *Le campagne emiliane nell'epoca moderna* (Milan, 1957)
  Lotte agrarie in Italia. La Federazione nazionale dei lavoratori della terra, 1901–1926 (Milan, 1960)

INDEX

Abbadia San Salvatore 147, 178
Abbatemaggio, Gennaro: demobilized sergeant 160; former boss in the camorra 163–4; member of the executive of the Florence *fascio* 164
absenteeism: of industrial workers 109; of landlords 23, 82, 85
Accademia dei Georgofili; and ideology of *mezzadria* 8–9, 14, 16, 26, 43; as base for organization of landlords 59; opposes employment of *braccianti* 49–50; opposes welfare payments 12
Adami, Valentino 202
affittuari: support fascism 78–9, 94
Agnelli, Giovanni 122, 132
Agnoletti, Ferdinando 159
agrari, see landlords
Agrarian Association, *see* Tuscan Agerarian Association
Agrarian Federation of Ferrara 82
agricultural population: census figures (1921) 232 n 19; census figures for Emilia (1921) 232 n 19
alcoholism, and industrial workers 108–9
Aldi Mai, Gino: landlord 13; Liberal deputy 56; supports fascism 56, 58, 133
Alfa Romeo company 143
Altobelli, Argentina 74
America; grain from 21
anarchists 115, 138
Ancona, mutiny at 139
Andriani, Dino: secretary of Grosseto Agrarian Association 57; secretary of Grosseto *fascio* 57; squadrist 64
animal husbandry 17, 22, 45, 59, 73
A Noi, fascist newspaper 133
Ansaldo company 130–2
Aosta, Emanuele Filiberto, Duke of 57
Apulia 1, 3, 21, 36

arbitration boards, demanded by trade unions 44–5
arditi 160, 164
arditi del popolo 104, 231–2 n 18
Arezzo (city): and congress of AAT 50; fascism 247 n 80
Arezzo (province): agitation of day labourers 44; Chamber of Commerce 113; elections of 1920 54–5; fascism 8, 57, 113, 141, 148, 184, 197, 247 n 80; fascist agrarian program in 71, 74, 95–104; mining industry 140–2; modernization of agriculture 22–3, 26, 28, 30, 59–60; strikes of 1919 44
Armani, Evaristo 57
army: conditions of soldiers in the First World War 37; crisis of discipline in 1917 40; defeat at Caporetto 40; demobilization 157–8, 161–2; fails to repress squadrism 199–200; helps to found Lucca *fascio* 200; mutiny at Ancona 190; opposition to socialism 190–2; and peasants in the First World War 37; pro-fascism of commanding officers 202–3; provides squads with arms and transport 198, 203–4; size of 37; tolerates illegal *fasci* at military academies 198–9; troops join fascism 198–201; veterans support fascism 158–60, 165–6; for *carabinieri* see also police and *carabinieri*
Arno Valley: employment of *braccianti* 31–2, 73; fascist agrarian program 71, 95–6; mining industry 141, 152; modernization of agriculture 22–3, 31–2; peasant proprietors 92; squadrism 57; strikes by *braccianti* 51, 73; stronghold of fascism 95–6, 152
Asciano 172
Avanti!, socialist newspaper 195

Azione comunista, communist newspaper 146

Bachi, Riccardo 130–1
bailiffs, see *fattori*
Baiocchi, Adolfo 149
Balbo, Italo 206
Baldesi, Gino: opposes revolution 145; rejects resistance to fascism 103; secretary of CGL 103
Ballila, fascist newspaper 97
Banca Commerciale 128, 132
Banchelli, Umberto: and Citizens' Defence Alliance 61, 133–4, 147; as fascist 148
Bandi, Gino 192
Bandiera socialista, socialist newspaper 196
Bandini, Mario 28
Banti, Athos Gastone 151
Bargagli, Marquis Alfredo 58
Bastianini, Giuseppe 155
Bastogi contract 29
Bastogi, Count Giovanni Angelo 29–30
Berti, Roberto, prefect of Massa Carrara 117
Bertone, Mauro Michele: defies the government 196; openly pro-fascist 189, 196; prefect of Siena 189
Biella 108, 128
Bisenzio Valley 108
black market 35
Bocchi Bianchi, Rolando 57
Bocciardo, Arturo 128
Boccini, Mario 160
Bolla, G. Gastone 23
Bologna 199, 205–6
Bondi, Max: director of Ilva 129–30; director of Max Bondi Bank 130; expelled from parliament 130; and financial speculation 130–1; and maladministration 130: owner of *Nazione* 134, 150–1; supports the Citizens' Defence Alliance, 133–4; supports fascism 133, 151
Bonomi, Ivanoe: attempts to repress fascism 151, 184–5, 192; opposes railwaymen's union 174–5; prime minister 117; target of police resentment 194; yields to fascist pressure 117
Boragno, Antonio: prefect of Grosseto 188, 201; sympathetic to landlords 188
Borgo San Lorenzo 60
Borrelli, Alfonso 197–8
Borro estate 57
Bosi, Luigi 113
Bottini, Colonel 198

Bowring, John 19
braccianti: effects of war on 34–41; numbers of 232 n 19; relations with fascism 88—9, 101–3; relations with *mezzadri* 71–4; role in Tuscan agriculture 31–2; and union movement 49–51
bread riots (1919): mass participation in 146; persuade state to use price controls 46–7; soviets control trade 138
brigandage 145
broad beans 22
Broglia, Giuseppe 122
Bruni, Enrico 159
Buitoni company: manufactures pasta 113; organizes fascism at San Sepolcro 113; uses squads for labour discipline 113
Buitoni, Fosco: attempts to murder socialist deputy 113; finances San Sepolcro *fascio* 113; manager of Buitoni company 113; member of executive of San Sepolcro *fascio* 113
Buitoni, Silvio: director of Arezzo Chamber of Commerce 113; member of executive of San Sepolcro *fascio* 113; owner of Buitoni company 113
Bulgarini, Colonel 158

Cadorna, General Luigi 38
Calamai, Bruno 111
Calcaterra, Major 200
Cambrai Digny, Countess 57
camorra 163–4
Camparini, Angelo 28
camporaioli 31–2, 73
Capanni, Italo 159–60
capoccia: fascism 99–199; as force of conservatism 18; head of *mezzadro* family 17–18; opposed by younger peasants 37, 99 , 217 n 74; powers of 18
Capoquadri, Tito 57
Caporetto 40, 157, 191
Cappelletti, Cesare 113
Capponi, Countess Luisa 58
Capponi, Marquis 12
carabinieri, see police and *carabinieri*
Carbonai, Guido: director of *Riscossa* 172; fascist deputy 172; former army officer 159; investigates corruption in Florence *fascio* 165; railroad employee 172; secretary of Florence *fascio* 159
Carrara, Lieutanant Orazio, and illegal *fascio* at Lucca military academy 198
Castellani, Dino: criminal 164; ex-socialist 161–2; former army officer 159; leader of squadrism in Grosseto province 159,

202; provincial secretary of Grosseto fascism 164
Cavina, Giulio 171
ceramics industry: active role in fascism 105; Richard-Ginori company and fascism at Sesto Fiorentino 113–14
Chayes, Vittorio 149
chemical industry: links with landlords 125–6; political orientation of 106; *see also* Donegani, Guido; Montecatini company
Chernov, Victor 39
Chiana Valley: fascist agrarian program 71; fascist union movement 63, 68; first peasant strikes in Tuscany 41–2; modernization of agriculture 22, 26, 30–1, 41, 59; peasant proprietorship 92; size of *poderi* 28; strikes by *braccianti* 512, 73; stronghold of fascism 92–8; *see also* Chianciano, Chiusi, Foiano della Chiana, Montepulciano, Pozzo
Chianciano 41
Chiesa, Eugenio 115
child labour: in agriculture 11, 212 n11; in industry 140
Chiostri, A. G. 53
Chiostri, Manfredo: fascist deputy 160; former army officer 159–60; leader of Florence fascism 247
Chiurco, Giorgio Alberto: advocate of land to the peasants 97; leader of squadrism in Grosseto providence 228 n 208; medical student 160, 258 n 118; organizer of fascist union movement 67–8; organizer of Sienese squadrism 57, 64; secretary of Siena *fascio* 64, 160
Chiusi 41
Chiusure 57
cholera 26
Church: and ideology of *mezzadria* 43; as an institution of conservatism 20; religiosity of peasants undermined by modernization 33; reports declining living standards of *mezzadri* 27
Ciano, Count Costanzo: admiral 150, 158, 191; fascist deputy 150, 158; industrial lobbyist 133, 150; leader of Livorno *fascio* 155; and Orlando shipyards 155, 191
Ciliberti, Manlio: former army officer 159, 161; founder of Siena *fascio* 159; law student 160; secretary of Siena *fascio* 160
Cimadori, Giorgio 165
Citizens' Defence Alliance: anti-socialist militia 60–1, 147; appeals to war veterans 158; financed by big business 133–4; organizes strike-breaking 168; precursor of fascism, 60, 80; supported by landlords 60–1
Ciullini, Leone 160
Civil Code 18, 44, 48
Civitella Marittima 57
clover 22
Colla e Concimi company 125
collocamento di classe: cause of conflict between *braccianti* and *mezzadri* 98, 100; central issue in class struggle in the Po Valley 49–50; instrument of Tuscan *braccianti* 85, 98, 101; means of workers' control in agriculture 49
Communist Party (PCI) 104, 146
conscription 20, 35–6, 38–9
Confagricoltura, *see* General Confederation of Agriculture
Confindustria, *see* General Confederation of Industry
Conti, Ettore 132
cooperative movement: destroyed by squadrism 169; undermines retail trade 169
Coppini, Eufrasio 159, 172
Corradini, Camillo 184–5, 189, 199
Corrado, General Giulio 158
Corsini, Prince Andrea 58
Corsini, Chiara 58
corvée labour 9
Cremona 206
criminals, and fascism 160–5
crop systems, under *mezzadria* 9, 13, 16–17, 21–3, 29–30, 34, 92–3, 206
Cuocolo trial 164
Credito Italiano, bank 128
Cucirini Cantoni Coates company 112–13
Cusona estate 24

Danesi, Gaetano 102
D'Antona, Serafino 160
day labourers, *see braccianti, terrazzieri*
De Ambris, Alceste 81
De Bernardinis, police commissioner 111, 171
debt (of *mezzadri*): increasing burden with modernization 24–5, 29; means of obtaining unpaid labour 11; temporary decrease during war 36, 93; weakens bond of peasants to social order 32
decimazione 38
De Larderel, Count Francesco 127
Dell'Amico, Francesco: and family as squadrists 116–17; hires only fascist

union members 115; marble quarry owner 115
Del Vivo, Luigi: Empoli glass manufacturer 114; gives public speech on behalf of fascism 57; landlord 114
De Martino, Achille: prefect of Pisa 146; removed because of his anti-fascism 189; threatened by fascist march on Pisa 189
demobilization 157–8, 161–2
D'Eufemia, Emilio: fears socialist power 193; opposes strikes 55–6; prefect of Siena 55, 193; views fascism as an ally 193
Di Donato, Gennaro: prefect of Lucca 112, 200–1; views fascism as an ally 194
diet (of *mezzadri*) 9, 21, 27, 216 n 60
Difesa, socialist newspaper: advocates revolution 42; editors resign to found *Azione comunista* 146; supports factory council movement 139; surprised by militancy of *mezzadri* 42, 74
Difesa agricola, landlords' newspaper: advocates long-term repression 62; reports secession of *fattori* from AAT 88
Di Frassineto, Count Alfredo: demands removal of prefect of Grosseto 188; president of the AAT 188
Di Gennaro, Filippo 202
Dindelli, Valentino: commander of squads at San Sepolcro 164; employee of Buitoni company 113; misappropriates funds of fascist branch 164
Dionigi, Marquet 255 n 88
Di Tarsia, Inspector General: describes alienation of workers from PSI at Prato 178–9; reports role of criminals in fascism 163; reports social bases of fascism at Prato 95, 110–11
division of labour: on estates under *mezzadria* 12; within *mezzadro* families 17, 29
domestic industry: decline of 106; as resource of *mezzadri* 17
Donegani, Guido: chairman of the board of Montecatini 125; closely linked with agriculture 125–8; defends fascism at Carrara 149–50; owner of marble quarries 116; personal envoy of Mussolini 126; speculative entrepreneur 131–2; supports fascist strike-breaking 148–9; supports intransigent fascism 125–6; uses fascists to restore labour discipline 115–16; welcomes March on Rome 126
Donini, Alberto 63
Duboin, Major Mario 201

Dumini, Amerigo: demobilized sergeant 160; leader of the Citizens' Defence Alliance 147; organizer of squadrism 162–3, 256 n 88

Economic Unions, *see* fascist unions
economy: crisis of *mezzadria* 14, 20–1, 28–9, 31–3, 41–2, 53–5, 92–3, 99–100, 206; crisis of 1921 97, 101–3, 109, 151–2, 157; inflation 34–6, 46–7, 89, 92, 136–7, 141, 166–8, 177, 221 n 119, 244 n 48; markets 11, 20–3, 29–33, 124; reconversion crisis 107–9, 128–32; standard of living 8–13, 20–1, 24–33, 34–7, 124–5; stunted home market for industry 124–5, 127–8, 131; tariffs 21, 131–2; taxation 20–1, 24, 32, 47, 53–5, 106, 108, 143, 170–1; unemployment 41, 71, 78, 91, 102, 157–8, 162, 166, 177; *see also* inflation, markets, taxes, unemployment
education, and effects on *mezzadria* 20, 35
Einaudi, Luigi 129
Elba island 141–2, 147
elections: of 1919 54, 108, 134, 139, 158; of 1920 54–5, 137–8, 146, 193; of 1921 188
electrical industry: links with landlords 128; Mineraria finances Florence *fascio* 133; Mineraria supports Citizens' Defence Alliance 133–4, 136; monopoly of Mineraria and Società Ligure-Toscana 127–8; *see also* Società Elettrica e Mineraria del Valdarno
emigration: beginning of mass peasant emigration 27; causes of 217 n 68; closing of emigration routes after the war 101; fascists advise peasants to emigrate 84; as source of peasant savings 93; traditionally lacking in Tuscany 20
Emilia: fascism in 56, 71–81, 105, 195, 205; *mezzadria* in 47; and peasant proprietorship 92; rural union movement in 49–50, 72–4, 98; statistics of agricultural population 232 n 19
employment offices (*uffici del lavoro*): as instruments of fascist unions 101–2
Empoli: fascist agrarian program 83; glass industry 114; notables support fascism 57, 114; peasant movement 48; uprising of 1921 78
estimates (*stime*), and *mezzadria* 10, 36, 44
eviction: as central issue in rural class conflict 85, 90; as an instrument of power for landlords 10, 16, 19–20, 37,

39, 43–4, 48–9, 66, 68, 90–1, 151–2, 234–5 n 56; suspended during the First World War 37, 90; of urban tenants 170–1
exchange of labour, among *mezzadri* 19, 32–3, 73
extortion, practised by squads 113, 165

Fabbricotti, Guido: commands mounted squadrists 116, 189; marble quarry owner 116; victimizes union activists 116
Facta, Luigi 185–6
factory councils and internal committees: abolished in employers' counter-offensive 152; absent in small factories 177; and conflict in the mining industry 140–2; considered unacceptable by industrialists 139; continue production during factory occupations 144; depot councils and soviets of railwaymen 173; in the metal industry 142; in Prato textile factories 108–9; spread in industry during the war 137; Turin as leading centre 139
factory occupations: AIT condemns Giolitti 145; begin with employers' offensive 142–3; extent of the movement in Tuscany 144; and formation of communist faction at Florence 146; industry rallies to fascism 146–7; in metal industry 142; Orlando brothers demand use of the army 144; 'Red Guards' try to extend movement to the peasants 146; strategy of Giolitti 246 n 76; supported by railway workers 173; union leaders and PSI contain movement 145–7; viewed with alarm by prefects and police 193
Falce, socialist newspaper: dilutes program of socialization 74; reports alienation of *mezzadri* from the PSI 100
family: effect of war on 37; decline of *mezzadro* family 28–9, 37, 124, 217–18 n 74; facilitates estate management 17–18; fascists pledge to restore 99–100; internal organization of *mezzadro* family 16–18; as legal fiction 17–18
farm councils (*consigli di fattoria*): established by *mezzadri* in Siena 49, 77, 222 n 125; as instruments of peasant self-management 77, 98; as threat to bailiffs 85
fascist movement: agrarian program of 81–5, 95–6, 98, 99–100, 167; appeals to farm workers 88–91, 96, 101–3; appeals to industrial workers 175–9; appeals to peasants 92–101; appeals to petty bourgeoisie 165–71; develops from Citizens' Defence Alliance 60–2; distinguishing features in Tuscany 72–81; establishes union movement 62–9; leading role of Florence *fascio* 147–8, 2456–7 n 80; organizes tax resistance 171; and railwaymen 171–5; recruits *fattori* 85–8, 96, 101; recruits landlords 56–69, 83–4; regional congress at Livorno 83, 135–6; as response to socialist violence 55–6, 103–4; and students 160–1, 165; supported by big business 121–56; supported by provincial industry 104–17; and use of violence 70–1, 77–8, 80, 88, 103, 109–13, 117, 151–3, 163, 165, 184–5, 196–7, 199–204, 207–8; and war veterans 157–60, 165
fascist unions: and landlords 62–4, 67–8; as means of labour discipline 65–9; and squadrism 64
Fattore toscano, bailiffs' newspaper 29
fattori: and AAT 59, 86–8, 228 n 199, 234 n 46; association of 29, 86, 234 n 46; and fascism 57, 85–8, 94, 96, 101; functions of 13–14, 16, 29–30, 216; as heroes of fascist propaganda 87; numbers of 86, 234 n 47; as purchasers of land 79, 86; secede en masse from the AAT to join fascism 87–8; social origins of 13, 19–20, 234 n 42; as targets of union anger 75, 225 n 154
fattorie: numbers of 210 n 10; organization of 8, 16–17, 99
Federation of Marble Industrialists 116
Federazione Italiana Operai Metalllurgici (FIOM) 143, 145–6, 156
Fera, Cesare 129–30
Ferrara: develops national fascist agrarian program 71; and labour militancy of Umberto Pasella 161; landlords provide land for fascist peasants 82, 96–7; pioneer of squadrism 199, 205; *see also* Emilia
Ferré, General Leopoldo 202–3
fertilizers 12, 17, 22–3, 26, 29–30, 34, 45–6
Fiamma, Liberal newspaper: adopts fascist cause as its own 58–9
FIAT company 129, 132
Figino, Captain Giuseppe 203
Filippi, Eugenio 156
Fiume 139

Florence (city): as centre of landlords' interests 4, 52, 59–60; as directing centre for Tuscan fascism 7, 80, 136, 147–8, 203–6, 208, 246 n 80; and election of 1920 137; labour movement in 139–40, 144; uprising of 1921 77–8

Florence (province): and agitation of *braccianti* 50–1; and Citizens' Defence Alliance 60–1, fascism 8, 57, 60–1, 70, 114, 159, 164–5, 171–2, 255 n 88; fascist agrarian program in 71; and local elections of 1920 54–5; and strikes of 1919 44

Florio, Federico: demobilized officer 159–60; dies on punitive expedition 160; leader of squadrism at Prato 110

fodder crops 9, 22, 24

Foiano della Chiana, fascist military occupation of 201, 203–4, 208

food industry: Buitoni company 113; and fascism 105–7, 121–2; links with the countryside 105–7

Foraboschi, Ezio 148–9

France 18–19, 21

Frigerio, Pietro: former prefect of Rovigo 189; prefect of Pisa 189; supports fascism 189, 194

Frilli, Alfredo 161

Frullini, Bruno: Florence squadrist leader 80; former army officer 161–2; reports industrial financing of fascism 80; reports supply of army weapons to fascism 204

Gallori, Guido 159

Gasperini, Giovanni: and fascism 262 n 41; prefect of Livorno 262 n 41

Gaudino, Inspector General L. 98, 193–4

Gavorrano 178

General Confederation of Agriculture 63, 188

General Confederation of Industry (Confindustria): limits its reliance on fascism 121–3, 126; re-imposes factory discipline 143; rejects factory councils 139; Tuscan industry as intransigent faction of 132

General Confederation of Labour (CGL): adopts positivist view of economic crisis; becomes bureaucratized 75; conveys pledges of land to the peasants 40; direct labour militancy in Tuscany 51; opposes revolution 142–3, 145–7; rejects violence as a weapon against fascism 103–4

generations, conflict of under *mezzadria* 17, 28–9, 37, 99–100, 217–18 n 74

Georgofili, *see* Accademia dei Georgofili

Germany 123

Giacomelli, Persindo: organizes *fascio* at Piombino 135; organizes *fascio* at Prato 109; organizes tax resistance 109; squadrist 163; unemployed 162

Giandi, Angelino 160

Ginori Conti, Piero 127–8

Ginori Lisci, Lorenzo 127–8

Giolitti, Giovanni: attempts to repress fascism 184–6, 259 n 1; and 'National Bloc' 188; proposes tax reforms 143; strategy during factory occupations 143–7, 246 n 76; and system of Liberal rule 33, 35, 41, 143–4, 185–6; weakness in 1920–1 185–6, 194; yields to fascist pressure 188–90

Giorni, Italiano 159

Giovinezza, fascist newspaper: defends the mining industry 153–4; develops fascist agrarian program 83–5, 95; edited by Idalberto Targioni 83

Giustiniani, Enrico 57

Grandi, Dino 206

grapes 13, 16, 30, 34, 36

Grazioli, Carlo 192

Grazioli, Fabbrizio 192

Grosseto (city): fascism in 178, 258 n 118; military occupation by fascists 80, 201–2; as place of punishment for state officials 196

Grosseto (province): as centre of latifundism 7; fascism 56–8, 64–5, 141; fascist occupation of Grosseto and Roccastrada 201–3; local elections of 1920 54–5; migrant labour 7; mining industry 140–1; as place of punishment for state officials 195–6

gruppi di competenza 87

Guicciardini, Count Leone 58

Guicciardini, Count Niccolò 58

Guicciardini, Count Piero 58

Guicciardini, Francesco 21, 23–4, 26

Guicciardini, Paolo 61

Gutierrez, Dario: prefect of Grosseto 187–8; removed because of his anti-fascism 188

Henderson, James 112–13

hepatitis 26

hoarding 35

House of Savoy 40

housing, of *mezzadri* 9, 26–7

hygiene 26–7, 35

Idea fascista, fascist newspaper 172
Ilva company: capital value of 129; finances *Popolo d'Italia* 134; financial speculation 128–9; horizontal and vertical integration 127–8; maladministration under Max Bondi 130–1; monopoly of steel industry 127; opposes Giolitti and tax reforms 143; reconversion crisis 134, 136; steel production of 129; supports fascism 133–4, 136, 149, 152; and union movement 141–2; and uprising at Piombino 138
imponibile di mano d'opera: cause of conflict between *braccianti* and *mezzadri* 73, 98, 100; central issue in class struggle in the Po Valley 49–50; instrument of Tuscan *braccianti* 85, 98, 101; means of workers' control in agriculture 49
Incontri, Marquis Carlo Lodovico 58
Incontri, Marquis Roberto 58
Industrial Association of Carrara 116
industry: and fascism 2, 104–56, 208–9; finances fascism 116, 148–9, 151, 155; and the First World War 34, 107, 128–32, 136–7; funds the Citizens' Defence Alliance 133–5, 136; and links with agriculture 105–7, 124–8; purges workers 151–3; rejects Giovanni Giolitti 142–7; *see also* chemical, electrical, food, marble, mining, shipbuilding and wool industries
inflation: as cause of division between *braccianti* and *mezzadri* 89–90; creates crisis for agriculture 34, 46–7; 92, 221–2 in 119; radicalizes the labour movement 140–1; undermines living standards of workers 34–6, 136–7, 177, 244 n 48; undermines position of middle classes 165–6; used by fascists to create urban hostility towards *mezzadri* 167–8
internal committees: *see* factory councils and internal committees
Interprovincial Miners' Federation 140–2
Intrepido, fascist newspaper 26–7, 84–5
irrigation 13, 88
Isola, Paolo 161
Isonzo front 38
Isotta Fraschini company 130
Italian Chamber of Labour 64, 67, 178

Japan 123
judges, and fascism 190–3

Labour Office of Siena 102

landlords: defend *mezzadria* 8–9, 12–14, 21–2, 210 n 2, 211 n 3; demand public works 50; invest in industry 126–7; lose confidence in the state 53–5, 60–2; national congress at Rimini 54; oppose welfare reforms 53; as organizers of fascism 55–62, 70–1, 77, 80, 82–3, 90–1, 96–7, 110–11, 121–4, 133–5, 148, 187–8, 192, 206–7, 225 n 157; as propagandists of peasant proprietorship 40; relations with tenants 8–16, 19–20, 23–6, 30, 213 n 28, 214 n 44, 216 n 55; size of property holdings 59, 227–8 n 190; and tenant strikes 41–56, 106–7; *see* Tuscan Agrarian Association
landlords (urban): and socialist local government 170–1; support fascism 170–1
Land Office of Ferrara 82, 96–7
Landogno, Franco 159, 161
Lanza, Renato 149
Lanzillo, Agostino 123, 208
Lardarello 127
Lascialfare, Ezio: founder of Florence fascism 171–2, 247 n 80; founds illegal *fascio* at Lucca military academy 198; railroad official 172
Latifundia 7, 41, 82
Latium, *see* Lazio
Lavagnini, Spartaco 200
Lazio 1, 41
League of Socialist Communes 170
Leghorn, *see* Livorno
Lelli, Dante 172
Leo, Colonel Costantino 158
Leo XIII, Pope 43
Liberals: defend fascist unions 63; defend *mezzadria* 15; government authority dissolves 185–90; join fascism 149; Landlords alarmed by weakness of the Liberal state 53–4; Liberal deputies defend fascism 56; Liberal parties collapse in elections 53, 137–8; Liberal parties sanction joint membership in the fascist movement 58; Liberal press supports fascism 58–9, 150–1; lost parliamentary majority 53; weakness of postwar governments 185–7; Young Liberals join squadrism 58
Livorno (city): Association of Building Owners 171; Chamber of Commerce 148–9; fascism 135, 147–9, 150, 154–6, 158–9, 176, 200; labour movement 139–40, 142, 149; as 'little Russia' 137; port of 126; uprising of 1921 78

Livorno (province): fascism in 7, 148; local elections of 1920 54–5
lock-outs: by Alfa Romeo 143–4; by marble quarry owners 117; by Orlando shipyards 154–6; by Prato wool manufacturers 111; by Società Elettrica e Mineraria del Valdarno 153
logaioli 31
Lucca (city): fascism supported by industry 176; fascism supported by the petty bourgeoisie; founding of *fascio* 147; military supports fascism 198–9; police support fascism 192; war veterans and fascism 158, 160; workers oppose fascism 176–7
Lucca (province): Catholic unions in 112; fascism 7, 57, 84, 112–13; local elections of 1920 54–5; and relative lack of class tensions 112, 194–5; textile industry 112–13
Lucchesi, Antonio 111
Lupi, Dario 153
Lutrario, Inspector General 198
Luzzati, Gino 149
Luzzatto, Artruro 129–30, 134

machinery (agricultural) 9–10, 22–4, 29–31, 34, 46
Magnani, Marino 141
Magni, Fortunato, 110
Magona d'Italia company 127
Malagoli, Luigi 135
Malaparte, Curzio 162
malnutrition 26
Mantovani, Vico 82, 96
marble industry: anarchist labour movement 115; extreme political orientation of 114–15; supports fascism 105, 112, 114–17; uses squadrism to impose labour discipline 115–16
March on Rome 1–2, 53, 79, 177, 187, 204–5
Marches 54
Maremma 28, 137, 148
Mariotti, Alessandro 111
markets: as pressure to modernize agriculture 11, 20–3, 29–33; as sources of subversion among *mezzadri* 33
Marmifera Nord Carrara company 127
Martelli, Alessandro 50
Marx, Karl 18–19, 43
Masino, Federico: prefect of Siena 189; removed because of his anti-fascism 189; resents posting to Siena 196, 262 n 42
Massa-Carrara: Chamber of Labour 115–16; and elections of 1920 54–5;

fascism 7, 114–17, 126, 148–50, 169, 185, 192
massaie 21, 28, 99
Mazzini, Carlo Massimiliano 12
Mendici, Andrea 161
Merloni, Giovanni 141
Meschi, Alberto 115
mezzadri: agitation of 41–9, 51–5, 73–5, 167–8, 208–9; and anti-fascist resistance 77–8, 231–2 n 18; and conflict of generations 28–9, 37, 99–100; and domestic industry 17, 106; effects of war on 33–41; as employers of wage labour 98, 100; and fascism in the Po Valley 71–3, 76–7, 81–3; and fascism in Tuscany 77–81, 83–5, 89–96, 98–104; isolation of 18–20, 32, 38–9, 124, 214 n 43, 214 n 44; lack pension and welfare 12–13, 48; numbers of 232 n 19; position of 8–33, 68–9; savings of 100; and security of tenure 15–16, 19, 32, 52; *see also mezzadria, poderi*
mezzadria: backwardness of 11–12, 16–17, 19; as a barrier to industry 124–5, 128; crisis of 14, 20–1, 28–9, 31–3, 41–2, 53–5, 92, 93, 99–100, 206; effects of war on 33–42, 43; and family structure 17–18, 28–9, 37, 99–100, 124, 217 n 74; geographical distribution of 1–2, 7–8, 71–2, 101; ideology of 8–14, 43, 61, 167, 210 n 2, 211 n 3; and intensity of labour 10–13, 20, 26–8, 36–7, 48, 91, 212 n 11; modernization of 11, 20–33, 99, 207, 218 n 79; reform of by peasant unions 43–9, 51, 52–3; and self-sufficiency 12–13, 16, 32; terms of contract 8–11, 19–20, 24–5, 30, 43–9, 68–9; and urban middle classes 168, 208–9; *see also mezzadri, poderi*
Modigliani, Giuseppe Emanuele 200
monopoly: as feature of Tuscan industry 104, 127–8
Montanari, Ezio 172
Montanari, Mario 172
Monte Amiata 137, 141
Monte Amiata company: Gino Luzzatti 149; links with landlords 127; supports fascism 149; threatened by miners' militancy 140–1
Montecatini company: colludes with fascist unions 133; Guido Donegani as chairman of the board 125; links with agriculture 125–6; threatened by miners' militancy 140–1; *see also* Guido Donegani

Montepulciano 68, 193, 201
Montevarchi 57
Moore, Barrington 207
Mugello 27, 28; Citizens' Defence Alliance 60–1; fascist unions 67; peasant strikes 47
Mulinaccio estate 25–6
Mussolini, Benito 1–2, 81–2, 121–3, 126, 134–5, 157, 164, 184, 205
Muzi, Oscar 198

Naples 163–4
National Agrarian Party 63
'National Bloc' 188
National Corporation of Agricultural Labour 88
nationalization of the lands, see socialization of the land
Nazione, Liberal newspaper: chosen as model for fascist journalism 151; defends fascist agrarian program 167–8; justifies squadrism 151–2; owned by Max Bondi 134; reports militancy of landlords 62; supports Citizens' Defence Alliance 134; supports fascist movement 150–1
Nicolai, Francesco 67
Nievole Valley 57, 112
Nitti, Francesco Saverio 175, 185–6, 194
Nuovo giornale, Liberal newspaper: Athos Gastone Banti as editor 151; campaigns for fascism 151; discusses discipline at Richard-Ginori factory 152; discusses economy of Prato industry 107; linked with Max bondi 150–1; reports alienation of police from the state 194–5

Oddi, Patrizio 64, 68
Odero, Attilio 130
Officine Galileo company: capital of 129; precision instruments 127; purges workers 249 n 110; supports fascism 133; and workers' control 139, 146, 149
olive oil 9
olives 13, 16, 34, 36
Olivetti, Gino 139
Olivieri, Carlo: alarmed by pro-fascism of authorities 197, 199–200; alarmed by subversion 194; close collaborator of Giolitti 195; and fascism 261–2 n 41; prefect of Florence 90, 148, 171, 179, 184
Ora nostra, socialist newspaper 189
Ordine nuovo, communist newspaper: criticizes bureaucratization of peasant unions 76; elaborates theory of workers' control 139; model for *Difesa* newspaper 139; views Tuscany as model of anti-fascist resistance 77
Orlando, Guiseppe: locks out workers 154–5; and Orlando shipyards 154–6; supports fascism 132–3, 148, 154–6; urges use of the army to end factory occupations 144
Orlando, Luigi: cooperates with fascist plan to march on Livorno 154–6; and financial speculation 131; and financial speculation 131; links with Costanzo Ciano 150, 154–5; locks out workers 154–5; member of the boards of SMI, Credito Italiano and Società Elettrica e Mineraria del Valdarno 127–8; negotiates with Ministry of the Navy 154, 156; and Orlando shipyards, 127;l president of the Ligure-Toscana 128; supports fascism 132–3, 148; urges use of the army to end factory occupations 144
Orlando Count Rosolino: director of Ilva 129–30; supports fascism 133, 154–6

Pacini, Carlo, 159
Pacinotti, Antonio 149
Paese, newspaper 196
Palazzo Medici-Riccardi (Florence): occupied by fascists 199–200
Palermo 40
Palizzolo de Ramione, Colonel Giuseppe 199
Paolella, Inspector General: describes collusion of authorities with fascism 197, 201–2; reports bases of fascism at Carrara 116; reports defeat of *mezzadri* by fascism 101; threatened by squadrists 202
partnership: as ideology under *mezzadria* 8–9, 14–15, 30, 43, 69; as objective of the union movement 43, 45–9
Pasella, Umberto: former revolutionary 161; organizer of Tuscan fascism 163; secretary of fascist movement 135, 198; urges appeals to veterans 159
Pasqualini, Luigi: director of Officine Galileo 149; supports fascism 133, 149; vice-president of AIT 149
paternalism: AAT attempts to revive 61–2; advocated by P. F. Serragli 45; example of Mulinaccio estate 213 n 28; falls into disuse 23, 124; Guicciardini attempts to revive 23–4; as means of social control 15, 124
Patria, newspaper of the wool industry:

defends squadrism 111; explains industrial offensive against unions 108; opposes both PSI and PPI 110; praises fascist unions for breaking strikes 109
patriarchy: as barrier to subversion 17–18; as basis for landlords' authority 15; as cause of conflict of generations 28–9, 37, 99; fascists pledge to retore 99–100; and structure of *mezzadro* family 17
Patrizi, Edmondo 172
patronage: instrument of power of bailiffs 86; landlords' patronage jeopardized by socialists 54; provided by fascist unions 68, 102
Peasant Brotherhoods, *see* fascist unions
peasant proprietors: in Arno and Chiana valleys 92; and effects of the war 91–3; numbers of 91–2, 232 n 19; support fascism 78–9, 94–8
peasants, see *affittuari*, *braccianti*, *mezzadri*, *mezzadria*, peasant proprietors
Pedriali, Vittorio 96–7
pellagra 26, 216 n 60
Pellegrini, Filippo 192
pensions: demanded by *mezzadri* 48; opposed by landlords 53; peasants lack 12–13, 48; provided for industrial workers 12
Pericoli, Vincenzo 189
Perrone brothers (Mario and Pio) 122
Perrone Compagni, Dino: and Citizens' Defence Alliance 61; demobilized NCO 160; founds Arezzo *fascio* 247 n 80; leader of Tuscan fascism 162–3, 165; organizes fascist threat to march on Livorno 154–5; presses government to remove anti-fascist officials 189; unemployed 162
Peruzzi de' Medici, Marquis 61
petty bourgeoisie: alienated by socialist antipathy 166–7; declining social standing 166–7; and inflation 166–8; opposes strikes in public services 168; supports Citizens' Defence Alliance 168; supports fascism 165–71; threatened by socialist cooperatives 169; threatened by socialist tax reforms 170–1
Philipson, Dino 149
Piazzesi, Mario 158
Piccioli, Arturo 149
Piccolomini, Count Girolamo: vice-president of Siena branch of the AAT 57; squadrist 57
piece work 50, 140
Piedmont 20, 143

Pierazzi, Ferdinando 57
Pieri, Goffredo 176
Piombino: and factory occupations 144; fascism in 147, 149, 159, 162; and uprising of 1920 138
Pirelli, Alberto 132
Pisa (city): Chamber of Commerce 171; and farm workers' congress 90; fascism in 135, 159–61, 169, 172, 189, 257 n 118; uprising of 1921 78
Pisa (province): and agitation of *braccianti* 49–51, 73; as centre of commercialized agriculture 22–3, 26; fascism 8, 72, 102–3; local elections of 1920 54–5; peasant proprietors 92–4; and strikes of 1919 44–9; *see also* Arno Valley
Pistoia: elects socialist town council 137; factory occupations 144; fascist violence 185
poaching 13
Pocherra, Bernardo 116
poderi: artificially created by landlords 90–2; declining size of 27–9, 90–1, 93, 217 n 69; and intensity of labour 27–9; as peasant farms 8–11; numbers of per *fattoria* 210 n 1; relations with the *fattoria* 126–17, 218 n 76; and stability of tenure 15–16, 32, 68–9; and tenant demand for self-management and tenant self-sufficiency 16–18
Poggi, Leone 134
police and *carabinieri*: fail to intervene against squadrists 96–7, 201–3; growing loss of confidence in the state 192–6; harass union members 187, 196–7, 200; join fascism 198, 200; links with middle classes and notables 190–2; officers removed for opposing fascism 111, 188–90; oppose strikes 53, 187; pro-fascism of the commanding officer of the *carabinieri* 202–3; provide squads with arms and transport 198; take part in punitive expeditions 199–200; view fascism as an ally 193–4
political Catholicism, *see* Popular Party
Polverelli, Gaetano 81, 83–4
Pontedera: fascism 159, 17–8; landlords alarmed by union organization of *braccianti* 50; tax reforms of socialist town council 170; uprising of 1921 78
Ponzio, General Giacomo 203
Popolo d'Italia, Mussolini's newspaper: financed by big business 133–5; supported by Tuscan industry 136
Popular Party (PPI): electoral success of 54; organizes industrial workers

112–13; organizes *mezzadri* 42–9, 51–5, 63, 65, 70, 108–10, 112
Portoferraio: centre of steel industry 132; elects socialist town council 137; factory occupations 144
Poulantzas, Nicos 123–4
Po Valleys, *see* Emilia
Pozzo della Chiana 114, 177
Prato: alliance of industrialists and landlords to support fascism 110–11, 169; conflict over workers' control in industry 108–9; and election of 1920 137; eviction of tenants 90; fascism 107–12, 117, 147, 160, 169, 178–9, 185, 189, 225 n 157, 238 n 114; tax resistance against socialist local government 109–11; textile industry 107–9, 128–9; Union of Industrialists 109; wool workers' strike of 1921 109
prefects: affected politically by the prestige of their postings 195–6; ordered to repress fascist violence 184–5; oppose socialism 190–2; replaced for antio-fascism 189; removed for sympathy with the left; view fascism as an ally 1903, 196 *see also* Bertone, Mauro Michele; Boragno, Antonio; De Martino, Achille; D'Eufemia, Emilio; Frigerio, Pietro; Gasperini, Giovanni; Masino, Federico; Oliveri, Carlo; Pericoli, Vicenzo; Rocco, Raffaele; Verdionois, Edoardo
price controls 35, 39, 96–7
prisoners of war, employed in agriculture 35
proleterianization, of *mezzadri* 23–33
protection rackets: run by squads at Florence 165; run by squads at San Sepolcro 113
public works: demanded by landlords 50, 101; and employment of *mezzadri* 88

Ragionieri, Ernesto 33
railroads: armed strike-breaking directed by the state 175–6; as crucial instruments of power 174–5; employees support fascism 171–5; railwaymen support factory occupations 144; struggle for workers' control 173
Rapalano 64
rationing 35, 39
Ravagli, Pietro 141
Ravenna 206
religion, as instrument of social control 9–10, 14, 20
republican party 35, 115, 162

Resto del carlino, landlords' newspaper 40, 54
revolts, *see* uprisings
Ricasoli, Baron Luigi 58
Ricci, Renato: defeats prefect's attempt to disarm his squads 117, 149–50; fascist boss of Massa Carrara 115, 160; former army officer 159–60; relations with marble industrialists 117; supported by Guido Donegani 149–50
Richard-Ginori company: establishes fascism at Sesto Fiorentino 113–14; imposes work discipline 152, 249 n 110
Ridolfi, Luigi 57–8
'right to work' 53, 56, 109
Rimini: national landlords' congress 59
Rinnovamento, Liberal newspaper 174
Riscossa, fascist newspaper: develops fascist agrarian program 83–5, 95; edited by Idalberto Targioni 83; Guido Carbonai as deputy director 172
Risveglio, socialist newspaper 188
Roccastrada: fascist military occupation 202–3, 208
Rocco, Raffaele: prefect of Grosseto 188; sympathetic to landlords 188
Romagnoli, Carlo 111
Rome 41, 184, 187–8, 190, 192, 195; *see also* March on Rome
Rossi, Filippo 159
Rotigliano, Edoardo: fascist 122, 133, 149; finances fascism 149; property speculator 149; spokesman for Ilva 149
Rovigo 189, 206
Russian Revolution 39–40, 137

Salandra, Antonio 194
Salvagnoli, Vincenzo 9
San Frediano (quarter of Florence), uprising of 1921 78
San Giovanni Valdarno: factory occupation 144; fascism 152–3; iron mines of Società Elettrica e Mineraria del Valdarno 134; uprising of 1921 78
San Miniato: agitation of *braccianti* 51; fascism 197–8
San Sepolcro: Buitoni company 113; centre for fascism in the Tiber valley 113, 184; fascism in 113, 159, 184, 239 n 135
Santa Croce (quarter of Florence): uprising of 1921 78
Santini, Paolo 159, 161
Sardinia 178
Sarrocchi, Gino: leader of AAT 56; Liberal leader 15; pro-fascist 56, 58; theorist of *mezzadria* 15–16

Sarzana: Carlo Scarfoglio castigates government 151; fascists collect funds for squadrists killed 165; funds collected embezzled 165; police open fire on squadrists 186
savings: accumulated by *fattori* 85–6; accumulated by *mezzadri* 36–7, 92–4; increase peasant proprietorship 86, 92–4
Scandici, uprising of 1921 78
Scarfoglio, Carlo: chosen as model for fascist journalism 151; defends squadrism 151; editor of *Nazione* 151; supports fascist agrarian program 167
Scorza, Carlo: demobilized army officer 159–60; fascist boss of Lucca 112; opposed by the working class 176; supported by marble industry 112; supported by middle classes 165–6; supported by war profiteers 176
Scotti, Stefano 159
Scroffa, Ildebrando 68
Scure, fascist newspaper: choses *Nazione* as model for fascist journalism 151; develops fascist agrarian program 95–6; opposes union influence on railroads 174; reports role of students in fascism 160
Secchiari, Ottaviano 116
Seisoldi, Umberto 172
Serpieri, Arrigo 46
Serragli, Pier Francesco: advocates paternalism 23, 45; defends landlords' rights 48–9; former mayor of Florence 24; industrialist 127; president of AAT 57, 68; supports fascism 24, 57, 62, 133
Sesto Fiorentino 113–14, 249 n 110
shipbuilding industry: cooperates with fascism in threat of march on Livorno 154–6; links with agriculture 126–67; negotiates with Ministry of the Navy; political orientation of 106–7; role of Costanzo Ciano 150; supports Mussolini 133; threatened by Livorno labour movement *see also* Orlando, Giuseppe; Orlando, Luigi; Orlando shipyards
shopkeepers: declining economic position 166; join fascism 165–6, 169; threatened by socialist cooperatives 169; *see also* petty bourgeoisie
Siena (city) 21: elections of 1920 137; fascism 147, 160, 172, 175, 192; uprising of 1921 78
Siena (province) 171; Chamber of Labour 77, 171; commercialization of agriculture 22–3; elections of 1920 54–5; farm councils 77; fascism 8, 56, 58–9, 87–8, 98, 114, 158–9; fascist agrarian program 71, 95–104; fascist unions 57, 63; first agricultural strikes in Tuscany 41–2; as socialist stronghold 54, 77, 195; strikes of 1919 44
Sismondi, Leonard Simonde de 15–17, 26
socialism: based on ideology of *mezzadria* and partnership 43; *mezzadria* as a barrier against 8–9, 13–14, 18–19, 21–2, 31, 42
Socialist Party (PSI): agrarian program of 72–6, 81–3, 96, 98; and *braccianti* 49–51, 72–4, 88–9, 98, 101–2; bureaucratization of 75–7; electoral successes 54, 108, 137, 170; and factory occupations 145; and the First World War 35; land question 40–1, 72–5, 81, 96; and local government 35–6, 54–5, 105–6, 137–8, 170–1; organization of industrial workers 108–10; organization of *mezzadri* 42–9, 51–6, 62–3, 65, 72–7, 79, 85–6, 94, 98–101, 193; and the Russian Revolution 39; weaknesses of 72–7, 91, 97–101, 103–4, 142, 145–6, 166–8, 173, 178–9, 191
socialization of the land: national policy of the PSI 72–3, 81, 96; rejected by Tuscan socialists 74–5
Società Boracifera di Lardarello: landlords as members of the board 127; links with fascism 133, 149; links with Ilva and the Mineraria 128; threatened by militancy of miners 140–2
Società Elettrica e Mineraria del Valdarno: factory occupations 144; locks out workers 153; monopoly of lignite 127; oligopoly in electrical industry 127; supported by fascist deputies in negotiations with the state 153–4; supports Citizens' Defence Alliance 133–4, 136; supports fascism 133, 152–3; uses squadrism to discipline workers 152–3; vertical and horizontal integration 127–8
Società Ligure-toscana 127–8
Società Magona d'Italia 127–8, 149
Società Mineraria del Siele 127, 140
Società per la Strade Ferrate Meridionali 127
Soffici, Ardengo 207
soil erosion 34
Sonnino, Sidney 211
special tribunals 38
Spinelli, Ferdinando 164
Spriano, Paolo 70

squadrism: adopted by Ilva and the Mineraria to enforce labour discipline 152–3; breaks wool workers' strike at Prato 109; cooperation between squadrists and police 78, 201–3; destroys the cooperative movement 169; failure of socialists to organize self-defence 178–9; forms of violence used 70–1, 184–5, 201–2; as important in fascist unions 66–7, 109–10; as key factor in defeat of union movement 55; occupation of Foiano della Chiana 203; occupation of Grosseto 201–2; occupation of Roccastrada 202; opposed by the police at Sarzana 186; and the railroads 187; reaches peak in mid 1921 188; reasons for extreme violence in tuscany 80–1; and recruitment of peasant proprietors 94–5; role of criminals 163–4; used by landlords to enforce evictions 90; tolerated by the police 196–7; used by marble quarry owners 116; used by wool manufacturers 110–11; used to repress uprising in Florence 77–8
Starace, Achille 164–5
steel industry: and control of the press 150–1; favours fascism 133; and Ilva 127, 129–30; links with landlords 126–7; and monopoly 127–8; position in the AIT 106, 136; position in Confindustria 132; and reconversion crisis 130–1; rejects Liberal government 136; uses squads to enforce labour discipline 152–3
strikes: absence during the war 35; alienate *fattori* 85, 88; first strikes by *mezzadri* (1902 and 1906) 41–2; general strike at Piombino 138; general strike at Viareggio 138; general strike in Piedmont 143; 'legalitarian strike' (1922) 148–9; by marble quarriers 112, 115; by *mezzadri* in 1919 42–9, 51; by *mezzadri* in 1920 51–4; middle classes alienated by strikes in the public services 168; by miners 140–2; by Prato wool workers 108–9; by railroad workers 173–4; solidarity strikes to support FIOM 144; threatened by fascist unions 64; traditional absence of 14; unavailable as a weapon by the AAT 63; as weapon of anti-fascist resistance 77
students: support Citizens' Defence Alliance 168; support fascism 157, 160–1, 165–6
sugar beet 22–3, 30

sugar industry 105
Switzerland 20

Tamburini, Tullio: commander of Florence squads 160, 162–3; discharged army officer 159–60, 162; unemployed 162
Tappari, Alberto 159
Tarchiani, Nello 158
Targioni, Idalberto: appeals to *braccianti* against *mezzadri* 89; develops fascist agrarian program 83–5, 95–6; editor of *Riscossa* and *Giovinezza* 83; fascist union organizer 64, 66–8; former socialist union official 64, 161–2
tariffs 21
taxes: burden on *mezzadri* 12, 20–1, 24, 32; business taxes 108, 143, 170; cattle tax 21, 44, 47; family taxes 21, 170; and fascist propaganda 171; grist tax 21; as instrument of socialist local government 54–5, 170–1; land taxes 21, 47, 53–5; salt duties 21; tax reform demanded by *mezzadri* 44, 47; tax reforms opposed by industry 143, 171; tax reforms opposed by landlords 47, 53, 171; tax reforms opposed by urban middle classes 106, 171
Telegrafo, Liberal newspaper 150–1
terrazzieri: disillusioned with socialist unions 91; employed on estates 88–9; join fascism 91, 96
Terzaghi, Michele 61
textile industry see wool industry
Tiber Valley: agitation of *braccianti* 51; centre of commercialized agriculture 22; fascism at San Sepolcro 113; squadrism 184
Tiezzi, Angelo
tobacco 22–3, 30
Togliatti, Palmiro 78–9, 195
Toniolo, Giuseppe 11, 15–16
Toscana, Liberal newspaper 147
tradesmen: see shopkeepers
Tramontano, Giovanni 160
transfer payments, low level under *mezzadria* 12–13
Trieste 205
Trigona, Emanuele 127
Trigona, Vincenzo 127
Turati, Filippo 103
Turin 20: factory councils 139; uprising of 1917 40
Tuscan Agrarian Association (AAT): branch presidents campaign for fascists 56–7; centralization of 60, 80; congress of 1920 50–1; defended by fascists 83;

divides land among peasants 97, 102–3;
endorses fascist price campaign 169;
finances fascism 56, 110, 122–3, 225
n 157; forms political alliance with
fascists at Prato 95, 110–11, 171, 225
n 157; founding of 59; membership 60,
228 n 199, 228 n 204; mourns Federico
Florio 110; opposes Liberal regime
50–1, 53–5, 60–1, 87–9; opposes
welfare provisions for peasants 53;
organizes pro-fascist press campaign 56;
relations with *fattori* 86–8; resistance
fund 56; supports Citizens' Defence
Alliance 60–1; supports fascist unions
57, 62–9; and union demands 47, 52,
223 n 136, 224 n 137, 234 n 56; uses
squadrism to evict tenants 90;
weaknesses of 63
Tuscan Industrial Association (AIT):
alarmed by labour militancy 145–6;
finances fascism 110, 148–9; leaders join
fascist movement 149–51; opposes
Giolitti during factory occupations
144–57; as right wing of Confindustria
136; supports fascist price campaign
150, 169; supports fascist tax resistance
campaign at Prato 109–10, 171

Umbria 54
unemployment: and demobilized soldiers
157–8, 161–2; as an instrument of
power for big business 154; and rural
support for fascism 71, 78–9, 91,
101–2; statistics, 1919–21 236 n 83;
and urban support for fascism 158, 162
Unification of Italy 20, 35
Unione Italiana Concimi 125
Unione Italiana Miniere Pirite 125
Union of Wool Manufacturers 109–10
uprisings: Empoli, Livorno, Pisa,
Pontedera, Siena, San Giovanni
Valdarno (1921) 78; Florence and Siena
(1921) 200; Piombino and Viareggio
(1920) 138; Turin, 1917 40

Vaccari, Marcello 159
Vai family 26
Veneto 54
Venice 40
Verdinois, Edoardo: faces threat of fascist
march on Livorno 154–6; and fascism
262 n 41; prefect of Livorno 154
vetch 22
veterans: alienated by PSI acceptance of
deserters as candidates 157–8; appeals
of Citizens' Defence Alliance and fascism

158; demobilization crisis 157, 159,
161–2; enlisted men and the left 158;
junior officers and the right 158–60;
senior officers and fascism 158; veterans'
association and fascism 159
Vetri, Giuseppe 158
Viareggio: occupation of factories 144;
uprising of 1920 138
vignaioli 31
Villari, Pasquale 8
violence: defended by *Nazione* as a tool of
fascism 151; enhanced by role of
veterans 160; increased by role of
criminals 163; as an instrument of
squadrism 70–1, 117, 165, 184–5,
196–7, 199–204, 207–8; rejected by the
socialist party 55–6, 103–4; special
importance for Tuscan fascism 77–8,
80; used by *fattori* 88; used by mining
industry to impose discipline 141, used
by Prato notables to repress subversion
109–13; used to crush subversion at
Grosseto 201–2; used to crush workers'
resistance at Florence 200; used to
repress socialism at Roccastrada 202–3;
see also squadrism
Vitali, Dario 160

Weber, Max 15
welfare, provisions for *mezzadri* 12–13,
35–6, 48, 53
wheat 16, 22, 34, 46
wine 9
women: and domestic industry 17; as
heads of sharecropping families 17;
hired during the war 35; and over-work
under *mezzadria* 10–12, 36–7; provide
welfare under *mezzadria* 12; *see also*
family, patriarchy
wool industry: expansion during the war
107–8; Prato as centre 107;
reconversion crisis 107–8; resistance to
unions 108; supports fascism 109–12,
121–2
work day, of *mezzadri* 26–7
workers (farm), see *braccianti, terrazzieri*
workers (urban): anarchist militancy at
Massa-Carrara 115–16; anti-fascist
resistance 77–8, 103–4; 231–2 n 18;
artisans and fascism 177–8; and bread
riots 138; disillusioned with PSI 156,
178–9; factory occupations 142–7;
indifference of Livorno workers to
fascism 154–5; isolated in postwar
politics 166–8; join fascist branches
175–9; join fascist unions 175–6;

militarized during the war 128, 136–7; organization of miners 140–2; organization of Prato wool workers 108–9; organization of railroad workers 171–5; politicized by the war 136–7; under-represented within fascism 176–7; victimization of activists 109, 113, 115–16, 151–2; and welfare payments 12; and workers' control 137–8, 139–42
workers' control: in industry 137, 139–46; on railways 173
world War I: as catalyst for industrial workers' militancy 136–8; as catalyst for peasant movement 14, 33–41, 43; economic effects of 46–7, 92–4, 128–9, 131, 137
written contracts: abuses of unwritten contracts in *mezzadria* 10; demanded by sharecroppers' unions 43–5

Young, Arthur 213
Young Liberals' Association, and squadrism 58

Zamboni, Luigi: former army officer 159; leader of Citizens' Defence Alliance 147; leader of fascism at Prato 111; provincial secretary of Flroence fascism 159 Zibordi, Giovanni 195
Zoni, Edilio 159

WITHDRAWN